SERMONS

PREACHED IN LENT,

ON GOOD-FRIDAY,

AND ON EASTER-DAY.

NINETY-SIX SERMONS

BY THE

RIGHT HONOURABLE AND REVEREND FATHER IN GOD,

LANCELOT ANDREWES,

SOMETIME LORD BISHOP OF WINCHESTER.

PUBLISHED BY HIS MAJESTY'S SPECIAL COMMAND.

VOL. II.

NEW EDITION.

WIPF & STOCK · Eugene, Oregon

Wipf and Stock Publishers
199 W 8th Ave, Suite 3
Eugene, OR 97401

Ninety-Six Sermons by the Right Honourable and Reverend Father in God,
Lancelot Andrewes, Sometime Lord Bishop of Winchester, Vol. II
By Andrewes, Lancelot
ISBN 13: 978-1-61097-383-0
Publication date 3/31/2011
Previously published by James Parker and Co., 1882

EDITOR'S PREFACE.

THE same plan has been pursued in the present as in the preceding volume, and although, from circumstances which it is unnecessary to explain, the same time has not been occupied in its preparation for the press, equal pains have been taken with a view to attain the greatest possible accuracy.

The number of Sermons now published is twenty-two, of which six were preached during Lent, three on Good-Friday, and the remaining thirteen, out of eighteen, the whole series upon the Resurrection, on Easter-day.

Of those delivered during Lent, four were preached before Queen Elizabeth at Greenwich, St. James's, and Hampton Court, between the years 1589 and 1594; and the last two were preached before the Court at Richmond and Greenwich on the fifth of March, and the fourth of April, 1596.

The topics touched upon in the Lent Sermons are, briefly, the following: That the strength of a land is in its pillars, the worship of God, and the due administration of Justice; That the Most High is to be recognised as the chief Head of every government, to Whom all civil rulers are subordinate; That as our Saviour accepted with favour, and as a good work, the anointing of His natural body by Mary Magdalene, so He will no less graciously accept whatever is done for His body mystical, the Church; That from the lamentable fall of Lot's wife, we learn the necessity of perseverance in the course of well-doing; That from the miserable state of the rich man tormented in Hades, we are taught the necessity of considering what we shall be hereafter; and that from the example of St. Paul, we find that love for souls, if sincere, will not be disheartened, however it may be requited. Such is a general outline of this series of Sermons, and as the temper of the times in which the Bishop lived was not altogether unlike our own, so it will be found that the truths therein evolved are such as may well be appreciated by ourselves.

The Sermons upon the Passion are only three in number. The second and third were preached before King James I. at Whitehall and Greenwich, on the sixth of April 1604, and the twenty-ninth of March 1605. The first was preached at the Court on the twenty-fifth of March 1597. They will be found to enter fully, but most reverently, into the subject of our Saviour's unexampled sufferings, both mental and bodily; to investigate the causes and motives which led to the death of the Son of God for us and for our salvation; to point out the inestimable benefits which have resulted to mankind from the propitiation thereby made for the sins of the whole world; and to enforce the necessity of "looking unto Jesus, the Author and Finisher of our faith," for a due sense and reception of the blessings purchased in His blood.

Of the thirteen Sermons which are here given on the Resurrection, twelve were preached at Whitehall before King James I. The remaining one, the thirteenth, was also preached before the King at Durham Cathedral, and the whole were delivered during the period commencing with Easter-day 1606, and ending with Easter-day 1618, both inclusive.

Of these Discourses it is not necessary to give any lengthened analysis. Plain, Scriptural, and Catholic, they speak for themselves, and while every topic of weight and moment, whether derived from the Law, or from the Prophets and Psalms, or from the Apostolic writings, is treated in a manner at once searching and satisfactory, the Student in Theology will hardly fail to derive from their serious perusal both instruction and encouragement;—instruction in points of doctrine, and encouragement to set his affections on things above, "where Christ sitteth at the right hand of God."

The texts at the head of each Sermon are, as before, for the most part from the Genevan Bible. The chief variations are verbal, and the most important are inserted in a note below[a].

With respect to quotations generally, it is perhaps necessary again to caution the reader, that he must not expect to find the exact passages referred to. For the most part the substance only is given, and therefore it is possible that in some few instances the Editor may have been mistaken in his reference. In all cases however which appeared at all

[a] The variations are given in italics—

SERMONS PREACHED IN LENT.

Serm. I. & II. No variation.
Serm. III. Mark xiv. 4—6. Ver. 5.
. . . . . and they *murmured* . . . . .
Serm. IV. V. & VI. No variation.

SERMONS PREACHED ON GOOD-FRIDAY.

Serm. I. No variation.
Serm. II. Lament. i. 12. . . . . *this* way. *Behold and see* if ever there *be* sorrow like *unto* My sorrow . . . . wherewith the Lord *hath afflicted* Me in the day of *His fierce* wrath.
Serm. III. No variation.

SERMONS PREACHED ON EASTER-DAY.

Serm. I. & II. No variation.

Serm. III. Mark xvi 1—7. . . . . . . *that they might* . . . *anoint* Him. Ver. 2. . . . . when the sun was *now risen.*
Serm. IV., V., VI., VII., & VIII. No variation of the least importance.
Serm. IX. Philip. ii. 8—11. Ver. 8. . . . *became* obedient. Ver. 9. *Wherefore* God. . . . Ver. 10. . . . of *things* in Heaven, and *things* in Earth, and *things* under the Earth.
Serm. X. John ii. 19. . . *in* three days. . .
Serm. XI. 1 Pet. 3, 4. Ver. 3 . . . . God *even* the Father. Ver. 4 . . . to an inheritance *immortal* . . . . and that *withereth* not, reserved in Heaven *for us.*
Serm. XII. No variation of the least importance.
Serm. XIII. 1 Cor. xi. 16. If any man *lust* to be contentious. . . . .

doubtful, the words "*vide*" or "*confer*" have been used, but wherever a reference is enclosed in brackets without this addition, there the reader will invariably find the quotation intended by the bishop.

J. P. W.

Magdalene College,
The Feast of the Annunciation,
1841.

CONTENTS.

SERMONS PREACHED IN LENT.

SERMON I.

(Page 3.)

Preached before Queen Elizabeth, at Greenwich, on Wednesday, the Eleventh of March, A.D. MDLXXXIX.

Psalm lxxv. 3.

The earth and all the inhabitants thereof are dissolved: but I will establish the pillars of it.

SERMON II.

(Page 16.)

Preached before Queen Elizabeth, at Greenwich, on the Twenty-fourth of February, A.D. MDXC., being St. Matthias's Day.

Psalm lxxvii. 20.

Thou didst lead Thy people like sheep, by the hand of Moses and Aaron.

SERMON III.

(Page 37.)

Preached before Queen Elizabeth, at St. James's, on Wednesday, being the Thirtieth of March, A.D. MDXCIII.

Mark xiv. 4—6.

Therefore some disdained among themselves, and said, To what end is this waste of ointment?

For it might have been sold for more than three hundred pence, and been given to the poor. And they grudged against her.

But Jesus said, Let her alone, why trouble ye her? she hath wrought a good work on Me.

SERMON IV.

(Page 61.)

Preached before Queen Elizabeth, at Hampton Court, on Wednesday, being the Sixth of March, A.D. MDXCIV.

Luke xvii. 32.

Remember Lot's wife.

SERMON V.

(Page 78.)

Preached in the Court at Richmond, on Tuesday, being the Fifth of March, A.D. MDXCVI.

Luke xvi. 25.

Son, remember that thou, in thy life time, receivedst thy pleasure (or good things;) and likewise Lazarus pains: Now therefore is he comforted, and thou art tormented.

SERMON VI.

(Page 98.)

Preached in the Court at Greenwich, on Sunday, being the Fourth of April, A.D. MDXCVI.

2 Corinthians xii. 15.

And I will most gladly bestow, and will be bestowed for your souls, though the more I love you, the less I am loved.

SERMONS PREACHED UPON GOOD-FRIDAY.

SERMON I.

(Page 119.)

Preached at the Court, on the Twenty-fifth of March, A.D. MDXCVII., being Good-Friday.

Zechariah xii. 10.

And they shall look upon Me, Whom they have pierced.

SERMON II.

(Page 139.)

Preached before the King's Majesty, at Whitehall, on the Sixth of April,
A.D. MDCIV., being Good Friday.

Lamentations i. 12.

*Have ye no regard, O all ye that pass by the way? Consider,
and behold, if ever there were sorrow like My sorrow, which
was done unto Me, wherewith the Lord did afflict Me in the
day of the fierceness of His wrath.*

SERMON III.

(Page 159.)

Preached before the King's Majesty, at Greenwich, on the Twenty-ninth of
March, A.D. MDCV., being Good-Friday.

Hebrews xii. 2.

*Looking unto Jesus the Author and Finisher of our faith; Who
for the joy that was set before Him, endured the cross, and
despised the shame; and is set at the right-hand of the
throne of God.*

SERMONS OF THE RESURRECTION.

PREACHED ON EASTER-DAY.

———

SERMON I.

(Page 189.)

Preached before the King's Majesty at Whitehall, on the Sixth of April,
A.D. MDCVI., being Easter-day.

ROMANS vi. 9—11.

*Knowing that Christ, being raised from the dead, dieth no more;
death hath no more dominion over Him.*

*For, in that He died, He died once to sin; but in that He liveth,
He liveth to God.*

*Likewise think (or account) ye also, that ye are dead to sin, but
are alive to God in Jesus Christ our Lord.*

SERMON II.

(Page 209.)

Preached before the King's Majesty at Whitehall, on the Fifth of April,
A.D. MDCVII., being Easter-day.

1 Corinthians xv. 20.

*But now is Christ risen from the dead, and was made the first
fruits of them that sleep.*

SERMON III.

(Page 224.)

Preached before the King's Majesty, at Whitehall, on the Twenty-seventh of
March, A.D. MDCVIII., being Easter-day.

Mark xvi. 1—7.

*And when the Sabbath day was past, Mary Magdalene, and
Mary the mother of James, and Salome, brought sweet ointments, that they might come and embalm Him.*

*Therefore early in the morning, the first day of the week, they
came unto the sepulchre, when the sun was yet rising.*

*And they said one to another, Who shall roll us away this stone
from the door of the sepulchre?*

*And when they looked, they saw that the stone was rolled away;
for it was a very great one.*

*So they went into the sepulchre, and saw a young man sitting
at the right side, clothed in a long white robe; and they
were afraid.*

*But he said unto them, Be not afraid: ye seek Jesus of Naza-
reth, Which hath been crucified; He is risen, He is not here;
Behold the place where they put Him.*

*But go your way and tell His disciples, and Peter, that He
will go before you into Galilee: there shall ye see Him, as
He said unto you.*

SERMON IV.

(Page 241.)

Preached before the King's Majesty at Whitehall, on the Sixteenth of April,
A.D. MDCIX., being Easter-day.

John xx. 19.

*The same day then, at night, which was the first day of the
week, and when the doors were shut where the Disciples
were assembled for fear of the Jews, came Jesus and stood
in the midst, and said to them, Peace be unto you.*

SERMON V.

(Page 256.)

Preached before the King's Majesty at Whitehall, on the Eighth of April,
A.D. MDCIX., being Easter-day.

Job xix. 23—27.

*Oh that my words were now written! Oh that they were
written even in a book!*
And graven with an iron pen in lead, or in stone for ever!
*For I am sure that my Redeemer liveth, and He shall stand
the last on the earth* (or, and I shall rise again in the last
day from the earth.)
*And though after my skin worms destroy this body, I shall see
God in my flesh.*
*Whom I myself shall see, and mine eyes shall behold, and none
other* for me, *though my reins are consumed within me.* (Or,
and this hope is laid up in my bosom.)

SERMON VI.

(Page 274.)

Preached before the King's Majesty at Whitehall, on the Twenty-fourth of
March, A.D. MDCXI., being Easter-day, and being also the day of the beginning
of his Majesty's most gracious reign.

Psalm cxviii. 22.

*The Stone Which the builders refused, the same Stone is become
(or* made) *the Head of the corner.*

SERMON VII.

(Page 294.)

Preached before the King's Majesty at Whitehall, on the Twelfth of April,
A.D. MDCXII., being Easter-day.

1 Corinthians v. 7, 8.

*Purge out therefore the old leaven, that ye may be a new
lump, as ye are unleavened; for Christ our Passover is
sacrificed for us:*
*Therefore let us keep the Feast, not with old leaven, neither
with the leaven of maliciousness and wickedness; but with
the unleavened bread of sincerity and truth.*

SERMON VIII.

(Page 314.)

Preached before the King's Majesty at Whitehall, on the Eighteenth of April,
A.D. MDCXIII., being Easter-day.

Colossians iii. 1, 2.

*If ye then be risen with Christ, seek those things which are
above, where Christ sitteth at the right hand of God.*
*Set your affections, or minds, on things which are above; and
not on things which are on the earth.*

SERMON IX.

(Page 328.)

Preached before the King's Majesty at Whitehall, on the Twenty-fourth of April,
A.D. MDCXIV., being Easter-day.

Philippians ii. 8—11.

*He humbled Himself, made obedient unto death, even the
death of the Cross.*
*For this cause hath God also highly exalted Him; and given
Him a Name above every name.*
*That at the Name of Jesus every knee should bow, of those in
Heaven, and in earth, and under the earth.*
*And that every tongue should confess, that Jesus Christ is the
Lord, to the glory of God the Father.*

SERMON X.

(Page 349.)

Preached before the King's Majesty at Whitehall, on the Ninth of April,
A.D. MDCXV., being Easter-day.

John ii. 19.

*Jesus answered and said, Dissolve (or destroy) this Temple, and
within three days I will raise it up again.*

SERMON XI.

(Page 369.)

Preached before the King's Majesty at Whitehall, on the Thirty-first of March,
A.D. MDCXVI., being Easter-day.

1 Peter i. 3, 4.

*Blessed be God and the Father of our Lord Jesus Christ,
Which according to His abundant mercy hath begotten us
again unto a lively hope, by the resurrection of Jesus Christ
from the dead,
To an inheritance incorruptible and undefiled, and that fadeth
not away, reserved in Heaven for you.*

SERMON XII.

(Page 389.)

Preached before the King's Majesty, in the Cathedral Church at Durham, on the
Twentieth of April, A.D. MDCXVII., being Easter-day.

Matthew xii. 39, 40.

*But He answered and said unto them, An evil and adulterous
generation seeketh a sign, but no sign shall be given unto it,
save the sign of the Prophet Jonas :
For as Jonas was three days and three nights in the whale's
belly, so shall the Son of Man be three days and three nights
in the heart of the earth.*

SERMON XIII.

(Page 410.)

Preached before the King's Majesty at Whitehall, on the Fifth of April,
A.D. MDCXVIII., being Easter-day.

1 Corinthians xi. 16.

*But if any man seem to be contentious, we have no such custom,
neither the Churches of God.*

SERMONS PREACHED IN LENT.

A SERMON

PREACHED BEFORE

QUEEN ELIZABETH, AT GREENWICH,

ON WEDNESDAY, THE ELEVENTH OF MARCH, A.D. MDLXXXIX.

PSALM lxxv. 3.

*The earth and all the inhabitants thereof are dissolved; but I
will establish the pillars of it.*

*Liquefacta est terra, et omnes qui habitant in ea: Ego confirmavi
columnas ejus.*

[*The earth and all the inhabitants thereof are dissolved; I bear up
the pillars of it.* Engl. Trans.]

IT was Moses, the Man of God, that by special direction
from God first began, and brought up this order, to make
music the conveyer of men's duties into their minds. And Deu. 31. 19.
David sithence hath continued it, and brought it to perfection in this book, as having a special grace and felicity in
this kind; he for Songs, and his son Solomon for Proverbs.
By which two, that is, by the unhappy adage, and by a wanton song, Satan hath ever breathed most of his infection and
poison into the mind of man.

In which holy and Heavenly use of his harp, he doth, by
his tunes of music, teach men how to set themselves in tune. Ps. 15.
How not only to tune themselves, but how to tune their [passim.]
households. And not only there, but here in this Psalm, Ps. 101.
how to preserve harmony, or, as he termeth it, how to sing [passim.]
ne perdas, to a commonwealth. So saith the inscription, [Vid. S.
which St. Augustine very fitly calleth the key of every August.
En. in Ps.
Psalm. 139. (140.)
1. et Serm.
For the time of setting this song, by general consent of all 27. de Tit.
expositors, being the latter end of the long dissension be- et Vers.
prior.
tween the Houses of David and Saul, evident it is, the estate Ps. 95.]

B 2

SERM.
I. of the land was very near to a *perdas*, and needed *ne perdas* to be sung unto it.

For, besides the great overthrow in the mountains of Gilboa, given by the enemy, wherein the King and three of his sons were slain, and a great part of the country surprised by the Philistine, the desolation of a divided kingdom was come upon them too. For within themselves they were at *Cujus est terra?* even at civil wars. At the beginning but "a play"—so Abner termeth it, but "bitterness at the end," as the same Abner confesseth. Surely, it was a weak state and low brought: so much doth David imply in the fore part of the verse, that he found the land a weak land, by means the strength and pillars of it were all out of course by the misgovernment of Saul. But then withal in the latter part of the verse he professeth, he will leave it a land of strength, by re-establishing the pillars, and re-edifying the state new again. "The earth," &c.

1 Sam. 31.7.

2 Sam. 3.12.
2 Sam. 2.14.
2 Sam. 2.26.

The style whereof runneth in the terms of Architecture, very aptly resembling the government to a frame of building; the same set upon and borne up by certain bases and pillars, the strength whereof assureth, or the weakness endangereth the whole; and David himself to a skilful builder, surveying the pillars, and searching into the decays; repairing their ruins, and setting them into course again.

The division. Whereout ariseth naturally the entreaty of these four points:

I.   That the weakness or strength of a land, is a point of important consideration.

II.   That the strength of a land is in the pillars; and what they are.

III. That the upholding of those pillars appertaineth to David.

IV. How, and in what sort, Saul weakened them in his time; and David in his made them fast.

I.   First, David had read that, among the instructions delivered by Moses to the spies, the very first and chief of all was, Whether the land were weak or strong. So he had read, and so he believed it to be; and so it is. For sure, in such lands where this is their song, "The earth is weak," their music is all out of tune. For the note is such as affecteth the inhabitants with fear. 1. Fear, in the inhabitant, for

Num. 13.19.

these two, 1. *Virtus testacea*, and 2. *Cor cereum*, "strength Ps. 22.14, like a potsherd," and "a heart like wax:" a weak land, and ^{15.} a fearful inhabitant, go together. 2. Courage, in the enemy: for where Rabshakeh knoweth but so much, that the land Isa. 36.12. is weak, you shall not entreat him to speak any thing but Hebrew.

This music is heavy, and therefore David saw the song must be new set. And so he doth set it new, changing it into a more pleasant note, "But I will strengthen it." And when the note is so changed, "in that day shall this song Isa. 26.1. be sung in the land of Judah, We have a strong city; salvation hath God set for the walls and bulwarks of it."

This music hath life in it, and hearteneth the inhabitant afresh; quaileth the enemy and resolveth the neighbour to say, "Thine are we, O David, and on thy side, thou son of 1Chr.12.18. Jesse." When a prince may say of his land, as Moses did of Judah, "His own hands are sufficient for him" (if the Deu. 33.7. Lord help him) "against all his enemies;" and the land may say of the Prince that which Solomon setteth down as the high commendation of a Prince, that he is *Rex Alkum*, that is, *ne surgito*, "rise not;" no rising against him, for Pro. 30. 31. that they which have risen had better have sat still. And they both may send word to the enemy, if he threaten to come and visit them, the word that Joash sent; "Tarry at 2 Kings 14. home, and provoke not evil against thyself." This music ^{10.} is blessed, and such hath hitherto been the song of our nation.

What Samuel said, when he pitched the stone of help, we 1 Sam.7.12. cannot deny, but we may say the same, "Thus far hath God holpen us;" Whose arm is not shortened though Pharaoh's heart be hardened. Hitherto, "Salvation hath God set for our walls and bulwarks," and our prince, Prince Alkum; and our enemy hath not "boasted himself at the putting off his 1 Kings 20. armour, as at the buckling it on;" and our neighbours glad ^{11.} to "lay hold of our skirts and say, We will be yours, for we Zach. 8. 23. see God is with you:" the great blessing of God having been upon us, "Thou shalt lend to many nations, but shalt borrow Deu. 28.12. of none." Such hath hitherto been our song; and such may it long be—yea, ever, O Lord! And that it may so be, David teacheth the way of keeping it so still, namely, by setting fast

S E R M.
I.
the pillars of it. Which is the second principal point; what this strength is, and what the pillars are that bear it up.

II. The Holy Ghost, speaking of strength, nameth two, as indeed

Gen. 32. 28. the Scripture knoweth no more : 1. The strength of Jacob, and 2. the strength of Israel. 1. Of Jacob supplanting, or prevailing over men ; 2. and of Israel, prevailing with God.

1. Jacob's strength I call whatsoever the counsel or might

Gen. 27. 6. of man affordeth ;—his prudent forecast, whereby he over-
Gen. 30. 37. reached Esau and Laban ; and his bow and sword, whereby
Gen. 48. 22. he won from the Amorite. Under these two I comprehend all human strength, the strength of Jacob.

2. But when all is done, we must reserve and keep a strength

Ps. 59. 9. for God, saith David. Who, if He forsake Alexandria, though
Nah. 3. 8. it have the sea for his ditch, it shall be carried captive :
Ps. 78. 9. Who, if He forsake Ephraim, though they be " well harnessed and carry bows," they shall " turn themselves back
Deu. 33. 7. in the day of battle." Therefore, ever *Dominus* cometh in. " Judah's own hands are sufficient to help," *si Tu Domine,*
Ps. 127. 1. " if Thou Lord help him against the enemy :" and *Nisi Dominus,* " If that the Lord do not keep the house, and watch the house, and make fast the pillars, all is in vain." Join,
Pro. 30. 1. saith the Wise Man, Ithiel, that is *Dominus mecum,* and then Ucal, that is, *Prævalebo,* will not tarry from you; Ucal and He go ever together. Sever, saith David, *Hi in curribus, hi in equis,* from *in nomine Domini,* the next news you
Ps. 20. 8. shall hear of them is, *Ibi ceciderunt, &c.* " There they are brought down and fallen." Therefore we must allow Israel a strength also, without which Jacob's forecast shall fail; for
Ps. 33. 10. " He casteth out the counsels of princes," and his sword too.
Ps. 89. 43. For, He can " rebate[1] the edge of the sword."

[1 *i. e.*
blunt.]
Two strengths then there are, and these two David here termeth two pillars, that we may know what be the pillars of the land. For such was the manner of the Jewish building— arch-wise, upon two main pillars to set it. We may see it by
Jud. 16. 19. Samson's desire so to be placed as the two supporters of the Temple might be in his two hands, that bowing them all the Church might come down upon their heads. Such an arch of government doth David here devise, and two pillars bearing it up. He telleth us they be two, and he telleth us what they be, for he hath already named them in the two former uses;

1. *Celebrabimus Te Jehova* in the first; and 2. *Justitias judi-cabo* in the second. God, and Right, the pillars; the worship of God, and the execution of justice or right. With these two he beginneth, and with these two again he taketh his farewell; the regard of religion in the ninth, and the care of [Ps. 75. 9, justice in the last. These two he teacheth us; for these two, 10.] he saith, God taught him. "God" saith he, "the Strength 2Sam.23.3. of Israel, spake to me and said, Thou shalt bear rule over men, 1. doing justice, and, 2. guiding them in the fear of God." So that these two are the pillars: 1. God, and 2. Right; Justice and the fear of God. These two give strength to that, and to all lands: 1. *Celebrabimus Te Jehova ;* and 2. *Justitias judicabo.* These two decay all, and weaken the land; 1. *Negligimus te Jehova;* and 2. *Injurias judicabo.*

God is a pillar; so is His most common name in the 1. Hebrew—Adonai, "My pillar." And His Son, a Rock; not Mat. 16. 18. only Peter's Rock, but David's Rock too; the Rock both of 2Sam. 22.2. Church and Kingdom. And His Spirit, a Spirit not of holi-ness only and truth, but "a Spirit of judgment" to them that Isa. 28. 6. sit on the throne; and "a Spirit of strength for them that keep the battle from the gate." And His favour, "a Shield," Ps. 5. 12. and His Name, *turris fortissima.* And therefore *Celebrabimus* Pro. 18. 10. *Te Jehova,* We will praise Thy Name: for "the nearer Thy Ps. 75. 1. Name is to us" and we to it, "the more wondrous works wilt Thou declare towards us." "Arise, O God, into Thy resting- Ps. 132. 8. place, Thou and the ark of Thy strength :" therefore the ark sendeth forth a strength. And Solomon, when he called the two pillars, which he set at the temple gate, Strength and Jachin Steadiness, meant, that out of that gate there proceeded and Boaz. 1 Kings strength and stablishing to the whole realm. 7. 21.

Even the strength and stablishing of *Si credideritis stabilie-* Isa. 7. 9. *mini,* by which not only the devil's "darts" are repelled in the Eph. 6. 16. spiritual, but "the armies of the aliens are put to flight" in Heb. 11. 34. the earthly warfare. Therefore Moses made such reckoning of *Celebrabimus,* that having recounted, as the strength of Cain's progeny, their inventing of the tent, making of the flute of brass, and iron works, he opposeth to them all, as able Gen. 4. to match them all, in the posterity of the sons of God, the 20-22. invocation of His Name, begun and set on foot, first, by Gen. 4. Enoch, as the main pillar of strength which the people of God 17.

trust to. And St. Paul is bold, 1 Tim. 2. 1, where, laying, as it were, the chamber-beams and stories of each Christian government;—Princes first, by whose means peace, and quietness; from thence knowledge of the truth; from it, godly and honest life; and from them, salvation; as the base or pillar of all, and that which beareth up, and giveth strength to all, setteth Prayer; prayer to be made, that so princes preserved; that so peace maintained; that so knowledge intended; that so a godly and honest life practised; that so salvation attained. Reckoning invocation as a special pillar of each estate; and as a prerogative royal, prayer for all men, but above all men for princes. Thus doth religion strengthen us, and is Israel with God: and not with God only, but is Jacob also, and prevaileth with men too.

Indeed, nothing prevaileth so much, nor worketh so deep, with man, as doth it; and, no men more fast and faithful, than *quorum Deus corda tetigit.* David therefore, undertaking in this verse to stablish the pillars, sheweth how he will do it in the next; *dicam,* by telling them their duty out of divinity; by laying before them *Deus est judex,* God's judgment, and the dregs of the cup which He holdeth in His hand. To make so many men so many pillars, well and wisely said the heathen man, *Odium oportet peccandi, non metum facias.* To hate sin is the pillar, to fear it is not; for fear will fall away if his understanding be removed, and where the duty is not grounded on *Deus est judex,* it is no pillar to be built on. Certain it is, that, except God's laws, all laws, fear of sin they breed; but a kind hatred or conscience of sin, they breed not. Well may they bind the hand, fetter the foot, and imprison the body: there is nothing can imprison the heart or thought, save *arma militiæ nostræ.* And thus is Religion a pillar among them also.

For sure, the *Christian* duty of bearing wrong, where it is well persuaded, doth mainly strengthen the *Civil* of doing no wrong; and the Christian, of departing with our own charitably, doth strengthen the Civil of not taking other men's injuriously; and so, of the rest. That he called it not amiss, that called Divinity the backbone of the Prince's law; and consequently, Religion of the commonwealth. So that, not only Moses and Paul by calling on the Name of God, but

[Conf.
Ciceron.
de Legib.
1. 14. et
Horat.
Epist. I.
16. 52.]

Elias and Jeremy, by teaching the will of God—not by prayer only, but by preaching—are the one, "an iron pillar," the other, "the chariot and horsemen of Israel," in his time. Jer. 1. 18. 2 Kings 13. 14.

Now if all men had faith, *dicam* would have served, and this one pillar have been enough; but because all men have not religion, but there be in the "world evil and absurd men," therefore needed the second, therefore needed *Justitias judicabo.* Indeed, *meliores sunt,* 'the better part be they,' *quos dirigit amor,* 'whom love leadeth;' but *plures sunt quos corrigit timor,* 'the greater by far, that fear driveth.' Even such as will not be "led with the cords of a man," that is, inducements of religion and reason, but they "must be held with bit and bridle," that is, the curb of justice. 2. 2 Thes. 3. 2. Hos. 11. 4. Ps. 32. 9.

Which kind of men are of two sorts; therefore it is *Justitias.* 1. The enemy or Egyptian smiting Israel from without; 2. The injurious Israelite wronging his brother, from within. Why then, *Sit nobis Rex,* say the people, which is a perfect comprehension of this pillar of justice to do them right, and to defend them by war, when need is, against the foreign enemy; by justice, when cause is, against the domestical oppressor. Against the one Jehoshaphat placeth "garrisons," that is, against outward hostility; against the other he ordaineth "judges," that is, inward injury. Ex.2.11.13. 1 Sam.8.19. 2 Chron. 17. 2. 2 Chron. 19. 5.

Dicens Cyro, saith God, *Pastor meus, &c.* "which say to Cyrus," the mighty monarch, "Thou art My shepherd." A shepherd, by pastoral justice, to see the flock safe from without, and quiet from within. From without, to keep "the wild boar of the forest" from spoiling our lives and goods, and from within, the "ravenous wolf from making havoc of our souls." Will you know what these two mean? "O My people," saith God, "remember what Balak the king hath devised against you"—speaking of a foreign prince, of the boar, "and what Balaam hath answered him"—speaking of a false Prophet, of the wolf. The case is very like ours, and God grant us a thankful remembrance and meditation of it; of the long intelligence between Balak and Balaam for our overthrow, and how graciously and marvellously God hath delivered us! Isa. 44. 28. Ps. 80. 13. Acts 20. 29. Mic. 6. 5.

Now, as without the fold these beasts be busy, and God therefore hath "girt the prince with a sword;" so within also there are certain "fed rams," saith Ezekiel, that with their Ps. 45. 3. Ez. 34. 20, 21.

SERM. horns push, and with their heels lay out against the poor
I. ―― weak sheep (that with *vis* and *fraus*, 'deceit' and 'violence'
keep evil rule within;) against whom He hath given into
Ps. 45. 6. their right hand a sceptre, that by the arrest of the sceptre
they might be quiet from within, and by the edge of the
1 Tim. 3. 9. sword, safe from without; so intending the "mystery of
1 Tim. 4. 7. godliness," and the knowledge thereof, and after it "the
exercise of godliness," and the practice thereof; that so,
after *Stabiliatur Regnum meum* in this life by Justice, we
may come to *Adveniat Regnum Tuum* in the life to come by
Religion. And this is the second pillar, yielding us Jacob's
Gen. 32. 10. strength, who, as we said, was furnished both with "his staff"
to see good order in his flock, and with his sword and bow
Gen. 48. 22. against the Amorite.

Thus have we the two pillars of the earth, each strengthening other; Religion rooting Justice within; Justice fencing
Religion without, and they both making an arch of government irremoveable.

III. Yet, these two pillars, as strong and as steady as they are,
except they be looked to and upheld, except they have an
upholder and that a good one, Religion will cleave, and Justice
bend, and they both sink, and the whole frame with them.
Therefore mention is made here of a person put in trust with
the bearing them up, which is the third point.

Which person is here, *Ego autem*, the first, that is, David;
the first and the chief person in any government. He it is
upon whom both these lean; he is the head, that guideth these
two arms; he, the breath of life in both these nostrils; yea,
of all the body, saith Jeremy of Josias. Even *christus Domini*,
Lam. 4. 20. "the anointed of the Lord is the breath of all our nostrils."

Familiar it is and but mean, but very full and forcible, the
Is. 22. 23. simile of Esay; wherein he compareth the prince to "a nail
driven into a wall," whereon are hanged all, both the vessels of
service and the instruments of music; that is, he bears them
up all. And great cause to desire God, fast may it stick and
never stir, this nail: for if it should, all our cups would batter
with the fall, and all the music of our choir be marred; that
Phil.
Judæ. is both Church and country be put in danger. Which God
περὶ τοῦ willing to shew, saith Philo Judæus, He did place the fifth
τίς ὁ τῶν
θείων commandment, which is the crown commandment, ὡς ἐν

μεσορίῳ, 'as it were, in the middle,' and confines of both τραγμάτων
tables; those touching Religion, and those touching Jus- κληρονό-
tice; that with one arm he might stay Religion, and with med.]
the other stay Justice, and so uphold both.

And, where such support ·hath wanted, both have lain on
the ground. For, both of Micah's idolatry, that is corrupt Jud. 17.
religion, and of the villany offered at Gibeah, and of the out- 1, 2, &c.
rage committed by them of Dan, both in rifling houses, and 19. 25, &c.
sacking whole towns, that is, of open injustice, God rendereth
no cause but this, *non erat Rex;* the pillars went down, *ego*
wanted. Without which, that is, an established government,
we should have no commonwealth, but a wild forest, where
Nimrod and his crew would hunt and chase all others; Gen. 10. 8.
no commonwealth, but a pond where the great fish would Hab. 1. 14.
devour the small; nothing but a sort of "sheep scattered Num. 27. 17
without a shepherd," saith Moses. No more *oves pascuæ,* Ps. 95. 7.
"sheep of the pasture," when their governor is gone, but
oves occisionis, "sheep for the slaughter." *Non populus, sed* Ps. 44. 22.
turba, 'no people, but a rout;' no building, nor pillars, but
a heap of stones. Therefore a joyful noise "is the shout of Nu. 23. 21.
a king" among them.

Joyful indeed every way, but joyful especially if this *ego*
be not Saul, but David. David, which giveth strength unto
the pillars, and not Saul, an impairer or weakener of them.
It is David's complaint in the forepart, he found the land
weak when he came to it. So Saul had left it. It is his
promise that as Saul by his slackness had brought the estate
low, so he by his vigilance would raise it up again. And this
is the last point, how Saul decayed, and David restored the
pillar again.

The Wise Man saith, that "evil looking to will decay the IV.
principals of any building;" and that was Saul's defect, as the Ecc. 10. 18.
Scripture recordeth. Religion first: instead of *Celebrabimus,*
Negligimus Jehovam. King David, in his oration to the states
of his realm before his first Parliament, testifieth, "the ark 1 Chron.
was not sought to in the days of Saul;" that pillar was 13. 3.
not looked to. Sought to it was, after a sort, religion; but
nothing so as it should. "Come let us have the ark," saith 1 Sam. 14.
he; and then, "Go to, it skills not greatly, carry it back 18, 19.
again;" which, what was it but to play fast and loose with

SERM.
I.

Acts 24. 25.
Eph. 5. 16.

2 Sam. 6. 16.

1 Sam. 21. 4.

Acts 18. 17.

Hos. 13. 2.

1 Kings
14. 15.

Deu. 33. 27.

Zach. 11. 4.

1 Sam. 13.
22.

2 Sam. 1. 18.

religion? To intend Paul, as Felix saith, at our idle time; and not to "redeem time," to that end? Judge of Religion's case by the reverence of the Ephod. A daughter of his own bringing up, Michal, saw David for honour of the ark wear it, and "despised him in her heart." Judge of it by the regard of the Priest, the keeper of the ark : for very love to it, that calling was kept so low and bare that they were tied to the allowance of their shew-bread; the High-Priest had not a loaf in his house besides. This was the first root of his kingdom: the ark not sought to, the Ephod in contempt, the priesthood impoverished : *et Saulo nihil horum curæ*, 'and Saul regarded not any of these things.'

Such another indifferency for Church matters we find in Jeroboam. "Tush," said he, jestingly, "let them kiss the calves and spare not." Let it go which way it will. But therefore God sends him word by Ahijah, "that Israel should be as a reed in the water," bowing to and fro, at the devotion of every wave and every wind, without any steadiness. And was it not so? Search the Chronicles. So, God saw this mind in Saul to His ark and was wroth; withdrew from him His religious and good Spirit, and sent upon him a profane and furious spirit, which carried him on first to a sinful life, and never left him till it had brought him to a shameful death. And God was even saying His *disperdas* to the kingdom, but David here entreated for a *ne perdas*, and promised a better care of *celebrabimus Jehovam*.

Now, where Religion thrives not, the other of Justice will not hold long; when one staff is broken, the other holdeth not whole long after. And surely his justice was suitable to the former, to his weak regard of religion; that also was weak too.

1. Weak towards the enemy. It is said, there was want of necessary furniture of armour and munition in his days. And there had been defect in teaching them to shoot, which David supplied at his entrance. 2. Weak at home too, where he did not *justitias*, but *injurias judicare*.

The parts of Justice are two, as we find in the tenth verse. 1. To exalt the horns of the righteous, 2. and to break the horns of the wicked.

1. For the first. Reason was, and so was promise too,

that David should have been rewarded with Merab his 1 Sam. 18.
eldest daughter's marriage. I know not how, one Adriel, an 17. 19.
obscure fellow, never to have been named but to shew such
an one put David by, had his horn exalted above him. This
for reward.

2. And his punishment was no better. Merciful to Agag, 1 Sam. 15. 9.
whose horns should have been broken, and in Ahimelech's 1 Sam. 22.
case too rigorous, putting him, and eighty-four more, to the 17.
sword for a dozen of bread.

And whereas, in kindly justice, the rigour of *frangam cornua* cometh not at first, but clemency giveth gracious warning, with *Dicam imprudentibus.* So, without regard thereof, Pa. 75. 4.
as upon any displeasure, without any word at all, his javelin 1 Sam. 18.
went straight to nail men to the wall, they knew not wherefore. 11.
1 Sam. 19.
Thus did justice decay after religion, and one pillar fall upon 10.
another, whereof ensued his overthrow, and the land dan- 1 Sam. 20. 33.
gerously sick of the palsy. Whereof David complaineth, and Pa. 60. 2.
prayeth, " Heal the sores thereof, for it shaketh."

Now David, as when he read Abimelech's mishap in the [Jud. 9. 53.]
Book of Judges, he made his use of it, as appeareth 2 Sam. 2 Sam. 11. 21.
11. 21; so here when he saw what had turned Saul to
damage, took warning by it (*ruina præcedentium, admonitio
sequentium*), and, to make the land strong, falleth to under-
set the pillars.

And first, of the first, that is, the stone which Saul and his
builders cast aside. For, coming to the kingdom, he conse-
crates all his laws with his act *de Arcâ reducendâ;* whereat he 1 Chron.
would needs be present in his own person, because it touched 13. 2, 8.
Celebrabimus Jehovam, and that with some disgrace, as Michal
imagined; but he was resolute in that point, he could receive
no dishonour by doing honour to God's ark. And, when it was
brought back, set such an order for the service of it by the 1 Chron. 26.
Levites, for maintenance so bountiful, so reverend for regard, passim.
so decent for order, so every way sufficient, as the care of
the Temple might seem to reign in his heart. As indeed it
did, and as he professeth, " he could not sleep" till he had set Pa. 132. 3.
a full order for God's matters, and brought this pillar to perfection. Which his care was *secundum cor Dei,* and God
would signify so much by the ceremony in the Coronation of
the kings of Judah. Wherein, putting not only the diadem

S E R M.
L.
2 Kings 11.
12.
Isa. 22. 22. imperial, but the Book of the Law also, upon the king's head, it was intended that Book should be as dear to them as their crown, and they equally study to advance it. And in putting the sceptre of justice in their hands, and in laying the key of the House of David on their shoulders, what else was required, but as they executed the one with their hand, so they should put to the other, arm and shoulder and all? that is, as David here expresseth it, two *celebrabimuses* to one *judicabo*.

Thus was strengthened the first pillar, and for the second the Holy Ghost giveth him an honourable testimony; I speak not of his military justice, I need not—therein he was trained 2 Sam. 8. 15. up, but that in peace, "he executed judgment and justice to Ps. 99. 4. all his people." "The king's power," saith he, "loveth judgment,"—not power in injury, but power in judgment, saith 2 Cor. 13. 10. David; "power to edification," saith St. Paul, "not to destruction;" that is, to build up, not to decay the building. Therefore, virtue and valour wanted not their reward in his Ps. 75. 6. time. He professeth after in this Psalm, the wind should blow no man to preferment, out of what quarter soever it came, but God by His graces should point them to it. And 1 Chron. 11. 10, &c. sure, the diligent description the Holy Ghost useth of his worthies and men of place, sheweth him to have been most exact in this point: first, his three; and then after, his 2 Sam. 23. 8, &c. thirty in their order; and that those "thirty attained not unto the first three," but every one esteemed and regarded, in his worthiness.

And for depressing the wicked, it was his morning work, Ps. 101. 8. as he testifieth, and that, as himself here sets down, in a most heavenly order, with *dicam* first, as being set over men, and Hos. 11. 4. therefore willing to "lead them with the cords of men," that is, fair and gentle, yet effectual persuasions. And never did Pro. 19. 12. the dew of Heaven more sweetly refresh the grass, than doth a favourable saying pierce the inferior from the mouth of a prince. Therefore, there was no estate in the land, but in this book, I will not say he mildly said, but he even sweetly, Ps. 101. 1-8. sung their several duties unto them. To his court, his Ps. 45. pas.
Ps. 82. 1-8. Church, his Judges; his commons, all in one. I will add this, Ps. 144.
passim. that if David offended in ought, herein it was, in that he used 2 Sam. 15. 3. *dicam* too much, and *frangam* not often enough. Absalom could object it, when it served his turn; and when David

was to leave the world, it lay on his conscience, his clemency 1 Kings 2. 5, &c.
used in Joab's and Shimei's case. " A dear and precious Pa. 72. 14.
thing is the meanest blood in the eyes of David"—so he
saith. And that made his people more afraid *for* him than
of him, and to value his life at " ten thousand" of their own ; 2 Sam. 18. 3.
and that, so many subjects, so many of his guard ; not, so
many subjects, so many conspirators, as Saul complained. 1 Sam. 22. 8.

Yet, because clemency is but one foot of the throne, and Pro. 20. 28.
severity at some other time (for, *cum accepero tempus,* time Ps. 75. 2.
must be kept in this music) doth no less support it ; therefore, where saying will not serve, nor singing, *frangam* must
sometimes be used ; where the rod contemned, let the sword Ez. 21. 9, 10.
be drawn. It is God's own course. If he, for all *dicam,* lift
up his horn against God or good orders, saw off his horn ; if
he do still *mutilá fronte minitari, caput ejus mittetur ad te,* 2 Sam. 20.
was David's justice ;—Take off his head. For *dicam* is the 21.
charm he speaketh of, which, if the viper stop not his ear, Ps. 58. 5.
will do him good ; if it do not, *contunde in theriacam,* he
must be bruised and made into mithridate[1], that others may [1 "One of
be amended by him, seeing he would not be amended by the capital medicines of
others. the shops, consisting

Thus did David repair Saul's ruins ; these are his steps, of a great number of
thus did he shew himself as good as his promise here, a skilful ingredients,
upholder of these two main pillars, which bear up and give name from
strength to every land. And by this means he changed both its inventor
the nature and name of his country ; finding it *Jebus,* that is, dates, King
conculcata, and so indeed it was, a city contemned and trod- Quincy,
den down with every foot ; and leaving it a new name, Jeru- cited in
salem, and so it was, *Salem Jeru,* a city to be feared and Johnson.]
envied of all round about it. So the land grew strong, and
the pillars fast ; and David, for his fastening, in favour with
God and man. God, Whom he praised, graciously assisting
him ; and men, whom he preserved, willingly serving him.

The Lord Who hath sent forth the like strength for our
land, stablish the good things which He hath wrought in us !
The Lord so fasten the pillars of our earth, that they never
be shaken ! The Lord mightily uphold the upholder of them
long, and many years ; that we may go forth rejoicing in His
strength, and make our boast of His praise, all our life long !

Which our gracious God, &c.

A SERMON

PREACHED BEFORE

QUEEN ELIZABETH, AT GREENWICH,

ON THE TWENTY-FOURTH OF FEBRUARY, A.D. MDXC. BEING
ST. MATTHIAS' DAY.

PSALM lxxvii. 20.

Thou didst lead Thy people like sheep, by the hand of Moses and Aaron.

[*Deduxisti sicut oves populum Tuum, in manu Moysis et Aaron.* Latin Vulg.]

[*Thou leddest Thy people like a flock by the hand of Moses and Aaron.* Engl. Trans.]

SERM. II.

Ps. 77. 7—9.

SOME, either present or imminent danger, and that no small one, had more than usually distressed the Prophet at the writing of this Psalm; wherewith his spirit, for a while, being tossed to and fro in great anguish, as may appear by those three great billows in the seventh, eighth, and ninth verses, yet at last he cometh to an anchor in the tenth verse, "upon the remembrance of the right hand of the Most High." Which right hand, in one even tenor throughout all ages, not only to that of David's, but even to this of ours, hath ever shewed itself a right hand of pre-eminence and power, in the two points in the latter part of the Psalm specified, the especial matter of his and all our comfort. 1. The final confusion of his enemies, though for a while exalted until this verse. 2. The final deliverance of His people, though for a while distressed in this verse. Which twain, of many Psalms are the substance, and of this now before us; and indeed, all the whole story in a manner is nothing else but a calendar of these two. That the Lord of Hosts, the God of Israel, is *El Nekamoth,* "a God of vengeance" against His enemies; and but a letter changed, is *El Nechamoth,* "a God of comfort" unto His people. That His Cherubims hold a flaming sword to repress the one, and have their wings spread to shadow and succour the other. That His creatures—the cloud from above is a mist of darkness to confound the Egyp- Ex. 14. 20. tians; and the same cloud a pillar of light to conduct the Israelites. That the water from beneath, to the Egyptian is a gulf to devour them, but to the Israelite, "a wall of de- [Ex.14.22.] fence on their right hand and on their left." We need not to seek far; in the Psalm next before, and again in the Psalm next after this, you shall find these two coupled; as indeed for the most part they go still together.

And as they go still together, so still they end in the safe-guard of the Church. Of all prophecies, of all judgments, of all miracles, past or present, new or old, that is the key and conclusion. The last verse, if I may so say, of the Deluge was the rainbow; of the Egyptian bondage was the Feast of Passover; and even here in this Psalm, after it hath in the four verses next before rained and poured down, and lightened and thundered, and Heaven and earth gone toge-ther, there doth in this verse ensue a calm to God's people. This is the blessed period that shutteth up the Psalm: Them that hated Thy people, or dealt unkindly with Thy ser-vants, them Thou drownedst and destroyedst; but "Thy people Thou leadest like sheep by the hands of Moses and Aaron."

And in these two may all kingdoms and countries read their own destinies, what they are to hope for or to fear, at the hands of God. If they be *Lo-ammi*, "not His people," [Hos. 1. 9.] they may look back, what they find in the verses before, and that is storm and tempest. If they be His, and we I trust are His—and more and more His He daily make us! this verse is for us, that is, safe and quiet conduct; "Thou didst lead Thy," &c.

In which verse there is mention of three persons: 1. God. The sum. 2. God's hand. 3. God's people. 4. And of a blessing or benefit issuing from the first, that is, God; conveyed by the second, that is, God's hands, Moses and Aaron; and received by the third, that is, God's people; and it is the benefit of good guiding or government. This is the sum of the verse.

As for order, I will seek no other than as the Holy Ghost The divi-sion.

ANDREWES. c

SERM. hath marshalled the words in the text itself. Which of itself
II. is right exact; every word in the body of it containing matter
worth the pausing on.

1. First, in the foremost word. *Tu,* God Who vouchsafed
this benefit.

2. And secondly, in *Duxisti.* The benefit itself of guiding
from Him derived.

3. And thirdly, derived to His people, the parties that receive it.

4. And fourthly, derived to His people by His hands, which
hands are Moses and Aaron, the means that convey it.

The first I. " Thou leadest Thy people," &c. To begin with God,
part. Who beginneth the verse, by Whom and to Whom we lead,
"Thou." and are led, and in Whom all right leading both beginneth
and endeth.

Ps. 78. 52. It is Thou, saith the Psalmist, that leadest Thy people, and
in the next Psalm it is " He that carried His people in the
wilderness like a flock." Who is that *He,* or this *Thou?* It
is God, saith the Prophet in the sixteenth verse.

That is, whosoever be the hands, God is the Person, He is
the *Tu.* Whose names soever we hear, whose hands soever
we feel, whose countenance soever we behold, we must yet
look up higher, and see God in every government. To Him
we must make our apostrophe, and say, " Thou leadest," &c.
For He it is leadeth properly; and in strict propriety of
speech Moses and Aaron lead not, but God by the hands
of Moses and Aaron. And that thus it is, that God is the
Person that leadeth, and all other but hands under Him and
unto Him, the Prophet giveth us in this same verse matter
of three marks of difference between Him and them.

1. The first is in *Duxisti.* " Thou didst lead," saith the
Prophet, didst and dost lead—didst then and dost still: but
Thou didst lead by Moses and Aaron; so dost Thou not now.
The hands are changed. Then, Moses and Aaron; after,
Joshua and Eleazar; after, Othniel and Phinehas; after,
Ps. 102. 27. others; *sed Tu idem es,* " but Thou art the same still, and
Thy years shall not fail." As if he should say; Their years
indeed fail, and come to an end: within so many years they
were not so led, and within so many more they shall not be.
But God hath a prerogative, that He is *Rex a Sæculo,* and

Rex in Sæculum; was "our King of old," and "shall be our King for ever and ever." Ps. 74. 12. Ps. 146. 10.

The second is in *populum Tuum*, "Thy people;" another 2. limitation. For this people are, in the fifteenth verse before, said to be "the sons of Jacob and Joseph:" so far stretcheth [Ps. 77. 15.] Moses' line, and no farther. But, *Tu duxisti*, God's line *ivit in omnem terram*, "goeth over all nations, even to the utter- Ps. 19. 4. most parts of the world." God's leading hath no marches. This people and all people are His; and He by special pre- rogative is *Rex universæ terræ*, "King" not of one people, or Ps. 47. 7. of one country or climate, but "of all the people of the whole earth."

The third is, *per manus*, "by the hands." For as He 3. guideth the people by the hands, so He guideth the hands themselves, by whom He guideth; ruleth by them, and ruleth them; ruleth by their hands, and ruleth in their hearts; is both "the Shepherd of Israel," leading them Ps. 80. 1. like sheep, and farther leadeth Joseph also, their leader, *tanquam ovem*, "like a sheep." That is, they be *reges gentium*, 'kings of the nations,' but He is *Rex regum*, "King 1 Tim. 6. 15. over kings themselves." Moses and they with him be ἡγούμενοι, "guides," as St. Paul calleth them; but Jesus Heb. 13. 17. Christ is Ἀρχηγὸς, "the Arch-guide." Aaron and his family Heb. 12. 2. be ποιμένες, "shepherds," as St. Peter termeth them; but Jesus Christ is Ἀρχιποιμὴν, "the high and sovereign Shep- 1 Pet. 5. 4. herd over all." Why then *dicite in gentibus*, "tell it out Ps. 96. 10. among the nations," saith the Prophet, "that God is King;" that He is the *Tu*, the Leader, the perpetual, the universal, principal Leader of His people.

From which plain note, that the Lord is Ruler, the Psalmist himself draweth a double use, containing matter both of comfort and fear.

1. Of comfort, in the ninety-seventh Psalm: *Dominus* Ps. 97. 1. *regnavit, exultet terra;* "the Lord is Ruler, or Leader, let the earth rejoice."

2. Of fear, in the ninety-ninth Psalm: *Dominus regnavit,* Ps. 99. 1. *contremiscat populus;* "the Lord is Ruler, or Leader, let the people tremble."

First, from God's ruling, matter of joy. For if we will be 1. ruled by Him, He will appoint over us a ruler "according to 1 Sam. 13. 14.

SERM.
II.
———
Ps. 21. 3.
Ps. 132. 18.
Ps. 89. 29.

His own heart;" He will "prevent her with the blessings of goodness;" He will deliver the power of Sisera into her hands; "He will clothe her enemies with shame, and make her crown flourish on her head, and set the days of her life as the days of Heaven."

Ps. 99. 1.

2. Secondly, matter of fear too. "The Lord is Ruler, let the people tremble." For if they fall to be unruly, He can

Ps. 76. 12.

vindemiare spiritum principum, as easily 'gather to Him' "the breath of a Prince," as we can slip off a cluster from the vine. He can send them a Rehoboam without wisdom, or a Jeroboam without religion, or Ashur a stranger, to be their

Hos. 10. 3.

King; or, which is worst of all, *nullum regem,* a disordered anarchy, *quia non timuimus Jehovam.* Therefore *exultantes et trementes,* 'in joy and trembling' let us acknowledge God and His supreme leading, that our parts may be long in *Dominus regnavit, exultet terra,* "The Lord doth lead us, let the land rejoice."

Yet one point more out of this *Tu,* by comparing it with the verses before, on which it dependeth; that as it is the Person and Power of God that is chief in every rule, so not every power, but even that very power of His, "whereby He worketh wonders." For the Prophet, in the

Ps. 77. 14.

fourteenth verse, having said of God, "Thou art the God That

Ps. 77. 18.

doest wonders," and so particularising, "Thou thunderest from Heaven, Thou shakest the earth, Thou dividest the

Ps. 77. 19, 20.

sea," at last cometh to this *Thou;*—"Thou leadest the people." Very strange it is, that he should sort the leading of the people with God's wonders, and that not only among them all, but after them all, as chief of all; recount the government of the people, as if it were some special miracle. And indeed a miracle it is, and whosoever shall look into the nature and weight of a Monarchy will so acknowledge it. The rod of government is a miraculous rod—both that

Exod. 4. 3.

of Moses, for it would turn into a serpent, and back again;

Nu. 17. 8.

and Aaron's rod too, for of a dry and sear stick it came to blossom again, and to bear ripe almonds; to shew, that every government is miraculous, and containeth in it matter of wonder, and that in two respects.

1. For whereas there is naturally in every man a seeking his

Ezek. 11. 3.

own ease, to lie soaking in his broth, as Ezekiel speaketh;

not to be *custos fratris*, nor to afflict and vex his soul with the Gen. 4. 9.
care of others; it is surely supernatural to endure that cark
and care which the governors continually do—a matter that
we inferiors can little skill of; but to read *Eâ nocte dormire* Esther 6. 1.
non potuit rex, "Such a night the King could not sleep;"
and again, Such a night "no meat would down with the Dan. 6. 18.
King, and he listed not to hear any music." To endure
this, I say, is supernatural; and it is God which, above all
nature, by His mighty Spirit worketh it in them.

Again, whereas there is in every inferior a natural wildness
or unwillingness to brook any ruler or judge over them, as Nu. 16. 12,
was told Moses flatly to his face, for by nature the people &c.
are not like sheep; it is not certainly any power of man, but
a mere supernatural thing, to keep the nations of the earth
in such awe and order as we see them in. *Quis potest*, saith 1Kings 3.9.
Solomon, "Who is able to manage this mighty multitude,"
so huge in number, so unruly in affection? *Nonne potestatem* Joh. 19. 10.
habeo ? "Have not I power," saith Pilate? But our Saviour
Christ very fitly telleth him, Power he hath indeed, but it is
not *innata*, but *data desuper ;* and except it were given him Joh. 19. 11.
from above, he should have none at all. It is *Tu duxisti* that
doth it; even Thou, O Lord, and Thine Almighty power,
that holdest them under. And very fitly from the wonder in
appeasing the sea, in the last verse before, doth the Prophet Ps. 77. 19.
pass in this to the leading of the people. Their natures are
alike, himself in one verse matcheth them; "Thou rulest the Ps. 65. 7.
raging of the sea, and the noise of the waves, and the mad-
ness of the people." That is, no less unruly and enraged by
nature is the multitude, than the sea. No less it roareth,
Dirumpamus vincula eorum, and *Nolumus hunc regnare super* Ps. 2. 3.
nos, when God unlooseth it. Of one and the same power it Lu. 19. 14.
proceedeth, to keep them both within their banks. Thou
that calmest the one, charmest also the other.

Wherefore when we see that careful mind in a Prince, I
will use Moses' own words, to carry a people in her arms, as Nu. 11. 12.
if she had conceived them in her womb, as no nurse, nor
mother more tender; and again, when we see this tumultuous and tempestuous body, this same sea of popularity kept
in a quiet calm, and infinite millions ebbing and flowing as it
were, that is, stirring and standing still, arming and disarm-

S E R M.
II.
Mat. 8. 9.

ing themselves, killing and being killed, and all at the mono-.
syllables of one person, "Go and they go, Come and they
come, Do and they do it;" let us see God sensibly in it, and
the power of God, yea, the miraculous power of God; and
say with the Prophet, "Thou art the God That doest wonders,
Thou leddest Thy people like sheep by the hands of Moses
and Aaron." And so much for the first part, first word, and
Person.

II.
The
second
part.
Duxisti.
Ex. 17. 15.
Isa. 9. 6.
Ps. 82. 1.

The second word compriseth the benefit issuing from God,
which is a leading or conduct, the second part. A word of
great compass, and includeth many leadings under it. For,
to be our Jehovah-Nissi, our "Standard-bearer," and to lead
our forces in the field; to be our "wonderful Counsellor,"
and to lead that honourable board; to sit in the midst of
our Judges, and to lead them in giving sentence;—all these
and more than these are all in *duxisti*. And all these are
especial favours; but the chief of all, and that whereof all
these are but the train, is the leading us in His heavenly
truth, and in the way of His Commandments, to the land of
the living. All the rest attend upon this; this is chief, and
therefore the leading of principal intendment.

And in this leading there be these four points. For that
it be a leading, it must be orderly without straying, skilfully
without erring, gently without forcing, and certainly without
missing our journey's end. First, orderly without straying;
led and not wandered. Second, skilfully without erring; led
and not missed. Third, gently without forcing; led and not
drawn. Fourth, certainly without missing; led, and not led
about, ever going, but never coming to our place of repose.

1. In the first whereof, we are but let see the wandering and
stayless estate we were in, till God vouchsafed to send us this

Ezek. 34.
5, 6.

gracious conduct; *sicut oves*, like Ezekiel's "stray sheep,
straggling upon every valley and upon every hill." The very
case these people here were in, when God in mercy sent them

Ex. 5. 12.

these two guides, scattered all over the land to seek stubble.
Which estate of theirs, is the express pattern of the world,
wandering in vanity, picking up straws, and things that shall

Wis. 1. 12.

not profit them, "seeking death in the error of their life," till
God look mercifully upon them, and from this wild wandering reduce them into the right way.

Which right way is the second point; for else it is not 2. *duxisti,* but *seduxisti;* and as good no leading at all, as misleading. Now this right way, if we ask where it lieth, the Prophet will tell us, " Thy way, O God, is in the Sanctuary;" Ps. 77. 13. that is, it is the word of God which is the load-star, when God is the Leads-man. *Sicut oves* it must be, and this is the voice of the true Shepherd to be listened to of all his flock, that will not rove and run headlong into the wolf's den. This is the " pillar of the cloud" in regard of this people here, Ex. 14. 19, to be kept in view of all those that will not perish in the &c. wilderness, wherein is no path. Indeed it is both 1. " the pillar of the cloud" before, directing us in the way; 2. and the voice of the shepherd behind us, as Esay saith, telling us Isa. 30. 21. when we miss, and crying, *Hæc est via, ambulate in eâ,* " This is the way, the right way, walk in it."

And in this way our guiding must be mild and gentle, else 3. it is not *duxisti* but *traxisti;* drawing and driving, and no leading. *Leni spiritu non durâ manu,* rather by an inward sweet influence to be led, than by an outward extreme violence to be forced forward. So did God lead this people here. Not the greatest pace, I wis, for they were a year marching that they might have posted in eleven days, as Deu. 1. 2. Moses saith. No nor yet the nearest way neither, as Moses telleth us. For he fetched a compass divers times, as all Ex. 13. 18. wise governors by his example must do, that desire rather safely to lead, than hastily to drive forward. " The Spirit Isa. 63. 14. of God leadeth this people," saith Esay, " as an horse is ridden down the hill into a valley;" which must not be a gallop, lest horse and ruler both come down one over another, but warily and easily. And *sicut oves* still giveth us light, seeing the text compareth it to a sheep-gate. Touching which kind of cattle, to very good purpose, Jacob, Gen. 33. 13. a skilful shepherd, answereth Esau, who would have had Jacob and his flocks have kept company with him in his hunting pace. " Nay not so, sir," saith Jacob, " it is a tender cattle that is under my hands, and must be softly driven, as they may endure; if one should overdrive them but one day, they would all die," or be laid up for many days after. Indeed, Rehoboam left ten parts of his flock 1 Kings 12. behind, only for ignorance of this very point in *duxisti.* 10, 11.

SERM.
II.

For when in boisterous manner he chased them before him, telling them what yokes he would make for them—a far unmeet occupation for a prince to be a yoke-maker—they all shrunk from him presently, and falsified his prophecy clean. For whereas he told them sadly, " His little finger should be as big as his father's whole body," it fell out clean contrary; for his whole body proved not so big as his father's little finger. A gentle leading it must be, and in the beginning such was the course. Therefore ye have the Kings of Canaan in Genesis for the most part called by the name of Abimelech, that is, *Pater Rex*, a King in place, a Father

Nu. 12. 3.

in affection. Such was Moses our leader here, "a meek man above all the men on the earth." Such was David

2 Sam. 3. 39.

himself, who full bitterly complaineth, "Ah, these sons of Zeruiah are too hard, too full of execution for me." And, to end this point, thus describeth he his good prince in the

Ps. 72. 6.

seventy-second Psalm; " He shall come down," not like hail-stones on a house-top, but " like the dew into a fleece of wool," that is, sweetly and mildly, without any noise or violence at all.

Last of all. All this reducing and right leading and gentle leading must end in an end; they must not go and go still *in infinitum ;* that is no leading but tiring outright. It must

Ps. 23. 2.

be *sicut oves,* whom the good Shepherd, in the three and twentieth Psalm, leadeth to a place, and to a place meet for them, "where there is green pasture by the waters of comfort." So was it in this people here. They were led out of Egypt to sacrifice to God, and to learn His law in the Mount of God, Sinai; and from thence also to Sion itself, His own rest, and holy habitation. And even so our people are led from the wanderings of this world unto the folds of God's Church, where, as the Prophet saith in the seventy-third

Ps. 73. 24.

Psalm, first God " will a while guide them with His counsel, and after will receive them into His glory." And this is the end of all leading. To bring us all from the vain proffers of the world, which we shall all find, as Solomon found it,

Ecc. 1. 2.

vanitas vanitatum et omnia vanitas, to the sound comfort of His word in this book, which is indeed *veritas veritatum et omnia veritas ;* in the knowledge and practice whereof, when they shall have fulfilled their course here, God will bring

them to His own rest, to His Heavenly Jerusalem, where is
and ever shall be *felicitas felicitatum et omnia felicitas.*

But in this life here, we come no farther than "the Ps. 78. 54.
borders of His Sanctuary," as he telleth us in the next
Psalm, in the way whereof if God lead us *constanter,* 'constantly,' not after our wanton manner, out and in when we
list, all the other inferior leadings shall accompany this one.
For this leading leadeth them all. He shall lead our Counsellors, that they shall advise the counsels of His own heart;
He shall lead our Judges, that they shall pronounce the
judgments of His own mouth; He shall lead our forces into
Edom, the strong cities and holds of the enemy; He shall
lead our navy in the sea by unknown paths to the place it
would go; and I can say no more. Through all the dreads
and dangers of the world, through the perils of the Red sea,
through the perils of the desert, through the malice of all
our enemies, He shall safely lead us, and surely bring us to
His promised kingdom, where we shall "see the goodness of Ps. 27. 13.
the Lord in the land of the living." And this is the benefit,
and thus much for that part.

The value of which benefit we shall the better esteem, if The Third
we consider the state of the parties on whom it is bestowed, part.
set down in these words *populum Tuum;* which is the third *Populum*
part. That all this good is for the people, worthy not so *Tuum.*
much as the least part of it. For, what is the people? Let *Populum.*
Moses speak for he knew them, *Siccine popule stulte et insi-* Deu. 32. 6.
piens? And Aaron too, for he had occasion to try them,
"This people is even set on mischief." And, if you will, Ex. 32. 22.
David also, *Inter belluas populorum.* And to conclude, God Ps. 68. 30.
Himself, *Populus iste duræ cervicis est.* This is the people. Ex. 32. 9;
We may briefly take a view of all these. 33. 3.

Will you see the folly and giddiness of this multitude? ye
may, Acts 19. There they be at the town-house, some cry- Acts 19. 32.
ing one thing, some another; "and the more part knew not
why they were come together." Therefore Moses truly said,
it was a fond and giddy-headed people.

Will ye see the brutishness of the people? In the twenty- Acts 22. 23.
second of Acts, you shall see them taking up a cry, upon a
word spoken by St. Paul, and "casting off their clothes and
throwing dust into the air," as if they were quite decayed

SERM. of reason; that David truly might say, *Inter belluas popu-*
II. *lorum.*

Will ye see the spite and malice of the people? In the
Nu. 16. 41. sixteenth of Numbers, for Korah's death they challenge
Moses and Aaron, "ye have persecuted and killed the
people of the Lord." Yet neither did Moses once touch
them, but God Himself from Heaven, by visible judgment,
shewed them to be as they were. Neither were Korah and
his crew the people of God, but the sons of Belial. But
that is their manner, in despite of Moses, if for aught they
like him not, presently to canonize Korah and his complices,
and make them the saints of God. That Aaron said truly of
[Ex. 32. them, "This people is even set on mischief."
22.]
1 Sam. 8. Lastly, if ye will see their headstrongness, look upon them
19, 20. in the eighth of the first of Samuel, where having fancied
to themselves an alteration of estate, though they were
shewed plainly by Samuel the sundry inconveniences of the
government they so affected, they answer him with "No"—
for that is their logic, to deny the conclusion—"but we will
be like other countries about us, and be guided as we think
[Deu. 32. 5.] good our ownselves." That, of all other, God's saying is
most true, "It is a stiff-necked and headstrong generation."

And yet, for all these wants, so well weening of themselves as they need no leading, they; every one among
them is meet to be a leader, to prescribe Moses, and con-
trol Aaron in their proceedings. So that, where God setteth
the sentence thus, "Thou leddest Thy people like sheep by
the hands of Moses and Aaron;" might they have their
wills, they would take the sentence by the end, and turn it
thus, 'Thou leddest Moses and Aaron like sheep by the
hands of Thy people.'

Tuum. And this is the people, *populus.* And surely, no evil can
be said too much of this word people, if ye take it apart by
itself, *populus* without *Tuus,* 'the people,' and not "Thy
people." But then, here is amends for all the evil before,
in this word *Tuus;* which qualifieth the former, and maketh
them capable of any blessing or benefit.

A common thing in Scripture it is thus to delay one word
Mat. 18. 15. with another. *Si peccaverit in te frater tuus: peccaverit*
stirs our choler straight, but then *frater* makes us hold our

hand again. *Tolle festucam ex oculo. Festucam,* " a mote ?" Lu. 6. 41, 2.
our zeal is kindled presently to remove it; but then *ex oculo,*
the tenderness of the part tempers us, and teacheth us to
deal with it in great discretion. And so it is here; *populus*
so unruly a rout as Moses and Aaron would disdain once to
touch them; but when *Tuus* is added, it will make any of
them not only to touch them, but to take them by the hand.
For it is much that lieth upon this pronoun *Tuus;* indeed,
all lieth upon it, and put me *Tuus* out of the verse, and
neither God respecteth them, nor vouchsafeth them either
Moses to govern, or Aaron to teach, or any heavenly benefit
else. For *populus* is unworthy of them all; but for *Tuus,*
nothing is too good.

For there is in *Tuus,* not only that they be men, and not
beasts; freemen, and not villains; Athenians or English-
men, that is, a civil not a barbarous people—the three considerations of the heathen ruler; but that they be God's
own people and flock; and that is all in all. His people,
because " He made them;" and so, the lot of His inherit- Ps. 100. 3.
ance. His people again, because " He redeemed them" from Ps. 77. 15.
Egypt with His mighty arm; and so His peculiar people.
His people the third time, because He redeemed their souls
by His sufferings; and so, a people purchased most dearly,
purchased even with the invaluable high price of His most 1 Pet. 1. 18,
precious blood. This is that that sets the price on them. 19.
For over such a flock, so highly prized, so dearly beloved,
and so dearly bought, it may well beseem any to be a guide.
Moses, with all his learning; Aaron, with all his eloquence;
yea, even " kings to be their foster-fathers, and queens to be Isa. 49. 23.
their nurses." No leading, no leader too good for them. I
conclude with St. Augustine upon these words; *Quamdiu
minimis istis fecistis fratribus meis, fecistis et mihi. Audis
minimis,* saith he, *et contemnis,* ' Thou hearest they be the
base people, the minims of the world, and thou settest thy
foot on them;' *Audi et fratribus,* 'Take this with thee too,
that they be Christ's brethren thou leadest:' *et mihi crede,
non est minima gloria horum minimorum salus,* ' and trust me,
it is no poor praise to protect this poor flock, but a high service it is, and shall be highly rewarded.' Christ will take
and reward it, as done to Himself in person.

Sicut oves standeth doubtful in the verse; and may be referred, either to the manner of leading—thus, " Thou leadest
like sheep;" or, to the persons led—thus, " Thy people like
sheep." There we touched it before in *duxisti*, in every of
the four manners of leading; and here now we take it in
again with the people to whom it may have reference. And
indeed, there is no term that the Holy Ghost more often
sendeth for than this of His flock to express His people by,
for in the estate of a flock they may best see themselves. As
here it is added respectively to *duxisti*, to let them see, both
what interest they have in it, and what need they have of it.
I mean of government.

1. First, as a note of difference between *Ammi* and *Lo-ammi*,

Thy people, and the people; God's people, and strange children. Every people is not *sicut oves,* nor every one among
the people. There is a people, as the Psalmist speaks, *sicut*

equus et mulus, " like the untamed horse or mule, in whom
is no understanding;" and among the people there be too
many such. Surely, by nature we are all so, wild and un-

broken as the ass-colt, saith Job. Which wildness of nature
when they are untaught, and taught to submit themselves to
government; to become gentle and easy to be led *sicut oves*
—led to feeding, led to shearing, to feed those that feed
them; tractable of nature, and profitable of yield; it is a
good degree and a great work is performed on them. For
by it, as by the first step, they become God's people. For
His people are *populus sicut oves*, and they that are not His,
are *populus sicut hirci*, ' a people like he-goats,' in nature
intractable, in use unserviceable.

Now, being His people, they come to have an interest in
duxisti, the benefit. For *populus sicut oves* must be led
gently; but *populus sicut hirci* must be driven forcibly.
Duxisti is not for both; it is a privilege. And if there be
any retain their wild nature, or degenerate from sheep into
goats, as divers do daily; for them Aaron hath a rod to sever
them from the fold by censure of the Church. And if that
will not serve, Moses hath another which he can turn into a
serpent and sting them; yea, if need so require, sting them
to death by the power secular. For *nachah* is leading, and,
the sound remaining, *nacah* is smiting; and a necessary use

of both. The one for Thy people like sheep who will be led; the other for the strange children like goats, who will not stir a foot farther than they be forced. And this is the interest.

But now again, when they be brought thus far to be like 2. sheep, they are but like sheep though; that is, a weak and unwise cattle, far unable to guide themselves. Which shew-eth them their need of good government, and though they be the people of God, yet that Moses and Aaron be not superfluous. For, a feeble poor beast we all know a sheep is; of little or no strength for resistance in the world, and therefore in danger to be preyed on by every wolf. And as of little strength, so of little reach. None so easily strayeth of itself, none is so easily led awry by others. Every strange whistle maketh the sheep; every *ecce hîc* maketh the people Mat. 24. cast up their heads, as if some great matter were in hand. 23, 24.

These two defects do mainly enforce the necessity of a leader. For they that want sight, as blind men, and they that want strength, as little children, stir not without great peril, except they have one to lead them. And both these wants are in sheep, and in the people too.

If then they be *sicut oves,* "like sheep," what is both their wisdom? Sure to be in the unity of a flock. And what is their strength? Truly to be under the conduct of a shep-herd: in these two is their safety. For if either they single themselves and stray from the fold; or if they be a fold and yet want a shepherd, none more miserable than they. And indeed in the Holy Ghost's phrase it is the ordinary note of a private man's misery, to be *tanquam ovis erratica,* "as a Isa. 53. 6. stray sheep from the flock;" and of the misery of every es-tate politic, to be *tanquam grex absque pastore,* "as a flock Mat. 9. 36. without a shepherd." Therefore, guiding they need—both the staff of unity, "Bands," to reduce them from straying, Zach. 11. 7. and the staff of order, "Beauty," to lead them so reduced. And would God they would see their own feebleness and shallowness, and learn to acknowledge the absolute neces-sity of this benefit; in all duty receiving it, in all humility *Duxisti* praying for the continuance of it, that God break not the *sicut oves.* fold, and smite not the shepherd for the flock's unthank- *sumus sicut oves.* fulness!

SERM.
II.
The fourth part.

Per manus Mosis et Aaronis.

By the hands of Moses and Aaron. This part of the verse that is behind, and containeth the means by whom God conveyeth this benefit to His people, had had no use, but might well have been left out and the verse ended at *populum Tuum*, if *author alienæ potentiæ perdit suam* had been God's rule. For He needed no means but immediately from Himself; *sine manibus* could have conveyed it, without any hands save those that made us, that is His Almighty power, but without any arm or hand of flesh, without Moses or Aaron, without men or angels, He was able Himself to have led us. And *a principio fuit sic;* for a time He did so, of Himself immediately, and of His own absolute sovereignty held He court in the beginning, and proceeded against Adam, Eve, Cain, the old world, and there was none joined

Ps. 74. 12.

in commission with Him. He only was our "King of old," saith the Psalmist; and for a space, the justice that was done on earth, He did it Himself. And as He held court before all, so will He also hold one after all. *Veniet, veniet, qui male judicata rejudicabit dies,* 'There will come a day, there is a day coming, wherein all evil-judged cases shall be judged over again.' To which all appeals lie, even from the days of affliction in this world, as sometimes they be, to the day of judgment in the world to come.

This estate of guiding being wholly invested in Him, there being but one God and one Guide, He would not keep it unto Himself alone as He might, but it pleased Him to send

Ps. 105. 26.

"Moses His servant, and Aaron whom He had chosen," to associate them to Himself in the commission of leading, and to make *hominem homini deum,* 'one man a guide and god to another.'

Per manum.

And those whom He thus honoureth, 1. First, the Prophet calleth God's hands, by whom He leadeth us; 2. and secondly telleth us who they be,—Moses and Aaron.

Ps. 103.

God's hands they be; for that by them He reacheth unto us *duxisti,* and in it religion and counsel and justice and victory, and whatsoever else is good. "He sendeth His word to Moses first, and by him," as it were through his hand, "His statutes and ordinances unto all Israel."

And not good things only, but if they so deserve, sometimes evil also. For as, if they be virtuous, such as Moses

and Aaron, they be the "good hand" of God for our be- [Ezr. 7. 9.]
nefit, such as was upon Ezra; so if they be evil, such as
Balak and Balaam, they be the "heavy hand" of God for [Job 33. 7.]
our chastisement, such as was upon Job. But the hand of
God they be both. And a certain resemblance there is between this government and the hand; for as we see the
hand itself parted into divers fingers, and those again into
sundry joints, for the more convenient and speedy service
thereof; so is the estate of government, for ease and expe-
dition, branched into the middle offices, and they again as
fingers into others under them. But the very meanest of
them all, is a joint of some finger of this hand of God.
Nazianzen, speaking of rulers as of the images of God, compareth the highest to pictures drawn clean through, even to
the feet; the middle sort to half pictures drawn but to the
girdle; the meanest to the lesser sort of pictures drawn but
to the neck or shoulders. But all in some degree carry the
image of God.

Out of which term, of " the hands of God," the people first
are taught their duty, so to esteem of them, as of God's own
hands; that as God ruleth them by " the hands of Moses
and Aaron," that is, by their ministry, so Moses and Aaron
rule them by the hands of God, that is, by His authority. It
is His name they wear, it is His seat they sit in, it is the rod
of God that is in Moses' and Aaron's hands. If we fall down
before them, it is He that is honoured; if we rise up against
them, it is He that is injured; and that *peccavi in Cœlum et
in te,* must be our confession, " against Heaven and them," Lu. 15. 21.
but first against Heaven and God Himself, when we commit
any contempt against Moses or Aaron.

1. And the rulers have their lesson too. First, that if they 1.
be God's hands, then His Spirit is to open and shut them,
stretch them out, and draw them in, wholly to guide and
govern them, as the hand of man is guided and governed
by the spirit that is in man. Heavenly and divine had those
hands need be, which are to be the hands and to work the
work of God.

2. Again, they be not only hands, but *manus per quam*, that
is, hands *in actu*. Not to be wrapped up in soft fur, but by
which an actual duty of leading is to be performed. Moses'

SERM.
II.

Exod. 4. 6.

own hand, in the fourth of Exodus, when he had lodged it in his warm " bosom, became leprous ;" but being stretched out, recovered again.   Hands *in actu* then they must be ; not loosely hanging down or folded together in idleness, but stretched out; not only to point others but themselves to be foremost in the execution of every good work.

3. Thirdly, *manus per quam ducuntur*; that is, as not the "leprous hand" of Moses, so neither the "withered hand" of Jeroboam stretching itself out against God, by misleading His people and making them to sin.   "Leading back again into Egypt"—a thing expressly forbidden ; either to the oppression and bondage of Egypt, or to the ignorance and false worship of Egypt, from whence Moses had led them.   For as they be not entire bodies of themselves but hands, and that not their own but God's; so the people they led are not their own but His, and by Him and to Him to be led and directed.   So much for " God's hands."

1 Kings 13. 4.

Deu. 17. 16.

Moses and Aaron.

This honourable title of the " hand of God," is here given to two parties, Moses and Aaron, in regard of two distinct duties performed by them.   Ye heard how we said before, The people of God were like sheep in respect of a double want ; 1. want of strength by means of their feebleness; 2. and want of skill by means of their simpleness.   For this double want here cometh a double supply, from the hand 1. of strength, and 2. of cunning; for both these are in the hand.

1. It is of all members the chief in might, as appeareth by the diversity of uses and services it is put to.   *In potentatibus dextræ*, saith the Prophet.

Ps. 20. 6.

2. And secondly, it is also the part of greatest cunning, as appeareth by the variety of the works which it yieldeth, by the pen, the pencil, the needle, and instruments of music. *In intellectu manuum*, saith the Psalmist, in the end of the next Psalm ; and, " let my right hand forget her cunning."

Ps. 78. 72.

Ps. 137. 5.

This hand of God then by his strength affordeth protection to the feebleness of the flock, and again by his skill affordeth direction to the simpleness of the flock.   And these are the two substantial parts of all leading.

These twain, as two arms, did God appoint in the wilderness, to lead His people by.   Afterward over these twain did He yet set another, even the power and authority regal, in

1 Sam. 15. 17.

place of the head, as Himself termeth it; and to it, as supreme, united the regiment of both. The consideration of which power I meddle not with, as being not within the compass of this verse, but only with the hands of regiments Ecclesiastical and Civil. Which, as the two cherubims did the ark, overspread and preserve every estate. One, saith Jehoshaphat, dispensing *res Jehovæ,* "the Lord's business," the other dealing *in negotio regis,* 'the affairs of estate.' One, saith David, intending "the worship of the tribes," the other, the "thrones for justice." One, saith Paul, being for us in τὰ πρὸς Θεὸν, "things pertaining to God;" the other in τὰ βιωτικὰ, "matters of this present life." The one *pro aris,* the other *pro focis,* as the very heathen acknowledge. [2 Chron. 19. 6.] [2 Chron. 19. 11.] [Ps. 122. 4,5.] [Rom. 15. 17.] [1 Cor. 6. 3.]

1. These two are the hands, necessary to the body, and necessary each to other. First, they be both hands; and the hands, we know, are pairs. Not Moses the hand, and Aaron the foot, but either and each the hand. As they be the pair of hands, so be they also a pair of brethren. Not Moses *de primis,* and Aaron *de novissimis populi;* not Moses the head, and Aaron the tail; not Moses a *quis,* as St. Hierome speaketh out of the twenty-second of Esay, and Aaron a *quasi quis;* but both of one parentage, both one man's children.

2. Secondly, being both hands, neither of them is superfluous, no more to be spared, than may the hands; but both are absolutely necessary, and a maimed and lame estate it is, where either is wanting. The estate of Israel, in the seventeenth of the Judges, without a civil governor proved a very mass of confusion. The very same estate, in the second of Chronicles, chap. 15. *sine sacerdote docente,* no less out of frame. Miserable first, if they lack Joshua, and be as "sheep wanting that shepherd." And miserable again, if they lack Jesus, and "be as sheep wanting that Shepherd." Moses is needful, in the want of water, to strike the rock for us, and to procure us supply of bodily relief. Aaron is no less. For he in like manner reacheth to every one food of other kind, which we may worse be without, even "the Bread of life," and water out of "the spiritual Rock," which is Christ Jesus. Moses we need, to see our forces led against Amalek, for safeguard of that little we hold here in this life; and Aaron no less, to preserve our free hold in everlasting life: for the great [Judg. 17. 6.] [2 Chr. 15. 3.] [Nu. 27. 17.] [Mat. 9. 36.] [Ex. 17. 6.] [Joh. 6. 48. 51.] [1 Cor. 10. 4.] [Ex. 17. 8, &c.]

D

SERM.
II.
Eph. 6. 12.

and mighty κοσμοκράτορες, the legions of our sins, the very forces of the prince of darkness are overthrown by the spiritual weapons of Aaron's warfare. Moses may not be spared from sitting and deciding the causes which are brought before him. No more may Aaron, whose *Urim* giveth answer in doubts no less important; and who not only with his *Urim* and *Thummim* giveth counsel, but by his incense and sacrifice obtaineth good success for all our counsels. In a word, if Moses' rod be requisite to sting and devour the wicked, Aaron's is also to receive the good and to make them to fructify. If Moses' hand want with the sword to make us a way, Aaron's hand wants too, with the key to give us an entrance. And thus much will I say for Aaron—for the devil hath now left to dispute about Moses' body, and bendeth all against him —that the very first note of difference in all the Bible to know God's people by, is, that as Cain and his race began at the city walls first, and let religion as it might come after, any it

Gen. 4. 26.

skilled not what; so the posterity of Seth, the people of God, begun at the Church, *et cœptum est invocari*, at the worship of God and His Tabernacle; as the point of principal neces-

Lu. 10. 42.

sity in their account, and as Christ reckoned it, *unum necessarium*. And truly if we be not *populus*, "a people," but *populus Tuus*, "God's people," we will so esteem it too. For as for justice and law, and execution of them both, *taliter fecit omni populo*, it is every where to be had, even among the very Heathen and Turks themselves. So is not God's truth and

Ps. 76. 1.

religion, and the way of righteousness. No; *notus in Judæá Deus*, saith the Prophet in the last Psalm;—that is only to be

[Ps. 147.
20.]

had in the Church, and *Non taliter fecit omni populo*, "He hath not dealt so with every people." Every "people have not knowledge of His laws." So that if the governor be not merely *pastor agrestis*, 'a rural shepherd,' such as are in the fields, and the people of God in his eyes no better than *pecora campi;* so that if he keep them one from goring another with their horns, and one from eating up the other's lock of hay, all is well and no more to be cared for of Gallio; but that he be like the great Shepherd, the Good Shepherd, the Prince of

1 Pet. 2. 25.

Shepherds, Who was *Pastor animarum,* as St. Peter calleth Him, "a Shepherd of souls;" to see also that they be in good plight, that they be led in the way of truth. It will easily be yielded to, that *per manum Mosis* is no full point, but needeth an Aaron to be joined to it. Moses himself saw this, and therefore in the fourth of Exodus, when he had divers times shifted off this sole leading, while God stood still upon *ecce mittam te;* at last when God came farther and said, *ecce Aaron frater tuus,* Ex. 4. 14. *mittam eum tecum,* that contented him, and then he undertook it; as knowing these were like hands maimed, the one without the other, but that Moses and Aaron make a complete government.

3. And what should I say more? They be hands, and the body needeth them both. They be hands, and they need each other. Moses needeth Aaron, for Moses' hands are heavy and need a stay; and Aaron it is that keepeth them steady, by continual putting the people in remembrance that they be subject to principalities; by winning that at their hands by his continual dropping his word upon them, which Moses, for the hardness of their hearts, is fain to yield to. By strengthening mainly Moses' *debita legalia,* ' duties of Parliament and common law,' by his *debita moralia,* ' duties of conscience and divinity.' And whatsoever action Moses doth imprison, Aaron imprisoneth all the thoughts any ways accessary to the action. Which thoughts if they may run at liberty, the action will surely be bailed or make an escape, and not be long kept in durance. And so many ways doth Aaron support, and make both more easy and more steady, the hands of Moses.

And Moses, for his part, is not behind, but a most jealous preserver of Aaron's honour and right every where. Every where mild save in Aaron's quarrel, and with those only that murmured against Aaron, and said he took too much upon him. Take but his prayer for all, because I would end, his prayer made for Aaron by name, in the thirty-third of Deuteronomy, and these three points in it. " Bless, O Lord, his substance ;" Deu. 33. 11. —therefore he would never have heard, *ut quid perditio hæc ?* that all is lost that is spent on Aaron's head. Then, " accept the work of his hands ;"—therefore he would never easily have excepted to, or with a hard construction scanned all the doings of Aaron. Last of all, " Smite through the loins of them that rise up against him ;"—therefore he would never

SERM.
II.

1 Sam. 22.
17.

2 Tim. 3. 8.

Jude, ver. 9.

have strengthened the hand of his evil willers, or said with Saul to Doeg, " Turn thou and fall upon the Priests."

To conclude, Moses and Aaron both have enemies. As Aaron hath Korah and Dathan that repine at him, so hath Moses too Jannes and Jambres that would withstand him. And he that at one time disputes about the body of Aaron, may also hereafter, for he hath done it heretofore, dispute about the body of Moses. It is good therefore they be respective each to other; Aaron help Moses in his lot; and Moses, Aaron in his; that they stand in the gap one for another; and so their unity be hand in hand as the unity of brethren, strong and hard to break as the bars of a palace.

The Lord, by Whose Almighty power all governments do stand, those especially wherein the people are led in the way of His Sanctuary; as He hath graciously begun to lead us in that way, so leave us not till we have finished our course with joy! Knit the hearts of Moses and Aaron, that they may join lovingly; teach their hands, and fingers of their hands, that they lead skilfully; touch the hearts of the people, that they may be led willingly; that by means of this happy conduct, surely without error, and safely without danger, we may lead and be led forward, till we come to the fruition of His promise, the expectation of our blessed hope, even the eternal joys of His celestial Kingdom, through Jesus Christ our Lord! To Whom, &c.

A SERMON

PREACHED BEFORE

QUEEN ELIZABETH, AT ST. JAMES'S,

ON WEDNESDAY, BEING THE THIRTIETH OF MARCH, A.D. MDXCIII.

MARK xiv. 4—6.

*Therefore some disdained among themselves, and said, To what
end is this waste of ointment?*

*For it might have been sold for more than three hundred pence
and been given to the poor. And they grudged against her.*

*But Jesus said, Let her alone, why trouble ye her? she hath
wrought a good work on Me.*

*Erant autem quidam indigne ferentes intra semetipsos, et dicentes,
Ut quid perditio ista unguenti facta est?*

*[Poterat enim unguentum istud vænumdari plus quam trecentis
denariis, et dari pauperibus. Et fremebant in eam.*

*Jesus autem dixit, Sinite eam, quid illi molesti estis? Bonum opus
operata est in Me.* Latin Vulg.]

*[And there were some that had indignation within themselves, and
said, Why was this waste of the ointment made?*

*For it might have been sold for more than three hundred pence, and
have been given to the poor. And they murmured against her.*

*And Jesus said, Let her alone, why trouble ye her? she hath
wrought a good work on Me.* Engl. Trans.]*

THIS action of waste, which by some is brought, and by
Christ our Saviour traversed, was against a woman, saith St.
Mark the verse before; which woman, as St. John hath it, Joh. 11. 2.
was Mary Magdalene, now a glorious Saint in Heaven, some
time a grievous sinner upon earth.

St. Augustine noteth; Of all those that sought to Christ,
she was the only sinner that for sin only, and for no bodily
grief or malady at all, sued and sought to Him. Of whom

SERM.
III.

being received to grace, and obtaining a *quietus est* for her many sins, a benefit inestimable, *et quod nemo scit nisi acceperit*, 'which they only know and none but they that have received it,' as much was forgiven her, so much she loved.

Lu. 7. 47.

And seeking by all means to express her *multam dilectionem propter multam remissionem*, as Christ saith ver. 8. ὁ ἔσχεν ἐποίησεν, nothing she had was too dear. And having a precious confection or ointment of *nardus*, the chief of all ointments, and in it of πιστικὴ, the chief of all *nardi ;* and in it too not of the leaf, but of the very choice part thereof, of the spike or flower—both for the making true, and for the value costly, that did she bestow. And that frankly, for she did not drop but pour ; not a dram or two, but a whole pound ; not reserving any, but breaking box and all ; and that not now alone, but three several times, one after another.

This she did ; and, as it may seem, the coherence fell out not amiss. This outward ointment and sweet odour she

Ps. 45. 7.
1 Joh. 2. 20.
2 Cor. 2. 14.

bestowed on Christ for "the oil of gladness,"—for the "spiritual anointing" (as St. John), and the "comfortable savour of His knowledge" (as St. Paul calls it), He bestowed on her.

This, as it was well done, so was it well taken of Christ ; and so should have been of all present but for Judas, saith St. John. Who, liking better *odorem lucri ex re qualibet*, than any scent in the apothecary's shop, seeing that spent on Christ's head that he wished should come into his purse, repined at it. But that so cunningly, in so good words, with so colourable a motion, 1. that it was a needless expense— indeed, "a waste ;" 2. that it might have been bestowed much better to the relief of many poor people ; as that he drew the disciples, some of them, to favour the motion, and to dislike of Mary Magdalene and her doing. So that both they and he joined in one bill ; but he of a wretched covetous mind, they of a simple plain intent and purpose, thinking all that was well spoken had been well meant.

Which action of theirs, for that it was brought not only against her that bestowed it, but even against Christ also that admitted it, though not so directly ; as it were against her with *ut quid perditio ?* against Him with *ut quid permissio ?* for that also it might be a dangerous precedent in ages to come, if nothing were said to it, and shut all boxes and bar all ointments for ever; our Saviour Himself taketh on Him to plead her cause. Not only excusing it in *sinite illam*, as no "waste," but also commending it in *bonum opus*, as "a good work;" that the ointment was not so pleasant to His sense, as her thankfulness acceptable to His Spirit; that the ointment, which then filled the house with the scent, should fill the whole world with the report of it; and as far and wide as the Gospel was preached, so far and wide should this act be remembered, as well for her commendation that did it, as for our imitation that should hear of it.

We see both the occasion and sum of these words read, which may aptly be said to contain in them a disputation or plea about Mary Magdalene's act, whether it were well done or no. Whereof there are two principal parts: Judas, with some other *ad oppositum*, 'against it,' to have Mary Magdalene reformed, and her box converted to better uses: Christ for it, and against them: *sinite*, that He would have it stand, yea that He would have it acknowledged, for that it was *bonum opus*.

In the entreating whereof, these three points I purpose: The division. I. First of Judas' motion; and in it 1. The speech itself, I. *ut quid perditio, &c.?* 2. The speaker—"some" of them; 3. The mind or affection, "thought much."

II. Secondly, of Christ's apology; and in it 1. That it is II. sufferable; 2. That it is commendable; 3. The reason of both, *in Me;* for that on Him.

III. Last of all, laying both together: the former, that it III. is "a good work;" the latter, that "yet grudged at;" that good actions oft-times meet with evil constructions; therefore, 1. though we do well, yet we shall be evil spoken of; and again, 2. though we be evil spoken of, yet we must proceed to do well. The use we shall make is briefly, *ex factis facienda discere,* 'by report of that which hath been done heretofore, to learn what to do in like case hereafter.' Whereof that I may so speak, &c.

Of the tongue the Psalmist saith, it is "the best member" I. we have; and St. James, it is the worst, and it marreth all Judas' motion. the rest. The nature of the tongue, thus being both good and 1. The speech. bad, maketh that our speech is of the same complexion, good *Ut quid* and bad likewise. Whereof this speech here is a pregnant *perditio?* Ps. 108. 1. Jas. 3. 8.

example.   Good in substance, as I shall shew presently; evil
in circumstance, as we shall afterward see, as neither well
meant nor well applied.

In the speech I commend two good things : 1. The abuse
noted, *ut quid, &c.*   2. The use set down, *potuit, &c.*   Not
only the defect—not thus wasted; but the provision how—
"turned into money, and distributed to the poor."

We begin with the first : *Ut quid perditio, &c.?*   Surely a
good speech and of good use, and to be retained.   Religion
and reason both teach us, in all things, to regard both *quid*
and *ut quid;* no less to what end we do, than what we do,
and both of them censure not only what is done to an evil end
wickedly, but what is done to no end vainly.   *Quem fructum,*
Rom. 6. 21. "what fruit," saith St. Paul—a good question; and if it have
Lu. 13. 7. none, *ut quid terram occupat,* "why troubleth it the ground?"
saith Christ.   So that religion alloweth not waste, censureth
idleness, and in all things calleth us to our *ut quid hæc?*

And this as in all things, in waste of time, waste words,
addle questions, so yet chiefly in that which we call *bonum*
utile.   The very goodness of which things is in their use, and
they no longer good than they have an use, which if they lose
they cease to be good.   So that in them not only those things
that are misspent upon wicked uses, but even those also that
are idly spent to no use, they are lost, lavished, and no good
cometh of them.   And therefore in them, *ut quid perditio*
indeed? is well said.   This they learned of Christ Himself,
Who, in the gathering of the broken meat, gave charge, *ut ne*
Joh. 6. 12. *quid perdatur,* "that no waste should be made."   Indeed, *ut*
quid perditio ulla?   "whereto either this or any waste at all?"
So that religion is an enemy to riot, and good husbandry is
good divinity.

It is God's will, that of our goods *justitia condus sit,* 'justice should be purveyor,' and they rightly gotten; *tempe-*
rantia promus, 'temperance the steward,' and they not waste-
1. fully spent.   Consequently, neither waste in buying: but as
Joh. 13. 29. Christ ὧν χρείαν ἔχομεν. Not ὧν χρῆσιν, but ὧν χρείαν, 'not
whereof we may have use, but whereof we have need' and
cannot be without it.

2.   Neither waste in spending: οἰκονομία 'a dispensation,' not
a dissipation ; a laying forth, not διασκορπισμὸς, 'a casting

away;' a wary sowing not a heedless scattering; and a sowing χειρὶ, οὐ θύλακι, 'by handfulls, not by basket fulls,' as the heathen man well said.

Neither waste in giving; not making χάριτας, πόρνας, the a. Graces, which be virgins, not prostituting them and making them common, but as the Apostle's rule is, καθότι ἄν τις χρείαν Acts 2. 45. εἶχε, "as need shall require." So that to all, to needless laying out, to superfluous expense, to unnecessary largess, *ut quid perditio?* may be said. The reason whereof is well set down; that, if we waste it in needless expenses, we shall not have enough for necessary charges; if we lavish out in wasting, we shall leave but little for well-doing. Whereof our times do yield plenteous testimony, in which Nabal's waste, which being a subject makes a feast like a king; the Assyrian's 1 Sam. 25. waste, every mean person in apparel like a young prince; Gen. 33. 1. Esau's waste, in carrying a retinue of four hundred at his heels; Shallum's waste, in enclosing ourselves in cedar, and Jer. 22. 15. lifting up our gate on high: once for all, I protest, and desire it may be graciously received, I do not so much as in thought once aim at the estate of the highest, whose glory I wish to match, yea, to surpass, " Solomon in all his royalty;" but this riotous mis-spending, where no need is, hath eaten up our Christian bestowing where need is. Less waste we must have, if we will have more good works. It is truly called *perditio;* it is the loss and destruction of all our good deeds, and I pray God it be not also of our reward for them.

Ut quid perditio is a fault, but *ut quid perditio hæc* is a greater. For *hæc* wanteth not his emphasis, but is as if he should say, If the sum had been little, or the value small, it might have been borne; if twenty or thirty pence, it might have been winked at; but if it come once into the hundreds, so great a sum, so much—verily it may not, it ought not to be suffered.

Thus much for *perditio,* " the idle waste," the abuse. Now followeth Judas' plot, the use he wisheth it put to. For first he maketh a perfect valuation and estimate of what it would rise to, and it may seem strange how he should be so skilful an auditor of the price of rich ointments, but he hit it well, for so saith Pliny, the best *nardus* was so worth; and that is [Vid. Plin. a material point. For the greater the sum, the more colour N. H. 12. 12. 26; of complaint: *ut quid perditio ulla,* but specially *ut quid per-* 13. 2.]

ditio hæc unguenti, " of so rich an ointment ?" Then from his
audit he cometh to his motion, *potuit vendi, &c.* Sale to be
made, the money to be divided, and the poor to be relieved.
This is his supplication, and this second is better than the
former. Indeed, *ut quid perditio* may be the speech of a
niggard; but this second that followeth, cannot but proceed
from a liberal mind;—*potuit vendi, &c.* In that he speaketh not
to have it spared, but to have it converted to better uses.
And this is a blessed conjunction, when honest sparing and
charitable relieving, when frugality and liberality go together.
Such is this motion, whereto no man can take exception.
Naturally our bowels yearn, and we have an inward compassion at the misery of our brethren; and God's law willeth
not to hide ourselves from our own flesh, but when we have
served our need, to give to the poor.

The motion then is both frugal and charitable; and besides,
if we look more narrowly into it, there appeareth great zeal
in it. All waste things he wisheth the poor had. Yea, it
seemeth he reckoneth it waste that the poor is not the better
for; that to be misspent that might be better spent, and is not.
And very exactly driveth to this point; that our goods may
go, not to some end, nor to some good end, but to the very
best end of all, the relief of the poor. Sure, when I consider
the sobriety, bounty, zeal of the speech, I think many wise
heads could not in so few words have contrived a better or
more pithy motion; that that which is otherwise lavished upon
one may be employed to the benefit of many; that these so
many hundreds may be bestowed rather in nourishment, than
in ointment; rather on necessary relief, than upon needless
delight; rather on a continual good, than on a transitory
smell; rather that many hungry bellies filled, than that one
head anointed. Sure, howsoever it was meant or applied, the
speech, in itself considered, is to very good purpose; even
Judas' speech, without Judas' application.

2.
The per-
sons that
speak.
"Some" of
them.
Prov. 24. 26.
We be now to enquire of the person by whom, and after, of
the intent wherewith it was spoken.

We are naturally carried of a good speech to enquire the
author: partly, in an honest inclination, as Solomon saith,
"to kiss the lips of him that answereth upright words;" partly,
because it is a matter of importance, not only to weigh *quid*

dicatur, but *quis dicat.* Τρόπος ἔσται ὁ πείθων τοῦ λέγοντος οὐ λόγος, 'Many times we be more persuaded with the mind of the speaker, than with the body of the speech ;' and their positions move not so much, as do their dispositions. It is very material in all, and so in this, to ask, *Quis hic loquitur ?* For who can choose but speak all good of the speech ? Surely if we had not been told otherwise, *Zelotæ vocem,* 'we must needs have thought it to have been Simon Zelotes.' *Zelotæ vocem putas, Iscariotæ est ;* 'one would imagine it was Simon the Zealous; it is not so, it was Judas the Covetous.' "Some of them," saith St. Mark. "Of His Disciples," saith St. Mat- Mat. 26. 8. thew. And namely Judas, saith St. John, who first stood up ; Joh. 12. 4. and took this exception; and, after him, some others. So that it was Judas, and by his persuasion some besides; for if he had not stirred, they would have taken it well enough : such is the danger of sinister speeches. Let us begin with Judas.

And here first, we begin somewhat to suspect, that it cometh from Judas. Judas, it was well known what he was. At that very instant that this very *ut quid* was in his mouth, his fingers were in Christ's coffers, and one might have said it to him, *Ut quid, &c.* And for all he spake against waste, he wasted and made havoc of his Master's goods; and a little after he might have been charged with a worse matter, and yet he prefers motions. Christ telleth us what he was, *filius perditionis;* and this term marreth all, that "the child of perdition" should find fault with perdition. The case is like, when they that have wasted many pounds complain of that penny waste which is done on Christ's body, the Church. Or, when they that in all their whole dealings, all the world sees, are unreformed, seriously consult how to reform the Church. When they that do no good with their own, devise what good may be done with Mary Magdalene's; they that have spent and sold and consumed themselves, and never in their whole lives shewed any regard of the poor ; when they talk of charitable uses—*O dolor!* saith Augustine : *Quis tulerit?* saith [Juvenal, the Poet. *Ut quid perditio ?* doth but evil fit their mouths. Sat. 2. 24.] God help us, when Judas must reform Mary Magdalene !

This is a grief; would this alone ! But a greater grief it is to see how he is matched in this complaint; that in this mur-

muring some other, divers well-disposed and of the better
sort of Christ's Disciples join with him, and take part against
Mary Magdalene. Who, rather carried with the speech than
heeding the speaker, were drawn into the society of the same
repining. And this sure is *scandalum magnum*, when evil
counsel meeteth with easy belief, and subtilty findeth cre-
dulity. When the Pharisees can persuade John's disciples
Mark 2. 18. to muster with them and say, "Why do we and John's disciples fast?" whom you cannot but say are good men, whatsoever you think of us. When Judas can say, Why do I, and
Christ's own disciples reprove this? So it is with us;—not to
see *homines perditos queri de perditione*, 'them speak of waste
that have wasted themselves,' for that might be digested; but
to see grave and good men err the same error, and draw
in the same line with them. But no doubt that which carried
these here leadeth them too,—Pretences; that which was able
to deceive Christ's Disciples, deceiveth them too. And this is
the difference; that the Disciples in a good meaning went
with him, because they saw he said well; but Judas, upon a
greedy covetous mind, to have his own turn served. For, *cui
bono?* if it had come to the poor, who should have had the
distribution? It was his office; so that it may be he spake
for himself. Which did plainly appear by the issue. For
upon better information given by Christ, the Disciples were
answered and remained content. But Judas grew enraged
and fell from evil to worse, from covetise to malice, from
sacrilege to treason; even to this dangerous resolution,
vendere nardum, or, if not, *vendere Christum*, and to subvert
Him That he might not spoil. For all the world, as some
in our time that sought help of authority, while they had
hope that way to prevail; but when that came not, since
begin to hold they will and may do it without stay for
authority, and seek to subvert the state they cannot form
to their fancy. My hope is and so is my prayer, that those
which have hitherto been carried with their plots and pretences, now they be informed and see what the truth is, may
do as the Disciples, leave Judas in his murmuring, and let
Mary Magdalene be quiet.

1.   That which we learn of this part is; 1. From Judas, that a
good speech may drop out of an evil mouth. As sure, setting

aside that the hands be Esau's, the voice might become Jacob Gen. 27. 22.
well enough. This instruction we have from Judas; it was
God's will that even he should preach and we learn some
good lessons by him. And this we may learn: that no waste
is to be made; and if we learn it, even he shall cooperate to
our good. And as from him we have this speech for our
economy, so from Caiaphas, as bad as he, we have another Joh. 11. 50.
full as good for our policy. That speech, which St. Bernard
can never enough commend, *melius est ut pereat unus quam
unitas.* Both evil meant I grant, but both well spoken where
their place is. So it pleaseth God that we should hear His
"wisdom justified," not only out of the mouth " of her own Mat. 11. 19.
children," but even out of the mouths of the children of
folly. That He might condemn evil things even by evil
men; and evil men, *non ex ore Suo,* not from His own, but
from their own mouths, and so their condemnation be just.

From the Disciples' too easy belief we learn *credit omni* Pro. 14. 15
verbo, not to trust phrases and oiled speeches too fast; never
by the list to conclude of the cloth. Seeing not only *vasa
electionis,* but *filii perditionis,* say well. But if we hear
much ado about *ut quid perditio,* to stay and think, May not
this be Judas that speaketh now as once it was? And if it
be, to suspect when he speaks well. Of this assuring ourselves, what St. Paul telleth us of sadly, that not only Mary
Magdalene shall be reformed, and her ointment maligned,
and the poor opposed, but even Christ Himself preached,
obtentu, " under pretence." Therefore it standeth us in hand Phil. 1. 16.
to look to the disposition as well as the position; and not to
run headlong to say straight *ut quid* as fast as they. So
much for the speaker.

With the person by whom we propound the affection ₃.
wherewith it is spoken. For as the person is a presump- The af-
tion; so if this can be had, it maketh a full evidence. And fection
that is in these words ἀγανάκτησις ἐν ἑαυτῷ, that " he spoken.
thought much with himself." *Indigne
ferentes, et
intra se di-
centes.*

The speech for the poor, if it be kindly, doth naturally
come from the compassion of charity, and not from the
grudging of a greedy desire, as this is said to do; and so
should we have conceived of this, that from the care of the
poor, no doubt, but that the Spirit of God maketh a window

S E R M.
III.
Joh. 12. 6. in his breast, and lets us see the secrets of his heart, and telleth us it was not the care of the poor. *Non, quia pertinebat ad eum de pauperibus,* but *quia fur erat,* because he "bare the bag," and took order it should never be over heavy, but that he might well bear it, and thought all too much that went beside it.

Which is a point of great use to be understood. It is one of the mysteries of iniquity, that, ever there be two *quias* belonging to bad purposes, as St. Mark saith. 1. One ἐν ἑαυτοῖς, "within," in heart : 2. the other, λέγοντες, without, "in speech." Another *quia* they "think in their hearts," and another they "speak in our ears," which is the *non quia.* 1. The one a true cause, inwardly intended ; 2. the other, only a colour outwardly pretended. As in this ; the true *quia,* ἐν ἑαυτοῖς, a wretched humour to provide for himself ; the pretenced *quia,* λέγοντες, a charitable affection to pro-Joh. 12. 19. vide for the poor. All sins have so. *Mundus sequitur Eum,* Joh. 11. 48. the true cause—envy ἐν ἑαυτοῖς. But they told another Mat. 2.8-16. *quia* — λέγοντες, *Venient Romani,* the safety of the state. Herod would learn where he might find Christ, the cause in deed to murder Him, the cause in show to worship Him.

Intra se.   It is no new thing, but common and usual, in all exceptions to religion ; the true cause is ἀγανάκτησις, " a thinking all too much," a thinking all is *perditio,* all lost that cometh not to us, that we gain not by. We see it was the true reason the men of Shechem made among themselves, why they would become of Jacob's religion, and be circum-Gen. 34. 23. cised ; *Nonne omnia quæ habent nostra erunt?* " Shall not all they have be ours ?" It was the very reason whereby Haman went about to persuade Ahasuerus to suppress the Esther 3. 9. Jews' religion ; Let it be done, and I will weigh so many thousands to the King's coffers. And in the New Testament it was the very reason Demetrius there useth : O, cry for Acts19. 25. Diana, magnify her, *Quia inde nobis erit acquisitio,* " we shall be all gainers by it." God knows this is the true cause, and the analogy of religion to many. It was so to Judas ; and God grant the like be not found in Israel !

Dicentes.   Now though this be the true, yet this in nowise must come into λέγοντες, and be spoken. If Judas had dealt plainly he should have framed his speech ; *Ut quid perditio?*

potuit vendi et mitti in crumenam meam; but that had been too harsh, for that had been plain sacrilege; and of sacrilege St. Paul seems to say, it is, if not worse, yet as bad as idolatry. " Thou that pullest down idols, committest thou Rom. 2. 22. sacrilege?" As if he held as good a false religion, as a spoiling religion. Therefore that must be kept ἐν ἑαυτῷ, and not come into λέγοντες, but it must be shrouded, as indeed the heathen man said, Μόνον δεῖται προφάσεως ἡ πονηρία, 'bad attempts need only an handsome pretence;' for with the rest they can dispense; with God and His word, and fear and conscience and all; and so a pretence had, it is all they desire.

Now no pretence more fit to make them perfect maskers, than St. Paul's " vizor," μόρφωσις εὐσεβείας; and St. Peter's 2 Tim. 3. 5. " cloke," ἐπικάλυμμα; the "vizor of godliness," and the [1 Pet. 2. 16.] " cloke of religion." And such was Judas' here, a charitable careful provision for the relief of the poor. Whom, though the Holy Ghost saith expressly, he cared not for one jot, Joh. 12. 6. yet maketh he them his stalking-horse, and *pauperibus* is the point; that is it he seeketh for, and, God knoweth, nothing else.

This his sacrilegious wicked humour he covereth under zeal of the poor; and so, to hide one fault committeth two. First sacrilege, then hypocrisy.

And "it is no new thing under the sun," as Solomon Pro. 26. 23. tells us, to "gild a potsherd with gold foil," that is, to overlay a false heart with zealous lips. Absalom's vow was the 2 Sam. 15. mask for his conspiracy against David. Jezebel's fast, her 1 Kings vizor for the oppressing of Naboth. And here we have an 21. 9. invective against waste, a supplication for the poor, in Judas' mouth, and yet " seven abominations in his heart." Pro. 26. 25.

Is it not heaviness unto death to consider this? Well said the Wise Man; " O wicked abomination, whence art thou come to cover the earth with deceit!"

But more need had we to beware than complain. And indeed all we learn from this point, is *novisse et odisse,* ' to know and avoid.' To know such there be as cover sacrilege with zeal, and with good uses cover no good intents. To know them, and to avoid them. And the better to do that, to mark the end of him that here used it, and see what be-

came of him; how from this sin, by God's just judgment, he
fell to *perditio;* and from it, after to make away himself.
To whom in that case truly might have been said, *ut quid
perditio,* indeed? But this was his end in this life, and in
the other he hath "his portion with hypocrites," and they
with him "in the lake of fire and brimstone."

So much for the 1. speech itself, 2. for the speaker, and in
him both his person, 3. and his intent.

Now as justice would, let us hear *alteram partem.* These
are shrewd presumptions; yet let us not resolve, but stay
till Christ have said; and if He mislike it too, sell it and
spare not.

"But Jesus," &c. There was, saith St. Gregory, no error
of the Disciples, *præsente Magistro,* 'while Christ was present with them,' but it was *salutaris error, quia totius mundi
sustulit errorem,* 'a wholesome and profitable error, for it rid
the world of an error for ever after.' We may well apply it
to this. We should have been of Judas' mind, and that,
that carried the Disciples, have gone for current, had not
our Saviour Christ overruled the case, and stayed the sale of
Mary Magdalene's ointment; and in staying it said enough
to stop their mouths for ever, that make the like motions.

Which to do the more firmly, albeit Christ might well
have excepted to Judas' person as unfit—what, the son of
perdition talk of perdition! Or laid open his intent as
wicked and execrable, *ut quid hoc sacrilegium? Ut quid hæc
hypocrisis?*—yet the more sufficiently to do it, he waves
both, and joins issue upon the very point itself; admitting
all had been simply and honestly both said and meant.

Wherein He keepeth this order; first propoundeth that
what was done, it was sufferable, and she not to be troubled
for it; *Sinite illam, &c.* Secondly, it was a good work; and
therefore she not only to be excused, but to be commended
for it. Thirdly, the reason and warrant of both, *in Me*—for
that it was done upon Him, on Whom nothing that is bestowed can be said to be lost, but must and ought to be said
to be well bestowed. So that there is a full answer to every
point of Judas' bill: *ut quid* for *ut quid; ut quid molestia
hæc?* for *ut quid perditio? Potuit vendi* is answered with
sinite, 'let alone;' *perditio,* with *bonum opus;* and *pauperibus*

with *in Me*, Who is of more value than many poor, after
Whom it may well become the poor to be served.

To begin then with the first. *Sinite illam*, saith Christ.
Not as they hoped, *sistite illam*, 'stay her'—indeed it is but
a waste work she is about; but *sinite illam*, "let her alone,
the work is good," suffer her to proceed. His meaning is;
Such acts as this was, are to be let alone, and they that so
disposed, not to be troubled. Sure He foresaw many would
be meddling, many *ut quids* would be framed, and many
potuits devised, and much business be made, about Mary
Magdalene's ointment, and about works of that nature; that
every otherwhile, some motions, petitions, plots would be
framed about the altering of it. To this day they will not let
her alone, but disquiet her still. He hath therefore left in
His Gospel these words, as a fit answer, to stay their hands,
and stop their mouths, for ever. *Sinite illam*, 'let them be,
suffer them to remain;' *ut quid molestia hæc?* a meet reply
to *ut quid perditio hæc?* to the world's end.

And this request, to my poor conceit, is very reasonable;
if, in this kind, any thing may be allowed for reasonable. It
is not, *imitamini illam*, or *adjuvate illam;* 'do ye the like con-
tribute to her charge,' further and help her what you may;
which yet He would have us. That would Judas never be
got to; if Christ had wished him to like cost, what ado then
would there have been! But this, Do but let her alone; if
you will not further, yet hinder her not, trouble her not.
That she hath spent, of her ability she hath done it; she
hath not had of you one penny toward her three hundred,
nor she asketh you none. Seeing you are at no cost, why
should it grieve you? If you like not to follow her, yet let
her alone.

And may not the same in like reason be said and entreated
at this day? That what our Fathers and Elders in the
Christian Faith bounteously employed on Christ; what they,
I say, have that way dedicate, if we will not add to it
and imitate them, yet we will let it alone and not trouble
them; and at least be not with Judas, if we like not or list
not to be with Mary Magdalene. On *Christ* it is, I dare
boldly say; and if I say it, I shall have all the ancient
Fathers on my side; and if I say it, St. Paul will warrant

E

me, who, in 1 Cor. 12. 12, expressly calleth the Church
Christ's Body. And he might well do it: the first speech
Christ ever spake to him, Himself calleth the Church *Me*—
the word He useth. On Christ it is spent, any part of Christ,
be His glory more than other; and on that office and calling
of the Church, which St. Paul, who best knew the dignity of
it, calleth "the glory of Christ." This I say under correc-
tion, is as me thinketh not unreasonable; that seeing what
superstition hath defiled is removed and gone, touching that
which is remaining it be said, *Sinite illam.*

From this first degree of *sinite*, our Saviour Christ ascendeth
to a higher; and lest we should mistake, as if He bare with
her good mind and meaning rather than allowed the work,
He tells us the very work itself is good; and so pleads and
justifies it, not as sufferable only, but as commendable. For
that is the meaning of *bonum opus operata est.*

Wherein, first, He answereth the principal reason, *perditio
est.* You may sell, saith Judas, it is but waste: you must
let it alone, saith Christ, it is *bonum opus.* So that as His
former, of *sinite*, crossed the motion; so this, of *bonum opus*,
overthroweth the reason, *perditio.*

In which our Saviour Christ looseth the knot, and teacheth
us a point; to enquire first, *Ecquid perditio*, 'Whether it be
a waste?' before we come to *Ut quid*, 'To what end is it?' If
it be waste, it is well and truly said; but this He pleadeth
is not any, unless, which God forbid, good works be waste
with us. And therefore joineth issue upon the word *hæc*;
that is, that is done upon him is no waste at all, as Judas
termeth it; but, as He christeneth it by a new name, *bonum
opus.* Therefore his reproof is nothing, *tanquam cadens in
materiam indebitam*, 'as lighting upon an unmeet matter,'
which deserveth no reproof, but rather commendation.

Indeed, if Judas sometime before had said it to Mary
Magdalene, in the days of her former vanity, when she
wasted thus much, and peradventure many a penny more, on
her riot and wantonness; then indeed, *ut quid perditio hæc?*
had hit right. But now it was not on herself, but on Christ's
head, it is out of season. As if our age now would apply
to Nabal's riotous feasts, to the Assyrians' superfluous suits,
to Esau's superfluous retinue, to the endless building Jeremy's

findeth fault with, to our manifold idle excesses many ways; to every and each of these, an *Ut quid perditio?* there now it were right, there indeed were the true place of *Ut quid perditio?* But this is, among many, a strong illusion of these days; that whereas there are abroad in the world so many true wastes, so much in ointments and perfumes upon our-selves, so many hundred *denarii,* indeed no man can tell what, daily lavished; we can neither see ourselves, nor pa-tiently hear of others, *ut quid perditiones hæ?* Here all is well—all is well bestowed. Neither *ut quid,* nor *potuit dari pauperibus;* the poor never comes in our head. No where but in Christ ought is amiss. Only in that that is meant to Him, and spent on Him, there comes out our *ut quid,* there comes the poor into our mind. No way to provide for them but by sale of Christ's ointment. That is the waste, and none but that; and none but that is maligned. We are perfect auditors, we can exactly reckon how many hundreds Christ wasteth; but who keepeth any account of his own? To ourselves too much is too little; to Him, too little is too much. And three hundred pence that way bestowed, is greater eyesore than three hundred pounds, I dare be bold to say, to not so good uses.

Thus it is, and it is to be lamented that thus it is. But Christ teacheth us better, if we will learn of Him and let Judas go, that we may better bestow our *ut quid* any where than upon Him. And we shall find it true : the day will come, when that only that goeth to Him, shall be found to be no *perditio;* and all else *perditio* indeed, whatsoever or upon whatsoever. To be lost indeed, and no fruit to come of it. That which is "sown in the flesh, to be lost in corruption;" Gal. 6. 8. that which on the belly, εἰς ἀφεδρῶνα: that which on the [Mark 7. back, in rags; that which on building, in rubbish; that which 19.] to our heirs, in prodigality, riot, and excess; and that which is *in Me,* shall prove no *perditio,* "waste," lost or lavished, but *bonum opus,* "a good deed;" to be rewarded with a blessed remembrance on earth, and with a crown of glory in the Kingdom everlasting.

Thus, you see, Judas is answered, and the work quit from the name of *perditio.* So far from *perditio,* that it is *bonum opus.* "A good work," indeed ; as proceeding from a good

SERM.
III.

mind, possessed with the virtue of virtues, thankfulness. For mercy bestowed on Him, Who only is good and goodness itself; Who here alloweth it for good, causeth it to be registered in His Gospels for good, in the day of judgment shall pronounce it good; rewardeth it for good in this world, with a good name; in that to come, with all the good of His Kingdom, where no good is wanting.

8.
The reason : *in Me.*

The third remaineth,—"upon Me," wherein properly is meant His natural body of flesh, which should not alway be with us. But they of whom we have learned to interpret the Scriptures, in a manner all extend it to His mystical Body too; and, as they think, by good consequence. That seeing He gave His natural Body to be bought and sold, rent and torn, crucified and slain for His Body mystical; His Body mystical is certainly dearer to Him, and better He loveth it. And then, if He will accept that is done to the less, and make it *bonum opus;* He will much more that which is done to the more beloved; and it shall never go for less, never did I am sure. The Scriptures record, as a good work, that that was

Acts 4. 37.

laid down at "the Apostles' feet," no less than this that was laid upon Christ's own head; and in them, Ananias a Church-

Luke 22. 3.

robber, and Judas a Christ-robber, both in one case. "Satan"

Acts 5. 3.

is said to have "filled both their hearts" in that act; and like evil end came to both; and both are good remembrances for them that seek and say as they did. Yea, which would not be content to detain a part—Ananias and Judas went no farther—but would seize of all gladly, if a gracious Lady did not say, *Sinite.*

To conclude, it is St. Augustine, and so say all the rest; *Tu intellige et de Ecclesiâ, quia qui aliquid de Ecclesiâ prædatur Judæ perditio comparatur:* 'Understand this of the Church, and spare not; for he that taketh any thing— I say any thing, from it, is in Judas' case:' for the sin certainly, for the punishment as it pleaseth God.

Now we know what is meant by *in Me;* it is no waste word. We will consider it first as a reason of the two former, and then as a special answer to that of the poor.

It answereth *Ut quid?* "To what end?" why, *in Me,* " to Me," and for My sake.

It answereth *perditio; in Me*—why, it is spent on Christ, "on Me," on Whom nothing that is spent is misspent.

It yieldeth a reason of *sinite*, "spare her;" if not her, yet spare Me, trouble Me not. Ye cannot scrape off the ointment but with My trouble.

And a reason of *bonum opus est;* for His *in Me* is warrant sufficient, why the work is to be reckoned good. Yea, in saying it is not only good done, but done to Him, He giveth it a dignity, and lifteth up this work above.

But especially, it answereth the weight of Judas' reason, *pauperibus*, "the poor." Our Saviour Christ plainly sheweth that Judas is mistaken that draweth a diameter, and maketh opposition between devotion toward Christ, and alms to the poor. Tabitha was good to the poor, Mary Magdalene to Christ. Must we put Mary Magdalene to death, to raise Tabitha again? and is there no other way? Yes indeed, *Sinite illam*, saith Christ in this verse—let this stand; and Mark 14. 6. yet do those good too, *date eleemosynam*, in the next. There be other means to provide for the poor, than by the sale of Christ's ointment; and we are not in pretence of them to omit this, or any office or duty unto Christ.

Pauperibus is not the only good work; this is also. And of the two, if any to be preferred, it is *in Me*: He certainly to be served first. To which work, not only those of wealth, Mary Magdalene with her three hundred pence; but even poor and all—the poor widow with her mites is bound, as we Mark 12.42. see; even to add something even to the offerings of God; and if not with *nardus*, yet with oil to anoint His head, as Himself requireth. This, I say, if both could not stand. But, thanks be to God, there be ways they may both stand; and not one fall, that the other may rise. Malachi telleth us a way, and it is a special one; to do as this virtuous woman here; *Inferte in Apothecas Meas*, "bring into Mine Mal. 3. 10. (that is, My Church's) treasures," and I will break the windows of Heaven and send you such plenty, as you and the poor both shall eat and have enough, and yet leave in abundance. So that we see the next and kindliest way to have Judas' complaint redressed, is to speak and labour that Mary Magdalene's example may be followed.

Secondly, by *in Me* it plainly appeareth, how Christ

SERM. ,standeth affected to works of this kind. For permitting
III.
——— them, standing for them, defending and commending them,
He sheweth plainly, He will be content with such as it is.
For, albeit He were the very pattern of true frugality, and an
enemy to all excess, yet this service, chargeable as it was, He
well alloweth of. Shewing us this, that as He is *Christus*
Acts 10. 38. *Patris*, anointed by God His Father, *Quem unxit Dominus*, so
also He will be *Christus noster*, and that passively anointed
Joh. 11. 2. by us, *Quem unxit Maria*. That as here He commendeth
Mary Magdalene for the supply of it, so He giveth Simon
Lu. 7. 46. an item, *oleo caput Meum non unxisti*, for being defective in
this duty.

I would gladly ask this question : If the ointment may be
sold, as Judas saith, and bought lawfully, and they that buy
may lawfully use; if they may use it, why may not Christ?
Num solis stultis apes mellificant ? 'Do bees make honey, and
nardus bear ointment, for wicked men only?' May any that
pays for it, and may not Christ? Is He only of all other
incapable or unworthy ?

If it be because it is more than needs, let that be a reason
of all. Let the law hold us, as well as Him. But if no man
but allows himself a more liberal diet and proportion of port
than in strict terms is needful, for all the poor, why should
,we bind Christ alone to that rule? Except we mean to go
farther with him, and not only except to Mary's ointment,
but even to Simon's feast also; *Ut quid unguentum hoc?*
.then. *Ut quid convivium hoc*, too? seeing a smaller repast
might serve, and the rest be given to the poor. So that his
allowance shall be just as much, and no more, than will serve
to hold life and soul together. But as He, without any bar
or *ut quid*, alloweth us not only *indumenta* for nakedness, but
ornamenta for comeliness ; not only *alimenta* for emptiness,
but *oblectamenta* for daintiness ; so good reason it is we think
not much of His *nardus*, and tie Him only to those rules
from which ourselves plead exemption.

.I demand again, If ointment might be spent on Aaron's
head under the Law, seeing a greater than Aaron is here,
why not on His too? I find that neither under the Law
He liked of their motion, What should the Temple do with
cedar? neither under the Gospel of theirs, What should

Christ's head to do with *nardus?* But that, to his praise he is recorded in the Old Testament that said, "Shall I dwell in my ceiled house, and the Ark of God remain under goats'-skins?" And she, in the New, that thought not her best ointment too good for Christ's head. Surely, they in Egypt had their service of God, it may be in a barn, or in some corner of an house. Yet when Moses moved a costly Tabernacle, no man was found that once said, Our fathers served God well enough without one, *Ut quid perditio hæc?* After that, many Judges and Prophets and righteous men were well when they might worship before the Ark, yet when Solomon moved a stately Temple, never any was found that would grudge and say, Why the ark is enough; I pray God, we serve God no worse than they, that knew nothing but a tent—*Ut quid perditio hæc?* Only in the days of the Gospel, which of all other least should, there steps up Judas, and dareth to say that against Christ's Church that no man durst ever either against Moses' tent, or Solomon's Temple.

And if Christ had taken it well, or passed it in silence, or said *Sinite illum,* 'suffer Judas' motion to take place,' we might have had some show. But seeing, He saith *Molestus est* to Judas, *Sinite illam,* 'suffer Mary to go forward;' and not that only, but *bonum opus* too; why should any, after Judas, be thought worthy the answering?

Surely, as the Gospel in this duty hath, and so ought to exceed the Law; so in the Gospel, we here and our country above all other. I will but say with Chrysostom, *Appende Christum ô homo;* do but construe these two words, *in Me,* aright; poise and prize Who it is, *et sufficit.* It is Christ Jesus, Who hath not spared to anoint us with His own blood, and our souls with all the comforts and graces of His Holy Spirit. If toward us neither blood nor life were too dear on His part, shall on ours any *nardus* be too dear, or any cost too much, that is on Him bestowed?

Perhaps our particular will more move us. It is Christ That created for us nard and all other delights whatsoever, either for use and necessity we have; or for fruition and pleasure we enjoy. It is He That hath enriched us that we be able to bestow it, by this long prosperity, plenty, and peace, as no other kingdom under Heaven. Is there any

1 Chron. 17. 1.

good mind can think that this is an indignity? that He is not worthy, hath not deserved, and doubly deserved this, and ten times more, at our hands?

An extraordinary conceit is entered into the world, by a new found gloss, to make whatsoever we like not, or list not to do ourselves, *extraordinary;* and so some deem of this as extraordinary, and whereof no example is to be made. No ancient writer is of that mind, but that for us it was written; and that, *Vade tu et fac similiter,* may be written upon her box. But be it so. Why may not I wish on our parts, Let us be extraordinary? For God hath not dealt ordinarily with us of this land; He hath not been to us a wilderness or a barren land, but hath, even our enemies being judges, been extraordinary in His goodness toward us all. And sure in us ordinary common thankfulness is not enough. Shall I set myself to recount His benefits? An easy matter to find entrance; but when then should I make an end? In one I will abridge them all. We spake of ointment. Verily, Christ hath anointed over us, and given us a most gracious sovereign, by whose happy and blessed reign we long have—and longer may we He grant!—enjoyed both the inward and outward anointing; the inward, the holy and heavenly comfort of God's truth, and true " oil of gladness ;" the outward, of earthly plenty and delight, which nard or any rich confection may afford; and, in a word, whatsoever happiness can fall to any nation under Heaven. From the holy oil of whose anointing, as the " dew of Hermon on Sion," and as "Aaron's ointment upon the skirts of His clothing," there daily droppeth upon this whole realm pure nard, or if anything else be more precious, whether in these earthly, or in those Heavenly blessings. I speak no more than we all feel. This is that one I spake of, and in this one is all—even the Lord's anointed. Whom, I make no question, but the Lord hath, and will more and more bless, for that her Highness hath said, as Himself said, *Sinite illam.* And blessed be God That hath put into her heart so to say, to like well of *Ut quid perditio,* but to have it so applied. I doubt not but this heroical virtue, among many others, shall make her sceptre long to flourish, shall make her remembrance to be in blessing to all posterity, and shall be, among other, her rejoicing in the

Lu. 10. 37.

Ps. 45. 7.

Ps. 133. 2, 3.

day of the Lord, and an everlasting crown of glory upon her head.

This is that ointment I spake of, that itself alone may make us all confess, we have received from Christ extraordinary mercy, and are therefore to return more than ordinary duty. *Non taliter fecit omni,* nay, *non taliter fecit ulli populo;* " He Ps. 147. 20. hath not dealt so with every, nay, not so with any people," as with us ; and therefore not any people to deal so thankfully with Him again.

This, if it were extraordinary. Howbeit, if antiquity may be admitted judge, this, as " a good work," is to be ordinary with us. Since every thing done in this kind to Christ's Church, only upon a thankful regard, is with them reckoned a dram of Mary Magdalene's ointment.

At least, if we will not come so far as *operata est,* we do yet thus far favour it as to yield to *Sinite illam;* seeing Mary Magdalene, that gave it, paid for it, and it never came out of our purse.

And now this question being thus dilated, it is every man's duty, saith Theophylact, to set down, *cujus partis sit,* 'whose [Theophyl. part he will take, whose mind he will be of.' Whether with in Evang. Marc. Enar. Judas, *Perditio est;* or with Christ, *Bonum opus est;* whether c. 14.] *Potuit vendi,* or *Sinite illam.*

But I trust we will stand to Christ's judgment, and rather take part with Him for Mary Magdalene, than with Judas against her; that we may be with Mary Magdalene, that are of her mind, which at the hour of death we all shall desire.

The entrance I make. From this unhappy conjunction of III. Mary's good work and Judas' evil speech, this first considera-The doc- trine. tion offereth itself, nothing pleasant, but wholesome and re- 1. That quisite to be called to mind of all that mean to do well. That works are things well done shall be evil taken, and often good affections maligned. have no good constructions, and that received with the left hand that is reached with the right.

For this her act that was well done, if Christ knew what it was to do well, yet we see it is disdained, grudged at, and she molested for it;—all three are in my text. Whence we learn, Be a thing done to never so good purpose, yet some Judas will mutter and malign, and come forth with his *Ut quid?* some Judas will cast his dead fly into Mary Magdalene's box of ointment.

No one creature had so good experience of this as this poor woman had. Three special virtues of hers the Gospels record, and in every one of the three she was repined at. 1. When, in the bitterness of her soul she shewed her repentance with tears, Simon the Pharisee did what he could to disgrace her. 2. When, in an hungry desire to receive comfort by the word of Grace, she shewed her devotion in sitting at Christ's feet, Martha, her own sister, made complaint of her. 3. And now here again the third time; when, in an honest regard of her duty she sheweth her thankfulness for comfort received, Christ's own Disciples both grudge and speak against her. So that, if she washeth His feet with tears, it contents not; if she anoint His head with balm, it is matter of mislike; if she sit still and say nothing, it is all one; still Mary is found fault with, ever her doings stand awry.

This is the lot and portion of all those that will follow their steps. Not only we of private estate, but even great personages, as Nehemias by Geshem[1], to bring detriment to the state by favouring the Church's case. Even princes: David by Shimei, to be a bloody persecutor, when, if in any thing he offended, it was in too much lenity. Even Christ Himself the Son of God, Who neither could have His feet, but Simon the Pharisee—nor His head anointed, but Judas His Apostle, malign and speak against it.

So that not only *regium est,* as the heathen said, *bene cum feceris, audire male,* 'to have evil speech for good deeds,' but *divinum,* a heavenly thing, as Christ saith, *de bono opere lapidari.*

This is their lot. And it serveth us to two purposes. 1. For judgment; to see this evil disease under the sun—the evil aspect which the world looks with on Mary Magdalene. Whereby many times that which is commended in Heaven is condemned in earth, and Judas' bag carrieth away even from Christ's. Whereby many times all good is said of them by whom little good is done, and some men's *flagitia,* which the heathen story lamenteth in Drusus, shall find more favour and be better rewarded than Drusus, *optime cogitata,* the good counsel and course of many a better man.

Lu. 7. 39.

Lu. 10. 40.

Neh. 6. 6.
[¹ Gashmu.]

2 Sam. 16. 7.

Joh. 10. 32.

Such is the deceitfulness of the sons of men upon the Ps. 62. 9.
weights. It serveth us, I say, to see and to sorrow at, and
to say with Augustine, *Væ tibi miser, bonus odor occidit te!*
'Miserable man that thou art, how art thou choked with so
good a scent!' To sorrow it, and to prepare ourselves to it,
and resolve that though we do well, yet we shall be evil
spoken of.

That first, and second this for practice. That though we 2.
be evil spoken of, yet not to be dismayed or troubled with this done. Yet to be
hard measure, but to go on and do as Mary Magdalene did;
not once, or twice, but three several times, one after another;
neither to hold our hand or shut our box, nor spare our
ointment, if things well done be evil taken. To look not to
Judas on earth, who disliketh, but to Christ in Heaven Who
approveth it, and in all three cases made answer for Mary
Magdalene, against Martha, Simon, and Judas, and all her
accusers. To know that that which in Judas' divinity is *perditio*, in Christ's divinity is *bonum opus*. In regard therefore
of our own duty, to be resolute with the Apostle, *Quod facio,* 2 Cor. 11.
hoc et faciam, "What I do, that will I do." In respect of mis- 12.
construction with them, *Mihi pro minimo est;* because we may 1 Cor. 4. 3.
truly say and in the sight of God, *sicut deceptores et veraces,* 2 Cor. 6. 8.
"as deceivers, yet true;" or, with Mary Magdalene, as wasters,
yet well-doers. Assuring ourselves, that it is well done; and
shall be both commended on earth and rewarded in Heaven.
On earth; for posterity shall better like of the shedding, than
of the sale of this ointment. In Heaven; for the day will
come, *qui male judicata rejudicabit,* 'when all perverse judgments shall have judgment against them;' and Mary Magdalene shall look cheerfully on Him on Whom she bestowed it,
and Judas ruefully behold Him from Whom he sold it.

This is Mary Magdalene's part, as Christ telleth; that howsoever Mary Magdalene be, in Simon's house, or in a corner,
found fault with, amends shall be made her; and as wide as
the world is, and as far as the Gospel shall sound, "she shall Mark 14. 9.
be well spoken of." Yea, when the great and glorious acts
of many monarchs shall be buried in silence, this poor box of [Vide S.
nardus shall be matter of praise, and never die. And contrary, in cap. 26.
howsoever Judas' motion may find favour and applause in S. Mat.
the present, yet posterity shall dislike and discommend it; Hom. 81.]

and he be no less infamous and hateful, than Mary famous and well spoken of, in all ages to the end of the world.

This is her portion from Christ; her soul refreshed with the sweet joys of Heaven, and her name as *nardus* throughout all generations. This is his lot from the Lord; a name Mat. 24.51. odious and loathsome to all that hear it, and his " portion with hypocrites," in the lake of fire and brimstone. From which, &c.

To which, &c.

A SERMON

PREACHED BEFORE

QUEEN ELIZABETH, AT HAMPTON COURT,

ON WEDNESDAY, BEING THE SIXTH OF MARCH, A.D. MDXCIV.

LUKE xvii. 32.

Remember Lot's wife.

[*Memores estote uxoris Lot.* Lat. Vulg.]

[*Remember Lot's wife.* Engl. Trans.]

A part of the Chapter read this morning, by order of the Church, for the Second Lesson.

THE words are few, and the sentence short; no one in Scripture so short. But it fareth with sentences as with coins: in coins, they that in smallest compass contain greatest value are best esteemed; and in sentences, those that in fewest words comprise most matter, are most praised. Which, as of all sentences it is true; so specially of those that are marked with *memento*. In them, the shorter the better; the better, and the better carried away, and the better kept; and the better called for when we need it. And such is this here; of rich contents, and withal exceeding compendious. So that, we must needs be without all excuse, it being but three words and but five syllables, if we do not remember it.

The sentence is our Saviour's, uttered by Him upon this occasion. Before, in verse 18, He had said, that "the days of the Son of Man should be as the days of Lot," in two respects: 1. In respect of the suddenness of the destruction that should come; 2. and in respect of the security of the people on whom it should come. For the Sodomites laughed at it; and Lot's wife, it should seem, but slightly regarded it. Being then in Lot's story, very fitly and by good consequence out of that story, He leaveth us a *memento* before He leaveth it.

SERM.
IV.

There are in Lot's story two very notable monuments of God's judgment. 1. The lake of Sodom, 2. and Lot's wife's pillar. The one, the punishment of resolute sin; the other, of faint virtue. For the Sodomites are, an example of impenitent wilful sinners; and Lot's wife of imperseverant and relapsing righteous persons.

Both these are in it; but Christ, of both these, taketh the latter only. For two sorts of men there are, for which these two items are to be fitted: 1. To those in state of sin that are wrong, the lake of Sodom. 2. To those in state of grace that are well, if so they can keep them, Lot's wife's pillar. To the first in state of sin, Moses propoundeth "the vine of Deu. 32. 32. Sodom and grapes of Gomorrah," *quæ contacta cinerescunt,* 'that if ye but touch them turn to ashes.' To the other in state of grace, Christ here, Lot's wife's pillar. To the one Jer. 8. 4. Jeremy crieth, *Qui cecidit, adjiciat ut resurgat.* To the other 1Cor.10.12. St. Paul; *Qui stat, videat ne cadat.* Agar, that is departed Gen. 21. 18. from Abraham's house with her face toward Egypt, the Angel calleth to return, and not to persevere : Lot's wife, that Gen. 19. 17. is gone out of Sodom, and in the right way to Zoar, the Angel willeth to persevere and not to return. So that to them this *memento* is by Christ directed, that being departed from the errors of Ur are gone out from the sins of Sodom, are entered into the profession of the truth, or into the course of a virtuous life. So that, if we lay it to ourselves, we shall lay it aright; that Lot's wife be our example, and that we sprinkle ourselves with the salt of her pillar, *ne putrescamus,* that we turn not again to folly, or fall away from our own steadfastness. And, if it be meant to us, needful it is that we receive it. A point no doubt of important consideration and necessity, as well for religion to call on, as for our nature to hear of. First, for religion : her glory it is no less to be [Acts 21. able to shew *antiquos Discipulos,* "old professors," as Mnason 16.] was, than daily to convert and make new proselytes. And therefore, with Christ, we must not ever be dealing with Mat. 11. 28. *venite ad me;* but sometimes too, with *manete in me.* That Joh. 15. 4. hath his place—not ever with *stimuli,* 'goads' to incite men to, but otherwhile with *clavi,* 'nails' to fasten them in. For, as nature hath thought requisite as well the breasts to bring up, as the womb to bring forth; and philosophy holdeth *tueri* of no less regard than *quærere;* and with the lawyers, *habendum* is not the only thing, but *tenendum* needful too; and the physician as careful of the regiment, and fearful of the recidivation[1], as of the disease and cure; so Divinity is respective [1 relapse.] to both—both to lay the groundwork surely, *ne corruat,* 'that it shake not' with Esay's *nisi credideritis;* and to roof it Isa. 7. 9. carefully, *ne perpluat,* 'that it rain not through' and rot the principals, with Paul's *si permanseris, alioquin excideris et tu,* Rom.11.22.

Needful then for religion, to call on this virtue; and as for religion to call on, so for our nature to be called on. Wherein, as there is *tenellum quid,* " a tender part" not able to endure the cross, for which we need the virtue of patience; so is there also ἀψίκορόν τι, 'a flitting humour,' not able to endure the tediousness of any thing long; for which we no less need the virtue of perseverance. The Prophet, in the seventy-eighth Psalm, saith, our nature is as a bow, which, when it is Ps. 78. 57. bent to his full, except it be followed hard till it be sure and fast, starts back again, and is as far off as ever it was. The Apostle compareth it to "flesh," as it is, which will *sine sale* Rom. 7. 18. *putrescere,* and if it be not corned, of itself bringeth forth corruption. And to help this our evil inclination forward, there be in all ages dangerous examples to draw us on. The Israelites, after they had passed the Red Sea and all the perils of the desert, and were now come even to the borders of Canaan, even there say, *Bene nobis erat in Ægypto,* " We Ex. 16. 3. were better in Egypt;" "let us make a captain and return Nu. 11. 18. thither." The Romans, in the New, at the first so glorious Nu. 14. 4. professors that St. Paul saith, " All the world spake of their Rom. 1. 8. faith;" after, when trouble arose, and St. Paul was called *coram,* of the same Romans he saith, *Nemo mihi adfuit, sed* 2 Tim.4.16. *omnes deseruerunt,* "None stood by me, all shrunk away." And in these dangerous days of ours, the falling away quite of divers, and some such as have said of themselves with Peter, *Etsi omnes, non ego;* and others have said of them, Mat. 26.33. *Etsi omnes, non ille.* The declining of others, which, as Daniel's image, decay by degrees; from a head of fine gold Dan. 2. 32, fall to a silver breast, and from thence to loins of brass, and &c. thence to legs of iron, and last to feet of clay; the wavering and amaze of others that stand in the plain, with Lot's wife, looking about, and cannot tell whether to go forward to little

SERM.
IV.

The division.
I.

II.

III.
[S. August.
En. in Ps.
75(76). 12.]

I.
The use of
stories in
general.
Isa. 62. 6.

Heb. 2. 1.

Jas. 1. 23,
24.

Job 10. 9.

Job 7. 7.

Eccl. 11. 8.

Job 8. 9.

Zoar or back again to the ease of Sodom; shew plainly that Lot's wife is forgotten, and this is a needful *memento,* "Remember Lot's wife." If then it be ours, and so nearly concern us, let us see, *quantum valent hæ quinque syllabæ.*

I. First, Christ sending our memory to a story past; of the use of remembering stories in general.

II. Secondly, Of this particular of Lot's wife, and the points to be remembered in it.

III. Thirdly, How to apply those points, that, as St. Augustine saith, *condiant nos, ut sal statuæ sit nobis condimentum vitæ,* 'that the salt of this pillar may be the season of our lives.'

The Prophet Esay doth call us that stand in this place, the Lord's remembrancers; as to God for the people by the office of prayers, so from God to the people by the office of preaching. In which office of preaching, we are employed as much about *recognosce,* as about *cognosce ;* as much in calling to their minds the things they know and have forgot, as in teaching them the things they know not, or never learnt. The things are many we have commission to put men in mind of. Some touching themselves : for it is many times too true which the philosopher saith; *Nihil tam longe abest a nobis quam ipsi nos,* 'Nothing is so far from our minds, as we ourselves.' For naturally, as saith the Apostle, we do παραῤῥύειν, "leak and run out;" and when we have looked in the glass, we straight "forget our fashion again." Therefore we have in charge to put men in mind of many things, and to call upon them with divers *mementos. Memento quia sicut lutum tu,* "remember the baseness of our mould what it is." *Memento quia vita ventus,* "remember the frailness of our life how short it is." *Memento tenebrosi temporis,* "remember the days of darkness are coming," and they be many. All which we know well enough, and yet need to be put in mind of them.

But the storehouse, and the very life of memory, is the history of time : and a special charge have we, all along the Scriptures, to call upon men to look to that. For all our wisdom consisting either in experience or memory—experience of our own, or memory of others, our days are so short, that our experience can be but slender; *tantum hesterni*

sumus, saith Job, and our own time cannot afford us obser-
vations enough for so many cases as we need direction in.
Needs must we then, as he here adviseth, *interrogare gene-* Job 8. 8.
rationem pristinam, "ask the former age," what they did in
like case; search the records of former times, wherein our
cases we shall be able to match, and to pattern them all.
Solomon saith excellently, *Quid est quod fuit? Quod futurum* Eccl. 1. 9.
est. "What is that that hath been? That that shall be."
And back again, What is that that shall be? That that hath
been. *Et nihil novum est sub sole,* "and there is nothing
under the sun" of which it may be said, It is new; but it
hath been already in the former generations. So that it is
but turning the wheel, and setting before us some case of
antiquity which may sample ours, and either remembering
to follow it if it fell out well, or eschew it if the success were
thereafter. For example, By Abimelech's story King David
reproveth his captains for pursuing the enemy too near the 2 Sam. 11.
wall, seeing Abimelech miscarried by like adventure; and so 21.
maketh use of remembering Abimelech. And by David's
example, that, in want of all other bread, refused not the
shew-bread, Christ our Saviour defendeth His Disciples in Mark 2. 25.
like distress, and sheweth that, upon such extremity, *ne-
cessitas* doth even *legem Legi dicere,* 'give a law even to the
Law itself.'

Seven several times we are called upon to do it: 1. *Me-* Deu. 32. 7.
mento dierum antiquorum, saith Moses. 2. *Recordamini pri-* Isa. 46. 9.
oris Seculi—Esay. 3. *State super vias antiquas*—Jeremy. Jer. 6. 16.
4. *Investiga patrum memoriam*—Job. 5. *Exemplum sumite* Job 8. 8.
Prophetas—James. 6. *Rememoramini dies priscos*—Paul. Jas. 5. 10.
7. Remember Lot's wife—Christ here; that is, to lay our Heb. 10. 32.
actions to those we find there, and of like doings to look for
like ends. So read stories past, as we make not ourselves
matter for story to come.

Now of and among them all, our Saviour Christ after a II.
special manner commendeth unto us this of Lot's wife. Of Of this of
Lot's wife.
which thus much we may say, that it is the only one story,
which of all the stories of the Old Testament He maketh
His choice of, to put in His *memento;* which He would
have them which have forgotten to remember, and those
that remember never to forget. Oft to repair to this story,

F

and to fetch salt from this pillar: that they lose not what they have done, and so perish in the recidivation of Lot's wife.

Then to descend into the particulars. I find in stories two sorts of *memento*: 1. *Memento et fac,* 'remember to follow;' 2. *Memento et fuge,* 'remember to fly the like.' Mary Magdalene's ointment, an example of one; Lot's wife's salt-stone, an example of the other. Or to keep us to this story, Lot looked not back, till he came safe to Zoar; *memento et fac.* Lot's wife did, and died for it; *memento et fuge.*

The verse before sheweth, why Christ laid the *memento* upon her. Μὴ καταβάτω, μὴ ἐπιστρεψάτω, that we should not turn or return back, as she did; that we should not follow her, but when we come at this pillar, turn at it and take another way. That is, we should "remember Lot's wife," but follow Lot; remember her, but follow him.

Now in either of both *mementos,* to follow, or to fly, we alway enquire of two points, and so here, 1. *quid fecit,* 2. *quid passa est;* what they did whose story we read, and how they sped—the fact and the effect. The fact, vice or virtue; the effect, reward or punishment.

Both which concerning this unfortunate woman we find Gen. 19. 26. set down in one verse, in the nineteenth of Genesis, what she did; that "she drew back," or "looked back"—this was her sin. The effect, that she was turned into a salt stone—this was her punishment. And these two are the two memorandums concerning her to be remembered. First, of her fault.

1.
Her fault. The Angel had given charge to Lot and his company, in the seventeenth of that chapter, "Scape for thy life, stay not in the plain, look not once behind thee lest thou perish." "Scape for thy life"—She trifled for all that as if no peril were. "Stay not in the plain," yet stayed she behind. "Look not back lest thou die." She would and did look back, to die for it. So that she did all that she was forbid, and regarded none of the Angel's words, but despised the counsel of God against her own soul. This was her sin, the sin of disobedience, but consisteth of sundry degrees by which she fell, needful all to be remembered.

1. The first was; that she did not *severe custodire man-* 1. Waver-
datum Dei, 'strictly keep her to the Angel's charge,' but ing.
dallied with it, and regarded it by halves; that is, say what
he would, she might use the matter as she would; go, or
stay and look about as she list. Such light regard is like
enough to have grown of a wandering distrust; lest haply,
she had left Sodom in vain, and the Angel feared them with
that which never should be. The sun rose so clear and it
was so goodly a morning, she repented she came away.
Reckoning her sons-in-law more wise in staying still, than
Lot and herself in so unwisely departing. Which is the sin
of unbelief, the bane both of constancy and perseverance.
Constancy in the purpose of our mind, and perseverance in
the tenor of our life.

2. From this grew the second, That she began to tire and 2. Fainting.
draw behind, and kept not pace with Lot and the Angels.
An evil sign. For ever fainting is next step to forsaking;
and *sequebatur a longe,* a preparative to a giving clean over.
Occasionem quærit, saith Solomon, *qui vult discedere ab* Pro. 18. 1.
amico, "he that hath not list to follow, will pick some quarrel or other to be cast behind."

3. This tiring, had it grown of weakness or weariness or 3. Looking
want of breath, might have been borne with; but it came of back.
another cause, which is the third degree. It was, saith the
text, at least to look back, and to cast her eye to the place
her soul longed after. Which sheweth, that the love of
Sodom sticked in her still; that though her feet were come
from thence, her heart stayed there behind; and that in look
and thought she returned thither, whither in body she might
not; but possibly would in body too, if as Nineveh did, so
Sodom had still remained.

4. Looking back might proceed of divers causes: so might 4. Pre-
this of hers, but that Christ's application directs us. The ferring
Sodom to
verse before saith, "Somewhat in the house;" something left Zoar.
behind affected her, of which He giveth us warning. She
grew weary of trouble, and of shifting so oft. From Ur to
Haran; thence, to Canaan; thence, to Egypt; thence, to
Canaan again; then to Sodom, and now to Zoar; and that,
in her old days, when she would fainest have been at rest.
Therefore, in this wearisome conceit of new trouble now to

begin, and withal remembering the convenient seat she had
in Sodom, she even desired to die by her flesh-pots, and to
be buried in "the graves of lust;" wished them at Zoar that
would, and herself at Sodom again, desiring rather to end
her life with ease in that stately city, than to remove, and be
safe perhaps, and perhaps not, in the desolate mountains.
And this was the sin of restiness of soul, which affected her
eyes and knees, and was the cause of all the former. When
men weary of a good course which long they have holden,
for a little ease or wealth, or I wot not what other secular
respect, fall away in the end; so losing the praise and fruit
of their former perseverance, and relapsing into the danger
and destruction, from which they had so near escaped.

Behold, these were the sins of Lot's wife, a wavering of
mind, slow steps, the convulsion of her neck: all these caused
her weariness and fear of new trouble—she preferred Sodom's
ease before Zoar's safety. "Remember Lot's wife."

The aggra-
vation of
her fall.
This was her sin; and this her sin was in her made much
more heinous by a double circumstance, well worth the remembering; as ever weighty circumstances are matter of
special regard, in a story specially. 1. One, that she fell
after she had stood long. 2. The other, that she fell even
then, when God by all means offered her safety, and so
"forsook her own mercy."

[Jonah 2. 8.]

1. After so
long stand-
ing.
Job 6. 15.
Amos 8.
1. 2.
Hosea 6. 4.
Mat. 13. 20.
Exod. 8. 8.
Touching the first. These "winter brooks," as Job termeth
flitting, desultory, Christians, if they dry; these "summer
fruits," as Amos, if they putrify; these "morning clouds," as
Hosea, if they scatter; these "shallow rooted corn," if they
wither and come to nothing, it is the less grief. No man
looked for other. Pharaoh with his fits, that at every plague
sent upon him is godly on a sudden, and "O pray for me
now;" and when it is gone, as profane as ever he was, beginning nine times, and nine times breaking off again;—he
moves not much. To go farther. Saul that for two years,
Judas that for three, Nero that for five kept well, and then
fell away, though it be much yet may it be borne. But this
woman had continued now thirty years, for so they reckon
from Abraham's going out of Ur to the destruction of Sodom.
This, this, is the grief, that she should persist all this time,
and after all this time fall away. The rather, if we consider

yet farther, that not only she continued many years, but sustained many things in her continuance, as being companion of Abraham and Lot in their exile, their travel, and all their affliction. This is the grief, that after all these storms in the broad sea well passed, she should in this pitiful manner be wrecked in the haven. And when she had been in Egypt, and not poisoned with the superstitions of Egypt; when lived in Sodom, and not defiled with the sins of Sodom; not fallen away for the famine of Canaan, nor taken harm by the fulness of the city of the plain; after all this, she should lose the fruit of all this, and do and suffer so many things all in vain;—this is the first. Remember it.

The second is no whit inferior; that at that instant she 2. Now, woefully perished, when God's special favour was proffered to when best means of preserve her; and that when of all other times she had standing. means and cause to stand, then of all other times she fell away. Many were the mercies she found and felt at God's hand by this very title, that she was Lot's wife. For by it she was incorporated into the house and family, and made partaker of the blessings of the faithful Abraham. It was a mercy to be delivered from the errors of Ur; a mercy, to be kept safe in Egypt; a mercy, to be preserved from the sin of Sodom; a mercy, to be delivered from the captivity of the five Kings; and this the last and greatest mercy, that she was sought to be delivered from the perishing of the five cities. This no doubt doth mightily aggravate the offence, that, so many ways before remembered by God in trouble, she so coldly remembered Him; and that now presently, being offered grace, she knoweth not the day of her visitation; but being brought out of Sodom, and warned of the danger that might ensue, having the Angels to go before her, Lot to bear her company, her daughters to attend her, and being now at the entrance of Zoar, the haven of her rest; this very time, place, and presence, she maketh choice of to perish in, and to cast away that which God would have saved; in respect of herself, desperately; of the Angels, contemptuously; of her husband and daughters, scandalously; of God and His favours, unthankfully; forsaking her own mercy, and perishing in the sin of wilful defection.

"Remember Lot's wife," and these two; 1. That she

SERM.
IV.

"looked back," after so long time, and so many sufferings. 2. That she "looked back," after so many, so merciful, and so mighty protections. And remember this withal, That she "looked back" only, and went not back; would, it may be, but that it was all on fire. But, whether she would or no, or whether we do or no, this forethinking ourselves we be gone out, this faint proceeding, this staying in the plain, this convulsion of the neck, and writhing of the eyes back; this irresolute wavering, whether we should choose either bodily pleasures in perishing Sodom, or the safety of our souls in little Zoar, was her sin; and this is the sin of so many as stand as she stood, and look as she looked, though they go not back; but if they go back too, they shall justify her, and heap upon themselves a more heavy condemnation. So much for the sin, which we should remember to avoid.

2. Her punishment.

Now for her punishment, which we must remember to escape.

This relapse in this manner, that the world might know it to be a sin highly displeasing His majesty, God hath not only marked it for a sin, but salted it too, that it might never be forgotten.

Death.

Rom. 6. 23.

The wages and punishment of this sin of hers was it, which is "the wages of all sin," that is, "death." Death in her sure worthily, that refused life with so easy conditions, as the holding of her head still, and would needs look back and die.

The sound of death is fearful, what death soever; yet it is made more fearful four ways, which all be in this of hers.

1. Sudden.

1. We desire to die with respite: and sudden death we fear, and pray against. Her death was sudden:—back she looked, and never looked forward more. It was her last look.

2. In the act of sin.

2. We desire to have remorse of sin ere we be taken away; and death, in the very act of sin, is most dangerous. Her death was so. She died in the very convulsion; she died with her face to Sodom.

3. Unusual.

[See Num. 16. 29.]

3. We would die "the common death of mankind, and be visited after the visitation of other men;" and an unusual strange death is full of terror. Hers was so. God's own hand from Heaven, by a strange and fearful visitation.

4. Our wish is to die, and to be buried, and not to remain a spectacle above ground, which nature abhorreth. She so died as she remained a spectacle of God's wrath, and a by-word to posterity, and as many as passed by. For until Christ's time, and after, this monument was still extant, and remained undefaced so many hundred years. Josephus, a writer of good account, which lived after this, saith, Ἱστόρηκα αὐτὴν, ἔτι γὰρ καὶ νῦν διαμένει: 'I myself have seen and beholden it, for it stands to be seen to this day.' A reed she was; a pillar she is, which she seemed to be but was not. She was melting water; she is congealed to salt. Thus have we both her fault and punishment. Let us remember both; to shun the fault, that the penalty light not on us.

Now this pillar was erected, and this verdure given it, for our sakes. For, among the many ways that the wisdom of God useth to dispose of the sin of man, and out of evil to draw good, this is one and a chief one, that He suffereth not their evil examples to vanish as a shadow, but maketh them to stand as pillars for ages to come, with the heathen man's inscription, Ἐς ἐμέ τις ὁρέων εὐσεβὴς ἔστω, 'Look on me, and learn by me to serve God better.'

And an high benefit it is for us, that He not only embalmeth the memory of the just for our imitation, but also powdereth and maketh brine of the evil for our admonition; that as a scent from Mary Magdalene's ointment, so a relish from Lot's wife's pillar, should remain to all posterity.

Profane persons, in their perishing, God could dash to pieces, and root out their remembrance from off the earth. He doth not, but suffereth their quarters, as it were, to be set up in stories, *ut pœna impii sit eruditio justi*, 'that their punishment may be our advertisement.' Poureth not out their blood, nor casts it away, but saves it for a bath, *ut lavet justus pedes in sanguine peccatoris*, "that the righteous may wash their footsteps in the blood of the ungodly;" that "all," even the ruin of the wicked, "may co-operate to the good of them that fear God." This woman, in her inconstancy, could He have sunk into the earth, or blown up as saltpetre, that no remembrance should have remained of her. He doth not, but for us and for our sakes He erecteth a pillar: and not a pillar only to point and gaze at, but

Marginal notes:

4. Without burial.

[Joseph. Ant. Jud. lib. 1. c. 11.]

III. Our lesson from this.

[Herodot. Euterp. 141.]

Ps. 58. 10.

Rom. 8. 28.

SERM.
IV.

[¹ *i.e.* an antidote.]

1. Perseverance.

[¹ S. Bern. Epist. 32. ad fin. et 109. circ. med.]
2. Care.

Phil. 3. 13.

3. Fear.
[Vid. S. Bern. de don. S. S. Serm. init.]

Rom. 11. 20—22.

Considerations out of her fault.
1.

a "pillar or rock of salt," whence we may and must fetch wherewith to season whatsoever is unsavoury in our lives. And this, this, is the life and soul of memory; this is wisdom—the art of extracting salt out of the wicked, triacle¹ out of vipers, our own happiness out of *aliena pericula;* and to make those that were unprofitable to themselves, profitable to us. For sure, though Lot's wife were evil, her salt is good. Let us see then how to make her evil our good; see if we can draw any savoury thing from this example.

1. That which we should draw out, is perseverance, *Muria virtutum,* as Gregory calleth it, 'the preserver of virtues,' without which, as summer fruits, they will perish and putrify; the salt of the covenant, without which the flesh of our sacrifice will take wind and corrupt. But St. Augustine better, *Regina virtutum,* 'the Queen of virtues;' for that, however the rest run and strive and do masteries, yet *perseverantia sola coronatur*¹, 'perseverance is the only crowned virtue.'

2. Now perseverance we shall attain, if we can possess our souls with the due care, and rid them of security. Of Lot's wife's security, as of water, was this salt here made. And, if security, as water, do but touch it, it melts away presently. But care will make us fix our eye, and gather up our feet, and "forgetting that which is behind," *tendere in anteriora,* "to follow hard toward the prize of our high calling."

3. And, to avoid security, and to breed in us due care, St. Bernard saith, 'Fear will do it.' *Vis in timore securus esse? securitatem time;* "the only way to be secure in fear, is to fear security.' St. Paul had given the same counsel before, that to preserve *si permanseris,* no better advice than *noli altum sapere, sed time.*

Now, from her story these considerations are yielded, each one as an handful of salt to keep us, and to make us keep.

First, that we see, as of Christ's twelve which He had sorted and selected from the rest, one miscarried: *et illum gregem non timuit lupus intrare,* 'and that the wolf feared not to seize, no, not upon that flock:' and as of Noah's eight that were saved from the flood, one fell away too; so, that of Lot's four here, and but four in all, all came not to Zoar—one came short. So that of twelve, of eight, of four;

yea, a little after, of two, one is refused; that we may re- Lu. 17. 35.
member, few there be that scape from Sodom in the Angel's
company; and of those, few though they be, all are not safe
neither. Who would not fear, if one may perish in the
company of Angels !

Secondly, that as one miscarrieth, so not every one, but 2.
one that had continued so long, and suffered so many things,
and after all this continuance, and all these sufferings,
falls from her estate, and turns all out and in; and by
the inconstancy of one hour maketh void the perseverance of
so many years, and as Ezekiel saith, "In the day they turn Ezek. 18.
away to iniquity, all the former righteousness they have done, 24.
shall not be remembered."

Thirdly, that as she perisheth, so at the same time that 3.
Sodom; she by it, and it by her. That one end cometh to
the sinner without repentance, and to the just without perseverance. One end to the abomination of Sodom, and to the
recidivation of Lot's wife. *Et non egredientes, et egredientes
respicientes;* 'they that go not out of her perish, and they
that go out of her perish too if they look back.' *Lacus
Asphaltites* is a monument of the one; Lot's wife's salt-
stone a memorial of the other.

Lastly, that as one perisheth, and that such an one, so that 4.
she perisheth at the gates, even hard at the entry of Zoar;
which of all other is most fearful—so near her safety, so
hard at the gates of her deliverance; remember, that near
to Zoar gates there stands a salt-stone.

These very thoughts, what her case was these four ways,
and what ours may be who are no better than she was, will
search us like salt, and teach us, that as, if we remember
what we have been, we may, saith St. Bernard, *erubescere;* so,
if we remember what we may be, we may *contremiscere;* that
we see our beginnings, but see not our ending; we see our
stadium, not our *dolichum.* And that, as we have great need
to pray with the prophet, "Thou hast taught me from my Ps. 71. 18.
youth up until now—forsake me not in mine old age, now
when I am grey-headed;" so we had need stir up our
care of continuing, seeing we see it is nothing to begin
except we continue: nor to continue, except we do it to
the end.

SERM.
IV.
Remember, we make not light account of the Angel's

Mat. 16. 22.
serva animam tuam; blessing ourselves in our hearts, and
saying, *non fiet tibi hoc;* we shall come safe, go we never
so soft, Zoar will not run away.

Remember, we be not weary to go whither God would
have us—not to Zoar, though a little one, if our soul may
there live; and never buy the ease of our body, with the
hazard of our soul, or a few days of vanity with the loss of
eternity.

Remember, we slack not our pace, nor stand still on the
plain. For if we stand still, by still standing we are meet
to be made a pillar, even to stand still, and never to remove.

Remember, we look not back, either with her on the vain
Joh. 21. 20. delights of Sodom left; or with Peter on St. John behind us,
to say, *Domine, Quid iste?* both will make us forget our
Lu. 9. 62. following. "None that casteth his eye the other way," is
εὔθετος, "meet" as he should be, "meet for the Kingdom
of God."

But specially remember we leave not our heart behind us,
but that we take that with us, when we go out of Sodom;
for if that stay, it will stay the feet, and writhe the eye, and
neither the one nor the other will do their duty. Remember,
that our heart wander not, that our heart long not. This
care, if it be fervent, will bring us perseverance.

Out of her
punish-
ment.
Now, that we may the better learn somewhat out of her
punishment too; let us remember also, that as to her, so
to us, God may send some unusual visitation, and take us
suddenly away, and in the act of sin too.

Remember the danger and damage; it is no less matter
we are about, than *perdet animam.* Which if we do, we frus-
trate and forfeit all the fruit of our former well-continued
course; all we have done is vain. Yea, all that Christ hath
done for us is in vain; Whose pains and sufferings we ought
specially to tender, knowing that *supra omnem laborem labor
irritus,* 'no labour to lost labour;' and Christ then hath lost
His labour for us.

Gal. 3. 3.
Remember the folly; that "beginning in the Spirit" we
"end in the flesh;" turning our backs to Zoar, we turn our
face to Sodom; joining to a head of fine gold feet of clay,
and to a precious foundation a covering of thatch.

Remember the disgrace ; that we shall lose our credit and account while we live, and shall hear that of Christ, *Hic homo ;* and that other, *Quid existis in desertum videre ?* "A reed shaken with the wind." Mat. 11. 7.

Remember the scandal; that, falling ourselves, we shall be a block for to make others fall ; a sin no lighter, nor less, nor lighter than a mill-stone. Mat. 18. 6.

Remember the infamy ; that we shall leave our memory remaining in stories, among Lot's wife, and Job's wife, Demas and Ecebolius, and the number of relapsed, there to stand to be pointed at, no less than this heap of salt.

Remember the judgment that is upon them after their relapse, though they live, that they do even with her here *obrigescere,* ' wax hard and numb,' and serve others for a *caveat,* wholly unprofitable for themselves.

Remember the difficulty of reclaiming to good ;—" seven evil spirits" entering instead of one, that their " last state is worse than the first." Mat. 12. 45.

And lastly, Remember that we shall justify Sodom by so doing, and her frozen sin shall condemn our melting virtue. For they in the wilfulness of their wickedness persisted till fire from Heaven consumed them ; and they being thus obdurate in sin, ought not she, and we much more, to be constant in virtue ? And if the drunkard hold out till he have lost his eyes, the unclean person till he have wasted his loins, the contentious till he have consumed his wealth, *Quis pudor quod infelix populus Dei non habet tantam in bono perseverantiam, quantam mali in malo !* 'What shame is it, that God's unhappy people should not be as constant in virtue, as these miscreants have been, and be in vice !'

Each of these by itself, all these put together will make a full *memento,* which if she had remembered, she had been a pillar of light in Heaven, not of salt in earth. It is too late for her—we in due time yet may remember it.

And when we have remembered these, remember Christ too that gave the *memento ;* that He calleth Himself *Alpha* and *Omega*—not only *Alpha* for His happy beginning, but *Omega* for His thrice happy ending. For that He left us not, nor gave over the work of our redemption, till He brought it to *consummatum est.* And that on our part, *summa religionis* Rev. i. 8.

S E R M. *est imitari Quem colis*, 'the highest act of religion, is for the
IV.
Christian to conform himself, not to Lot's wife, but to Christ,
Whose name he weareth.' And though *verus amor non sumit
vires de spe*, 'true love indeed receiveth no manner strength
from hope,' but, though it hope for nothing, loveth nevertheless; yet to quicken our love, which oft is but faint, and
for a full *memento*, remember the reward. Remember how
Christ will remember us for it; which shall not be the wages
of an hireling, or lease-wise for time, and term of years, but
αἰῶνες αἰώνων, eternity itself, never to expire, end, or determine, but to last and endure for ever and ever.

Ezek. 9. 4.   But this reward, saith Ezekiel, is for those, whose foreheads
are marked with Tau, which, as Omega in Greek, is the last
letter in the Hebrew alphabet, and the mark of *consummatum
est* among them; they only shall escape the wrath to come.
And this crown is laid up for them, not of whom it may be
Gal. 5. 7.   said, *currebatis bene*, "ye did run well;" but for those that
2 Tim. 4. 7. can say with St. Paul, *cursum consummavi*, "I have finished
my course well."

And, thanks be to God, we have not hitherto wanted this
salt, but remembered Lot's wife well. So that this exhortation, because we have prevented and done that which it
calleth for, changeth his nature, and becometh a commendation, as all others do. A commendation I say; yet not so
much of the people, whose only felicity is to serve and be
subject to one that is constant—for otherwise we know how
wavering a thing the multitude is—as for the Prince, whose
constant standing giveth strength to many a weak knee
otherwise. And blessed be God and the Father of our Lord
Jesus Christ, that we stand in the presence of such a Prince,
who hath ever accounted of perseverance, not only as of
Regina Virtutum, 'the Queen of virtues,' but as of *virtus
Reginarum*, 'the virtue of a Queen.' Who, like Zerubbabel,
first by princely magnanimity laid the corner-stone in a
troublesome time; and since, by heroical constancy, through
many both alluring proffers and threatening dangers, hath
brought forth the Head-stone also with the Prophet's acclama-
[Zech. 4.7.] tion, "Grace, grace, unto it"—Grace, for so happy a beginning, and Grace for so thrice happy an ending. No terrors,
no enticement, no care of her safety hath removed her from

her stedfastness; but with a fixed eye, with straight steps, with a resolute mind, hath entered herself, and brought us into Zoar. It is a little one, but therein our souls shall live; and we are in safety, all the cities of the plain being in combustion round about us. Of whom it shall be remembered, to her high praise, not only that of the Heathen, *Illaque virgo viri;* but that of David, that all her days she served God "with a covenant of salt," and with her Israel, from the first day until now. And of this be we persuaded, that "He which began this good work in her, will perform it unto the day of Jesus Christ," to her everlasting praise, comfort, and joy, and in her to the comfort, joy, and happiness of us all.

Yet it is not needless, but right requisite, that we which are the Lord's remembrancers put you in mind, that as perseverance is the queen of virtues, *quia ea sola coronatur;* so is it also, *quia Satanas ei soli insidiatur,* 'for that all Satan's malice, and all his practices are against it.' The more careful need we to be, to carry in our eye this example. Which God grant we may, and that our hearts may seriously regard, and our memories carefully keep it, *Ut hæc columna fulciat nos, et hic sal condiat nos,* 'that this pillar may prop our weakness, and this salt season our sacrifice,' that it may be remembered, and accepted, and rewarded in the day of the Lord! Which, &c.

2 Chron. 13. 5.

[Phil. 1. 7.]

[S. Bernard, Epist. 32. ad fin.]

A SERMON

PREACHED IN

THE COURT AT RICHMOND,

ON TUESDAY, BEING THE FIFTH OF MARCH, A.D. MDXCVI.

LUKE xvi. 25.

Son, remember that thou, in thy life time, receivedst thy plea-sure (or, good things ;) and likewise Lazarus pains: Now therefore is he comforted, and thou art tormented.

Fili, recordare quia recepisti bona in vita tua, et Lazarus similiter mala : nunc autem hic consolatur, tu vero cruciaris.

[*Son, remember that thou in thy life-time receivedst thy good things, and likewise Lazarus evil things ; but now he is comforted, and thou art tormented.* Engl. Trans.]

SERM.   THIS Scripture hath the name given it in the very first
V.   words; *Recordare fili,* "Son, remember :"—it is a remem-brance.

There be many sermons of remembrance here on earth; this is one from Heaven, from the mouth of Abraham. Not now on earth but in Heaven, and from thence beholding, 1Cor.13.12. "not in a glass or dark speech," but *intuitive,* that which he Joh. 19. 85. telleth us; and "He that saw it bare witness, and His wit-ness is true."

Which may somewhat move attention ; or if that will not, let me add farther, That it is such a remembrance, that it toucheth our estate in everlasting life; that is, the well or evil hearing of this *recordare* is as much as our eternal life is worth. For we find both in it. That our comfort or torment eternal—comfort in Abraham's bosom, torment in the fire of hell—depend upon it; and therefore as much as we regard them, we are to regard it.

This remembrance is directed to a son of Abraham's, not so much for him, as for the rest. For it is to be feared, that both the sons of Abraham and the daughters of Sarah forget this point overmuch; and many of them, with this party here to whom it is spoken, never remember it till it be too late.

To Abraham's sons then, all and every one. But specially such of his sons as presently are in the state that this son here sometime was, of whom it is said, "He had received good things in his life." By virtue whereof, I find, this *recordare* will reach home to us; for that, we are within the compass of this *recepisti*. For truly the sum of our receipt hath been great, no nation's so great; and our *recordare* little, I will not say how little, but sure too little for that we have received.

Now albeit it be all our case, for we all have received, yet not all our case alike, but of some more than other. For, some have received in far more plentiful manner than other some, and they therefore more deeply interested in it. And look, who among us have received most, them it most concerneth; and they of all other most need to look to it.

If you ask, Why they more than others? For that, besides the duty, to whom a great *recepisti* is given, of them a great *recordare* will be required. The danger also helps them forward. For so it oft happeneth unhappily; that whereas *recepisti* is made, and so may well be, a motive for us to remember; so cross is our nature, none is so great an enemy to *recordare* as it. Our great receiving is oft occasion of our little remembering. And as a full diet in the vessels of our body, so a plenteous receipt breeds stoppings in the mind and memory, and the vital parts of our soul.

We have hereof a lively example before our eyes; and such an one, as if it move us not, I know not what will. A receipt for memories that suffer obstructions.

Our Saviour Christ unlocketh hell-gates to let us see it. In discovering what sighs and what sufferings are in the other world, He sheweth us one lying in them, to whom Abraham objecteth, that this frank receiving had marred his memory. And as He sheweth us his fault, so withal what came to him for it, that strange and fearful consequent; "Now therefore thou art tormented."

SERM.
V.
This example is told by our Saviour, in the fourteenth
verse, to other rich men, and troubled with the same lethargy.
Who when He put them in mind, It would not be amiss
Lu. 16. 9. while they were here, "to make them friends of that they
had received," that when this failed them, as fail them it
must, that "might receive them into everlasting tabernacles;"
forgat themselves so far, as they derided His counsel, not
[ἐξημυκτή-
ριζον
αὐτόν.
G. V.] in words, but *per mycterismum.* Which maketh Him fall
from parables to a plain story, for so it is holden by the best
interpreters, both old and later; and from everlasting tabernacles to everlasting torments; that howsoever they regarded
not His *recordare* on the earth, they had best give better
ear to Abraham's from Heaven.

It is His intent in reporting of it, that our remembering
[Vid. S.
Chrysost.
de Lazar.
con. 3.] of it should keep us from it. *Non vult mortem, et minatur
mortem ne mittat in mortem,* saith Chrysostom: 'He would
not have us in that place, yet He telleth us of that place, to
the end we never come in that place.'

Yea it is Abraham's desire too we should not be overtaken,
but think of it in time; and prevent it before it prevent us.
And therefore he lifteth up his voice, and crieth out of
Heaven, *Recordare fili.*

And not only Abraham, but he that was in the place itself,
and best knew the terror because he felt it—felt that in it as
he heartily wisheth and instantly sueth that they whom he
loveth or any way wisheth well to, may some way take warn-
Lu. 16.
27, 38. ing, *Ne et ipsi veniant,* "That they also come not into that
place of torments."

This use Christ on earth, Abraham from Heaven, and he
out of hell, wish we may have of it. And we, I trust, will
wish ourselves no worse than they: and therefore look to our
recordare, carry it in mind, and (in *recordare* there is *cor*
too) take it to heart, and by both in time take order, *Ne et
ipsi veniamus.*

The
division.
The verse itself, if we mark it well, is in figure and proportion an exact cross. For as a cross it consisteth of two
bars or beams so situate, as the one doth quarter the other.
"Thou receivedst good things, and Lazarus received evil."
These two lie clean contrary, but meet both at the middle
word, "Now therefore;" and there, by a new antithesis, cross

each other: ὁ δὲ, he that "received evil, is comforted;" and σὺ δὲ, "thou that didst receive good, art tormented." And to make it a perfect cross, it hath a title or inscription too set over it; and this it is, *Recordare fili.* And sure next to the cross of Christ, and the memory thereof, this cross of Abraham's invention and exaltation is of all others most effectual. And I verily persuade myself, if we often would fix it before our eyes, and well mark the inscription, it would be a special preparation to our passover, meaning by our passover our end, whereby pass we must ere long into another state, either of misery or bliss; but whether of misery or bliss, it will lie much in the use of this word *recordare.*

First then, we will treat 1. of the cross; after, 2. of the title. _{I.
II.}

We have in the cross two bars; but with both we will not meddle. For why should we deal with Lazarus? This place is not for him, nor he no room in this auditory. Therefore waving his part, in this other of the rich man's, we have two quarters, representing unto us two estates: 1. the upper part or head, *recepisti bona in vitâ*, his estate in this life; 2. the nether or foot, *jam vero torqueris*, his estate in the other.

Of these two: 1. That two they are. 2. Which they be. 3. And how they be fastened or tenanted the one to the other with the illative, "Now therefore."

To quarter out this cross. Two parts it stands of, which two parts are two estates. 1. One past, 2. the other present; the one in memory, the other in experience. Now both memory and experience—memory of things past, and experience of things present—are both handmaids to providence, and serve to provide for things to come. And of all points of providence, for that which is the highest point of all, that our memory of it keep us from experience of this place, this conclusion. _{1.
Of the
cross.}

These two are set down: 1. the one estate, in the words *vitâ tuâ:* 2. the other in the words *jam vero*, "but now." The former past with him, and yet present with us; for we yet "receive." The latter present with him, but with us yet to come, or rather I trust never to come; *jam vero torqueris.* _{1.
The upper
part of it;
the present estate,
*In vitâ
tuâ rece-
pisti.*}

1. The first is the life in *esse*, which we all now live;

G

which, though it be one and the same, yet is there in it a sensible difference, *pauper et dives obviaverunt,* of some poor and some rich every day meeting each other.

2. But *nemo dives semper dives;* and again, *nemo pauper semper pauper.* ' They that be rich in it shall not ever be rich, nor they that are poor, poor alway.' " It came to Lu. 16. 22. pass," saith the Scripture, " that the beggar died." *Mortuus est etiam et dives,* " and the rich man," for all his riches, died also. There ends the first estate.

3. But that end is no final end. For after *vitâ tuâ* there is a *jam vero* still, a second state in reversion to take place when the first is expired. Our hearts misgive us of some such estate; and, as the heathen man said, they that put it off with *quis scit ?* ' who can tell whether such estate be ?' shall never be able to rid their minds of *quid si ?* ' but what if such a one be,' how then ? But to put us that be Christians out of all doubt, our Saviour Christ by this story openeth us a casement into the other life, and sheweth us whither we go when we go hence.

1. First, that as in this life, though but one, yet there are two diverse estates; so death, though it be but one neither, hath two several passages; and through it, as through one and the same city gate, the honest subject walketh abroad for his recreation, and the lewd malefactor is carried out to his execution.

2. Two states then there be after death, and these two disjoined in place, dislike in condition; both set down within the verse; 1. one of comfort: 2. the other of torment.

3. And that both these take place *jam,* ' presently.' For immediately after his death, and while all his " five brethren" yet lived, and ere any of them were dead, he was " in his torments," and did not expect the general judgment, nor was not deferred to the end of the world.

4. And to make it a complete cross, for so it is, as the poor and rich meet here, so do they there also otherwhile; and go two contrary ways, every one to " his own place." Lazarus to his bosom, the rich man to his gulf; and one's misery endeth in rest, the other's " purple and fine linen" [S. Chry- in a flame of fire. *Vere stupendæ vices,* saith Chrysostom, sost. de ' Verily a strange change, a change to be wondered at;' to conc. 2.]

be wondered at and feared of those whom it may concern any manner of way, and at any hand to be had in remembrance.

To apply these two to the party we have in hand, and to 1. begin with the first estate first. Two things are in it set down by him; 1. the one in the word *fili;* 2. the other in the word *recepisti.*

First, That he was Abraham's son, and so of the religion 1. *Fili.* only true; and one that, as himself saith of himself, had had "Moses and the Prophets," though *tanquam non habens,* 'as though he had them not.' For little he used, and less he regarded them; yet a professor he was.

Secondly, as by nature Abraham's son, so by condition or 2. *Recepisti.* office, one of God's receivers. Receivers we are every one of us more or less, but yet in receipts there is a great latitude. Great between her that received "two mites," and him that received "a thousand talents." Between them that receive *tegumenta* only, 'covering for their nakedness,' and them that receive *ornamenta,* 'rich attire' also, for comeliness; and again, that receive *alimenta,* 'food for emptiness,' and *oblectamenta,* 'delicious fair for daintiness.' Now he was not of the petty, but of the main receipt. It is said; "he received good things," and it is told what these good things were—purple of the fairest, and linen of the finest; and *quotidie splendide,* "every day a double feast." Which one thing, though there were nothing else, asketh a great receipt alone. Here "rich," in this life; and who would not sue to succeed him in it? One would think this wood would make no cross, nor these premises such a "now therefore." But to him that was thus and had thus, all this plenty, all this pleasure, *post tantas divitias, post tantas delicias,* to him is this spoken, "but now thou art tormented." Which first estate, as it was rich, so it was short; therefore I make short with it to come to *cruciaris.* Which, though in syllables it is shorter, yet it is in substance, that piece to which he is fastened, in length of continuance far beyond it.

Cruciaris is but one word, but much weight lieth in it; 2. therefore it is not slightly to be passed over, as being The nether part of the cross. the special object of our *recordare,* and the principal part of The second state, *cruciaris.*

G 2

SERM. the cross indeed.   Two ways our Saviour Christ expresseth
  V.   it : 1. one while under the term βάσανος, which is ' torture ;'
       2. another under the term ὀδύνη, which is 'anguish of the
       spirit;' referring this to the inward pain, and that to the
       outward passion.   The soul being there subjected by God's
       justice, to sensual pain, for subjecting itself willingly to
       brutish sensuality in this life, it being a more noble and
       celestial substance.

       Of which pain St. Chrysostom noteth, That because many
       of us can skill what torment the tongue hath in extremity of
       a burning ague, and what pain our hand feeleth when from
       the hearth some spark lighteth on it; Christ chose to
       express them in these two.   Not but that they be incom-
       parably greater than these, yea far above all we can speak
       or think; but that flesh and blood conceiveth but what it
       feeleth, and must be spoken to as it may understand.   And
       it is a ground, that in terms here and elsewhere proportioned
       to our conceit, torments are uttered far beyond all conceit ;
       which, labouring to avoid, we may, but labouring to express,
       we shall never do it.

  1.   Yet to help them somewhat, we shall the more deeply
       apprehend them if we do but compare them ; as we may,
       and never go out of the confines of our own verse.

       With *recepisti*, first.   To consider this ; that his torment
       is in the present tense, now upon him, *cruciaris*: His good,
       all past and gone, *recepisti*.   Mark, saith St. Augustine, of
       his pleasure, *omnia dicit de præterito ; dives erat, vestiebatur,
       epulabatur, recepisti ;* 'He was rich, did go, did fare, had
       received ; was, did, and had; all past, and vanished away ;'

[1 One
part of a
pair of
deeds,
used for
'counter-
part.']

       all, like the [1]counterpane of a lease, expired, and our Abra-
       ham likeneth it to wages, received and spent beforehand.

       Secondly, If we lay together his torments, and *bona tua in
       vitá.*   For we shall find, they are of a divers scantling.   The
  2.   one had an end with his life; and *ó quam subito !* The other,
       when it beginneth once, shall never have an end.   That life
       is not like this.   No: if the lives of all—I say not, men,
       women, and children, but of all—and every of the creatures
       that ever lived upon the earth or shall live to the world's end,
       were all added one to another, and all spun into one life, this
       one exceedeth them all.   This then, I make no question, will

make another degree to think, *quod delectabat fuit momenta-* [Vid. S.
neum, quod cruciat est æternum. Bernard.
Sentent.

Thirdly, If we match it with *Lazarus autem,* that is, with "Viæ quæ
ducunt ad
the sight of others in that estate whence he is excluded; and, mortem,
&c.]
in them, with sorrow to consider what himself might have had 3.
and hath lost for ever. "There shall be," saith Christ of this Lu. 13. 28.
point, "weeping, and gnashing of teeth, to see Abraham,
Isaac, and Jacob, and all the Prophets, in the Kingdom of
God, and yourselves thrust out of doors." Not only "weeping" for grief that themselves have lost it, but "gnashing of
teeth" also for very indignation, that others have obtained it.
And of others not some other, but that *Lazarus iste,* one of
these poor people whom we shun in the way, and drive our
coaches apace to escape from; that of them, it may fall, we
may see some in bliss, "when they shall lie in hell like sheep," Ps. 49. 14.
saith the Psalmist, that walked on earth like lions. Will not
this bear a third?

But beyond all these, if we counterpoise it with the word 4.
παρακαλεῖται, "is comforted," with which Abraham hath set
it in opposition—"torment" opposed to "comfort;" that is,
torment comfortless, wherein no manner hope of any kind of
comfort. Neither of the comfort of mitigation; for, in the
verse next before, all hope, of κατάψυξις, 'relief,' is denied,
even to "a drop of water;" neither of the comfort of delivery Lu. 16. 24.
at last; for, in the verse next following, he is willed to know,
that by reason of the "great partition," their case is such, *ut* Lu. 16. 26.
non possint, that they cannot presently, or for ever, look for
any passage from thence, but must there tarry in torments
everlastingly. So neither comfort of relief, nor of delivery; nor
the poor comfort, which in all miseries here doth not leave us,

—— dabit Deus his quoque finem; [Virg. Æn.

An end will come: nay, no end will never come. Which 1. 199.]
never is never deeply enough imprinted nor seriously enough
considered. That this *now* shall be still *now,* and never have
an end; and this *cruciaris* be *cruciaris* for ever, and never
declined into a preter tense, as *recepisti* was. This is an
exaltation of this cross, above all else; none shall ever come
down from it, none shall ever beg our body to lay it in our
sepulchre.

Fifthly, if we lay it to *recordare.* For, may I not add to 5.

all these, that being in this case he heareth *recordare*, and is willed to " remember," when his remembering will do him no good; but though he remember it in sorrow and in the bitterness of his soul, yea though his sorrow be above measure sorrowful, it will profit him nothing? I say, grief both utterly comfortless, and altogether unprofitable.

These five make him that feels it here wish, that none of those he wisheth well may ever come there to know how hot that " fire," or how terrible that " torment" is.

These five words are all within the compass of the verse itself, and may serve every one as a nail to fasten our memory to this cross; that we may ever remember it and never forget it, and never forgetting it, never feel it.

This then is his cross. We long, I know, to have it taken down; our ears are dainty, and the matter melancholic, and we little love to hear it stood on so long. But Chrysostom [Conf. S. Chry- sost. de Lazar. con. 2.] saith well, of that fire: *Nunquid, si tacuimus, extinximus?* ' If we speak not of it, will it go out?' No, no: *sive loquamur, sive taceamus, ardet ille;* ' speak we, or keep we silence, it burneth still, still it burneth.' Therefore let us speak and think of it, and let it stand in the name of God; *et exercea- mus auditum*, saith the good Father, *ne ita mollescat*, ' and keep our ears in exercise, that they grow not nice.' If to hear of it be painful, to feel it will be more. The invention is to keep the exaltation, to take it up. For none so near it as they, *qui non tollunt, donec super-imponitur*, ' that take it not up till it be laid upon them.'

3.
The join- ing, or tenon. Jam vero. [¹ Deut. 32. 22.] Thus we have severally seen the counterpoints of this cross; the top, which is *in vitâ*, ' in this life;' and the foot, which reacheth *ad novissima inferni*, " to the bottom of hell ¹." It remaineth we tenon both these together, as antecedent and consequent: " Thou didst receive;" " Now therefore." 1. First, that they may be; 2. and then, how they may be joined.

1.   First then we find, that *recepisti* is as it ends; and that, by this example, it may end in *cruciaris*, and prove the one end of a heavy cross. Which first bringeth us out of admiration of the riches of this life. When we see that these " good things" which after the tax of the world are counted, and in a manner styled, the only good things, and in the deceitful

balance of this world weigh down "Abraham's bosom," be [S. Chry-
not ever demonstrative signs of God's special liking; nor Lazar.
they, *ipso facto*, highest in His favour that receive them in con. 3.]
greatest measure; nor peradventure, as Christ saith, so Lu. 16. 15.
highly accounted of in Heaven as they be on earth. Therefore, they that have them, not to reflect too much on them;
nor be *ideo inflati*, as saith St. Augustine, *quia obsericati*,
' as much pride in their soul as purple on their body.' And
they that have them not, not to *æmulari*, ' vex and grieve
themselves' at Nabal's wealth, Haman's preferment, this
man's table; seeing there cometh a *jam vero*, and when
that cometh, we shall see such an alteration in his state,
as he that wisheth him worst shall wish, that for every
" good thing" he received here he had received a thousand;
and, with St. Bernard, *ut omnes lapides converterentur in
rosas*, ' that every stone under his feet here had been turned
into a rose.' Such is his case now, and such theirs that
come where he is.

Is this all? No. But, as it bringeth us out of admiration, 2.
so it bringeth us into fear. For two things it offereth, either
of which is, or may be, matter of fear. 1. First, in that
he is Abraham's son. That Abraham hath of his seed in
hell, and that all his sons shall not rest in their father's
bosom. Which offereth us occasion to fear, for all our profession. For though he were a son too, and so acknowledged
by Abraham, yet there he is now.

2. In that he is of Abraham's rich sons, and one that
" received good things" in his life. Which ministereth new
matter of fear; that, as the Prophet saith, "Tophet is pre- Isa. 30. 33.
pared of old, and that even for great ones," for such as go in
purple, and wear fine linen, and fare full daintily;—even for
such is it prepared. Not as every prison for common persons, but as *tophet*, or the tower, for great estates. So that
it may seem either of both these have their danger at their
heels; for that they to him were, to many they are, and to
us they may be as antecedents to an evil consequent.

Men verily may flatter themselves; but sure I can never
think but there is more in this " Now therefore," than the
world will allow. And that this *recordare* of Abraham's is
not a matter so slightly to be slipped over. There is some

S E R M.
V.
Amos 6. 1.

Rom. 13.
13.
[S. August.
Confess.
lib. 8. 29.]
[Vid. S.
Hierou.
Epist. 22.
ad Eustoc
30.]
danger no doubt, and that more than will willingly be acknowledged, to such as are "wealthy and well at ease in Sion." St. Gregory confesseth by himself, that never any sentence entered so deep into his soul as this. And that, as *surgite mortui* was ever in St. Hierom's ear, and *non in comessationibus,* "not in surfeiting," in St. Augustine's, by which he was first converted; so this was with him, and he could not get it out of his mind. For he, sitting in the See of Rome, when it was grown rich and of great receipt, was as he saith still in doubt of *recepisti;* whether his exalting into that Chair might not be his recompense at God's hands, and all that ever he should receive from Him for all his service. And ever he doubted this *recepisti,* which we so easily pass over, and whether his case might not be like. Thus did the good Father, and, as I think, not unwisely; and would God, his example herein might make due impression, and work like fear, in so many as have in the eyes of all men "received the good things in this life!" For this may daily be seen every where, that divers that received them if ever any did, and that in a measure heaped up and running over, carry themselves so without remembrance or regard of this point, as if no such simile were in the Scripture as that of Mat. 19. 24. the needle's eye; no such example as of this rich man, no such *recordare* as this of Abraham which we have in hand.

It should seem, they have learned a point of divinity Abra2 Pet. 2. 15.ham never knew—Balaam's divinity I fear, "to love the wages of unrighteousness" and a gift in the bosom, and yet Nu. 23. 10. to cry *Moriatur anima mea,* his soul should go straight to Abraham's bosom for all that; and so, in effect, to deny Abraham's consequence.

We must then join issue upon the main point, we cannot avoid it; to enquire how this "Now therefore" cometh in; and how far and to whom this consequent holdeth. I demand then, Was he therefore "tormented," because he "received good things?" Is this the case of all them that wear purple and fare well in this life? Shall every one, to whom God reacheth such "good things" as these, be quit for ever "from Abraham's bosom? By no means. For *Cujus est sinus,* [S. August. in Ps. 51. c. 14. ad fin.] 'Whose is the bosom?' Is it not Abraham's? And what was Abraham? Look Gen. 13. 2. "Abraham was rich in cattle, in silver and gold." There is hope then for rich men, in a rich man's bosom. Then the bosom itself is a rich man's, though a Lazarus be in it. Yea though we find here Lazarus in it; yet elsewhere, we find, he is not all. For the great lord that bare rule under Queen Candace; the elect Acts 8. 27. lady; Joseph of Arimathea, and the Areopagite—grave and 2 Joh. 1. wise counsellors; the purple seller; and if the purple seller, [Mat. 27. 57.] why not the purple wearer? Yes, the purple wearers too Acts 17. 34. were in earth Saints as we read, and are we doubt not in Acts 16. 14. Abraham's bosom also. Dan. 5. 29.

It was not therefore because he was rich; for then must Abraham himself have been subject to the same sentence. Nay, one may so be rich, and so use his riches together, as they shall conclude in the other figure, and end in *solaris;* and no ways hinder, but help forward his account, and bring him a second *recipies* of the "good things" of that eternal life. And, if you mark it well, we have here in this Scripture two rich men; 1. One that giveth the *recordare;* 2. The other, to whom it is given. The example of a rich man, which rich men to avoid; the sentence of a rich man, which rich men to remember.

It is evident it was not for that he had "received good 1. things in this life," seeing as truly as Abraham said to him, "Son, remember, thou didst receive good things," so truly might he have rejoined, 'Father, remember, thou didst receive, &c.' It was not that.

Neither was it because he came by them unduly, by such 2. ways and means as the soul of God abhorreth; for it is, saith Bernard, *recordare quia recepisti*—not, *quia rapuisti*, or *quia* [S. Bernard. *decepisti*, ' by ravine or deceit.' Epist. 2. Ed. Ben.] 3.

Neither was it because he received them and wrapped them up. For as his receipts are in this verse, so his expences in the nineteenth. So much in purple and linen, so much in feasting.

Neither was it, because receiving plenty, he took his por- 4. tion of that he received in apparel or diet. For *Num solis stultis apes mellificant?* saith the philosopher; 'Do bees make honey, or worms spin silk, for the wicked or reprobate only?' Howbeit it cannot be excused, that being but *homo quidam,* he went like a prince; for purple was princes' wear.

Or that he feasted, and that not meanly, but λαμπρῶς, "in all sumptuous manner;" and that not at some set times, but καθ᾽ ἡμέραν, "day by day;" for this portion was beyond all proportion.

None of these it was. Yet we hold still some danger there is; there is some, and this *recordare* is not idle or needless.

[Vid. S. Bernard. Declam. 38. 47.] What was it then that brought him thither, or, as St. Bernard calleth it, what was his *scala inferni*, 'the ladder by which he went down to hell?' that we may know, what is the difference between Abraham's receipt and his; and when *recepisti* shall conclude with *cruciaris*.

[S. Chrysost. de Lazar. conc. 3.] St. Chrysostom doth lay the weight on the word *recepisti*, in his natural or proper sense. For it is one thing saith he, λάβειν, that is, *accipere*, 'to receive or take;' another, ἀπολάβειν, that is, *recipere*, to 'receive it as it were in full discharge and final satisfaction.' And the same distinction doth Mat. 6. 16. Christ Himself observe in ἔχειν and ἀπέχειν, in the sixth chapter of St. Matthew. Both have, and both receive; but they that do λάβειν, 'receive them' as a pledge of God's [Vid. S. Gregor. lib. 5. in cap. 4. Beati Job.] farther favour; but they that do ἀπολάβειν, "receive them as a full and complete reward," and have no more to receive, but must thereupon release and quit claim all demands in whatsoever else. *Tanquam arrham*, and *tanquam mercedem*, is the distinction in schools.

1. With God verily it is a righteous thing to let every man receive for any kind of good he hath done here. Yea, even the heathen for their moral virtues, as St. Augustine holdeth of the Romans, and the victories they received.

2. But righteous it is also, that the Reubenites, which choose their lot in Gilead on this side of Jordan, and there seat themselves, should not after claim their part too in the Land of Promise. Even so, that they that will have, and have their receiving time here, should not have it here and elsewhere also.

3. Then all is in the choice where we will lay our *recepisti*; whether here or there, in this or that life; in purple and silk, and the delights of the world, or in the rest and comfort of Abraham's bosom. Whether we will say; Lord, if I may so receive, that I may be received; if I may receive so the good

of this life, that I be not barred the other to come, *tanquam arrham,* ' as the earnest of a better inheritance,' *Ecce me.* But if my receiving here shall be my last receipt, if I shall receive them *tanquam mercedem,* ' as my portion for ever,' I renounce them; put me out of this receipt, and reserve my part in store for the Land of the living. And of evil: If it must come here or there, with St. Augustine, *Domine, hic ure, hic seca, ibi parce;* ' Let my searing and smart be here; there let me be spared;' and from *cruciaris,* 'torment' to come, *libera me, Domine.*

To very good purpose said the ancient Father; *Quisque dives, quisque pauper; Nemo dives, nemo pauper; Animus omnia facit.* ' It is somewhat to be rich or poor, it is nothing to be rich or poor; it is as the mind is; the mind maketh all.' Now, saith St. Chrysostom, what mind he carried is gathered out of Abraham's doubling and trebling. *Tu, tua,* and *tuá: recepisti tu, bona tua, in vitá tuá;* which words are working words, as he taketh them, and contain in them great emphasis. Understanding by *tua,* not so much that he had in possession as that he made special reckoning of, for that is most properly termed ours; *Animus omnia facit.*

This life is called ' his life;' not because he lived in it, but because he so lived in it as if there had been no other life but it. And in his account there was no other; Δὸς μοὶ τὸ σήμερον, λάβε σοὶ τὸ αὔριον, ' give him this life, let this day be his day, take to-morrow who will.' This did not Abraham; for he " saw a day," and that after this life, that re- joiced him more than all the days of his life. Joh. 8. 56.

This life as it was his life, so the good of it his good— *bona tua.* This his life, these the portion of his life; these he chose for his good; they his, and he theirs. They that make such a choice, their *recepisti* may well end in *cruciaris.*

This way St. Chrysostom, by the mind. St. Augustine taketh another by the memory, more proper to the Patriarch's meaning; and that four ways.

1. For, saith he, Abraham willing him to remember he had received such things, implieth, in effect, that he had clean forgotten that any such things he had ever received. Look how Esau speaketh, *Habeo bona plurima,* "I have Gen. 33. 9.

S E R M.
V.
———
Lu. 12. 19.
enough, my brother;" and, as his pew-fellow here, *Anima habes*, "Soul, thou hast goods enough;" even so for all the world it seemeth this party here he had them, sure he was he had them; but that he "received" them he never remembered. Now he is put in mind, *quia recepisti;* "Now, therefore, thou art tormented."

2. Now, not remembering he had received them, no marvel if he forgat why he received them, or with what condition; forgetting God in Heaven, no marvel if he remembered not Lazarus on earth. Verily, neither he nor any man receive [S. Chrysost. de Lazar. con. 2.] them as proprietaries, but as stewards and as accountants, as Christ telleth us above in this chapter. Not for ourselves only, or for our own use, but for others too; and among others, for Lazarus by name. If Lazarus receive not, it was his fault and not God's, Who gave him enough to supply his own uses and Lazarus' want too. For both which two, he and all receive that receive at God's hands. But he, it seemeth, received them to, and for himself, alone, and nobody else; that Abraham saith truly, *Recepisti tu—tu et nemo alius;* 'You and yours and nobody besides.' For his *recepisti* ended in himself, and he made himself *summam omnium receptorum*. For if you call him to account by the writ of *redde rationem*, this must be his audit: In purple and linen so much, and in belly-cheer so much; so much on his back, and so much on his board, and in them endeth the total of his receipt; except you will put in his hounds too, which received of him more than Lazarus might. This is indeed *recepisti tu solus*. This did not Abraham, for his receipt reacheth to strangers, and others besides himself; and Lazarus he received in his bosom on earth, or else he had never been in Heaven to have him there.

Will you see, "Now therefore," the consequent in kind? Therefore is this party now in the gulf, because living himself was a gulf; it is now *gurges in gurgite*, 'but one gulf in another.' While he lived, he was as a gulf swallowing all: "Now therefore," the gulf hath swallowed him. Remember this, for it is a special point. For if our purple and fine linen swallow up our alms; if our too much lashing on, to do good to ourselves, make us in state to do good to none but ourselves; if our riotous wasting on expenses of vanity,

be a gulf and devour our Christian employing in works of
charity; there is danger in *recepisti*, even the danger of
"Now therefore;" *gurges eras et in gurgitem projicieris,*
a gulf thou wert, and into the gulf shalt thou go.' Ever,
for the most part, you shall find these two coupled. In
Sodom "pride, and fulness of bread," with not stretching Ezek. 16.
the hand to the poor. In Judah great bowls of wine, and 49.
rich "beds of ivory," with little compassion on the misery of Amos 6. 4.
Joseph. And here going richly, and faring daintily, with
Lazarus' bosom and belly both empty. The saying of St.
Basil is highly commended, that ἀκόνη τῆς ἀσωτίας ἡ φιλο-
τιμία, 'Pride is prodigality's whetstone.' And so it is sure;
and sets such an edge upon it in our expenses, that it cuts so
deep into our receipt, and shares so much for purple and
linen, as it leaves but a little for Lazarus' portion. Sure so
it is: less purple must content us, and somewhat must be
cut off from *quotidie splendide*, if we will have Lazarus better
provided for.

This I have stood a little on, that it may be remembered.
It is Christ's special drift, both in the parable before and in
this story here; and "remember" it we must, if either as
in that we will be received into "everlasting tabernacles,"
or as in this we will be delivered from "everlasting torments."

3. Now I add that, in thus forgetting Lazarus to remember himself, he remembered not himself neither, but failed in
that too. For whereas he consisted of two parts, 1. a body,
and 2. a soul, he remembered the one so much as he quite
left the other out of his *memento*. For his *recepisti tu* was
his body, and nothing else. Now reason would, the body
should not take up the whole receipt, but that the poor soul
should be thought upon too. Purple and silk, and *Ede, bibe,*
they are but the body's part; but alms and works of mercy,
they, they, be the soul's. May not our souls be admitted
suitors, that we would remember them, that is, remember
Lazarus? for that is the soul's portion; for the other part,
he and we all remember fast enough.

4. Thus remembering neither God nor Lazarus, nay, nor
his own soul; his memory thus failing him, God provided
and sent some to put him in mind. Sure, as he had received

SERM.
V. those former "good things," so also had he received "Moses
and the Prophets" by his own confession; and in receiving
them, he had received a great benefit, and peradventure
greater in this than the other; and Moses had told him as
Deu. 32. 29. much as Abraham tells him now. *Utinam novissima pro-
viderent,* "Would God," saith Moses, "men would remember
the four *novissima ;*" 1. That there is a death; 2. there is
a judgment; 3. there is a Heaven; 4. there is a hell. But
Deu. 32. 22. of all the four, *Novissima inferni,* in the same chapter, "the
nethermost;" *Nunc igitur cruciaris,* 'the place of torments.'
Jer. 5. 31. The Prophets said as much. Jeremy—Ever think that an
end there will be, *Et quid fiet in novissimo,* "what shall
Isa. 33. 14. become of us in that end?" "Who among us," saith Esay,
"can endure devouring fire?" who can dwell with *ardores
sempiterni,* "everlasting burnings?" These he had, and if
he had heard these, it is plainly affirmed, *Audiant ipsos*
would have done it; they would have kept him from ever
coming in that place. But these also, living, he strove to
forget, and as ingenderers of melancholy to remove them far
away. And that he might the more easily do it, it was
thought not amiss to call their authority in question, whether
they were worth the hearing or no. It is in effect confessed
by him, that his "five brethren" and he were of opinion,
that the hearing of Moses and the Prophets was a motive
far unworthy to carry such men as they. An Angel from
Heaven, or "one from the dead," might perhaps; but the
books of Moses should never move them. It was not for
nothing he complaineth of his "tongue:" *illâ linguâ,* 'with
that tongue' he had scorned the holy oracles; peradventure that place wherein he now lay, with that tongue which
in that place feeleth the greatest torment, and from that
place the smallest comfort; both which it had before pro-
fanely derided.

Thus then you see his *scalam inferni,* the brief of his faults,
for which his receipt endeth in this bitter receipt of torments
[S. Chry-
sost. de
Lazar.
conc. 2. 3.]
Mat. 6. 2. without end. 1. Epicurism: no life but this, no good but
these here, good attire, good cheer. 2. This was his reward;
Amen, dico vobis, recepistis. St. Chrysostom's two. 1. Remembering neither God in Heaven, nor Lazarus on earth;
2. but being a *gurges,* a gulf of all that he received, himself.

3. No, not his own soul; 4. nor last of all, this place of torments before he was in it, and scorning at Moses for remembering him of it. This you see; and in him you see who they be over whom Abraham shall read the like sentence: *Qui habet aures, &c.*

Now then we have set up both sides of this cross, and fastened each part to other with "Now therefore;" let us affix the inscription and so an end. That is *recordare fili,* the want of which brought him thither, the supply of it shall keep us thence.

II.
The title:
Recordare
fili.

Fili recordare—optime dictum sed sero, 'excellently well said, but too late,' saith St. Bernard. For, alas! cometh Abraham in now with *recordare?* doth he now affix the title? why, it is too late. True it is so, but till now he would not suffer any to set it up. Before, while it was time, and when it might have done him good, then he would not endure it; now he is fain, when it is out of time, to know what in time might have done him good; and may do others, if in time they look to it. Indeed, to him now it is of no use in the world, but only to let him see by what justice he is where he is, and what he suffereth he suffereth deservedly. The best is, Abraham hath more sons than this son, and they may take good by it, and have use of that whereof he had none. With this son it is too late, with some other it is not. Not with us; we are yet upon the stage, our *jam vero* is not yet come. And for us is this inscription set up, and for our sakes both Christ reported, and St. Luke recorded this *recordare.*

If you ask What good is that? What is the good of exemplary justice? What good is it to see a malefactor punished, or to read in a paper the crime wherefore? What, but only that by reading what brought him thither, we may remember what will keep us from thence. The neglect of *recordare* is the cause he is there; why then *recordare fili,* and keep thee from thence. So with one view of this inscription, we read both his ruin and our own remedy.

This is the right use of this title; God forbid we should have no use of it, till we come where he is! But it is therefore set over his head in that life, that we may read it in this; read it and remember it; remember it, and never have title set over ours.

[S. Greg.
in Evang.
lib. 2.
Hom. 40.
6. init.]

It will be good then sometimes to keep some day holy to the exaltation of this cross, and to set this title before our eyes; to approach it and read it over; yea not once, but often to record this *recordare*. Indeed, it is that St. Gregory saith; *Recordatione magis eget versus iste quam expositione;* 'indeed it more needs a disposition to remember it, than an exposition to understand it.'

We are yet; how long we shall we know not, nor how soon *vitâ tuâ* will be gone, nor how quickly this *jam vero* will come in place. This we know; between his state and ours there is only a puff of breath in our nostrils. That this life, short though it be, and in a manner a moment, yet *hoc est momentum unde pendet æternitas;* 'on it no less matter dependeth than our eternity;' or bliss or bane, comfort or torment. That in that place, without all hope either of relief, escape, or end; and that from thence, neither our profession of truth, nor the greatness of our receiving shall deliver, but only this *recordare*. It standeth us then in hand to take perfect impression of this *recordare;* and as St. Augustine saith, *oblivisci quid simus, attendere quid futuri simus,* 'to forget what we now be, to consider what we shall be' without all question ere long, but we know not how soon; but oft it falleth, the shorter and sooner the less we think of it.

1. Three things then I wish for conclusion; 1. that we may remember; 2. remember in time; 3. remember effectually. That we may remember the fire, the thirst and the torments; and know what they mean by memory rather than by sense. Abraham from Heaven calls to us to that end; the party in hell crieth, *ne veniant et ipsi.*

2. That we do it in time, that we be not in his case, never "lift up our eyes" till we "be in hell," nor remember that may do us good till it be too late.

3. That we do it effectually from the heart; for there is a heart in *recordare*, and that this being our greatest business, we make it not our least care.

Our remembering will be effectual, if we pray to God daily we may so receive as we may be received. And our remembering shall be effectual, if it have the effect, that is, make us remember Lazarus. *Quotidie Lazarus,* you may find Lazarus if you seek him, every day; nay you shall find him, though you seek him not. Our present estate, by present occasion of the dearth now upon us, makes the memory more fresh than at other times it would be. Remember then, our being remembered there lieth on this their remembrance here, and upon their receiving our *recipies* or rather *recipieris.* And remember that day, wherein what we have received shall be forgotten, and what He hath received of us shall be remembered, and nothing else shall be remembered, but *quod uni ex minimis.* The attaining "everlasting Taber- Mat. 10. 42. nacles," the "avoiding everlasting torments," lie upon it. That which we remember now in Lazarus' bosom, shall be remembered to us again in Abraham's bosom. To which, &c.

A SERMON

PREACHED IN

THE COURT AT GREENWICH,

ON SUNDAY, BEING THE FOURTH OF APRIL, A.D. MDXCVI.

---

2 CORINTHIANS xii. 15.

*And I will most gladly bestow, and will be bestowed for your
souls, though the more I love you, the less I am loved.*

*Ego autem libentissime impendam, et superimpendar ipse pro ani-
mabus vestris, licet plus vos diligens, minus diligar.*

[*And I will very gladly spend and be spent for you; though the more
abundantly I love you, the less I be loved.* Engl. Trans.]

SERM.
VI.

THE words be St. Paul's, and to the Corinthians. And if
we neither knew whose they were, nor to whom, yet this we
might know by the words themselves, that it is love that
speaks, and unkindness that is spoken to. *Impendam—
superimpendar—libentissime.* This must needs be love; and
that, unkindness, that requiteth such love with such an
etsi; etsi minus diligar, "though, the more I love the less
I be loved."

1.
1 Cor. 15.
10.

Acts 18. 11.

2 Cor. 12.
14.

Many ways it may be manifest, that St. Paul loved the
Church of Corinth, more than many other loved them, for
he laboured more for them. By the time he spent with
them, a year and a half full—scarce with any so much. By
his visiting them three several times—not any so oft. By
two of his largest Epistles sent to them—not to any the like.
And in the one of them we see here, how frank and how
kind a profession he maketh, *in quâ omne verbum charitatis
igne vaporatur,* 'wherein every word carrieth a sweet scent
of love's perfume'—it is St. Gregory. These, each of these:
but all these together may prove his *magis diligam,* the
abundance of his love to Corinth.

Now there should be in love the virtue of the load-stone, 2. the virtue attractive, to draw like love to it again. There should be, but was not. For their little love appeared by their many unloving exceptions which they took to him. To his office: that he was but an Apostle of the second head, and no ways to be matched with the chief Apostles. To his 2 Cor. 12. person: that he was one of no presence. Somewhat good ^{11.} at an Epistle, but his person or presence nothing worth. To 2 Cor. 10. his preaching: that he was but ἰδιώτης τῷ λόγῳ, "not so 10. eloquent by much," as divers of them were; nor his sermons 2 Cor. 11. 6. *ex opere Corinthiaco*, 'of the Corinthian fashion.' Indeed, I know not how, but he could not hit on their vein.

This cold infusion of so faint regard on their parts might 3. have quenched his love. It did Apollos', for Apollos was once at Corinth, but found them so diverse to please, as he waxed weary and got him away; and when he was moved to return to them, πάντως οὐκ ἦν θέλημα, "his mind was 1 Cor. 16. not at all" to come there again as yet, saith St. Paul. It ^{12.} made Apollos give over. So might it St. Paul too. But him it did not. *Charitas quâ ædificabat*, 'the love wherewith he built' was like lime, slacked not but rather kindled with water. For notwithstanding all these, such was his zeal, and he *tantus zelator animarum*, that we see his affection, and we hear his resolution what it is. Unkind they might be, but no unkindness of theirs, or verdict never so hard, or censure never so sharp; no *minus diligar* should move him, or make him love their souls a whit the less.

Wherein, lest they might be jealous he sought to Corinth 4. so oft for the ore of it, because the soil was rich, there was good to be done, as men are ever that way quick-eyed; he appealed to all his former course with them, that he had sought nothing hitherto. Nothing he had sought, nor 2 Cor. 11. nothing he would seek. And to come to this our verse, not ^{8, 9.} only seek nothing, 1. but he would bestow; 2. bestow, and be bestowed himself; 3. and that, most willingly—indeed it is higher, ἥδιστα, "most gladly;" 4. and all this, to use Chry- [S. Chry-sostom's words, not ὑπὲρ τῶν οὐδὲ φιλούντων, 'for those that ^{sost. in loc.]} had not begun to love him first,' but ὑπὲρ τῶν οὐδ᾽ ἀντιφι-λούντων, 'for those that being loved first did not love him again.' 5. And that, not κατ᾽ ἴσα, 'in equal measure'—that

H 2

is not his complaint, but such as "the more" (it is fuller in the Greek, περρισσοτέρως, " the more abundantly") "they were loved, loved him the less for it." The degrees are many; and look how many degrees, so many several points of elevation.

5. All which when I consider, I cannot choose but marvel at his love, which truly is right admirable; and more at their *minus,* than his *magis.* But at his heroical spirit most of all, whom such and so great unkindness could not overcome. The rather, when I lay it to, and compare it with ours in these times; in which, a kind of love we have, such as it is, but such as will not endure St. Paul's assay ; or if in some degrees it do, if it be not respected straight—not as it deserveth, for so haply it is, but as it supposeth itself to deserve, if it be crossed with any unkindness, it groweth abrupt. Every *minus diligar* makes it abate; and far we are from this Christian magnanimity, to resolve with him in the eleventh chapter, *Quod facio, hoc et faciam,* "what I do, that I will do still." Or here, love I will still, "though the more I love the less I be loved."

2 Cor. 11.
12.

The thing loved, is the Corinthians' souls. And as Corinth itself was situate in a narrow land between two seas, so are they in the verse; having on the one side, the sea of self-love, in the former part ; and on the other, the gulf of unkindness, in the latter. Through either of which St. Paul maketh a first and second navigation, if haply he may so *adire Corinthum,* gain their souls to Christ, more precious to him than Corinth itself and all the wealth in it.

The division. I.
In the love two things are offered. For, in the former moiety of the verse, he is encountered with self-love, 1. which bestoweth nothing, 2. but least of all his life; 3. or if it do, it is not most gladly ; nay, not gladly at all. These three he beateth down : the first, with *impendam ;* the second, with *impendar ;* the third, with *libentissime.* Thus having vanquished the love of himself in the former, in the latter moiety uukindness riseth up. Unkindness in them for whom he had done all the former. Over which second enemy having a second conquest also, and triumphing over it with his *etsi,* he sheweth his love to be a love of proof, to have all the perfections and signatures of love; all which are within compass

of this verse. *Amor,* as in schools we reckon them, 1. *Impensivus;* 2. *Expensivus,* 3. *Intensivus,* and 4. *Extensivus.* The two former in the two verbs: 1. active, *impendam;* and 2. passive, *impendar;* "bestowing," or spending; "bestowed," or spent itself. The two latter in the adverb and the conjunction; 3. *Intensive,* straining itself to the highest degree, "most gladly;" and 4. *Extensive,* stretching itself to those that are farthest from love, and least deserve it; *Etsi minus diligar.* 1. "To spend;" 2. "To spend and be spent;" 3. "To spend and be spent most willingly." If the full point were there, it were enough. 4. But not only *libentissime,* but *libentissime etsi;* "most gladly," yea, "though the more he, the less they;"—that is all in all.

But then, lest we mistake our term of love, as easily we II. may, and confound it with lust, we must look to our *pro* in the second part. It is *pro animabus,* "soul-love," he meaneth all the while. "Love," the fruit of the Spirit; not lust, the Gal. 5. 22. weed of the flesh. Not of this flesh, sister to worms, and Job 17. 14. daughter to rottenness; but of the spirit allied to the Angels, and "partaker in hope of the Divine nature" itself. And 2 Pet. 1. 4. not of one only, but *animabus,* "of souls"—more than love of one soul; many souls, many thousands of souls, of a whole state or country. Them to love, and to them thus to prove our love, is it which St. Paul would teach, and it which we need to learn. These be the two parts. Whereof, &c.

To enter the treaty of the first part. We begin at the   I. four points: 1. *Impendam,* 2. *Impendar,* 3. *Libentissime,* and The love. 4. *Etsi.* If love be "an ensign," as Cant. 6, the colours. If Cant. 6. 4. it be "a band," as Hosea 11, the twists. If a scale, as Chry- Hos. 11. 4. sostom, the ascents. If an art, as Bernard, the rules of it. [S. Bernard. de Indeed, they talk much of an art of love, and books of verses Nat. et have been written of it; but above all verses, is *carmen hoc* Dignit. *amoris.* This verse hath more art than they all; and of this Divin. it may be said, *Me legat, et lecto carmine doctus erit;* 'learn [Ovid. Art. it and say you learned love.' To take them as they lie, and Amat. lib.1. with the first, first. *Ego vero impendam.* init.]

1. There was a world when one said, *Da mihi cor tuum et*   1. *sufficit;* 'bestow your heart on me, and I require no farther *Amor impensivus.* bestowing;' and the bestowing of love, though nothing but *Impendam.* love, was something worth.

SERM.
VI.

2. Such a world there was, but that world is worn out. All goeth now by *impendam.* Love and all is put out to interest. The other empty-handed love is long since banished the court, the city, and the country. For long since it is 1 Sam.22.7. that King Saul saw it, and said it to his courtiers that he was not regarded, but because he gave them fields, and vineyards, and offices over hundreds and thousands. Nor Acts 19. 24. yet Diana in the city of Ephesus, magnified there by the craftsmen, but because by her silver shrines they had there advantage. Nay nor Christ Himself neither in the country, Joh. 6. 26. but because they " ate of the loaves and were filled." For many miracles had they seen much greater than that, yet never professed they so much, *sicut tunc exaturati,* as when He bestowed a good meal on them.

3. Such is now the world's love, but specially at Corinth, where they do *cauponari amorem* indeed; set love to hire, and love to sale, and at so high a rate, as some were forced to give over, lest paying for love they might buy repentance too, and both too dear.

4. There is no remedy then; St. Paul must apply himself to time and place, wherein as all things else, so love depends upon *impendam,* yielding and paying.

5. Now, there is nothing so pliant as love, ever ready to transform itself to whatever may have likelihood to prevail; and if it be liberality, into that too. For, that love is liberal, nay prodigal, the Greek proverb noteth it that saith, The purse-strings of love are made of a leak blade; easily in sunder, and wide open with no great ado.

6. St. Paul therefore cometh to it; and as he maketh his 2 Cor. 12. case a father's case towards them in the verse next before, 14. so he saith with the kind father, *Ecce omnia mea tua sunt.* Lu. 15. 31. Father's love and all must be proved by bestowing.

7. Yea, " I will bestow." Now alas, what can Paul bestow? Especially upon so wealthy citizens? What hath 2 Tim. 4.13. he to part with, but his "books and his parchments?" Ware, at Athens perhaps somewhat; but at Corinth, little used and less regarded. Indeed, if silver and gold be all, and nothing else worth the bestowing, nothing will come under *impendam* but it; his bestowing is stalled. But, by the grace of God there is something else. There be talents—

so the world will call them when they list, howsoever they
esteem them scarce worth pence a piece. And there be
"treasures of wisdom and knowledge," in *Christo Jesu,* Col. 2. 3.
saith St. Paul. Indeed, so had St. Paul need to say; he
had best magnify his own *impendam,* for he hath nothing
else to make of. Nay, it shall not stand upon his valuation.
They that had both, both the wealth of Corinth and the
wisdom of Paul, and both in abundance, as being both of
them Prophets; the one of them, King David, preferreth
this *impendam* of Paul's before "gold, fine gold, much fine Ps. 19. 10.
gold;" and that we may know how much that *much* is,
"before thousands of gold and silver." This was no poor Ps. 119. 72.
Apostle. The other, King Solomon, saith directly; "There
is gold, and a multitude of rich stones; but the lips of know- Pro. 20. 15.
ledge—that is the precious jewel." And not policy, but
scientia sacrorum, prudentia; "the knowledge of holy things Pro. 9. 10.
is the wisdom" he meaneth. And it was no flourish, he was
in earnest. For it is well known he himself chose them 1 Kings
before the other when he was put to his choice, and that his 3. 9-12.
liking in that choice was highly approved by God's own
liking. The truth is, men have no sense of their souls till
they be ready to part with them; and then is St. Paul's
impendam called for, and never seriously before, when their
case is such that they can little feel what the bestowing
is worth.

And because they would not seek to feel it before, it is
God's just punishment they feel it not then. But if men will
labour to have sense of that part in due time, they should find
and feel such an estate of mind as none know but such as
have felt; surely such as they would acknowledge to be worth
an *impendam.* Indeed, this it is St. Paul can bestow, and
this it is Corinth needs; and the more wealthy it is, the
more. The other, as he hath it not, so they need it not,
that is, *aurum et argentum; quod autem habet,* "but that he Acts 3. 6.
hath," he is ready to bestow. What would we have more.
Fecit quod potuit, saith our Saviour in Mary Magdalene's case; Mark 14. 8.
and *dedit quod habuit,* in the case of the poor widow's mites; Mark 12. 44.
and that is as much as God doth, or man can require. But Lu. 21. 4.
be it little, or be it much, he that giveth all leaveth nothing
ungiven, and therefore his *impendam* is at the highest.

S E R M.   But when it is at the highest, the passive *impendar* is
VI. higher than it.   Much more to "be bestowed," than "to
2.
Amor ex- bestow."   And therefore it hath a *super-impendar* bestowed
pensivus.
Impendar. on it.   1. For first, they that bestow give but of their fruits;
but he that is bestowed giveth fruit, tree, and all.   In that,
the bestower remained unbestowed; here, he himself is in
the deed of gift too.   2. Secondly, before there was but one
act of bestowing only; here in one are both bestowing and
being bestowed, and there being *both* must needs be better
than one.   3. Thirdly, before, that which was bestowed, what
Heb. 12. 4 was it?   Our good, not our blood; our living, not our life.
Nondum ad sanguinem, "not yet so far as to the shedding of
blood."   Then, there is somewhat behind.   But if to the
shedding of that, then is it love at the farthest; if it be as
Cant. 8. 6. Solomon saith, *fortis sicut mors;* "dare throw death his
Joh. 15. 13. gauntlet."   *Majorem hoc nemo,* saith Christ; "greater love
hath no man than this, to bestow his life."   4. And indeed,
we see many can be content to bestow frankly, but at no
hand to be bestowed themselves.   Yea, that they may not be
bestowed, care not what they bestow.   For self-love crieth to
Mat. 16. 22. us, Spare our living; but in any wise, *propitius esto tibi,*
Job 2. 4. to spare our life.   "Skin for skin" is nothing but *impen-*
dere ne impendamur; 'to spend all we have, to spare ourselves.'   But hither also will St. Paul come from δαπανᾷν
to ἐκδαπανᾶσθαι, without any reservation at all of himself;
to do or suffer, "to spend or to be spent."

How "to be spent;" will he die?   Yea indeed.   What,
presently here at Corinth?   No, for at this time, and long
after he was still alive; and yet he said truly *impendar* for all
that.   For, as before we said, so say we in this.   If there be
no way "to be bestowed" but by dying out of hand, they
that in the field receive the bullet, or they that at the stake
have the fire set to them, they and they only may be said "to
be bestowed."   That is a way indeed, but not the only way;
but other ways there be beside them too.   As that is said "to
be bestowed," not only that is defrayed at one entire pay-
ment, but that which by several sums is paid in; especially,
if it be when it was not due, nor could not be called for.
This I mean: The Patriarch Lot, or the Prophet Jeremy,
that dwelling where sin abounded, and seeing and hearing,

" vexed their righteous souls" with the daily transgressions of 2 Pet.2.7,8. the people, and for their unkindness too; and thereby prevented their term, and paid nature's debt ere their day came, bestowed themselves say I, though not at once. For, hearts' grief and heaviness do more than bestow, for they even consume and waste a man's life. And Timothy, that by giving 1 Tim.4 13. attendance to reading, meditation, and study, grew into an ἀπεψία, and " often infirmities," and thereby shortened his 1 Tim.5.23. time by much, bestowed himself say I, though not at one instant. He that knew it, bare witness, that that course of life is " a wearying," yea, and a wearing of it too ; and spends Eco. 12. 12. another manner substance than the sweat of the brows. This then, for the present, was St. Paul's *impendar.* By intentive meditation, for his books and parchments took somewhat from his sum ; by sorrow and grief of heart, for *Quis scanda-* 2 Cor. 11. *lizatur et ego non uror ?* and that he said and said truly, *Quotidie morior,* he bestowed himself by inch-meal; and 1 Cor. 15. might avow his *impendar* before God or man. And so far it is the case of all them that be in this case—*Sal terræ,* as Mat. 5. 13. Christ termeth them ; which salt, by giving season, melteth itself away, and ceaseth in short time to be that it was. *Lux* Mat. 5. 14. *mundi,* " the light of the world," *aliis ministrando, seipsos consumendo,* ʻlighting others, and wasting themselves;ʼ that is, abridging their natural course, and drawing on their untimely diseases and death, before their race be half run.

But, to make it a perfect *impendar* and to give it his *super,* after all this he came to that other too. For so he did; in that point, like the poor labouring ox to which in the ninth 1 Cor. 9. 9. chapter of the former Epistle he resembleth his state, spending his time in earing the ground for corn, in inning the corn, in treading out the corn; his neck yoked, and his mouth muzzled, and in the end, when all is done, offered on the altar too and made a sacrifice of. It was his case, and thither he came at last; and therefore in both cases, he might truly say *impendar,* and *super-impendar* both.

But to elevate it yet a point higher we say, that as either 8. of these are much, and both exceeding much ; yet above both *Amor intensivus;* these is that, which though we handle third, it standeth first, *libentissime.* the adverb *libentissime.* True it is, which in divinity we say : with God the adverb is above the verb, and the inward affection wherewith, above the outward action or passion of *impendam* or *impendar*, either. With men it is so too. When a displeasure is done us, say we not, we weigh not so much the injury itself, as the malicious mind of him that did offer it? And if in evil it hold, why not in good much more? Not so much *impendar*, the thing which; as *libentissime*, the good heart wherewith it is bestowed. And will you see the mind wherewith St. Paul will do both these? By this adverb ἥδιστα you may look into his very heart. Bestow he will, and be bestowed too; and that, not *utcunque*, 'in any sort,' be contented to come to it, but willingly;—willingly, nay readily; readily, nay gladly; and the degree is somewhat, ἥδιστα, "most gladly," in the very highest of all, in the superlative degree. To spend, and spending to make no more reckoning of it than of chaff; nay it is more, to be glad of our loss, more glad than others would be of their gain. To be spent, and in being spent not to hold our life precious: nor so, but to rejoice in it, and as if death were advantage; *in hoc est charitas*, certainly. Death of itself is bitter, and loss is not sweet. Then, so to alter their natures as to find sweetness in loss whereat all repine, and gladness in death which maketh all to mourn, verily herein is love. Or, if not here, where? Nay, here it is indeed, and before now we had it not. For in flat terms he avoweth, in the thirteenth chapter before of his former Epistle, if we sever this from the other two, one may part with all his goods to feed the poor, and yet have no love; one may give his body to be burnt, and yet have no love. And then, though he do *impendere*, "bestow" all he hath; and though he do *impendi*, "be bestowed" himself, *nihil est*, 'he is nothing' if he want this affection, which is love indeed, the very soul of love, and the other but σκελετὸς, but the skin and bones, and indeed nought else but the carcass, without it. Therefore it was that St. Paul set this in the first place before the other two, because the other two be but ciphers, and after this the figure set, they be tens and hundreds, and have their valuation; but without it, of themselves they be but ciphers, just nothing. Thus much St. Paul hath said, in saying these three words, 1. *Impendam*, 2. *Impendar*, 3. *Libentissime*. Thus much they amount to.

　　And now must we pause a little to see what will become

[1 Cor. 13.
3.]

of all this, and what these three will work in the Corinthians.

We marvel at the love; we shall more marvel when we see what manner of men on whom it is bestowed. What his proofs are we have heard, how large and how loving, and thus far is he come, only to win favour and like mutual love at their hands, without eye to any other thing in the world. No *vestra;* no—but *vos* only. This is all. And not this, not so much; nay not so little as this will come. Which, if it did come, what singular thing were it? since the "very publicans do the like," love him that loveth them. Which we gather by his *etsi.* Wherein, as he may, in no loud and bitter manner he complaineth, but complaineth though; that seeking their love, and nothing else, so hard was his hap, he found it not. Not, in a greater, or as great a measure, as his; but *minus* for *magis*, and so he a great loser by it. The more, the higher, the nearer, his; the less, the lower, the farther off, theirs; so that little likelihood of ever meeting. *2 Cor. 12. 14.* *Mat. 5. 46.*

This is St. Paul's case, to meet with unkindness; and not only his, but Christ met with nine for one too. Indeed, it is common, and not to be noted but for commonness. *De ingratis etiam ingrati queruntur,* 'they that are unkind themselves inveigh against the unkindness of others.' And, as it was said of them that made Cæsar away, *Oderunt tyrannum, non tyrannidem,* so may it truly here; the persons that are unkind they hate, rather than the vice itself. Yet, even to know this, doth no hurt, what St. Paul met with in the Corinthians, and this too, that all unkind persons dwell not at Corinth. And as he to be pitied, so they to be blamed. All other commodities return well from Corinth; only love is no traffic. St. Paul cannot make his own again, but must be a great loser withal. We cannot but pity the Apostle in this *minus* of his. St. Augustine saith well; *Nulla est major ad amorem provocatio, quam prævenire amando. Nimis enim durus est animus, qui amorem etsi nolebat impendere, nolit tamen rependere.* 'No more kindly attractive of love, than in loving to prevent; for exceeding stony is that heart, which, though it like not to love first, will not love again neither;' neither first, nor second. Yet so hard were theirs that *Lu. 17. 14, 15, &c.*

SERM. neither one way nor other, *recte* nor *reflecte,* would either
VI. begin or follow. No, not provoked by all those so many
forcible means, that St. Chrysostom maketh a wonder at it,
Quomodo non converterentur in amorem, 'that they were not
melted and resolved into love itself.'

4. Which cold success openeth a way to the last point, the

Amor ex-
tensivus. point indeed of highest admiration, and of hardest imitation
Etsi minus
diligar. of all the rest, in the conjunction *Etsi.* Which conjunction is situated, much like Corinth itself, in a narrow land,
as it were between two seas; beaten upon the one with
self-love, upon the other with unkindness. Hitherto we
have had to do but with self-love, and his assaults; but now
unkindness also is up. These Corinthians, saith St. Paul,
my affection standeth toward them in all love. Love them
and spare not, saith self-love, but *tene quod habes.* Nay sure,
Impendam, " I will bestow it." Well, if there be no remedy—
But, hear you, *Propitius esto tibi,* for all that. Nay, nor that

Mat. 16. 22. neither. *Impendar,* " I will be bestowed myself too." *Potesne*
Mark 10.
38. *bibere calicem hunc,* saith self-love; and can you get it down,
think you? Yea, *libentissime,* " exceeding gladly." There
is the conquest of self-love.

But all this while he lived still under hope, hope of winning their love for whose sakes he had trod under foot the
love of himself; hope that it had been but *impendam* all the
while, he should have had returned his own again at least.
But at this *etsi* all is turned out and in. For this is as much
to say as all is to little purpose; for to his grief he must take
notice, they care for none of them, nor for him ever a whit
the more; yea, rather the less by a great deal. So that all
three be in vain; *et supra omnem laborem labor irritus,* 'no
labour to lost labour:' nor expense of life or goods to that is
spent in vain. For that is not *impendam,* but *perdam;* not
spent, but cast away. Therefore the former, though it were

[Eccl. 4. *funiculus triplex,* " a threefold cord," and not easily bro-
12.] ken, would not hold but fly in pieces, but for this *etsi.* To
have then an *etsi* in our love: this *etsi,* this εἰ καὶ εἰκῇ,
" though in vain," though our *impendam* prove a *perdam;*
that is it. To be able to turn the sentence and say, " though
the more I love the less I be loved, yet will I bestow;" yea,
" be bestowed," and that most " gladly," for all that. It

is hard, I confess; but *Solus amor erubescit nomen difficultatis,* 'love endureth not the name of difficulty,' but shameth to confess any thing too hard or too dangerous for it. For verily, unkindness is a mighty enemy, and the wounds of it deep. Nay there be that of themselves are most kind in all the three degrees before remembered, as was King David, and as all noble natures are; why self-love is nothing in their hands. But let them be encountered with unkindness, as David was in Nabal, they cannot stand the stroke; it woundeth deep, and the fester of discontentment more dangerous than it. Indeed, saith David, "this fellow," I see, "I have done all in vain for him, for he rewarded me evil for good; so and so do God to me, if he be alive to-morrow by this time." Mark it in him, and in others infinite; and you shall see, whom self-love could not, unkindness hath overcome; and who passed well along the other three, at *minus diligar* their love hath wracked, and from kind love been turned to deadly hate. 1 Sam. 25.
10-42.

But neither can this appal the Apostle, or dislodge his love; but through all the rest, and through this too, he breaketh with his *etsi,* and sheweth he will hold his resolution, maugre all unkindness. *Minus diligar* shall not do it; unkindness must yield, love will not.

And now we are come to the highest, and never till now, but now we are; that farther we cannot go. The very highest pitch of well-doing the heathen man saw in part; for he could say, *Beneficium dare et perdere,* 'to bestow love and lose it,' is well done; but that is not it. This is it; *Beneficium perdere, et dare,* 'to lose the first and yet bestow the second;' *etsi,* yea, though the first were lost. Seneca.

Yea, the love of loves, Christ's own love, what was it? *Majorem hâc charitatem nemo habet, quam ut vitam quis ponat pro amicis.* Whereto St. Bernard rejoineth well, *Tu majorem habuisti Domine, quia Tu vitam posuisti etiam pro inimicis:* 'Greater love than this hath no man, to bestow his life for his friends.' 'Yet Lord,' saith St. Bernard; 'Thou hadst greater, for Thou bestowedst Thy life for Thy very enemies.' And to this love it is that St. Paul aspireth, and near it he cometh; that in some sort we may likewise say to him, *Tu majorem habuisti Paule,* 'Yes thy love, Paul, was [S.Bernard.
Serm. de
Feriâ 4.
Hebdom.
Sanct.]

SERM.
VI.
greater, for thou art ready to do the like; not for thine enemies, but for thy unkind friends, the next degree to professed enemies. 1. "To spend;" 2. "To spend and be spent;" 3. "To spend and be spent, and that most gladly." 4. Not only "most gladly;" but "most gladly, yea though."

Thus you have now his double conquest: Over the love of himself first; and now, over *minus diligar,* an unkind repulse too. And, in sign of victory he setteth up his colours, even these four; 1. *Impendam,* 2. *Impendar,* 3. *Libentissime,* and 4. *Etsi.* But *etsi* is the chief; it is Christ's colour, and that no perfect love that wanteth *etsi.*

II.
The object
of his love.
Thus we have seen love in his highest ascendant, and heard love in his *magisterium,* the hardest and highest, and indeed the master-point of this art. Which setteth us new on work, to pass over into the second part, and to enquire what this object may be, so amiable, whereon St. Paul hath set his affection so, that for it he will do and suffer all this; and that, so willingly without any exception, so constantly without any giving over. All this is nothing but the zeal of souls, *zelus animarum faciet hoc;* it is for their souls, all this. For their souls; and let their bodies go.

1.
*Pro ani-
mabus,*
"for your
souls."
Which first draweth the diameter that maketh the partition between the two loves; the love which St. Paul found, and the love which St. Paul left at Corinth. For he found that which is *scelus corporum,* 'the body's unruly affection,' and infection too otherwhile; — if ever in any place, there it abounded—but he left *zelus animarum,* the soul's perfection. Indeed, it falleth out sometimes, that in carnal love, or rather lust than love, we may pattern all the former; and find, as the Wise Man speaketh, some one destitute of understanding, wasting his whole substance, hazarding his life, and that more willingly than wisely, perhaps to gain nothing but a scorn for his labour, and yet persisting in his folly still; and all this, in the passion of concupiscence to a vain creature; pleasing his fancy to the displeasing of God, and to the piercing of his soul one day with deep remorse for it; and except it do, to the utter ruin both of body and soul. We have here at Corinth, a strange example of it. Of one,—*ad cujus jacuit Græcia tota fores,* 'at whose doors, sundry of all sorts waited,' suing and seeking, and as one of them said, Buying

LAIS.
Demos-
thenes.
[Propert.
lib. 2.
El. 5, 2.]

repentance at too dear a rate[1]. But what need we sail to
Corinth? Even in our own age we have enow fond examples
of it; of love set awry and sorted amiss, diverted from the
soul where it should be bestowed, and lavished on the body,
where a great deal less would serve. It is St. Augustine's
wish; *O si excitare possemus homines et cum iis pariter exci-
tari, ut tales amatores, &c.!* 'O that we would in this kind
stir up others, and ourselves with them be stirred up, but
even to bestow such love on the immortal soul, as we see
daily cast away on the corruptible body!' What, but so
much, and no more? *Absit ut sic, sed utinam vel sic!* 'Till
it might be more, would God it were but as much in the
mean time!' Yet more, and much more should it be. *Sed
infelix populus Dei non habet tantum fervorem in bono, quantum mali in malo,* is St. Hierom's complaint. 'But the people of God unhappy in this point, hath not that courage or
constancy in the love of the Spirit, that the wicked world hath
in the lust of the flesh.' That courage! Nay, nothing like.
Ad erubescentiam nostram dico, "to our shame it must be
spoken." Look but to the first point, *impendam;* doth not
the body take it wholly up? And, if we fail in the lowest,
what shall become of the rest? Well, St. Paul's love is, and
ours must be if it be right, *pro animabus,* "soul-love," which
may serve for the first point of the sequestration.

But why *pro animabus,* what is there in the soul so lovely
that all this should be said or done for it? Why for souls?
Why? 1. Why, take the soul out of the body which so much
we dote on, but even half an hour, and the body will grow so
out of our love, so deformed, so ugly, so every way loathsome,
as they that now admire it will then abhor it; and they that
now cannot behold it enough, will not then endure once to
come near it, nor within the sight of it. This a natural man
would answer: The soul is to be regarded of the body, for it
maketh the body to be regarded. 2. But a Christian man
will say more for it. That the love of Christ must be the
rule of the love of Christians, and ours suitable to His. And
Christ hath valued the soul above the world itself, in direct
affirming that he, that to win the world hazards his soul,
makes but an unwise bargain; which bargain were wise
enough, if the world were more worth. *Appende animam*

[marginal notes:]

['Οὐκ ὠνοῦ-
μαι μυρίων
δραχμῶν
μεταμέ-
λειαν.]

1 Cor. 6. 5.

2.
The rea-
son.

Mat. 16. 26.

homo, saith Chrysostom, *et impende in animam :* 'If you would prize your souls better, you would bestow more on them.' This is nothing. Christ hath valued your souls—valued and loved them above Himself; Himself, more worth than many worlds, yea, if they were ten thousand. I come now to the point. Is Christ to be loved? Why, all that St. Paul hitherto hath professed, all and every part of it, it was but to the souls at second-hand. His eye was upon Christ, all the time of his profession. But because Christ hath by deed enrolled set over His love to men's souls, and willed us toward them to shew whatsoever to Him we profess; therefore, and for no other cause, it is, that he standeth thus affected. For that those souls Christ so loved, that He loved not Himself to love them. *Dilexisti me, Domine, plus quam Te, quando mori voluisti pro me*—it is Augustine. 'Dying for my soul, Lord, Thou shewedst, that my soul was dearer to Thee, than Thine own self.' In love then to Christ, we are to love them that Christ loved—not *sicut Seipsum* 'as Himself,' but *plus-quam Seipsum,* 'more than Himself;' and therefore hath

Mat. 19. 19. changed the *sicut* of the Law, *sicut teipsum,* "as thyself,"
Joh. 13. 34. into a new *sicut, sicut Ego vos,* "as I have loved you." And how did He love us? Even that He was the first that ever professed these four to us, 1. Did bestow, 2. was bestowed, 3. most gladly, 4. yea though the more He loved, the less we loved Him. Or, to give Him His right, a degree higher
Joh. 15. 24. than Paul; not, when we loved Him little, as faint friends, but hated Him greatly as sworn enemies. For He it was that professed this art, first. The words are indeed Christ's own; the primitive and most proper uttering them, belongeth to Him. None ever so fully or so fitly spake or can speak
Lu. 23. 34. them, as the Son of God on the cross, from the chair of His profession. And of Him there St. Paul learned *hoc carmen amoris.* Himself confesseth as much, in the fifth chapter of this Epistle, that it was love; not his own love, but Christ's love, *charitas Christi extorsit,* that brought these words from Him. His they be not, but *ore tenus;* the tongue his, but Christ the speaker. His they were; His they are, out of whose mouth, or from whose pen, soever they come.

    We are come then now, where we may read love in the very original; yea, in the most complete perfection that ever it was. *Profitente Christo,* 'Christ Himself, the professor,' saith 1. *Impendam* first; bestow He will. If you will make port-sale of your love, none shall outbid Him. Even whatsoever Himself is worth, He will bestow; His kingdom, and the fulness of joy and glory in it for ever.

2. *Impendar.* That? why *consummatum est,* it is done Joh. 19. 30. already; all, hands and feet, head and heart, opened wide; and all, even to the last drop of blood bestowed for us on His cross, where the love of souls triumphed over the love of His own life.

3. *Libentissime,* "most gladly." Witness that speech; "A baptism I have to be baptized with," and *quomodo* Lu. 12. 50. *coarctor,* "how am I pained till I be at it!" And that too, that to him that moved Him not to bestow, but favour Himself, He used no other terms than to the devil himself, "Avoid Satan." Proof enough, say I, how willingly He Mat. 16. 23. went, and how unwillingly He would be kept from it.

4. And for His *etsi,* would God it were not too plain! Both at His cross, where the louder their *crucifige,* with Lu. 23. 34. the more strong crying and tears He prayed *Pater ignosce;* and ever since, *usque hodie,* 'till now,' when all may see our regard is as little as His love great, and He respected as if He had done nothing for us. Every part of His love, and the profession of His love, but specially the *etsi* of His love passeth all. For Christ by deed enrolled hath set over His love to them. Which is that that setteth such a price upon them, and maketh them so amiable, if not in their own kindness and loveliness, yet in the love of Christ Himself. And it is the answer that David when he loseth his sleep, to Ps. 132. 4. think upon the people of God; that Moses, when he wearieth Ex. 18. 14. himself in hearing causes from morning to night; that ^18, &c. Joshua, when he fighteth the Lord's battles, and jeopards his life in the high places of the field; that any that wears and spends himself in the common cause, may make as well as St. Paul. Why it is *pro animabus,* "it is for souls," for safeguard of souls—those souls which Christ hath so dearly loved, and so dearly bought, and to our love so carefully commended: *Sicut Ego vos,* as He did or ever shall do for us, that we do for them. Whereto, if not the souls themselves, for the most part unthankful, yet this motive of love, of Christ's love, doth in a manner violently constrain us.

I

S E R M. For though nothing is less violent in the manner, yet in the
VI.
work nothing worketh more violent than it.

The appli-   I conclude then with St. Bernard's demand; *Quæ vero*
cation.
utilitas in sermone hoc? ' What use have we of all that hath
been said?' For he that wrote it is dead, and they to whom
it was written are gone; but the Scripture still remaineth,
and we are to take good by it.

1.   It serveth first to possess our souls of that excellent vir-
1 Cor. 13. tue, *Major horum,* " the greatest of the three;" nay, the vir-
13.
tue without which the rest be but ciphers; the virtue that
shineth brightest in Christ's example, and standeth highest
in His commendation, love.

2.   But love, the action of virtue, not the passion of vice.
Phil. 3. 21. Love, not of the body, the " vile body"—so the Holy Ghost
Pro. 6. 26. termeth it—but of the soul, "the precious soul" of man.
Love of souls; the more, the more acceptable. If of a city,
well; if of a county, better; if of a country or kingdom,
best of all.

3.   And for them, and for their love, to be ready to prove it
by St. Paul's trial; to open our *impendam,* to vow our *im-*
pendar, and as near as may be to aspire to the same degree
of *libentissime.* Verily, they that either, as the Apostle, for
the winning of souls; or for the defence and safety of souls,
many thousands of souls, the souls of an whole estate, in
high and heroical courage have already passed their *im-*
pendam; and are ready to offer themselves every day to
impendar, and with that resolute forwardness which we all
see, for it is a case presently in all our eyes; they that do
thus, no good can be spoken of their love answerable to the
desert of it. Heavenly it is, and in Heaven to receive the
reward.

4.   But when all is done, we must take notice of the world's
nature. For, as St. Paul left it, so we shall find it, that is,
we shall not perhaps meet with that regard we promise ourselves. St. Paul's *magis diligam* met with a *minus diligar.*

Therefore above all remember his *etsi.* For to be kind,
and that to the unkind; to know, such we shall meet with;
yea, to meet with them, and yet hold our *etsi,* and love
nevertheless; this certainly is that love, *majorem quâ nemo;*
and there is on earth no greater sign of a soul throughly
settled in the love of Christ, than to stand thus minded.

Come what will come, *magis* or *minus, si* or *etsi,* frown or
favour, respect or neglect; *Quod facio, hoc et faciam,* "What 2 Cor. 11.
I do, I will do," with eye to Christ, with hope of regard from 12.
Him, let the world be as it is, and as it ever hath been.

Samuel, this day in the first Lesson, when he had spent
his life in a well-ordered government that his very enemies
could no ways except to, in his old days was requited with
fac nobis Regem, only upon a humour of innovation. What 1 Sam. 8. 5.
then? Grew he discontent? No, *non obstante,* for all their
ingratitude, good man, this he professeth, "God forbid," 1 Sam. 12.
saith he, "I should sin in ceasing to pray for you; yea, I will 23.
shew you the good and right way of the Lord for all that."
That may serve to match this out of the Old Testament. For
here in like sort we have Paul's *minus diligar* before our
eyes; and we see, he is at his *libentissime etsi* for all that.
You learn then, as that *minus diligar* may come, so in case it
do come, what to do; even to consummate your love with a
triumph over unkindness. Learn this, and all is learned;
learn this, and the whole art is had.

And we have in this verse, and in the very first word of it,
that will enter us into this lesson.

First from *ego vero.* From his, and from our own persons, 1.
we may begin to raise this duty. When we were deep in our
minus diligar, and smally regarded Christ; nay, *cum inimici* Rom. 5. 10.
essemus, to take as we should, "when we were His enemies,"
of His over-abundant kindness it pleased Him to call us from
the blindness of error to the knowledge of His truth; and
from a deep consumption of our souls by sin, to the state of
health and grace. And if St. Paul were loved when he raged Acts 9. 1.
and breathed blasphemy against Christ and His name, is it
much if for Christ's sake he swallow some unkindness at the
Corinthians' hands? Is it much if we let fall a duty upon
them, upon whom God the Father droppeth His rain, and
God the Son drops, yea sheds His blood ὑπὲρ ἀχαρίστους Lu. 6. 35.
καὶ πονηροὺς, "upon evil and unthankful men?"

Surely if love, or well-doing, or any good must perish, 2.
which is the second motive, and be lost through some body's
default where it lighteth, much better it is that it perish in
the Corinthians' hands, than in Paul's; by them in their evil
receiving, than by him in his not bestowing; through their
unkindness, than through our abruptness. For so, the sin

S E R M.
VI.
——◦—— shall be theirs, and we and our souls innocent before God,
Impendatur per nos, pereat per illos.

But perish it shall not, which is the third point, though for
them it may. For howsoever of them it may be truly said,
'The more we love the less they ;' of Christ it never can, nor
ever shall be said. For St. Paul, for the little love at their
hands, found the greater at His. Though the more he loved,
the less they loved him ; yet the less they loved, the more
Christ loved him. Of Whom to be loved, even in the least
degree, is worth all the love of Corinth, and all Achaia too.
So that here we find that we missed all this while a *tamen* for
our *etsi*. Though not they, yet Christ. Which *tamen* maketh
amends for all. *Et vigilanti verbo usus est Apostolus ;* that
St. Paul spoke not at adventure, but was well advised when
he used the word *impendam*. For it is *impendam* indeed, not
perdam ; not lost, but laid out ; not cast away, but employed
on Him, for Whose love none ever hath or shall bestow
aught, but he shall receive a *super-impendar* of an hundred-
fold. And indeed, all other loves of the flesh, or world, or
whatsoever else, shall perish and come to nothing ; and of
this, and this only, we may say *impendam* truly.

So that, to make an end, though true it be that St. Bernard saith, *Perfectus amor vires non sumit de spe,* ' Perfect
love receives no manner strength from hope ;' yet for that our
love is not without his imperfections, all under one view we
may with one eye behold Christ's *magis diligam,* when we were
scarce in our *minus,* nay scarce loved Him at all ; and with
the other look upon *impendam,* that what we do herein,
though at men's hands we find no return, at Christ's we
shall, and it shall be the best bestowed service that ever
we bestowed, that we bestowed in this kind.

Now, would God, the same Spirit which here wrote this
verse would write it in our hearts, that those things are
thus ; that such a *rependam* there shall be, and we well
assured of it, *ut et nos converteremur in amorem,* ' that we
might be transformed into this love !' Which blessing,
Almighty God bestow on that which hath been said, for
Christ's, &c. !

[S. Ber-
nard. su-
per Cant.
Serm. 83.
circ. med.]

SERMONS

PREACHED UPON GOOD-FRIDAY.

A SERMON

PREACHED AT THE COURT,

ON THE TWENTY-FIFTH OF MARCH, A.D. MDXCVII., BEING GOOD-FRIDAY.

ZECHARIAH xii. 10.

And they shall look upon Me, Whom they have pierced.

Respicient in Me, Quem transfixerunt.

[*And they shall look upon Me Whom they have pierced.* Engl. Trans.]

THAT great and honourable person the Eunuch, sitting in his chariot, and reading a like place of the Prophet Esay, asketh St. Philip, "I pray thee, Of Whom speaketh the Prophet this? of himself, or some other?" A question very material, and to great good purpose, and to be asked by us in all prophecies. For knowing who the party is, we shall not wander in the Prophet's meaning. Acts 8. 34.

Now, if the Eunuch had been reading this of Zachary, as then he was that of Esay, and had asked the same question of St. Philip, he would have made the same answer. And as he out of those words took occasion, so may we out of these take the like, to preach Jesus unto them. For neither of himself, nor of any other, but of Jesus, speaketh the Prophet this; and "the testimony of Jesus is the spirit of this prophecy." Rev. 19. 10.

That so it is the Holy Ghost is our warrant, Who in St. John's Gospel reporting the Passion, and the last act of the Passion—this opening of the side, and piercing of the heart—our Saviour Christ saith plainly, that in the piercing the very words of the prophecy were fulfilled, *Respicient in Me Quem transfixerunt.* Joh. 19. 37.

Which term of piercing we shall the more clearly conceive,
if with the ancient writers, we sort it with the beginning
of Psalm 22, the Psalm of the Passion. For, in the very
front or inscription of this Psalm, our Saviour Christ is compared *cervo matutino*, " to the morning hart;" that is, a hart
roused early in the morning, as from His very birth He was
by Herod, hunted and chased all His life long, and this day
brought to His end, and, as the poor deer, stricken and
pierced through side, heart, and all; which is it we are here
willed to behold.

There is no part of the whole course of our Saviour Christ's
life or death but it is well worthy our looking on, and from
each part in it there goeth virtue to do us good; but of all
other parts, and above them all, this last part of His piercing
is here commended unto our view. Indeed, how could the
Prophet commend it more, than in avowing it to be an act of
grace as in the fore part of this verse he doth? *Effundam*
super eos Spiritum Gratiæ, et respicient, &c. as if he should
say; If there be any grace in us, we will think it worth the
looking on.

[Zech. 12.
10.]

Neither doth the Prophet only, but the Apostle also, call
us unto it, and willeth us what to " look unto" and regard,
" Jesus the Author and Finisher of our faith." Then specially, and in that act, when for " the joy of our salvation set
before Him He endured the cross, and despised the shame;"
that is, in this spectacle, when He was pierced.

Heb. 12. 2.

Which surely is continually, all our life long, to be done by
us, and at all times some time to be spared unto it; but if at
other times, most requisite at this time, this very day which
we hold holy to the memory of His Passion, and the piercing
of His precious side. That, though on other days we employ
our eyes otherwise, this day at least we fix them on this
object, *respicientes in Eum.* This day, I say, which is dedicated to none other end, but even to lift up the Son of Man,
as Moses did the serpent in the wilderness, that we may look
upon Him and live; when every Scripture that is read soundeth
nothing but this unto us, when by the office of preaching
Jesus Christ is lively described in our sight, and as the
Apostle speaketh, is " visibly crucified among us;" when in
the memorial of the Holy Sacrament, " His death is shewed

Joh. 3. 14.

Gal. 3. 1.

1 Cor. 11.

forth until He come," and the mystery of this His piercing so many ways, so effectually represented before us. This prophecy therefore, if at any time, at this time to take place, *Respicient in Me, &c.*

The principal words are but two, and set down unto us in The division. two points. I. The sight itself, that is, the thing to be seen; II. and the sight of it, that is, the act of seeing or looking. *Quem transfixerunt* is the object, or spectacle propounded. *Respicient in Eum,* is the act or duty enjoined.

Of which the object though in place latter, in nature is the former, and first to be handled; for that there must be a thing first set up, before we can set our eyes to look upon it.

Of the object generally, first. Certain it is, that Christ is here meant: St. John hath put us out of doubt for that point. I. The sight or object generally. I. Christ. And Zachary here could have set down His name, and said, *Respice in Christum ;* for Daniel before had named His name, Dan. 9. 26. *Occidetur Messias ;* and Zachary, being after him in time, might have easily repeated it. But it seemed good to the Holy Ghost and to him, rather to use a circumlocution ; and suppressing His name of Christ, to express Him by the style or term, *Quem transfixerunt.* Which being done by choice, must needs have a reason of the doing, and so it hath.

1. First, the better to specify and particularize the Person of Christ, by the kind, and most peculiar circumstance, of His death. Esay had said, *Morietur,* " Die He shall, and lay down Isa. 53. 10. His soul an offering for sin." 2. Die—but what death? a natural or a violent? Daniel tells us, *Occidetur ;* He shall die, Dan. 9. 26. not a natural, but a violent death. 3. But many are slain after many sorts, and divers kinds there be of violent deaths. The Psalmist, the more particularly to set it down, describeth it thus : " They pierced My hands and My feet ;" which is only Ps. 22. 16. proper to the death of the Cross. 4. Die, and be slain, and be crucified. But sundry else were crucified ; and therefore the Prophet here, to make up all, addeth, that He should not only be *crucifixus,* but *transfixus ;* not only have His hands and His feet, but even His heart pierced too. Which very note severs Him from all the rest, with as great particularity as may be ; for that, though many besides at other times, and some at the same time with Him were crucified ; yet the side and the heart of none was opened, but His, and His only.

SERM.
I.
2. Christ
pierced.

2. Secondly, as to specify Christ Himself in Person, and to sever Him from the rest; so in Christ Himself, and in His Person, to sever from the rest of His doings and sufferings, what that is that chiefly concerneth us, and we specially are to look to; and that is this day's work—Christ pierced.

1 Cor. 2. 2. St. Paul doth best express this: "I esteemed," saith he, "to know nothing among you, save Jesus Christ, and Him crucified." That is, the perfection of our knowledge is Christ; the perfection of our knowledge in, or touching Christ, is the knowledge of Christ's piercing. This is the chief sight; nay, as it shall after appear, in this sight are all sights; so that know this, and know all. This generally.

2.
The object
specially.
1. The
passion
itself:
Quid.

Now, specially. In the object, two things offer themselves; 1. The Passion, or suffering itself, which was, to be "pierced." 2. And the persons, by whom. For if the Prophet had not intended the Persons should have had their respect too, he might have said *Respicient in Eum Qui transfixus est ;*—which passive would have carried the Passion itself full enough— but so he would not, but rather chose to say, *Quem transfixerunt;* which doth necessarily imply the piercers themselves too. So that we must needs have an eye in the handling, both to the fact, and to the persons, 1. *quid,* and 2. *quibus,* both what, and of whom.

1. The
degree
thereof·
Transfixerunt.

In the Passion, we first consider the degree; for *transfixerunt* is a word of gradation, more than *fixerunt,* or *suffixerunt,* or *confixerunt* either. Expressing unto us the piercing, not with whips and scourges; nor of the nails and thorns, but of the spear-point. Not the whips and scourges, wherewith His skin and flesh were pierced; nor the nails and thorns wherewith His feet, hands, and head were pierced; but the spear-point which pierced, and went through, His very heart it-

Joh. 19. 34. self; for of that wound, of the wound in His heart, is this spoken. Therefore *trans* is here a transcendent—through and through; through skin and flesh, through hands and feet, through side and heart, and all; the deadliest and deepest wound, and of highest gradation.

2. The extent, *Me.*

Secondly, as the preposition *trans* hath his gradation of divers degrees, so the pronoun *me* hath his generality of divers parts; best expressed in the original. "Upon Me;" not, upon My body and soul. "Upon Me" Whose Person,

not Whose parts, either body without, or soul within; but
"upon Me," Whom wholly, body and soul, quick and dead,
"they have pierced."

Of the body's piercing there can be no question, since no 1. His
part of it was left unpierced. Our senses certify us of that— body.
what need we farther witness?

Of the soul's too, it is as certain, and there can be no doubt 2. His
of it neither; that we truly may affirm, Christ, not in part, soul.
but wholly, was pierced. For we should do injury to the
sufferings of our Saviour, if we should conceive by this
piercing none other but that of the spear.

And may a soul then be pierced? Can any spear-point
go through it? Truly Simeon saith to the blessed Virgin
by way of prophecy, that "the sword should go through her Lu. 2. 35.
soul," at the time of His Passion. And as the sword through
hers, so I make no question but the spear through His. And
if through hers which was but *anima compatientis*, through
His much more, which was *anima patientis;* since compassion
is but passion at rebound. Howbeit, it is not a sword of
steel, or a spear-head of iron, that entereth the soul, but a
metal of another temper; the dint whereof no less goreth
and woundeth the soul in proportion, than those do the
body. So that we extend this piercing of Christ farther than
to the visible gash in His side, even to a piercing of another
nature, whereby not His heart only was stabbed, but His
very spirit wounded too.

The Scripture recounteth two, and of them both expressly
saith, that they both pierce the soul. The Apostle saith it
by sorrow: "And pierced themselves through with many 1Tim. 6. 10
sorrows." The Prophet, of reproach: "There are whose Ps. 64. 3, 4.
words are like the pricking of a sword;" and that to the soul
both, for the body feels neither. With these, even with both
these, was the soul of Christ Jesus wounded.

For sorrow—it is plain through all four Evangelists; *Un-* With sor-
dique tristis est anima Mea usque ad mortem! "My soul is row.
environed on every side with sorrow, even to the death." Mark 14.
Cœpit Jesus tædere et pavere, "Jesus began to be distressed 34.
and in great anguish." *Factus in agoniá,* "being cast into 33.
an agony." *Jam turbata est anima Mea;* "Now is My soul Lu. 22. 44.
troubled." Avowed by them all, confessed by Himself. Yea, Joh. 12. 27.

S E R M.
I. that His strange and never else heard of sweat—drops of blood plenteously issuing from Him all over His body, what time no manner of violence was offered to His body, no man then touching Him, none being near Him; that blood came certainly from some great sorrow wherewith His soul was pierced. And that His most dreadful cry, which at once _{Mat. 27. 46.} moved all the powers of Heaven and earth, "My God, My God, &c." was the voice of some mighty anguish, wherewith His soul was smitten; and that in other sort, than with any material spear. For *derelinqui a Deo*—the body cannot feel it, or tell what it meaneth. It is the soul's complaint, and therefore without all doubt His soul within Him was pierced and suffered, though not that which—except charity be allowed to expound it—cannot be spoken without blasphemy. Not so much, God forbid! yet much, and very much, and much more than others seem to allow; or how much, it is dangerous to define.

With reproach.　　To this edge of sorrow, if the other of piercing despite be added as a point, as added it was, it will strike deep into any heart; especially, being wounded with so many sorrows before. But the more noble the heart, the deeper; who beareth any grief more easily than this grief, the grief of a contumelious reproach. _{Ps. 69. 26.} "To persecute a poor distressed soul, and to seek to vex Him that is already wounded at the heart," why, it is the very pitch of all wickedness; the very extremity that malice can do, or affliction can suffer. And to this pitch were they come, when after all their wretched villanies and spittings, and all their savage indignities in reviling Him most opprobriously, He being in the depth of all His distress, and for very anguish of soul crying, *Eli, Eli, &c.*, they stayed those that would have relieved Him; and void of all humanity _{Mat. 27. 49.} then scorned, saying; "Stay, let alone, let us see if Elias will now come and take Him down." This barbarous and brutish inhumanity of theirs, must needs pierce deeper into His soul, than ever did the iron into His side.

To all which if we it add, not only that horrible ingratitude of theirs, there by Him seen, but ours also no less than theirs by Him foreseen at the same time; who make so slender reckoning of these His piercings, and, as they were a matter not worth the looking on, vouchsafe not so much as to spend

an hour in the due regard and meditation of them; nay, not
that only, but farther by incessant sinning, and that without
remorse, do most unkindly requite those His bitter pains, and
as much as in us lies, "even crucify afresh the Son of God, Heb. 6. 6.
making a mock of Him and His piercings." These I say, for
these all and every of them in that instant were before His
eyes, must of force enter into, and go through and through
His soul and spirit; that what with those former sorrows,
and what with these after indignities, the Prophet might truly
say of Him, and He of Himself, *in Me,* "upon Me;" not
whose body or whose soul, but whom entirely and wholly,
both in body and soul, alive and dead, they have pierced and
passioned this day on the cross.

Of the persons;—which, as it is necessarily implied in the 2. The
word, is very properly incident to the matter itself. For it is persons,
usual, when one is found slain as here, to make enquiry, By *a quibus.*
whom he came by his death. Which so much the rather is
to be done by us, because there is commonly an error in the
world, touching the parties that were the causes of Christ's
death. Our manner is, either to lay it on the soldiers, that
were the instruments; or if not upon them, upon Pilate the
judge that gave sentence; or if not upon him, upon the people that importuned the judge; or lastly, if not upon them,
upon the Elders of the Jews that animated the people; and
this is all to be found by our quest of enquiry.

But the Prophet here indicted others. For by saying,
"They shall look," &c., "Whom they have pierced," he
intendeth by very construction, that the first and second
"They," are not two, but one and the same parties. And
that *they* that are here willed to look upon Him, are *they*
and none other that were the authors of this fact, even of
the murder of Jesus Christ. And to say truth, the Prophet's
intent is no other but to bring the malefactors themselves
that pierced Him, to view the body and the wounded heart
of Him, "Whom they have so pierced."

In the course of justice we say, and say truly, when a
party is put to death, that the executioner cannot be said to
be the cause of his death; nor the sheriff, by whose commandment he doth it; neither yet the judge by whose sentence; nor the twelve men by whose verdict; nor the law

SERM.
I.

itself, by whose authority it is proceeded in. For, God forbid we should indict these, or any of these, of murder. *Solum peccatum homicida;* sin, and sin only, is the murderer. Sin, I say, either of the party that suffereth; or of some other, by whose means, or for whose cause, he is put to death.

Now, Christ's own sin it was not that He died for. That is most evident. Not so much by His own challenge, *Quis ex vobis arguit Me de peccato?* as by the report of His judge, who openly professed that he had examined Him, and "found no fault in Him." "No, nor yet Herod," for being sent to him and examined by him also, nothing worthy death was found in Him. And therefore, calling for water and washing his hands he protesteth his own innocency of the blood of this "Just Man;" thereby pronouncing Him Just, and void of any cause in Himself of His own death.

It must then necessarily be the sin of some others, for whose sake Christ Jesus was thus pierced. And if we ask, who those others be? or whose sins they were? the Prophet Esay tells us, *Posuit super Eum iniquitates omnium nostrûm,* "He laid upon Him the transgressions of us all;" who should, even for those our many, great, and grievous transgressions, have eternally been pierced, in body and soul, with torment and sorrows of a never-dying death, had not He stepped between us and the blow, and received it in His own body; even the dint of the wrath of God to come upon us. So that it was the sin of our polluted hands that pierced His hands, the swiftness of our feet to do evil that nailed His feet, the wicked devices of our heads that gored His head, and the wretched desires of our hearts that pierced His heart. We that "look upon," it is we that "pierced Him;" and it is we that "pierced Him," that are willed to "look upon Him." Which bringeth it home to us, to me myself that speak, and to you yourselves that hear: and applieth it most effectually to every one of us, who evidently seeing that we were the cause of this His piercing, if our hearts be not too hard, ought to have remorse to be pierced with it.

When, for delivering to David a few loaves, Abimelech and the priests were by Saul put to the sword, if David did then acknowledge with grief of heart and say, "I, even I, am the cause of the death of thy father and all his house;"—when he

Joh. 8. 46.

Lu. 23. 14, 15.

Mat. 27.24.

Isa. 53. 4-6.

1 Sam. 22. 22.

was but only the occasion of it, and not that direct neither—may not we, nay ought not we much more justly and deservedly say of this piercing of Christ our Saviour, that we verily, even we, are the cause thereof, as verily we are, even the principals in this murder; and the Jews and others, on whom we seek to derive it, but only accessories and instrumental causes thereof. Which point we ought as continually, so seriously to think of; and that no less than the former. The former, to stir up compassion in ourselves, over Him that thus was pierced; the latter, to work deep remorse in our hearts, for being authors of it. That He was pierced, will make our bowels melt with compassion over Christ. That He was pierced by us that look on Him, if our hearts be not "flint," as Job saith, or as "the nether mill-stone," will Job 41. 24. breed remorse over ourselves, wretched sinners as we are.

The act followeth in these words; *Respicient in Eum.* A request most reasonable, to "look upon Him"—but "to look upon Him," to bestow but a look and nothing else, which even of common humanity we cannot deny, *Quia non aspicere despicere est.* It argueth great contempt, not to vouchsafe it the cast of our eye, as if it were an object utterly unworthy the looking toward. Truly, if we mark it well, nature itself of itself inclineth to this act. When Amasa treacherously was slain by Joab, and lay weltering in his blood by the way side, the story saith that not one of the whole army, then marching by, but when he came at him, "stood still 2 Sam. 20. and looked on him." 12.

II.
The act.
To look
upon Him.

In the Gospel, the party that goeth from Jerusalem to Jericho was spoiled and wounded and lay drawing on, though the Priest and Levite that passed near the place relieved him not, as the Samaritan after did; yet it is said of them, they "went near and looked on," and then passed on their way. Lu. 10. 32. Which desire is even natural in us; so that even nature itself inclineth us to satisfy the Prophet.

Nature doth, and so doth Grace too. For generally we are bound to "regard the work of the Lord, and to consider Ps. 28. 5. the operations of His hands;" and specially this work, in comparison whereof God Himself saith, the former works of His "shall not be remembered, nor the things done of old Isa. 43. 18. once regarded."

Yea Christ Himself, pierced as He is, inviteth us to it. For in the Prophet here it is not *in Eum*, but *in Me;* not 'on Him,' but "on Me Whom they have pierced." But more fully in Jeremy; for, to Christ Himself do all the ancient writers apply, and that most properly, those words Lam. 1. 12. of the Lamentation; "Have ye no regard all ye that pass by this way? Behold and see, if there be any sorrow like My sorrow, which is done unto Me, wherewith the Lord hath afflicted Me in the day of His fierce wrath."

Our own profit, which is wont to persuade well, inviteth Nu. 21. 8, 9. us; for that as from the brazen serpent no virtue issued to heal but unto them that steadily beheld it, so neither doth there from Christ but upon those that with the eye of faith have their contemplation on this object; who thereby draw life from Him, and without it may and do perish, for all Christ and His Passion.

And if nothing else move us, this last may, even our danger. For the time will come when we ourselves shall desire, that God looking with an angry countenance upon our sins, would turn His face from them and us, and look upon the face of His Christ, that is, *respicere in Eum;* which shall justly be then denied us, if we ourselves could never be gotten to do this duty, *respicere in Eum*, when it was called for of us. God shall not look upon Him at ours, Whom we would not look upon at His request.

In the act itself are enjoined three things: 1. That we do it with attention; for it is not *Me*, but *in Me;* not only "upon Him," but "into Him." 2. That we do it oft, again and again, with iteration; for *respicient* is *re-aspicient*. Not a single act, but an act iterated. 3. That we cause our nature to do it, as it were, by virtue of an injunction, *per actum elicitum*, as the schoolmen call it. For in the original it is in the commanding conjugation, that signifieth, *facient se respicere*, rather than *respicient*.

1.
With at-
tention.
*Respicient
in Eum.*
First then, not slightly, superficially or perfunctorily, but stedfastly, and with due attention, to "look upon Him." And not to look upon the outside alone, but to look into the very entrails; and with our eye to pierce Him That was thus pierced. *In Eum* beareth both.

1. "Upon Him" if we "look," we shall see so much

as Pilate shewed of Him;—*ecce Homo*, that He is a Man. And if He were not a man, but some other unreasonable creature, it were great ruth to see Him so handled.

2. Among men we less pity malefactors, and have most compassion on them that be innocent. And He was innocent, and deserved it not, as you have heard, His enemies themselves being His judges.

3. Among those that be innocent, the more noble the person, the greater the grief, and the more heavy ever is the spectacle. Now if we consider the verse of this text well, we shall see it is God Himself and no man that here speaketh, for to God only it belongeth to "pour out of the Spirit of grace," it passeth man's reach to do it; so that, if we look better upon Him, we shall see as much as the Centurion saw, that this party thus pierced "is the Son of God." The Son ^{Mat. 27. 54.} of God slain! Surely he that hath done this deed "is the ^{2 Sam. 12.} child of death," would every one of us say; *Et tu es homo,* ^{5-7.} "Thou art the man[1]," would the Prophet answer us. You ^{[1 See the} are they, for whose sins the Son of God hath His very heart-^{Vulgate.]} blood shed forth. Which must needs strike into us remorse of a deeper degree than before; that not only is it we that have pierced the party thus found slain, but that this party, whom we have thus pierced, is not a principal person among the children of men, but even the only-begotten Son of the Most High God. Which will make us cry out with St. Augustine, *O amaritudo peccati mei, ad quam tollendam necessaria fuit amaritudo tanta!* 'Now sure, deadly was the bitterness of our sins, that might not be cured, but by the bitter death and blood-shedding Passion of the Son of God.' And this may we see looking upon Him.

But now then, if we look *in Eum,* "into Him," we shall see yet a greater thing, which may raise us in comfort, as far as the other cast us down. Even the bowels of compassion and tender love, whereby He would and was content to suffer all this for our sakes. For that, whereas "no man had power to ^{Joh. 10. 18.} take His life from Him," for He had power to have commanded twelve legions of Angels in His just defence; and ^{Mat. 26. 53.} without any Angel at all, power enough of Himself with His *Ego sum,* to strike them all to the ground; He was content ^{Joh. 18. 6.} notwithstanding all this, to lay down His life for us sinners.

K

SERM.
I.

Joh. 15. 13.

The greatness of which love passeth the greatest love that man hath; for "greater love than this hath no man, but to bestow his life for his friends," whereas He condescended to lay it down for His enemies. Even for them that sought His death, to lay down His life, and to have His blood shed for them that did shed it; to be pierced for His piercers. Look how the former *in Eum* worketh grief, considering the great injuries offered to so great a Personage; so, to temper the grief of it, this latter *in Eum* giveth some comfort, that so great a Person should so greatly love us, as for our sakes to endure all those so many injuries, even to the piercing of His very heart.

2.
With ite-ration:
Re-aspi-cient.

Heb. 12. 3.

Secondly, *respicient*, that is, *re-aspicient;* not once or twice, but oftentimes to look upon it; that is, as the Prophet saith here, *iteratis vicibus*, to look again and again; or, as the Apostle saith, *recogitare*, "to think upon it over and over again," as it were to dwell in it for a time. In a sort, with the frequentness of this our beholding it, to supply the weakness and want of our former attention. Surely, the more steadily and more often we shall fix our eye upon it, the more we shall be inured; and being inured, the more desire to do it. For at every looking some new sight will offer itself, which will offer unto us occasion, either of godly sorrow, true repentance, sound comfort, or some other reflection, issuing from the beams of this heavenly mirror. Which point, because it is the chief point, the Prophet here calleth us to, even how to look upon Christ often, and to be the better for our looking; it shall be very agreeable to the text, and to the Holy Ghost's chief intent, if we prove how, and in how diverse sorts, we may with profit behold and "look upon Him" Whom thus we have "pierced."

1. *Respice et trans-figere.*

First then, looking upon Him, we may bring forth the first effect that which immediately followeth this text itself in this text, *Et plangent Eum :—Respice et plange.* First, 'look and lament,' or mourn; which is indeed the most kindly and natural effect of such a spectacle. "Look upon Him that is pierced," and with looking upon Him be pierced thyself; *respice et transfigere.* A good effect of our first look, if we could bring it forth. At leastwise, if we cannot *respice et transfigere,* 'look and be pierced,' yet that it might be *respice et compungere,* 'that with looking on Him we might be "pricked in our hearts,"' and have it enter past the Acts 2. 37. skin, though it go not clean through. Which difference in this verse the Prophet seemeth to insinuate, when first he willeth us to mourn as for one's only son, with whom all is lost. Or, if that cannot be had, to mourn as for a first-begotten son, which is though not so great, yet a great mourning; even for the first-begotten, though other sons be left.

And, in the next verse, if we cannot reach to natural Zech. 12. grief, yet he wisheth us to mourn with a civil; even with 11. such a lamentation as was made for Josias. And behold a greater than Josias is here. Coming not, as he, to an honourable death in battle, but to a most vile death, the death of a malefactor; and not, as Josias, dying without any fault of theirs, but mangled and massacred in this shameful sort for us, even for us and our transgressions. Verily, the dumb and senseless creatures had this effect wrought in them, of mourning at the sight of His death; in their kind sorrowing for the murder of the Son of God. And we truly shall be much more senseless than they, if it have in us no work to the like effect. Especially, considering it was not for them He suffered all this, nor they no profit by it, but for us it was, and we by it saved; and yet they had compassion, and we none. Be this then the first.

Now, as the first is *respice et transfigere,* 'look upon Him 2. *Respice* and be pierced;' so the second may be, and that fitly, *respice et transfige.* *et transfige,* 'look upon Him and pierce;' and pierce that in thee that was the cause of Christ's piercing, that is, sin and the lusts thereof. For as men that are pierced indeed with the grief of an indignity offered, withal are pricked to take revenge on him that offers it, such a like affection ought our second looking to kindle in us, even to take a wreak or revenge upon sin, *quia fecit hoc,* 'because it hath been the cause of all this.' I mean, as the Holy Ghost termeth it, a mortifying or crucifying; a thrusting through of our wicked passions and concupiscences, in some kind of repaying those manifold villanies, which the Son of God suffered by means of them. At leastwise, as before, if it kindle not our zeal so far against sin, yet that it may slake our zeal and affection to sin; that is, *respice ne respicias, respice Christum ne respicias peccatum.* That we have less mind, less liking, less acquaintance with sin, for the Passion-sake. For that by this means we do in some sort spare Christ, and at least make His wounds no wider; whereas by affecting sin anew we do what in us lieth to crucify Him afresh, and both increase the number, and enlarge the wideness of His wounds.

It is no unreasonable request, that if we list not wound sin, yet seeing Christ hath wounds enough, and they wide and deep enough, we should forbear to pierce Him farther, and have at least this second fruit of our looking upon Him; either to look and to pierce sin, or to look and spare to pierce Him any more.

Now, as it was sin that gave Him these wounds, so it was love to us that made Him receive them, being otherwise able enough to have avoided them all. So that He was pierced with love no less than with grief, and it was that wound of love made Him so constantly to endure all the other. Which love we may read in the palms of His hands, as the Fathers express it out of Esay 49. 16; for "in the palms of His hands He hath graven us," that He might not forget us. And the print of the nails in them, are as capital letters to record His love towards us. For Christ pierced on the cross is *liber charitatis,* 'the very book of love' laid open before us. And again, this love of His we may read in the cleft of His heart. *Quia clavus penetrans factus est nobis clavis reserans,* saith Bernard, *ut pateant nobis viscera per vulnera;* 'the point of the spear serves us instead of a key, letting us through His wounds see His very bowels,' the bowels of tender love and most kind compassion, that would for us endure to be so entreated. That if the Jews that stood by said truly of Him at Lazarus' grave, *Ecce quomodo dilexit eum!* when He shed a few tears out of His eyes; much more truly may we say of Him, *Ecce quomodo dilexit nos!* seeing Him shed both water and blood, and that in great plenty, and that out of His heart.

Which sight ought to pierce us with love too, no less than before it did with sorrow. With one, or with both, for both have power to pierce; but specially love, which except it had

Isa. 49. 16.

[S. Bernard. super Cant. Serm. 61. circ. med.]

*Joh.*11. 36.

3. *Respice et dilige.*

entered first and pierced Him, no nail or spear could ever
have entered. Then let this be the third, *respice et dilige;*
'look and be pierced with love of Him' that so loved thee,
that He gave Himself in this sort to be pierced for thee.

And forasmuch as it is Christ His Ownself That, resem- 4.
bling His Passion on the cross to the brazen serpent lift up *Respice et crede.*
in the wilderness, maketh a correspondence between their
beholding and our believing—for so it is John 3. 14.—we Joh. 3. 14.
cannot avoid, but must needs make that an effect too; even
respice et crede. And well may we believe and trust Him,
Whom looking a little before we have seen so constantly
loving us. For the sight of that love maketh credible unto
us, whatsoever in the whole Scripture is affirmed unto us of
Christ, or promised in His Name; so that believe it, and
believe all. Neither is there any time wherein with such
cheerfulness or fulness of faith we cry unto Him, "My Lord, Joh. 20. 28.
and My God," as when our eye is fixed upon "the print of
the nails, and on the hole in the side" of Him that was
pierced for us. So that this fourth duty Christ Himself
layeth upon us, and willeth us from His own mouth, *respice
et crede.*

And believing this of Him, what is there the eye of our 5.
hope shall not look for from Him? What would not He do *Respice et spera.*
for us, That for us would suffer all this? It is St. Paul's
argument, "If God gave His Son for us, how shall He deny Rom. 8. 32.
us any thing with Him?" That is, *respice et spera.* "Look
upon Him, and His heart opened, and from that gate of hope
promise thyself, and look for all manner of things that good
are.' Which our expectation is reduced to these two: 1. The
deliverance from evil of our present misery; 2. and the
restoring to the good of our primitive felicity. By the death
of this undefiled Lamb, as by the yearly Passover, look for
and hope for a passage out of Egypt, which spiritually is our
redemption from the servitude of the power of darkness.
And as by the death of the Sacrifice we look to be freed
from whatsoever evil, so by the death of the High Priest
look we for and hope for restitution to all that is good; even
to our forfeited estate in the land of Promise which is Heaven
itself, where is all joy and happiness for evermore. *Respice
et spera,* 'look and look for;' by the Lamb that is pierced to

S E R M. be freed from all misery, by the High Priest that is pierced
—— I. —— fruition of all felicity.

6.
Respice et
recipe.
Now, inasmuch as His heart is pierced, and His side opened; the opening of the one, and the piercing of the other, is to the end somewhat may flow forth. To which

[S. August. end, saith St. Augustine, *Vigilanti verbo usus est Apostolus,*
Tract. in
Joann.120.] 'the Apostle was well advised when he used the word

[Joh. 19. opening;' for there issued out "water and blood," which
34.] make the sixth effect, *Respice et recipe.* Mark it running out, and suffer it not to run waste, but receive it. Of the former, the water, the Prophet speaketh in the first words of

Zech. 13. 1. the next chapter, that out of His pierced side God "opened a fountain of water to the House of Israel for sin and for uncleanness;" of the fulness whereof we all have received in the Sacrament of our Baptism. Of the latter, the blood,

Zech. 9. 11. which the Prophet, in the ninth chapter before, calleth "the blood of the New Testament," we may receive this day; for it will run in the high and holy mysteries of the Body and Blood of Christ. There may we be partakers of the flesh of

Ps. 116. 13. the Morning Hart, as upon this day killed. There may we
1 Pet. 1. 19. be partakers of "the cup of salvation," "the precious blood"
Mat. 26. 28. "which was shed for the remission of our sins." Our part it
Heb.10. 29. shall be not to account "the blood of the Testament an unholy thing," and to suffer it to run in vain for all us, but with all due regard to receive it so running, for even therefore was it shed. And so to the former to add this sixth, *Respice et recipe.*

7.
Respice et
retribue.
And shall we alway receive grace, even streams of grace issuing from Him That is pierced, and shall there not from us issue something back again, that He may look for and receive from us that from Him have, and do daily, receive so many good things? No doubt there shall, if love which pierced Him have pierced us aright. And that is, no longer to hold you with these effects, *Respice et retribue.* For it will even behove us, no less than the Psalmist, to enter into

Ps. 116. 12. the consideration of *quid retribuam.* Especially since we by
[Mat. 13. this day both see and receive that, which he and many others
17.] desired to see, and receive, and could not. Or if we have
[Lu.17.16.] nothing to render, yet ourselves to return with the Samaritan, and falling down at His feet, with a loud voice, to

glorify His goodness, Who finding us in the estate that other Samaritan found the forlorn and wounded man, healed us by being wounded Himself, and by His own death restored us to life. For all which His kindness if nothing will come from us, not so much as a kind and thankful acknowledgment, we are certainly worthy He should restrain the fountain of His benefits, which hitherto hath flowed most plenteously, and neither let us see nor feel Him any more.

But I hope for better things—that love, such and so great love, will pierce us, and cause both other fruits, and especially thoughts of thankfulness to issue from us. Thus many, and many more if the time would serve, but thus many several uses may we have of thus many several respects, or reflexed lookings upon Him Whom we have pierced.

Thirdly, *facient se respicere.* For the Holy Ghost did easily foresee, we would not readily be brought to the sight, or to use our eyes to so good an end. Indeed, to flesh and blood it is but a dull and heavy spectacle. And neither willingly they begin to look upon it, and having begun are never well till they have done and look off of it again. Therefore is the verb by the Prophet put into this conjugation of purpose, which to turn in strict propriety is *respicere se facient*, rather than *respicient.* 'They shall procure or cause, or even enjoin or enforce themselves to look upon it;' or, as one would say, look that they look upon it.

For some new and strange spectacle, though vain and idle, and which shall not profit us how strange soever, we cause ourselves sometimes to take a journey, and besides our pains are at expenses too to behold them. We will not only look upon, but even cause ourselves to look upon vanities; and in them, we have the right use of *facient se respicere.* And why should we not take some pains, and even enjoin ourselves to look upon this, being neither far off, nor chargeable to come to, and since the looking on it may so many ways so mainly profit us? Verily it falleth out oft, that of Christ's; *violenti rapiunt illud*, nature is not inclined, and where it is not inclined, force must be offered, which we call in schools *actum elicitum.* Which very act by us undertaken for God,

3. With enforcement of themselves. Respicere se facient.

Mat. 11. 12.

and as here at His word, is unto Him a sacrifice right acceptable. Therefore *facias,* or *fac facias;* 'do it willingly, or do it by force.' Do it, I say, for done it must be. Set it before you and look on it; or if list not, remove it, and set it full before you: though it be not with your ease, *respice,* 'look back upon it' with some pain; for one way or other, look upon it we must.

The necessity whereof, that we may the better apprehend it, it will not be amiss we know, that these words are in two
Joh. 19. 37. sundry places two sundry ways applied. 1. Once by St. John in the Gospel, 2. and the second time again by Christ Himself in the Revelation. By St. John to Christ at His first coming, suffering as our Saviour upon the cross. By Christ to Himself at His second coming, sitting as our Judge
Rev. 1. 7. upon His throne, in the end of the world: "Behold He cometh in the clouds, and every eye shall see Him, yea, even they that pierced Him ;" *et plangent se super Eum omnes gentes terræ.* The meaning whereof is, Look upon Him here if you will; enjoin yourselves if you think good, either here or somewhere else; either now or then, look upon Him you shall. And they which put this spectacle far from them here, and cannot endure to "look upon Him Whom they have pierced," *et plangere Eum,* "and be grieved for Him," while it is time; a place and time shall be, when they shall be enforced to look upon Him, whether they will or no, *et plangent se super Eum,* 'and be grieved for themselves,' that they had no grace to do it sooner. Better compose themselves to a little mourning here, with some benefit to be made by their beholding, than to be drawn to it there when it is too late, and when all their looking and grieving will not avail a whit. For there *respicientes respiciet, et despicientes despiciet;* 'His look shall be amiable to them that have respected His piercing here, and dreadful on the other side to them that have neglected it.' And as they that have inured themselves to this looking on here, shall in that day
Lu. 21. 28. "look up and lift up their heads with joy, the day of their redemption being at hand ;" so they that cannot bring themselves to look upon Him here, after they once have looked upon Him there, shall not dare to do it the second time, but
Rev. 6. 16. cry to the mountains, "Fall upon us, and to the hills, Hide

us from the face of Him That sits upon the throne." Therefore, *respicient* is no evil counsel. No, though it be *facient se respicere.*

In a word, if thus causing ourselves to fix our eyes on Him we ask, How long we shall continue so doing, and when we may give over? let this be the answer; *Donec totus fixus in corde, Qui totus fixus in cruce.* Or if that be too much or too hard, yet *saltem,* 'at the least,' *respice in Illum donec Ille te respexerit,* 'Look upon Him till He look upon you again.' For so He will. He did upon Peter, and with His look Lu. 22. 61. melted him into tears. He that once and twice before denied Him and never wept, because Christ looked not on him, then denied and Christ looked on him, and "he went out and wept bitterly." And if to Peter thus He did, and vouchsafed him so gracious a regard, when Peter not once looked toward Him, how much more shall He not deny us like favour, if by looking on Him first we provoke Him in a sort to a second looking on us again, with the Prophet, saying; *Proposui Dominum coram me,* 'I have set Thee, O Ps. 16. 8. Lord, before me;' and again, *Respice in me, &c.* "O look Ps. 119.132. Thou upon me, and be merciful unto me, as Thou usest to do to those that love Thy Name." "That love Thy Name," which is *Jesus,* "a Saviour;" and which love that sight wherein most properly Thy Name appeareth, and wherein Thou chiefly shewest Thyself to be *Jesus* "a Saviour."

And to conclude, if we ask, How we shall know when Christ doth thus respect us? Then truly, when fixing both the eyes of our meditation "upon Him That was pierced,"— as it were one eye upon the grief, the other upon the love wherewith He was pierced, we find by both, or one of these, some motion of grace arise in our hearts; the consideration of His grief piercing our hearts with sorrow, the consideration of His love piercing our hearts with mutual love again. The one is the motion of compunction which they felt, who when they heard such things "were pricked in their hearts." The Acts 2. 37. other, the motion of comfort which they felt, who, when Christ spake to them of the necessity of His piercing, said; "Did we not feel our hearts warm within us?" That, from Lu. 24. 32. the shame and pain He suffered for us; this, from the comforts and benefits He thereby procured for us.

These have been felt at this looking on, and these will be felt. It may be at the first, imperfectly, but after with deeper impression; and that of some, with such as *nemo scit*, 'none knoweth,' but He that hath felt them. Which that we may endeavour to feel, and endeavouring may feel, and so grow into delight of this looking, God, &c.

A SERMON

PREACHED BEFORE THE

KING'S MAJESTY, AT WHITEHALL,

ON THE SIXTH OF APRIL, A.D. MDCIV. BEING GOOD-FRIDAY.

LAMENTATIONS i. 12.

Have ye no regard, O all ye that pass by the way? Consider, and behold, if ever there were sorrow like My sorrow, which was done unto Me, wherewith the Lord did afflict Me in the day of the fierceness of His wrath.

[*O vos omnes, qui transitis per viam, attendite et videte si est dolor sicut dolor Meus: quoniam vindemiavit Me ut locutus est Dominus in die iræ furoris Sui.* Lat. Vulg.]

[*Is it nothing to you, all ye that pass by? Behold, and see if there be any sorrow like unto My sorrow, which is done unto Me, wherewith the Lord hath afflicted Me in the day of His fierce anger.* Engl. Trans.]

AT the very reading or hearing of which verse, there is none but will presently conceive, it is the voice of a party in great extremity. In great extremity two ways: 1. First, in such distress as never was any, "If ever there were sorrow like My sorrow;" 2. And then in that distress, having none to regard Him; "Have ye no regard, all ye?" ^{A complaint.}

To be afflicted, and so afflicted as none ever was, is very much. In that affliction, to find none to respect him or care for him, what can be more? In all our sufferings, it is a comfort to us that we have a *sicut;* that nothing has befallen us, but such as others have felt the like. But here, *si fuerit sicut;* "If ever the like were"—that is, never the like was. ^{1 Cor. 10. 13.}

Again, in our greatest pains it is a kind of ease, even to find some regard. Naturally we desire it, if we cannot be delivered, if we cannot be relieved, yet to be pitied. It ^{Job 19 21.}

SERM. sheweth there be yet some that are touched with the sense
II. of our misery, that wish us well, and would wish us ease if
they could. But this Afflicted here findeth not so much,
neither the one nor the other; but is even as He were an
out-cast both of Heaven and earth. Now verily an heavy
case, and worthy to be put in this book of Lamentations.

Christ's   I demand then, "Of whom speaketh the Prophet this? of
complaint. himself, or of some other?" This I find; there is not any
of the ancient writers but do apply, yea in a manner appro-
priate, this speech to our Saviour Christ. And that this
very day, the day of His Passion, truly termed here the day
of God's wrath, and wheresoever they treat of the Passion,
ever this verse cometh in. And to say the truth, to take
the words strictly as they lie, they cannot agree, or be verified of any but of Him, and Him only. For though some
other, not unfitly, may be allowed to say the same words,
it must be in a qualified sense; for in full and perfect propriety of speech, He and none but He. None can say,
neither Jeremy, nor any other, *si fuerit dolor Meus,* as Christ
can; no day of wrath like to His day, no sorrow to be compared to His, all are short of it, nor His to any, it exceedeth
them all.

And yet, according to the letter, it cannot be denied but
they be set down by Jeremy in the person of his own people,
being then come to great misery; and of the holy city, then
Hos. 11. 1. laid waste and desolate by the Chaldees. What then? *Ex
Ægypto vocavi Filium Meum,* "out of Egypt have I called
Mat. 2. 15. My Son," was literally spoken of this people too, yet is by
Ps. 22. 1. the Evangelist applied to our Saviour Christ. "My God,
my God, why hast Thou forsaken me?" at the first uttered
Mat. 27. 46. by David; yet the same words our Saviour taketh Himself,
and that more truly and properly, than ever David could;
and of those of David's, and of these of Jeremy's, there is
one and the same reason.

Of all which the ground is that correspondence which is
between Christ, and the Patriarchs, Prophets, and people
1Cor.10.11. before Christ, of whom the Apostle's rule is, *omnia in figurâ
contingebant illis;* "that they were themselves types," and
their sufferings forerunning figures of the great suffering
of the Son of God. Which maketh Isaac's offering, and

Joseph's selling, and Israel's calling from Egypt, and that complaint of David's, and this of Jeremy's, appliable to Him; that He may take them to Himself, and the Church ascribe them to Him, and that in more fitness of terms, and more fulness of truth, than they were at the first spoken by David, or Jeremy, or any of them all.

And this rule, and the steps of the Fathers proceeding by this rule, are to me a warrant to expound and apply this verse, as they have done before, to the present occasion of this time; which requireth some such Scripture to be considered by us as doth belong to His Passion, Who this day poured out His most precious Blood, as the only sufficient price of the dear purchase of all our redemptions.

Be it then to us, as to them it was, and as most properly it is, the speech of the Son of God, as this day hanging on the cross, to a sort of careless people, that go up and down without any manner of regard of these His sorrows and sufferings, so worthy of all regard. " Have ye no regard? O all ye that pass by the way, consider and behold, if ever there were sorrow like to my sorrow, which was done unto me, wherewith the Lord afflicted me in the day of the fierceness of His wrath."

Here is a complaint, and here is a request. A complaint The parts. that we have not, a request that we would have the pains and Passions of our Saviour Christ in some regard. For first He complaineth, and not without cause, " Have ye no regard?" And then, as willing to forget their former neglect, so they will yet do it, He falleth to entreat, " O consider and behold!"

And what is that we should consider? The sorrow which He suffereth, and in it two things; the quality, and the cause. 1. The quality, *Si fuerit sicut;* 'if ever the like were;' and that either in respect of *Dolor,* or *Dolor Meus,* 'the sorrow suffered,' or 'the Person suffering.' 2. The cause: that is God That in His wrath, in His fierce wrath, doth all this to Him. Which cause will not leave us, till it have led us to another cause in ourselves, and to another yet in Him; all which serve to ripen us to regard.

These two then specially we are moved to regard. 1. Regard is the main point. But because therefore we regard

but faintly, because either we consider not, or not aright, we
are called to consider seriously of them. As if He should
say, Regard you not? If you did consider, you would; if
you considered as you should, you would regard as you ought.
Certainly the Passion, if it were throughly considered, would
be duly regarded. Consider then.

I.
II.
III.
IV.
So the points are two: 1. The quality, and 2. the cause of
His suffering. And the duties two: 1. To consider, and
regard; 2. So to consider that we regard them, and Him
for them.

The par-
ties to
whom.
" O all ye
that pass
by the way,
consider."
"Have ye no regard," &c.? To ease this complaint, and
to grant this request, we are to regard; and that we may
regard, we are to consider the pains of His Passion. Which,
that we may reckon no easy common matter of light moment,
to do or not to do as we list; first, a general stay is made of
all passengers, this day. For, as it were from His cross, doth
our Saviour address this His speech to them that go to and
fro, the day of His Passion, without so much as entertaining
a thought, or vouchsafing a look that way. *O vos qui transitis!*
" O you that pass by the way," stay and consider. To them
frameth He His speech, that pass by; to them, and to them
all, *O vos omnes, qui transitis,* "O all ye that pass by the
way, stay and consider."

Which very stay of His sheweth it to be some important
matter, in that it is of all. For, as for some to be stayed, and
those the greater some, there may be reason; the most part
of those that go thus to and fro, may well intend it, they
have little else to do. But to except none, not some special
person, is hard. What know we their haste? their occasions
may be such, and so urgent, as they cannot stay. Well, what
haste, what business soever, pass not by, stay though. As
much to say as, Be they never so great, your occasions; they
are not, they cannot be so great as this. How urgent soever,
this is more, and more to be intended. The regard of this is
worthy the staying of a journey. It is worth the considering
of those, that have never so great affairs in hand. So material is this sight in His account. Which serveth to shew the
exigence of this duty. But as for this point, it needeth not
be stood upon to us here at this time; we are not going by,
we need not be stayed, we have stayed all other our affairs

to come hither, and here we are all present before God, to
have it set before us, that we may consider it. Thither then
let us come.

That which we are called to behold and consider, is His Sorrow.
sorrow. And sorrow is a thing which of itself nature in‑
clineth us to behold, " as being ourselves in the body," which Heb. 13. 3.
may be one day in the like sorrowful case. Therefore will
every good eye turn itself, and look upon them that lie in
distress. Those two in the Gospel that passed by the wounded 1. Behold.
man, before they passed by him, though they helped him not Lu. 10. 32.
as the Samaritan did, yet they looked upon him as he lay.
But, this party here lieth not, He is lift up as the serpent in Joh. 3. 14.
the wilderness, that unless we turn our eyes away purposely,
we can neither will nor choose but behold Him.

But because, to behold and not to consider is but to gaze,
and gazing the Angel blameth in the Apostles themselves, we Acts 1. 11.
must do both—both "behold" and "consider;" look upon 2. Con-
with the eye of the body, that is "behold;" and look into sider.
with the eye of the mind, that is "consider." So saith the
Prophet here. And the very same doth the Apostle advise
us to do. First, ἀφορᾶν, to think upon Him, that is, to
"behold," and then ἀναλογίζεσθαι, to think upon Him, Heb. 12. 2.
that is, to "consider" His sorrow. Sorrow sure would be
considered.

Now then, because as the quality of the sorrow is, accord‑ The qua-
ingly it would be considered—for if it be but a common sor‑ lity, if ever
the like.
row the less will serve, but if it be some special, some very
heavy case, the more would be allowed it; for proportionably
with the suffering, the consideration is to arise;—to raise our
consideration to the full, and to elevate it to the highest
point, there is upon His sorrow set a _si fuerit sicut,_ a note of
highest eminency; for _si fuerit sicut,_ are words that have life
in them, and are able to quicken our consideration, if it be
not quite dead; for by them we are provoked, as it were, to
"consider," and considering to see whether ever any _sicut_
may be found to set by it, whether ever any like it.

For if never any, our nature is to regard things exceeding
rare and strange; and such as the like whereof is not else to
be seen. Upon this point then, there is a case made, as if
He should say, 'if ever the like, regard not this;' but if never

SERM. any, be like yourselves in other things, and vouchsafe this, if
II.
—— not your chiefest, yet some regard.

In the
three parts
of His
sorrow.

To enter this comparison, and to shew it for such. That
are we to do, three sundry ways; for three sundry ways,
in three sundry words, are these sufferings of His here expressed, all three within the compass of the verse.

1.　The first is מכאוב, *Mac-ob*, which we read "sorrow," taken
from a wound or stripe, as all do agree.

2.　The second is עולל, *Gholel;* we read "Done to me," taken
from a word that signifieth melting in a furnace, as St. Hierome noteth out of the Chaldee, who so translateth it.

3.　The third is הוגה, *Hoga*, where we read afflicted, from
a word which importeth renting off, or bereaving. The old
Latin turneth it *Vindemiavit me*, as a vine whose fruit is
all plucked off. The Greek, with Theodoret, ἀπεφύλλισέ
με, as a vine or tree whose leaves are all beaten off, and is
left naked and bare[a].

[Not the
LXX. but
an ἀλλ'. of
the Hexap.
which
however
reads ἐπεφ.
as does
Theo-
doret.]

In these three are comprised His sufferings—wounded,
melted, and bereft leaf and fruit, that is, all manner of
comfort.

1. Of the
quality.
First, of
His Pas-
sion.

Of all that is penal, or can be suffered, the common division is, *sensus et damni*, grief for that we feel, or for that
we forego. For that we feel in the two former, wounded in
body, melted in soul; for that we forego in the last, bereft
all, left neither fruit nor so much as a leaf to hang on Him.

1. *Pœna
sensus*, in
the body.

According to these three, to consider His sufferings, and to
begin first with the first. The pains of His body, His wounds
and His stripes.

Our very eye will soon tell us no place was left in His
body, where He might be smitten and was not. His skin
and flesh rent with the whips and scourges, His hands and
feet wounded with the nails, His head with the thorns, His
very heart with the spear-point; all His senses, all His parts
laden with whatsoever wit or malice could invent. His
blessed body given as an anvil to be beaten upon with the
violent hands of those barbarous miscreants, till they brought

Joh. 19. 5.　Him into this case of *si fuerit sicut*. For Pilate's *Ecce Homo!*
his shewing Him with an *Ecce*, as if he should say, Behold,
look if ever you saw the like rueful spectacle; this very

---

a The words *Vindemiavit* and ἀπεφύλλισε (*ἐπεφ.*) apply to *Gholel*, not to *Hoga*.

shewing of his sheweth plainly, He was then come into
woeful plight—so woeful as Pilate verily believed His very
sight so pitiful, as it would have moved the hardest heart of
them all to have relented and said, This is enough, we desire
no more. And this for the wounds of His body, for on this
we stand not.

In this one peradventure some *sicut* may be found, in the
pains of the body; but in the second, the sorrow of the soul,
I am sure, none. And indeed, the pain of the body is but
the body of pain; the very soul of sorrow and pain is the
soul's sorrow and pain. Give me any grief, save the grief of
the mind, saith the Wise Man; for, saith Solomon, "The
spirit of a man will sustain all his other infirmities, but a
wounded spirit, who can bear?" And of this, this of His
soul, I dare make a case, *Si fuerit sicut.*

"He began to be troubled in soul," saith St. John; "to
be in an agony," saith St. Luke; "to be in anguish of mind
and deep distress," saith St. Mark. To have His soul round
about on every side environed with sorrow, and that sorrow
to the death. Here is trouble, anguish, agony, sorrow, and
deadly sorrow; but it must be such, as never the like: so it
was too.

The estimate whereof we may take from the second word
of melting, that is, from His sweat in the garden; strange,
and the like whereof was never heard or seen.

No manner violence offered Him in body, no man touching Him or being near Him; in a cold night, for they were
fain to have a fire within doors, lying abroad in the air and
upon the cold earth, to be all of a sweat, and that sweat to
be blood; and not as they call it *diaphoreticus*, 'a thin faint
sweat,' but *grumosus*, 'of great drops;' and those so many, so
plenteous, as they went through His apparel and all; and
through all streamed to the ground, and that in great
abundance;—read, enquire, and consider, *si fuerit sudor sicut
sudor iste*; 'if ever there were sweat like this sweat of His.'
Never the like sweat certainly, and therefore never the like
sorrow. Our translation is, "Done unto Me;" but we said
the word properly signifieth, and so St. Hierome and the
Chaldee paraphrast read it, "melted Me." And truly it should
seem by this fearful sweat of His He was near some furnace,

Side notes:
2. *Pœna
sensus*, in
the soul.

Pro. 18, 14.

Joh. 12. 27.
Lu. 22. 44.
Mark 14. 33.
Mat. 26. 38.

Lu. 22. 44.

L

the feeling whereof was able to cast Him into that sweat, and
to turn His sweat into drops of blood.   And sure it was so ;
for see, even in the very next words of all to this verse, He
Lam. 1. 13. complaineth of it; *Ignem misit in ossibus meis,* "that a fire
was sent into His bones" which melted Him, and made that
bloody sweat to distil from Him.   That hour, what His
feelings were, it is dangerous to define; we know them not,
we may be too bold to determine of them.   To very good
purpose it was, that the ancient Fathers of the Greek Church
in their Liturgy, after they have recounted all the particular
pains, as they are set down in His Passion, and by all and by
every one of them called for mercy, do after all shut up all
with this, Δι' ἀγνωστῶν κόπων καὶ βασάνων ἐλέησον καὶ
σῶσον ἡμᾶς, ʻBy Thine unknown sorrows and sufferings,
felt by Thee, but not distinctly known by us, Have mercy
upon us, and save us !'

Now, though this suffice not, nothing near, yet let it suffice,
the time being short, for His pains of body and soul.   For
those of the body, it may be some may have endured the
like ; but the sorrows of His soul are unknown sorrows, and
for them none ever have, ever have or ever shall suffer the
like, the like, or near the like in any degree.

3.
*Pœna
damni,*
And now to the third.   It was said before, to be in distress,
such distress as this was, and to find none to comfort, nay not
so much as to regard Him, is all that can be said to make
His sorrow a *non sicut.*   Comfort is it by which, in the midst
of all our sorrows, we are *confortati,* that is strengthened and
made the better able to bear them all out.   And who is there,
even the poorest creature among us, but in some degree
findeth some comfort, or some regard at some body's hands ?
For if that be not left, the state of that party is here in the
third word said to be like the tree, whose leaves and whose
fruit are all beaten off quite, and itself left bare and naked
both of the one and of the other.

1.
Leaves.
And such was our Saviour's case in these His sorrows this
day, and that so as what is left the meanest of the sons of
men, was not left Him, not a leaf.   Not a leaf!   Leaves I
may well call all human comforts and regards, whereof He
[Joh. 1.11.] was then left clean desolate.   1. "His own," they among
whom He had gone about all His life long, healing them,

teaching them, feeding them, doing them all the good He could, it is they that cry, "Not Him, no, but Barabbas rather;" "away with Him," "His blood be upon us and our children." It is they that in the midst of His sorrows shake their head at Him, and cry, "Ah, thou wretch;" they that in His most disconsolate estate cry Eli, Eli, in most barbarous manner, deride Him and say, "Stay and you shall see Elias come presently and take Him down." And this was their regard.

But these were but withered leaves. They then that on earth were nearest Him of all, the greenest leaves and likest to hang on, and to give Him some shade; even of them some bought and sold Him, others denied and forswore Him, but all fell away, and forsook Him. Ἀπεφύλλισέ με, saith Theodoret, not a leaf left.

But leaves are but leaves, and so are all earthly stays. The fruit then, the true fruit of the Vine indeed, the true comfort in all heaviness, is *desuper,* 'from above,' is divine consolation. But *Vindemiavit Me,* saith the Latin text;—even that was in this His sorrow, this day bereft Him too. And that was His most sorrowful complaint of all others; not that His friends upon earth, but that His Father from Heaven had forsaken Him; that neither Heaven nor earth yielded Him any regard, but that between the passioned powers of His soul, and whatsoever might any ways refresh Him, there was a traverse drawn, and He left in the state of a weather-beaten tree, all desolate and forlorn. Evident, too evident, by that His most dreadful cry, which at once moved all the powers in Heaven and earth, "My God, My God, why hast Thou forsaken Me?" Weigh well that cry, consider it well, and tell me, *si fuerit clamor sicut clamor iste,* 'if ever there were cry like that of His:' never the like cry, and therefore never the like sorrow.

It is strange, very strange, that of none of the martyrs the like can be read, who yet endured most exquisite pains in their martyrdoms; yet we see with what courage, with what cheerfulness, how even singing, they are reported to have passed through their torments. Will ye know the reason? St. Augustine setteth it down: *martyres non eripuit, sed nunquid deseruit?* 'He delivered not His martyrs, but did He

Margin notes:
1. Withered leaves.
Joh. 18. 40.
Joh. 19. 15.
Mat. 27.25.
Mar. 15.
29. 36.

2. Green leaves.

Fruit.

Mat. 27. 46.

forsake them?' He delivered not their bodies, but He forsook not their souls, but distilled into them the dew of His heavenly comfort, an abundant supply for all they could endure. Not so here. *Vindemiavit Me*, saith the Prophet; *Dereliquisti Me*, saith He Himself;—no comfort, no supply at all.

[Vid. S. Leon. de Pass. Dom. Serm. 17.] Leo it is that first said it, and all antiquity allow of it, *Non solvit unionem, sed subtraxit visionem.* 'The union was not dissolved: true, but the beams, the influence was restrained,' and for any comfort from thence, His soul was even as a scorched heath-ground, without so much as any drop of dew of divine comfort; as a naked tree—no fruit to refresh Him within, no leaf to give Him shadow without; the power of darkness, let loose to afflict Him, the influence of comfort restrained to relieve Him. It is a *non sicut* this, it cannot be expressed as it should, and as other things may; in silence we may admire it, but all our words will not reach it. And though to draw it so far as some do, is little better than blasphemy, yet on the other side to shrink it so short as other some do, cannot be but with derogation to His love; Who, to kindle our love and loving regard, would come to a *non sicut* in His suffering; for so it was, and so we must allow it to be. This, in respect of His passion, *Dolor*.

Secondly, Of the quality of His Person. Now in respect of His Person, *Dolor Meus.* Whereof, if it please you to take a view even of the person thus wounded, thus afflicted and forsaken, you shall then have a perfect *non sicut*. And indeed the Person is here a weighty circumstance, it is thrice repeated—*Meus, Mihi, Me*, and we may not leave it out. For as is the Person, so is the passion; and any one, even the very least degree of wrong or disgrace, offered to a person of excellency, is more than a hundred times more to one of mean condition; so weighty is the circumstance of the person. Consider then how great the Person was; and I rest fully assured here we boldly challenge and say, *si fuerit sicut.*

1. Joh. 19. 5. *Ecce Homo!* saith Pilate first: a Man He is as we are, and were He but a Man, nay, were He not a Man, but some poor dumb creature, it were great ruth to see Him so handled as He was.

2. Mat. 27. 19. "A Man," saith Pilate, and a "just Man," saith Pilate's wife. "Have thou nothing to do with that just Man." And

that is, one degree farther. For though we pity the punishment even of malefactors themselves, yet ever most compassion we have of them that suffer and be innocent. And He Lu. 23. 14. was innocent; Pilate and Herod, and "the prince of this Joh. 14. 30. world," His very enemies, being His judges.

Now among the innocent, the more noble the person, the 8. more heavy the spectacle. And never do our bowels yearn so much as over such. "Alas, alas for that noble Prince," Jer. 22. 18. saith this Prophet;—the style of mourning for the death of a great personage. And He that suffered here is such, even a principal Person among the sons of men, of the race royal, descended from Kings. Pilate styled Him so in his title, Joh. 19. 22. and he would not alter it.

Three degrees. But yet we are not at our true *quantus.* 4. For He is yet more, more than the highest of the sons of men, for He is the Son of the Most High God. Pilate saw no farther but *Ecce Homo!* the centurion did, *vere Filius Dei* Joh. 19. 5. *erat Hic,* "now truly This was the Son of God." And here Mar. 15. 39. all words forsake us, and every tongue becometh speechless.

We have no way to express it but *a minore ad majus;*— thus. Of this book, the book of Lamentations, one special occasion was the death of King Josias; but behold a greater than Josias is here.

Of King Josias, as a special reason of mourning, the Prophet saith, *Spiritus oris nostri, christus Domini,* "the very Lam. 4. 20. breath of our nostrils, the Lord's anointed," for so are all good Kings in their subjects' accounts, he is gone. But behold, here is not *christus Domini,* but *Christus Dominus,* "the Lord's christ," but the "Lord Christ Himself;" and [Lu. 2. 11.] that not coming to an honourable death in battle as Josias did, but to a most vile reproachful death, the death of malefactors in the highest degree. And not slain outright as Josias was, but mangled and massacred in most pitiful strange manner; wounded in Body, wounded in Spirit, left utterly desolate. O consider this well, and confess the case is truly put, *si fuerit Dolor sicut Dolor Meus!* Never, never the like person; and if as the person is, the passion be, never the like Passion to His.

It is truly affirmed, that any one, even the least drop of blood, even the least pain, yea of the body only, of this so

great a person, any *Dolor* with this *Meus*, had been enough
to make a *non sicut* of it. That is enough, but that is not
all; for add now the three other degrees; add to this Person
those wounds, that sweat and that cry, and put all together,
and I make no manner question the like was not, shall not,
cannot ever be. It is far above all that ever was or can be,
abyssus est. Men may drowsily hear it and coldly affect it,
but principalities and powers stand abashed at it. And for
the quality both of the Passion and of the Person, that never
the like, thus much.

1.
Of the
cause.
　　Now to proceed to the cause and to consider it, for without it we shall have but half a regard, and scarce that.
Indeed, set the cause aside, and the passion, as rare as it is,
is yet but a dull and heavy sight, we list not much look
upon spectacles of that kind, though never so strange, they
fill us full of pensive thoughts and make us melancholic.
1. And so doth this, till upon examination of the cause we find
it toucheth us near; and so near, so many ways, as we
cannot choose but have some regard of it.

1.
God.

Lu. 22. 53.
　　What was done to him we see. Let there now be a quest
of enquiry to find who was doer of it. Who? who but the
"power of darkness," wicked Pilate, bloody Caiaphas, the
envious Priests, the barbarous soldiers? None of these are
returned here. We are too low by a great deal, if we think
to find it among men. *Quæ fecit Mihi Deus,* 'it was God
That did it.' An hour of that day was the hour of the
"power of darkness;" but the whole day itself, is said here
plainly, was the day of the wrath of God. God was a doer
in it; "wherewith God hath afflicted Me."

God's
wrath.
　　God afflicteth some in mercy, and others in wrath. This
was in His wrath. In His wrath God is not alike to all;
some He afflicteth in His more gentle and mild, others in
His fierce wrath. This was in the very fierceness of His
wrath. His sufferings, His sweat, and cry, shew as much;
they could not come but from a wrath *si fuerit sicut,* for we
are not past *non sicut,* no not here,—in this part it followeth
us still, and will not leave us in any point, not to the end.

2.
Sin.
　　The cause then in God was wrath. What caused this
wrath? God is not wroth but with sin, nor grievously wroth
but with grievous sin. And in Christ there was no grievous

sin; nay, no sin at all. God did it, the text is plain. And Not His:
in His fierce wrath He did it. For what cause? For, God
forbid, God should do as did Annas the high-priest, cause Joh. 18. 22.
Him to be smitten without cause! God forbid, saith Abra- Gen. 18. 25.
ham, "the Judge of the world should do wrong" to any!
To any, but specially to His own Son, that His Son, of
Whom with thundering voice from Heaven He testifieth, all
His joy and delight were in Him, "in Him only He was [Mat. 3. 17.]
well-pleased." And how then could His wrath wax hot to
do all this unto Him?

There is no way to preserve God's justice, and Christ's
innocency both, but to say as the Angel said of Him to
the Prophet Daniel, "The Messias shall be slain," וְאֵין לוֹ Dan. 9. 26.
ve-en-lo, "shall be slain but not for Himself." "Not for But other
Himself?" For whom then? For some others. He took men's.
upon Him the person of others, and so doing, justice may
have her course and proceed.

Pity it is to see a man pay that he never took; but if he
will become a surety, if he will take on him the person of
the debtor, so he must. Pity to see a silly poor lamb lie
bleeding to death; but if it must be a sacrifice, such is the
nature of a sacrifice, so it must. And so Christ, though
without sin in Himself, yet as a surety, as a sacrifice, may
justly suffer for others, if He will take upon Him their
persons; and so God may justly give way to His wrath
against Him.

And who be those others? The Prophet Esay telleth Ours.
us, and telleth it us seven times over for failing, "He took Isa. 53. 4-6.
upon Him our infirmities, and bare our maladies. He was
wounded for our iniquities, and broken for our transgressions:
the chastisement of our peace was upon Him, and with His
stripes were we healed. All we as sheep were gone astray,
and turned every man to his own way; and the Lord hath
laid upon Him the iniquity of us all." "All," "all," even
those that pass to and fro, and for all this regard neither
Him nor His passion.

The short is, it was we that for our sins, our many great
and grievous sins,—*Si fuerit sicut*, the like whereof never
were,—should have sweated this sweat and have cried this
cry; should have been smitten with these sorrows by the

fierce wrath of God, had not He stepped between the blow and us, and latched it in His own body and soul, even the dint of the fierceness of the wrath of God. O the *non sicut* of our sins, that could not otherwise be answered!

To return then a true verdict. It is we—we, wretched sinners that we are—that are to be found the principals in this act, and those on whom we seek to shift it, to drive it from ourselves, Pilate and Caiaphas and the rest, but instrumental causes only. And it is not the executioner that killeth the man properly, that is, they; no, nor the judge, which is God in this case; only sin, *solum peccatum homicida est,* 'sin only is the murderer,' to say the truth, and our sins the murderers of the Son of God; and the *non sicut* of them the true cause of the *non sicut* both of God's wrath, and of His sorrowful sufferings.

Which bringeth home this our text to us, even into our own bosoms, and applieth it most effectually to me that speak and to you that hear, to every one of us, and that with the Prophet Nathan's application; *Tu es homo,* "Thou art the
2 Sam.12.7. man," even thou, for whom God in "His fierce wrath" thus afflicted Him. Sin then was the cause on our part why we, or some other for us.

3.
Love of us.   But yet what was the cause, why He on His part? what was that that moved Him thus to become our surety, and to take upon Him our debt and danger? that moved Him thus
Isa. 53. 7. to lay upon His soul a sacrifice for our sin? Sure, *oblatus*
[See the
Vulgate.] *est quia voluit,* saith Esay again, "Offered He was for no other cause, but because He would." For unless He would, He needed not. Needed not for any necessity of justice, for no lamb was ever more innocent; nor for any necessity of constraint, for twelve legions of Angels were ready at His command, but because He would.

And why would He? No reason can be given but because He regarded us:—Mark that reason. And what were we? Verily, utterly unworthy even His least regard, not worth the
Rom. 5. 8. taking up, not worth the looking after. *Cum inimici essemus,* saith the Apostle; "we were His enemies," when He did it, without all desert before, and without all regard after He had done and suffered all this for us; and yet He would regard us that so little regard Him. For when He saw us

a sort of forlorn sinners, *non prius natos quam damnatos,* 'damned as fast as born,' as being "by nature children of Eph. 2. 3. wrath," and yet still "heaping up wrath against the day of Rom. 2. 5. wrath," by the errors of our life, till the time of our passing hence; and then the "fierce wrath of God" ready to overwhelm us, and to make us endure the terror and torments of a never dying death, another *non sicut* yet: when, I say, He was in this case, He was moved with compassion over us and undertook all this for us. Even then in His love He regarded us, and so regarded us that He regarded not Himself, to regard us.

Bernard saith most truly, *Dilexisti me Domine magis quam Te, quando mori voluisti pro me:* 'In suffering all this for us Thou shewedst, Lord, that we were more dear to Thee, that Thou regardest us more than Thine ownself;' and shall this regard find no regard at our hands?

It was sin then, and the heinousness of sin in us, that provoked wrath and the fierceness of His wrath in God; it was love, and the greatness of His love in Christ, that caused Him to suffer the sorrows, and the grievousness of these sorrows, and all for our sakes.

And indeed, but only to testify the *non sicut* of this His love, all this needed not that was done to Him. One, any one, even the very least of all the pains He endured, had been enough; enough in respect of the *Meus,* enough in respect of the *non sicut* of His person. For that which setteth the high price on this sacrifice, is this; that He which offereth it unto God, is God. But if little had been suffered, little would the love have been thought that suffered so little, and as little regard would have been had of it. To awake our regard then, or to leave us excuseless, if we continue regardless, all this He bare for us; that He might as truly make a case of *Si fuerit amor sicut amor Meus,* as He did before of *Si fuerit dolor sicut dolor Meus.* We say we will regard love; if we will, here it is to regard.

So have we the causes, all three: 1. Wrath in God; 2. Sin in ourselves; 3. Love in Him.

Yet have we not all we should. For what of all this? Our benefit What good? *Cui bono?* That, that, is it indeed that we will by it: Pertains it not regard if any thing, as being matter of benefit, the only thing to us?

SERM. in a manner the world regardeth, which bringeth us about to
II. the very first words again. For the very first words which
we read, "Have ye no regard?" are in the original, לוא אליכם
lo alechem, which the Seventy turn, word for word, οὐ πρὸς
ὑμᾶς; and the Latin likewise, *nonne ad vos pertinet?* Pertains
it not to you, that you regard it no better? For these two,
pertaining and regarding, are folded one in another, and go
together so commonly as one is taken often for the other.
Then to be sure to bring us to regard, he urgeth this: "Pertains not all this to you?" Is it not for your good? Is not
the benefit yours? Matters of benefit, they pertain to you,
and without them love and all the rest may pertain to whom
they will.

Consider then the inestimable benefit that groweth unto
you from this incomparable love. It is not impertinent this,
even this, that to us hereby all is turned about clean contrary; that "by His stripes we are healed," by His sweat we
refreshed, by His forsaking we received to grace. That this
day, to Him the day of the fierceness of God's wrath, is to
us the day of the fulness of God's favour, as the Apostle
2 Cor. 6. 2. calleth it, "a day of salvation." In respect of that He suffered,
I deny not, an evil day, a day of heaviness; but in respect
of that which He by it hath obtained for us, it is as we truly
call it a good day, a day of joy and jubilee. For it doth not
only rid us of that wrath which pertaineth to us for our sins;
but farther, it maketh that pertain to us whereto we had no
manner of right at all.

For not only by His death as by the death of our sacrifice,
by the blood of His cross as by the blood of the paschal
Ex. 12. 13. lamb, the destroyer passeth over us, and we shall not perish;
Nu. 35. 25. but also by His death, as by the death of our High Priest—
for He is Priest and Sacrifice both—we are restored from
our exile, even to our former forfeited estate in the land of
Rom. 5. 15. Promise. Or rather, as the Apostle saith, *non sicut delictum
sic donum;* not to the same estate, but to one nothing like
it, that is, one far better than the estate our sins bereft us.
For they deprived us of Paradise, a place on earth; but by
the purchase of His blood we are entitled to a far higher,
even the Kingdom of Heaven; and His blood, not only the
Mat. 26. 28. blood of "remission," to acquit us of our sins, but "the blood

of the Testament too," to bequeath us and give us estate in that Heavenly inheritance.

Now whatsoever else, this I am sure is a *non sicut*, as that which the eye by all it can see, the ear by all it can hear, the heart by all it can conceive, cannot pattern it, or set the like by it. "Pertains not this unto us" neither? Is not this worth the regard? Sure if any thing be worthy the regard, this is most worthy of our very worthiest and best regard.

Thus have we considered and seen, not so much as in this sight we might or should, but as much as the time will give us leave. And now lay all these before you, every one of them a *non sicut* of itself; the pains of His body esteemed by Pilate's *Ecce*; the sorrows of His soul, by His sweat in the garden; the comfortless estate of His sorrows, by His cry on the cross; and with these, His Person, as being the Son of the Great and Eternal God. Then join to these the cause: in God, "His fierce wrath;" in us, our heinous sins deserving it; in Him, His exceeding great love, both suffering that for us which we had deserved, and procuring for us that we could never deserve; making that to appertain to Himself which of right pertained to us, and making that pertain to us which pertained to Him only, and not to us at all but by His means alone. And after their view in several, lay them all together, so many *non sicuts* into one, and tell me if His complaint be not just and His request most reasonable. The recapitulation of all.

Yes sure, His complaint is just, "Have ye no regard?" None? and yet never the like? None? and it pertains unto you? "No regard?" As if it were some common ordinary matter, and the like never was? "No regard?" As if it concerned you not a whit, and it toucheth you so near? As if He should say, Rare things you regard, yea, though they no ways pertain to you: this is exceeding rare, and will you not regard it? Again things that nearly touch you you regard, though they be not rare at all: this toucheth you exceeding near, even as near as your soul toucheth you, and will you not yet regard it? Will neither of these by itself move you? Will not both these together move you? What will move you? Will pity? Here is distress never the like. Will duty? Here is a Person never the like. Will fear? Here is wrath never the like. Will remorse? Here are sins The complaint. The matter just.

SERM.
II.
never the like. Will kindness? Here is love never the like. Will bounty? Here are benefits never the like. Will all these? Here they be all, all above any *sicut*, all in the highest degree.

The manner earnest.
Truly the complaint is just, it may move us; it wanteth no reason, it may move; and it wanteth no affection in the delivery of it to us, on His part to move us. Sure it moved Him exceeding much; for among all the deadly sorrows of His most bitter passion, this, even this, seemeth to be His greatest of all, and that which did most affect Him, even the grief of the slender reckoning most men have it in; as little respecting Him, as if he had done or suffered nothing at all for them. For lo, of all the sharp pains He endureth He complaineth not, but of this He complaineth, of no regard; that which grieveth Him most, that which most He moaneth is this. It is strange He should be in pains, such pains as never any was, and not complain Himself of them, but of want of regard only. Strange He should not make request, O deliver Me, or relieve Me! But only, O consider and regard Me! In effect as if He said, None, no deliverance, no relief do I seek; regard I seek. And all that I suffer, I am content with it, I regard it not, I suffer most willingly, if this I may find at your hands, regard.

The regard of the creatures of it.
Truly, this so passionate a complaint may move us, it moved all but us; for most strange of all it is, that all the creatures in Heaven and earth seemed to hear this His mournful complaint, and in their kind to shew their regard of it. The sun in Heaven shrinking in his light, the earth trembling under it, the very stones cleaving in sunder, as if they had sense and sympathy of it, and sinful men only not moved with it. And yet it was not for the creatures this was done to Him, to them it pertaineth not; but for us it was, and to us it doth. And shall we not yet regard it? shall the creature, and not we? shall we not?

The benefit —It.
If we do not, it may appertain to us, but we pertain not to it; it pertains to all but all pertain not to it. None pertain to it but they that take benefit by it; and none take benefit by it no more than by the brazen serpent, but they that fix their eye on it. Behold, consider, and regard it; the profit, the benefit is lost without regard.

If we do not, as this was a day of God's fierce " wrath" The peril, If not.
against Him, only for regarding us; so there is another day
coming, and it will quickly be here, a day of like " fierce Ps. 90. 11.
wrath" against us, for not regarding Him. " And who
regardeth the power of His wrath?" He that doth, will
surely regard this.

In that day, there is not the most careless of us all but
shall cry as they did in the Gospel, *Domine, non ad Te per-* Mark 4.38.
tinet, si perimus? " Pertains it not to Thee, carest Thou not
that we perish?" Then would we be glad to pertain to Him
and His Passion. Pertains it to us then, and pertains it not
now? Sure now it must, if then it shall.

Then to give end to this complaint, let us grant Him His The re-
request, and regard His Passion. Let the rareness of it, the quest,—
Have some
nearness to us, let pity or duty, fear or remorse, love or regard.
bounty; any of them or all of them; let the justness of His
complaint, let His affectionate manner of complaining of this
and only of this, let the shame of the creatures' regard, let
our profit or our peril, let something prevail with us to have
it in some regard.

Some regard! Verily as His sufferings, His love, our good 1.
by them are, so should our regard be a *non sicut* too; that is, Our best
regard.
a regard of these, and of nothing in comparison of these. It
should be so, for with the benefit ever the regard should arise.

But God help us poor sinners, and be merciful unto us!
Our regard is a *non sicut* indeed, but it is backward, and in a
contrary sense; that is, no where so shallow, so short, or so
soon done. It should be otherwise, it should have our deepest consideration this, and our highest regard.

But if that cannot be had, our nature is so heavy, and 2.
flesh and blood so dull of apprehension in spiritual things, At least
some
yet at leastwise some regard. Some I say; the more the regard.
better; but in any wise some, and not as here no regard,
none at all. Some ways to shew we make account of it, to
withdraw ourselves, to void our minds of other matters, to
set this before us, to think upon it, to thank Him for it,
to regard Him, and stay and see whether He will regard us
or no. Sure He will, and we shall feel our " hearts pricked" Acts 2. 37.
with sorrow, by consideration of the cause in us—our sin;
and again, " warm within us," by consideration of the cause Lu. 24. 32.

in Him—His love; till by some motion of grace He answer us, and shew that our regard is accepted of Him.

And this, as at all other times, for no day is amiss but at all times some time to be taken for this duty, so specially on this day; this day, which we hold holy to the memory of His Passion, this day to do it; to make this day, the day of God's wrath and Christ's suffering, a day to us of serious consideration and regard of them both.

It is kindly to consider *opus diei in die suo,* 'the work of the day in the day it was wrought;' and this day it was wrought. This day therefore, whatsoever business be, to lay them aside a little; whatsoever our haste, yet to stay a little, and to spend a few thoughts in calling to mind and taking to regard what this day the Son of God did and suffered for us; and all for this end, that what He was then we might not be, and what He is now we might be for ever.

Which Almighty God grant we may do, more or less, even every one of us, according to the several measures of His grace in us!

A SERMON

KING'S MAJESTY, AT GREENWICH,

HEBREWS xii. 2.

Looking unto Jesus the Author and Finisher of our faith ; Who for the joy that was set before Him, endured the cross, and despised the shame; and is set at the right-hand of the throne of God.

Aspicientes in Authorem fidei, et Consummatorem Jesum ; Qui proposito Sibi gaudio, sustinuit crucem, confusione contempta ; atque in dexterâ sedis Dei sedet.

[*Looking unto Jesus the Author and Finisher of our faith ; Who, for the Joy that was set before Him, endured the cross, despising the shame, and is set down at the right hand of the throne of God.* Engl. Trans.]

ST. LUKE, though he recount at large our Saviour Christ's whole story, yet in plain and express terms he calleth the Passion θεωρίαν, "a theory or sight," which sight is it the Lu. 23. 48. Apostle here calleth us to look unto.

Of our blessed Saviour's whole life or death, there is no part but is "a theory" of itself, well worthy our looking on; for from each part thereof there goeth virtue to do us good. From each part; but of all, from the last part, or act of His Passion. Therefore hath the Holy Ghost honoured this last part only with this name, and none but this. This is the "theory" ever most commended to our view. To be looked on He is at all times, and in all acts; but then, and in that act, specially "when for the joy set before Him, He endured the cross, and despised the shame." Then, saith the Apostle, "look unto Him." St. Paul being elsewhere careful to shew the Corinthians, and with them us, Christ; and as to shew them Christ, so to shew them in Christ what that is that specially concerneth them to know or look unto, thus he saith: that though he knew many, very many things besides, yet he "esteemed not to know any thing but Jesus Christ," 1 Cor. 2. 2. *et Hunc crucifixum,* Him, "and Him crucified." Meaning *respective,* as they term it, that the perfection of our knowledge is Christ; and the perfection of our knowledge in or touching Christ, is the knowledge of His Cross and Passion. That the chief "theory." Nay, in this all; so that see this and see all.

The view whereof, though it be not restrained to any one time, but all the year long, yea all our life long, ought to be frequent with us;—and blessed are the hours that are so spent! yet if at any one time more than other, certainly this time, this day may most justly challenge it. For this day was this Scripture fulfilled, and this day are our ears filled full with Scriptures about it. So that though on other days we employ our eyes otherwise, yet that this day at least we would, as exceeding fitly the Apostle wisheth us, ἀφορᾷν, "cast our eyes from other sights," and fix them on this object, it being the day dedicate to the lifting up of the Son Joh. 12. 32. of Man on high, that He may draw every eye unto Him.

The occasion of the speaking is ever the best key to every speech. The occasion then of this speech was this. The Apostle was to encourage the Hebrews, and in them us all, to hold on the well-begun profession of Christ and His faith. This our profession he expresseth in the former verse in the terms of a race or game, borrowing his similitude from the games of Olympus. For from those games, famous then over all the world, and by terms from them taken, it was common to all writers of that age, both holy and human, to set forth, as in the running the laborious course, so in the prize of it, the glorious reward of a virtuous life.

Which race, truly Olympic, because they and we, the most of us, either stand still, or if we remove do it but slowly, and are ready to faint upon every occasion ; that we may run the sooner, and attain the better, two sights he sets before us to comfort us and keep us from fainting. One, a cloud of witnesses, in the first verse, that is the Saints in Heaven— witnesses as able to depose this race may be run, and this prize may be won, for they have run the one, and won the other long ago. These look on us now, how well we carry ourselves; and we to look to them, that we may carry ourselves well in the course we have undertaken.

On which cloud when we have stayed our eyes a while, and made them fit for a clearer object, he scattereth the cloud quite, and sets us up a second, even our blessed Saviour His ownself. And here he willeth us, ἀφορᾶν, "to turn our eyes from them," and to turn them hither, and to fasten them here on Jesus Christ, "the Author and Finisher of our Faith." As if he should say; If you will indeed see a sight once for all, look to Him. The Saints, though they be the guides to us, yet are they but followers to Him. He the Ἀρχηγὸς, "the Arch-guide," the Leader of them and us all [Heb.12.2.] —Look on Him. They but well willers to our faith, but neither authors nor finishers of it; He both. Both Author to call us to it, and set us in it; and Finisher to help us through it, and reward us for it:—Look to Him. *Hunc aspicite* is the Apostle's voice, the voice that cometh out of this cloud, for it is the wish of them all, even all the Saints; —*Hunc aspicite.* At His appearing therefore the cloud vanisheth. There is a time when St. James may say, "Take, my Jas. 5. 10. brethren, the Prophets for an example." But when He cometh forth That said, *Exemplum dedi vobis,* "I have given you Joh. 13.15. an example," *exemplum sine exemplo,* 'an example above all examples;' when He cometh in place, *Sileat omnis caro,* Zech. 2. 13. "Let all flesh keep silence." Let all the Saints, yea, the Isa. 6. 2. Seraphims themselves cover their faces with their wings, that we may look on Him, and let all other sights go.

Let us then turn aside to see this great sight. The prin- The division. cipal parts thereof are two: 1. The sight itself, that is, the I. thing to be seen; 2. and the sight of it, that is, the act of seeing it or looking on it.

The whole verse, save the two first words, is of the object or spectacle propounded. "Jesus the Author, &c." The two first words, ἀφορῶντες εἰς, is the other, the act or duty enjoined.

But as in many other cases, so here, *Et erunt primi novis-* [Mat. 19. *simi,* "the first must be last." For though the act, in the 30.] verse, stand foremost, yet in nature it is last, and so to be

M

handled. We must have a thing first set up before our
eyes, before we can set our eyes upon it.

Of the object then first: this object is Jesus, not barely,
but with His double addition of 1. "the Author," 2. "the
Finisher of our faith, Jesus." And in Him more particularly,
two theories or sights: 1. Of His Passion; 2. Of His Session.
1. His Passion, in these words: "Who for the joy," &c.
2. His Session, in these: "And is set," &c.

In the Passion, two things He pointeth at: 1. What He
suffered, 2. and what moved Him to it. 1. What He
suffered: the cross and shame. The cross He endured, the
shame He despised. 2. And what moved Him; "for a
certain joy set before Him."

II.   Then is to follow the act or duty of looking on this sight,
ἀφορῶντες εἰς. 1. Wherein first the two prepositions, 1.
'Ἀπὸ and 2. Εἰς, "from" and "to:" to look "from," and to
look "to." 2. Then the two verbs: 1. One in the verse
expressed, that is, ὁρᾶν in ἀφορῶντες. 2. The other of necessity implied, for we have never a verb in all the verse.
'Ἀφορῶντες is a participle, and but suspendeth the sentence,
till we either look back to the verb before; and so it is 1.
Ut curramus: or to the verse next after, and so it is 2. *Ne
fatigemur.* In the one is the theory or sight we shall see,
thus looking. In the other the *praxis* of this theory, what
this sight is to work in us; and that is a motion, a swift
motion, running. So to look on it that we run, and so to
run that we faint not.

And if the time will give leave, if our allowance will hold
out, then we will take a short view of the session; that He "is
set down." Wherein is 1. rest and ease opposed to His cross,
where He hung in pain. 2. And in "a throne;" wherein is
glory opposed to shame. 3. And "at the right hand of God,"
wherein is the fulness of both the joy wherein He sitteth, and
the joy which was set before Him, and which is set before us.

I.
The ob-
ject.
"The Au-
thor and
Finisher of
our faith,
Jesus."
To give the better aspect to the party Whom he presenteth to our view, that with better will we may behold
Him, before he name His Name he giveth Him this double
addition, as it were displaying an ensign, proclaiming His
style before Him; whereof these two are the two colours,
1. "The Author," 2. "The Finisher of our faith, Jesus."

"Author and Finisher" are two titles, wherein the Holy
Ghost oft setteth Him forth, and wherein He seemeth to
take special delight. In the very letters, He taketh to Him
the name of "Alpha" the Author, and again of "Omega" Rev. 1. 8.
the Finisher of the alphabet. From letters go to words: _{Rev. 21. 6.}
there is He *Verbum in principio,* "the Word at the begin- Rev. 22. 13.
ning." And He is "Amen" too, the word at the end. From _{Rev. 3. 14.}
words to books. *In capite libri scriptum est de Me,* in the Ps. 40. 7.
very "front of the book" He is; and He is Ἀνακεφαλαίωσις, Eph. 1. 10.
"the Recapitulation," or conclusion of it too. And so, go
to persons: there He is *Primus* and *novissimus,* "the first Rev. 1. 17.
and the last." And from persons to things; and there He
is, "the beginning and the end;" whereof ἀρχὴ, "the be- Rev. 1. 8.
ginning," is in Ἀρχηγὸς, the Author; and τέλος, "the end,"
is in Τελειωτὴς, the Finisher. The first beginning *a Quo,*
He "by Whom all things are made;" and the last end He, Col. 1. 16.
per or *propter Quem,* "by, for, or through Whom" all things
are made perfect.

Both these He is, in all things. And as in all things else,
so in faith, whereto they are here applied most fully and fitly
of all other. Therefore look not aside at any in Heaven or
earth for matter of faith, look full upon Him. He is worth
the looking on with both your eyes, He hath matter for
them both.

The honour that Zerubbabel had in the material, is no
less truly His in the spiritual temple of our faith. *Manus* Zech. 4. 9.
Ejus, "His hands" have laid the corner-stone of our belief,
and His hands shall bring forth the head-stone also, giving [1Pet. 1. 9.]
us "the end of our faith, which is the salvation of our souls."

Of our faith, and of the whole race of it He is the Author,
casting up His glove at the first setting forth. He is the
Finisher, holding out the prize at the goal end. By His
authority it is our course is begun; we run not without
warrant. By His bounty it shall be finished and crowned
in the end; we run not in vain, or without hope of reward.

But what is this title to the point in hand? So, as nothing can be more. "Author and Finisher," they are the
two points that move us to look to Him. And the very
same are the two points wherein we are moved to be like
to Him.

SERM.
III.

To fix our eye, to keep it from straying, to make us look on Him full, he telleth us He is both these. In effect as if he said, Scatter not your sight, look not two ways, as if He I shew you were to begin, and some other make an end. He I shew you doth both.

His main end being to exhort them, as they had begun well, so well to persevere; to very good purpose, He willeth them to have an eye to Him and His example, Who first and last ἀπὸ φάτνης ἄχρι σταυροῦ, 'from the cratch to the

Acts 1. 1. cross,' from St. Luke's time *quo cœpit Jesus facere et docere,*
Joh. 19. 30. "that He began to do and teach," to St. John's time that
Joh. 13. 1. He cried *consummatum est,* gave them not over *sed in finem usque dilexit eos,* but "to the end loved them." And so must they Him, if they do Him right. Both set out with Him, as " Author" by a good beginning; and hold out with Him, as " Finisher," to a far better end; and follow Him in both Who is both. Were He " Author" only, it would serve to step forth well at the first. But He is " Finisher" too: therefore we must hold out to the last. And not rend one of them from the other, seeing He requireth both—not either, but both—and is indeed Jesus, a Saviour of none but those, that follow Him as " Finisher" too, and are therefore

His Passion. marked in the forehead with Tau the last letter of the He-
Ezek. 9. 4. brew, as He Himself is Omega, the last of the Greek Alphabet. This is the party he commendeth to our view; "Jesus, the Author and the Finisher of our faith." For these two to look upon Him, and in these two to be like unto Him.

I. Our sight then is Jesus, and in Jesus what? you have called us hither, say they in the Canticles, to see your
Cant. 6. 13. Shulamite;—"what shall we see in Him?" What? saith the Spouse, but as "the company of an army," that is, many legions of good sights, an ocean or bottomless depth of manifold high perfections. We shall lose ourselves, we shall be confounded to see in Him all that may be shewed us, the object is too great. Two pieces therefore He maketh choice of, and but two, and presenteth Him to our eye in two forms only: 1. As hanging on the cross; 2. as sitting on the throne. 1. His Passion, and 2. His Session; these two. And these two, with very good and perfect correspondence to the two former. By the "cross," He is "Author;" by the

"throne," He is "Finisher of our faith." As man on the
"cross," "Author;" as God on the "throne," "Finisher."
"Author," on the "cross"—there He paid the price of our
admitting. "Finisher," on the "throne"—there He is the
prize to us of our course well performed, of the well-finish-
ing our race, the race of our faith.

And sure, with right high wisdom hath the Holy Ghost,
being to exhort us to a race, combined these twain. For in
these twain are comprised the two main motives, that set all
the world on running, 1. love, and 2. hope. The love He
hath to us in His Passion on the cross; the hope we have
of Him, in His Session on the throne. Either of these alone
able to move; but put them together, and they will move
us, or nothing will.

1. Love first. What moveth the mother to all the travail 1. The
and toil she taketh with her child? She hopes for nothing, motives thereto.
she is in years, suppose; she shall not live to receive any 1. Love.
benefit by it. It is love and love only. Love first.

2. And then hope. What moveth the merchant, and so 2. Hope.
the husbandman, and so the military man, and so all the
rest? All the sharp showers and storms they endure, they
love them not. It is hope, and hope only, of a rich return.

If either of these will serve us, will prevail to move us,
here it is. Here is love, love in the cross: "Who loved us, Eph. 5. 2.
and gave Himself for us, a sacrifice" on the cross. Here is
hope, hope in the throne: "To Him that overcometh will Rev. 3 21.
I give to sit with Me in My throne." If our eye be a
mother's eye, here is love worth the looking on. If our eye
be a merchant's eye, here is hope worth the looking after.
I know it is true, that *verus amor vires non sumit de spe;*—it
is Bernard. 'Love if it be true indeed, as in the mother, [S. Ber-
receiveth no manner strength from hope.' Ours is not such, per Cant.
but faint and feeble, and full of imperfection. Here is hope Serm. 83.
therefore to strengthen our weak knees, that we may run circ. med.]
the more readily to the high prize of our calling.

To begin then with His love, the love of His Passion, the 2. What
peculiar of this day. In it we first look to what He suffered, fered.
and that is of two sorts. 1. "The cross He endured;" 2.
"The shame He despised." 3. And then with what mind,
for the mind is worth all; and love in it sheweth itself, if

SERM. not more, as much as in the suffering itself:—but certainly
III. more. And this is His mind, *proposito Sibi gaudio*, as cheerfully as if it had been some matter of joy. Of both first,
jointly under one. Then severally each by itself.

1. "The   Two things are to us most precious, 1. our life and 2. our
cross" and reputation. *Pari passu ambulant*, saith the lawyer, 'they go
"shame"   arm in arm,' and are of equal regard both. Life is sweet:
jointly.   the cross cost Him His life. Honour is dear: shame bereft Him His honour. In the race which, before us and for
us, our blessed Saviour ran, these two great blocks, 1. death,
and 2. disgrace were in His way. Neither stayed Him. To
testify His love, over both He passed. Put His shoulders
under the cross and endured it, to the loss of His life. Set
His foot upon shame and despised it, to the loss of His
honour. Neither one nor other, life or honour, held He
dear, to do us good. O, if we should hazard but one of these
two, for any creature living, how much ado would we make
of it, and reckon the party eternally obliged to us! Or if any
should venture them for us, we should be the better every
time we saw him. O that it might be so here! O that
we would meet this love with the like measure! Certainly in
His Passion, the love of us triumphed over the love of His
life and honour both.

2. One view more of both these under one, and we shall by
these two discover two other things in ourselves, for which
very agreeable it was He should suffer these two, that by
these two of His for those two of ours He might make a full
satisfaction. It will shew a good congruity between our
sickness and His salve, between our debt and His discharge.

The mother-sin then, the sin of Adam and Eve, and their
motives to it, are the lively image of all the after-births of sin,
and the baits of sin for ever. Now that which moved them
to disobey, was partly pleasure, and partly pride. Pleasure
Gen. 3. 6. 5. —O the fruit was delightful to see and to taste. Pride—*eritis
sicut Dii*, it promised an estate equal to the highest. Behold
then in His Passion, for our pleasure His pain, and for our
pride, His shame and reproach. Behold Him in His patience,
enduring pain for our wicked lust; in His humility, having
Acts 3. 15. shame poured on Him for our wretched pride. "The Lord
1 Cor. 2. 8. of life," suffering death; "The Lord of glory," vile and igno-

minious disgrace. *Tanquam agnus*, saith the Prophet of Him, _{Jer. 11. 19.}
" as a lamb," pitifully slaughtered. *Tanquam vermis*, saith _{Ps. 22. 6.}
He of Himself, " as a worm," spitefully trod upon. So, by
His enduring pains and painful death, expiating our unlawful
pleasure; and by His sustaining shame, satisfying for our
shameful pride. Thus may we under one behold ourselves,
and our wicked demerits, in the mirror of His Passion.
Gregory saith well: *Dicendum erat quantum nos dilexit, ne
diffidere; dicendum erat et quales, ne superbire et ingrati esse.*
' How greatly He loved us, must be told us, to keep us from
distrust; and what we were when He so loved us, must
be told us, to hold us in humility, to make us everlastingly
thankful.' Thus far both under one view.

Now are we to part them, to see them apart. We shall _{2. " The cross" and "shame" severally.}
have much ado to do it, they are so folded and twisted
together. In the cross there is shame, and in shame there
is a cross, and that a heavy one.

The cross, the Heathen termed *cruciabile lignum,* ' a tree of _[Livii Hist. lib. 1. 26.]
torture;' but they called it also, *arborem infœlicem, et stipitem
infamem,* ' a wretched infamous tree' withal. So it was in
His crown; the thorns pricked Him—there was pain; the
crown itself was a mere mockery, and matter of scorn. So in
His robe; His purple body underneath in great pain certainly, His purple robe over it, a garment of shame and disgrace. All along the Passion, thus they meet still together.
In a word, the prints of His Passion, the Apostle well calleth _{Gal. 6. 17.}
stigmata Christi. Both are in that word; not only wounds,
and so grievous, but base and servile marks, and so shameful,
for so are *stigmata.* Thus shame and cross, and cross and
shame run interchangeably.

Yet since the Holy Ghost doth shew us them severally, so
to see them as He shews them. Enduring is the act of
patience, and patience hath pain for her object. Despising
shame is the property of humility, even of the highest humi- _{The cross.}
lity; not only *spernere se,* but *spernere se sperni.* First then
we must see the pain His patience endured—that is meant
by the cross; and then see the despising His humility despised
—that is meant by the shame. First then of His cross.

It is well known that Christ and His cross were never
parted, but that all His life long was a continual cross. At

SERM.   the very cratch, His cross first began.   There Herod sought
III.   to do that which Pilate did, even to end His life before it
began.   All His life after, saith the Apostle in the next verse,
Heb. 12. 3. was nothing but a perpetual " gainsaying of sinners," which
we call crossing; and profess we cannot abide in any of our
speeches or purposes to be crossed.   He was.   In the Psalm of
the Passion, the twenty-second, in the very front or inscription of it, He is set forth unto us under the term of a hart,
cervus matutinus, " a morning hart," that is, a hart roused
early in the morning; as from His birth He was by Herod,
and hunted and chased all His life long, and this day brought
to His end, and as the poor deer, stricken and wounded to the
heart.   This was His last, last and worst; and this we properly
call His cross, even this day's suffering.   To keep us then to
our day, and the cross of the day.   " He endured the cross."

" He endured."   Very enduring itself is *durum, durum
pati.*   Especially for persons of high power or place as the
Son of God was.   For great persons to do great things, is no
great wonder; their very genius naturally inclineth to it.
But to suffer any small thing, for them is more than to do
many great.   Therefore the Prophet placeth his moral for-
titude, and the Divine his Christian obedience, rather in
suffering than in doing.   Suffering is sure the more hard
of the twain.   " He endured."

If it be hard to endure, it must be more hard to endure
hard things; and of all things hard to be endured, the
[Arist. Eth. hardest is death.   Of the philosopher's πέντε φοβερὰ, 'five
3. 6. 3.] fearful things,' it is the most fearful; and what will not
a man, nay, what will not a woman weak and tender, in
physic, in chyrurgery, endure, not to endure death?   " He
endured" death.

And that if He endured, and no more but that, it might
suffice; it is worth all we have, for all we have we will give
for our life.   But not death only, but the kind of death is it.
Phil. 2. 8. *Mortem, mortem autem crucis,* saith the Apostle, doubting the
point; " death He endured, even the death of the cross."

The cross is but a little word, but of great contents; but
few letters, but in these few letters are contained *multa dictu
gravia, perpessu aspera,* ' heavy to be named, more heavy to
be endured.'   I take but the four things ascribed by the Holy

Ghost to the cross, answerable to the four ends or quarters of it. 1. *Sanguis Crucis,* 2. *Dolores Crucis,* 3. *Scandalum Crucis,* 4. *Maledictum Crucis :* that is, the death of the cross is all these four; a 1. bloody, 2. doleful, 3. scandalous, 4. accursed death.

Col. 1. 20.
Acts 2. 24.
Gal. 5. 11.
Gal. 3. 13.

1. Though it be but a cold comfort, yet a kind of comfort it is, if die we must, that our death is *mors sicca,* a dry, not *sanguis crucis,* not a bloody death. 2. We would die, when we die, an easy, not ὠδῖνες σταυροῦ, not a tormenting death. 3. We desire to die with credit if it might be; if not, without scandal—*scandalum crucis.* 4. At leastwise to go to our graves, and to die by an honest, ordinary, and by no means by an accursed death—*maledictum crucis.* In the cross are all these, all four. The two first are in " the cross," the two latter in " the shame." For " the cross," and " the shame" are in very deed two crosses; the shame, a second cross of itself.

To see then, as in a short time, shortly. That of the poet, 1. *nec siccâ morte tyranni,* sheweth plainly, it is no poor privilege to die without effusion of blood. And so it is. 1. For a blessing it is, and our wish it is, we may live out our time, and not die an untimely death. Where there is effusion of blood there is ever an untimely death.

[Juv. Sat. 10. 113.]

2. Yet every untimely death is not violent, but a bloody 2. death is violent and against nature; and we desire to pay nature her debt by the way of nature.

3. A violent death one may come to, as in war—*sanguis* 3. *belli* best sheweth it—yet by valour, not by way of punishment. This death is penal; not, as all death, *stipendium peccati,* but, as evil men's death, *vindicta sceleris,* an execution for some capital offence.

4. And not every crime neither. *Fundetur sanguis* is the 4. punishment of treason and other more heinous crimes, to die embrued in their own blood. And even they that die so, die not yet so evil a death as do they that die on the cross. It is another case where it is *sanguis mortis,* the blood and life go away together at once; another, when it is *sanguis crucis,* when the blood is shed, and the party still in full life and sense, as on the cross it was; the blood first, and the life a good while after. This is *sanguis crucis,* an 1. untimely,

2. violent, 3. penal, 4. penal in the highest degree; there
bleeding out His blood before He die, and then die.

When blood is shed, it would be no more than needs; shed
it would be, not poured out.   Or if so, at one part, the neck
or throat, not at all parts at once.   But here was *fundetur*,
havoc made at all parts; His Passion, as he termeth it, a
Mark 10. 38. second baptism, a river of blood, and He even able to have
been baptized in it, as He was in Jordan.   And where it
would be *summa parcimonia etiam vilissimi sanguinis,* 'no
waste, no not of the basest blood that is,' waste was made
here.   And of what blood? *Sanguis Jesu,* 'the blood of
Jesus.'   And Who was He? Sure, by virtue of the union
personal, God; and so this blood, blood of God's own bleeding, every drop whereof was precious, more precious than
that whereof it was the price, the world itself.   Nay, more
worth than many worlds; yea if they were ten thousand.
Yet was this blood wastefully spilt as water upon the ground.
The *fundetur* and the *Qui* here, will come into consideration,
both.   This is *sanguis crucis,* and yet this is not all neither;
there is more yet.

For the blood of the Cross was not only the blood of Golgotha, but the blood of Gabbatha too.   For of all deaths,
this was peculiar to this death, the death of the Cross; that
they that were to be crucified, were not to be crucified alone,
which is the blood of Golgotha, but they must be whipped
too before they were crucified, which is the blood of Gabbatha; a second death, yea worse than death itself.   And in
both these places He bled, and in either place twice.   They
rent His body with the 1. whips; they gored His head with
the 2. thorns—both these in Gabbatha.   And again, twice
in Golgotha, when they 1. nailed His hands and His feet;
when He was 2. thrust to the heart with the spear.   This is
sanguis crucis.   It was to be stood on a little, we might not
pass it.   It is that whereon our faith depends, *per fidem in*
Rom. 3. 25. *sanguine Ipsius.*   By it He is " Author of our faith," faith in
God, and peace with God, both; *pacificans in sanguine crucis,*
Col. 1. 20. " pacifying all with the blood of the Cross."

Now this bloody whipping and nailing of His, is it which
bringeth in the second point of pain; that it was not blood
alone without pain, as in the opening of a vein, but it was

blood and pain both. The tearing and mangling of His flesh with the whips, thorns, and nails, could not choose but be exceeding painful to Him. Pains, we know, are increased much by cruel, and made more easy by gentle handling, and even the worst that suffer, we wish their execution as gentle, and with as little rigour as may be. All rigour, all cruelty was shewed to Him, to make His pains the more painful. In Gabbatha they did not whip Him, saith the Psalmist, Ps. 129. 3. "they ploughed His back, and made," not stripes, but "long furrows upon it." They did not put on His wreath of thorns, and press it down with their hands, but beat it on with bats, to make it enter through skin, flesh, skull, and all. They did not in Golgotha pierce His hands and feet, but made wide Ps. 22. 16. holes like that of a spade, as if they had been digging in some ditch.

These were pains, and cruel pains, but yet these are not ὠδῖνες, the Holy Ghost's word in the text; those are properly "straining pains, pains of torture." The rack is devised as a most exquisite pain, even for terror. And the cross is a rack, whereon He was stretched, till, saith the Psalm, all Ps. 22. 14. His bones were out of joint. But even to stand, as He hung, three long hours together, holding up but the arms at length, I have heard it avowed of some that have felt it to be a pain scarce credible. But the hands and the feet being so cruelly nailed, parts of all other most sensible by reason of the texture of sinews there in them most, it could not but make His pain out of measure painful. It was not for nothing that *dolores acerrimi dicuntur cruciatus,* saith the heathen man, [Sed vid. 'that the most sharp and bitter pains of all other have their S. August. Tract. 36. 4 name from hence, and are called *cruciatus,*' "pains like those in Joan.] of the cross." It had a meaning that they gave Him, that He had for His welcome to the cross, a cup mixed with gall or myrrh, and for His farewell, a sponge of vinegar; to shew by the one the bitterness, by the other the sharpness of the pains of this painful death.

Now, in pain we know the only comfort of *gravis,* is *brevis;* if we be in it, to be quickly out of it. This the cross hath not, but is *mors prolixa,* 'a death of dimensions, a death long in dying.' And it was therefore purposely chosen by them. Blasphemy they condemned Him of: then was He to be stoned; that death would have despatched Him too soon. They indicted Him anew of sedition, not as of a worse fault, but only because crucifying belonged to it; for then He must be whipped first, and that liked them well, and then He must die by inch-meal, not swallow His death at once Heb. 2. 9. but "taste" it, as chap. 2. 9, and take it down by little and little. And then He must have His legs and arms broken, and so was their meaning His should have been. Else, I would gladly know to what purpose provided they to have a Joh. 19. 29. vessel of vinegar ready in the place, but only that He might not faint with loss of blood, but be kept alive till they might hear His bones crash under the breaking, and so feed their eyes with that spectacle also. The providence of God indeed prevented this last act of cruelty; their will was good though. All these pains are in the cross, but to this last specially the word in the text hath reference; ὑπέμεινε, which is, He must μένειν ὑπὸ, "tarry, stay, abide under it;" so die that He might feel himself die, and endure the pains of an enduring death.

And yet all this is but half, and the lesser half by far of *cruciatus crucis.* All this His body endured. Was His soul free the while? No; but suffered as much. As much? nay more, infinitely much more on the spiritual, than His body did on the material cross. For a spiritual Cross there was too: all grant a Cross beside that which Simon of Cyrene did help Him to bear. Great were those pains, and this time too little to shew how great; but so great that in all the former He never shrunk, nor once complained, but was as if He scarce felt them. But when these came, they made Him Heb. 5. 7. complain and cry aloud κραυγὴν ἰσχυρὰν, "a strong crying." In all those no blood came, but where passages were made for it to come out by, but in this it strained out all over, even at all places at once. This was the pain of the "press"—so Isa. 63. 3. the Prophet calleth it, *torcular,* wherewith as if He had been in the wine-press, all His garments were stained and gored with blood. Certainly the blood of Gethsemane was another manner of blood than that of Gabbatha, or that of Golgotha either; and that was the blood of His internal Cross. Of the three Passions that was the hardest to endure, yet that did He endure too. It is that which belief itself doth wonder how it doth believe, save that it knoweth as well the love as the power of God to be without bounds; and His wisdom as able to find, how through love it might be humbled, as exalted through power, beyond the uttermost that man's wit can comprehend.

And this is the Cross He endured. And if all this might "The have been endured, *salvo honore*, 'without shame or disgrace,' shame." it had been so much the less. But now, there is a farther matter yet to be added, and that is shame. It is hard to say of these two, which is the harder to bear; which is the greater cross, the cross or shame. Or rather, it is not hard. There is no mean party in misery, but if he be insulted on, his being insulted on more grieves him than doth the misery itself. But to the noble generous nature, to whom *interesse honoris est majus omni alio interesse,* 'the value of his honour is above all value;' to him the cross is not the cross, shame is the cross. And any high and heroical spirit beareth any grief more easily, than the grief of contemptuous and contumelious usage. King Saul shewed it plainly, who chose rather to run upon his own sword, than to fall into 1 Sam. 31. 4. the hands of the Philistines, who he knew would use him with scorn, as they had done Samson before him. And Judges 16. even he, Samson too, rather than sit down between the pil- 25. 30. lars and endure this, pulled down house and all, as well upon his own head, as theirs that so abused him. Shame then is certainly the worse of the twain. Now in his death, it is not easy to define, whether pain or shame had the upper hand; whether greater, *cruciatus,* or *scandalum crucis.*

Was it not a foul disgrace and scandal to offer Him the 1. shame of that servile base punishment of the whip, not to be offered to any but to slaves and bondmen? *Loris? liber sum,* [Terent. saith he in the comedy in great disdain, as if being free-born 2. 1. 28.] he held it great scorn to have that once named to him. Yet shame of being put out of the number of free-born men He despised, even the shame of being *in formâ servi.* Phil. 2. 7.

That that is servile, may yet be honest. Then was it not 2. yet a more foul disgrace and scandal indeed to appoint Him for His death that dishonest, that foul death, the death of malefactors, and of the worst sort of them? *Morte turpissimâ,* as themselves termed it; 'the most shameful opprobrious death of all other,' that the persons are scandalous that suffer it. To take Him as a thief, to hang Him between two thieves; nay, to count Him worse than the worst thief in the gaol; to say and to cry, *Vivat Barabbas, pereat Christus,* 'Save Barabbas and hang Christ !' Yet this shame He despised too, of being *in formâ malefici.*

3. If base, if dishonest, let these two serve; use Him not disgracefully, make Him not a *ridiculum Caput,* pour not contempt upon Him. That did they too, and a shame it is to see the shameful carriage of themselves all along the whole tragedy of His Passion. Was it a tragedy, or a Passion trow? A passion it was, yet by their behaviour it might seem a May-game. Their shouting and outcries, their harrying of Him about from Annas to Caiaphas, from him to Pilate, from Pilate to Herod, and from him to Pilate again; one while in purple, Pilate's suit; another while in white, Herod's livery; nipping Him by the cheeks, and pulling off His hair; blindfolding Him and buffeting Him; bowing to Him in derision, and then spitting in His face;—was as if they had not the Lord of glory, but some idiot or dizard[1] in hand. "Died Abner as a fool dieth?" saith David of Abner in great regret. O no. Sure, our blessed Saviour so died; and that He so died, doth equal, nay surpass even the worst of His torments. Yet this shame also He despised, of being *in formâ ludibrii.*

[1 i.e. blockhead.]
2 Sam. 3. 33.

Is there any worse yet? There is. For though contempt be bad, yet despite is beyond it, as far as earnest is beyond sport; that was sport, this was malice. Despite I call it, when in the midst of His misery, in the very depth of all His distress, they vouchsafed Him not the least compassion; but as if He had been the most odious wretched caitiff and abject of men, the very outcast of Heaven and earth, stood staring and gaping upon Him, wagging their heads, writhing their mouths, yea blearing out their tongues; railing on Him and reviling Him, scoffing at Him and scorning Him; yea, in the very time of His prayers deriding Him, even in His most mournful complaint and cry for the very anguish of His Spirit. These vile indignities, these shameful villanies, so void of all humanity, so full of all despite, I make no question, entered into His soul deeper than either nail or spear did.

into His body. Yet all this He despised, to be in *formâ reprobi.* Men hid their faces at this; nay, to see this sight, the sun was darkened, drew back his light, the earth trembled, ran one part from the other, the powers of Heaven were moved.

Is this all? No, all this but *scandalum,* there is a greater yet remaining than *scandalum,* and that is *maledictum crucis;* that the death He died was not only servile, scandalous, opprobrious, odious, but even execrable and accursed, of men held so. For as if He had been a very reprobate, in His extreme drought they denied Him a drop of water, never denied to any but to the damned in hell, and instead of it offered Him vinegar in a sponge; and that in the very pangs of death, as one for whom nothing was evil enough.

All this is but man, and man is but man, his glory is shame oftentimes, and his shame glory ; but what God curseth, that is cursed indeed. And this death was cursed by God Himself, His own mouth, as the Apostle deduceth. Gal. 3. 13. When all is said we can say, this, this is the hardest point of His shame, and the highest point of His love in bearing it. *Christus factus est maledictum.* The shame of a cursed death, cursed by God, is a shame beyond all shames, and he that can despise it, may well say *consummatum est,* there is no greater left for him to despise. O what contempt was poured upon Him! O how was He in all these despised! Yet He despised them all, and despised to be despised in them all. The highest humility, *spernere se sperni ;* these so many ways, *spernere se sperni.*

So have we now the cross, ξύλον δίδυμον, ' the two main bars of it,' 1. Pain. 2. Shame ; and either of these again, a cross of itself; and that double, 1. outward, and 2. inward. Pain, bloody, cruel, dolorous, and enduring—pain He endured. Shame, servile, scandalous, opprobrious, odious— shame He despised. And beside these, an internal cross, the passion of Gethsemane ; and an internal shame, the curse itself of the cross, *maledictum crucis.* Of these He endured the one, the other He despised.

These, all these, and yet there remaineth a greater than all these, even *quo animo,* ' with what mind,' what having in His mind, or setting before His eyes, He did and suffered all this, 3. *Quo animo.*

That He did it not *utcunque,* but *proposito Sibi,* ' with an eye
to somewhat He aimed at.'

We handle this point last, it standeth first in the verse.
And sure, if this as a figure stand not first, the other two are
but ciphers ; with it of value, nothing without it.

To endure all this is very much, howsoever it were. So to
endure it as to make no reckoning of it, to despise it is more
strange than all the rest. Sure the shame was great; how
could He make so small account of it? and the cross heavy;
how could He set it so light? They could not choose but
pinch him, and that extremely : and how then could He endure, and so endure that He despised them? It is the third
point, and in it is *adeps arietis,* ' the fat of rams,' the marrow
of the Sacrifice; even the good heart, the free forward mind,
the cheerful affection, wherewith He did all this.

There be but two senses to take this ἀντὶ in, neither amiss,
both very good, take whether you will. Love is in both, and
love in a high measure. 'Αντὶ, even either *pro* or *præ ; pro,*
' instead ;' or *præ,* ' in comparison.'

'Αντὶ, *pro,* "instead of the joy set before Him." What joy
was that? 'Εξῆν γὰρ Αὐτῷ ἐν οὐρανοῖς, saith Chrysostom,
' for He was in the joys of Heaven : there He was, and there
He might have held Him.' Nothing did or could force Him
to come thence, and to come hither thus to be entreated.

[Joh.3.16.] Nothing but *Sic dilexit,* or *Propter nimiam charitatem quâ*
Eph. 2. 4. *dilexit nos;* but for it. Yet was He content, "being in the
Phil. 2. 6. form of God," ἀντὶ "instead of it," thus to transform, yea to
deform Himself into the shape of a servant, a felon, a fool;
nay, of a caitiff accursed. Content to lay down His crown
of glory, and ἀντὶ "instead of it," to wear a crown of thorns.
Content, what we shun by all means, that to endure,—loss
of life; and what we make so great a matter of, that to
despise,—loss of honour. All this, with the loss of that joy
and that honour He enjoyed in Heaven; another manner
joy, and honour, than any we have here; ἀντὶ " for this," or
" instead of this."

But the other sense is more praised, ἀντὶ, *præ,* " in comparison." For indeed, the joy He left in Heaven was rather
περικειμένη than προκειμένη, joy, ' wherein He did already
sit,' than " joy set before Him." Upon which ground, ἀντὶ,

they turn *præ*, and that better as they suppose. For that is, in comparison of a certain joy, which He comparing with the cross and shame and all, chose rather to go through them all than to go without it. And can there be any joy compared with those He did forego? or can any joy countervail those barbarous usages He willingly went through? It seemeth, there can. What joy might that be? Sure none other, but the joy He had to save us, the joy of our salvation. For what was His glory, or joy, or crown of rejoicing, was it not we? Yes truly, we were His crown and His joy. In comparison of this joy He exchanged those joys, and endured these pains; this was the honey that sweetened His gall. And no joy at all in it but this—to be Jesus, "the Saviour" of a sort of poor sinners. None but this, and therefore pity He should lose it.

And it is to be marked, that though to be Jesus, "a Saviour," in propriety of speech be rather a title, an outward honour, than an inward joy, and so should have been *præ honore*, rather than *præ gaudio;* yet He expresseth it in the term of joy rather than that of honour, to shew it joyed Him at the heart to save us; and so as a special joy, He accounted it.

Sure, some such thing there was that made Him so cheerfully say to His Father in the Psalm, *Ecce venio,* " Lo Ps. 40. 7. I come." And to His disciples in earth, This, this is the Passover that *desiderio desideravi,* "I have so longed for," Lu. 22. 15. as it were embracing and even welcoming His death. And which is more, *quomodo coarctor!* "how am I pinched, or Lu. 12. 50. straitened," till I be at it! as if He were in pain, till He were in pain to deliver us. Which joy if ever He shewed, in this He did, that He went to His Passion with Psalms, and with such triumph and solemnity, as He never admitted all His life before. And that this His lowest estate, one would think it, He calleth His exaltation, *cum exaltatus fuero.* And Joh. 12. 32. when any would think He was most imperfect, He esteemeth and so termeth it, His highest perfection; *Tertio die perficior.* Lu. 13. 32. *In hoc est charitas,* "here is love." If not here, where? But 1 Joh. 4. 10. here it is, and that in his highest elevation. That the joys of Heaven set on the one side, and this poor joy of saving us on the other, He quit them to choose this. This those pains

N

and shames set before Him, and with them this joy, He chose them rather than forego this.

Those joys He forsook, and this He took up; and to take it, took upon Him so many, so strange indignities of both sorts; took them and bare them with such a mind, as He not only endured but despised; nor that neither, but even joyed in the bearing of them, and all to do us good. So to alter the nature of things as to find joy in death whereat all do mourn, and joy in shame which all do abhor, is a wonder Exod. 3. 2. like that of the bush.

This is the very life and soul of the Passion, and all besides but the σκελετὸς only, 'the anatomy,' the carcass without it.

II.
The act or duty. So have we now the whole object, both what, and with what mind. And what is now to be done? shall we not pause a while and stay, and look upon this "theory" ere we go any farther? Yes, let us. Proper to this day is this sight of the cross. The other, of the throne, may stay yet his time a day or two hence.

We are enjoined to look upon Him. How can we, seeing He is now higher than the heavens, far out of our sight, or from the kenning of any mortal eye? yes, we may for all that. As, in the twenty-seventh of the chapter next before, Heb.11. 27. Moses is said to have seen "Him That is invisible;" not with the eyes of flesh—so neither he did, or we can; but, as there it is, "by faith." So he did, and we may. And what is more kindly to behold "the Author" of faith, than faith? or more kindly for faith to behold, than her "Author" here at first, and her "Finisher" there at last? Him to behold first and last, and never be satisfied with looking on Him, Who was content to buy us and our eye at so dear a rate.

Our eye then is the eye of our mind, which is faith; and Heb. 12. 3. our *aspicientes* in this, and the *recogitantes* in the next verse, all one; our looking to Him here, is our thinking on Him there; on Him and His Passion over and over again, *Donec totus fixus in corde Qui totus fixus in cruce,* 'till He be as fast fixed in our heart as ever He was to His cross,' and some impression made in us of Him, as there was in Him for us.

In this our looking then, two acts be rising from the two,

prepositions; one before, ἀπὸ, in ἀφορῶντες, "looking from;" the other after, εἰς, "looking upon, or into."

There is ἀπὸ, "from," abstracting our eye from other objects to look hither sometime. The preposition is not idle, nor the note, but very needful. For naturally we put this spectacle far from us, and endure not either oft or long to behold it. Other things there be, please our eyes better, and which we look on with greater delight. And we must ἀφο-ρᾶν, 'look off of them,' or we shall never ὁρᾶν, 'look upon' this aright. We must, in a sort, work force to our nature, and *per actum elicitum*, as they term it in schools, inhibit our eyes, and even wean them from other more pleasing spectacles that better like them, or we shall do no good here, never make a true "theory" of it. I mean, though our prospect into the world be good, and we have both occasion and inclination to look thither oft, yet ever and anon to have an eye this way; to look from them to Him, Who, when all these shall come to an end, must be He that shall finish and consummate our faith and us, and make perfect both. Yea, though the Saints be fair marks, as at first I said, yet even to look off from them hither, and turn our eye to Him from all, even from Saints and all. But chiefly, from the baits of sin, the concupiscence of our eyes, the shadows and shows of vanity round about, by which death entereth at our windows; which unless we can be got to look from, this sight will do us no good, we cannot look on both together.

Now our "theory," as it beginneth with ἀπὸ, so it endeth with εἰς. Therefore look from it, that look to Him; or, as the word giveth it rather, "into Him," than to Him. *Εἰς* is 'into,' rather than 'to.' Which proveth plainly, that the Passion is a piece of perspective, and that we must set ourselves to see it if we will see it well, and not look superficially on it; not on the outside alone, but ὁρᾶν εἰς, 'pierce into it,' and enter even into the inward workmanship of it, even of His internal Cross which He suffered, and of His entire affection wherewith He suffered it.

And we may well look into Him; *Cancellis plenum est corpus*, 'His body is full of stripes,' and they are as lattices; *patent viscera per vulnera*, His wounds they are as windows, through which we may well see all that is within

1. Looking from: Ἀπὸ.

2. Looking up to: Εἰς, "into."

SERM.
III.
[S. Bernard. super Cant. Serm. 61. circ. med.]
Isa. 49. 16.
Joh. 19. 34.
[S. August. Tract. in. Joan. 120.]

Him. *Clavus penetrans factus est mihi clavis reserans*, saith St. Bernard; 'the nails and spear-head serve as keys to let us in.' We may look into the palms of His hands, wherein, saith the Prophet, He hath graven us, that He might never forget us. We may look into His side, St. John useth the word, "opened." *Vigilanti verbo*, saith Augustine, 'a word well chosen, upon good advice:' we may through the opening look into His very bowels, the bowels of kindness and compassion that would endure to be so entreated. Yea that very heart of His, wherein we may behold the love of our salvation to be the very heart's joy of our Saviour.

2.
To see,
ὁρᾶν.

Thus "looking from," from all else to look "into" Him, what then? then followeth the participle, we shall see. What shall we see? Nay, what shall we not see? What "theory" is there worth the seeing but is there to be seen? To recount all were too long: two there are in especial.

There is a theory medicinal, like that of the brazen serpent, and it serveth for comfort to the conscience, stung and wounded with the remorse of sin. For what sin is there, or can there be, so execrable or accursed, but the curse of the cross; what so ignominious or full of confusion, but the shame of it; what so corrosive to the conscience, but the pains of it; what of so deep or of so crimson a dye, but the blood of it, the blood of the Cross will do it away? What sting so deadly, but the sight of this Serpent will cure it? This is a principal theory, and elsewhere to be stood on, but not here. For this serveth to quiet the mind, and the Apostle here seeketh to move it and make it stir.

1 Tim. 2. 6.

There is then another "theory" besides, and that is exemplary for imitation. There He died, saith St. Paul, to lay down for us, ἀντίλυτρον, our "ransom;"—that is the former. There He died, saith St. Peter, to leave unto

1 Pet. 2. 21.

us ὑπογραμμὸν, *relinquens nobis exemplum*, "a pattern," an example to follow, and this is it, to this He calleth us; to have a directory use of it, to make it our pattern, to view it as our idea. And sure, as the Church under the Law needed not, so neither doth the Church under the Gospel need any other precept than this one, *Inspice et fac*, "see and do according to the theory shewed thee in the mount;" to them in Mount Sinai, to us in Mount Calvary.

Ex. 25. 40.

Were all philosophy lost, the theory of it might be found there. Were all Chairs burnt, Moses' Chair and all, the Chair of the Cross is absolutely able to teach all virtue new again. All virtues are there visible, all, if time would serve: now I name only those five, which are directly in the text.

1. Faith is named there; it is, it was most conspicuous there to be seen, when being forsaken of God, yet He claspeth as it were His arms fast about Him, with *Eli, Eli,* "My God, My God," for all that. 2. Patience in "endur- Mat. 27. 46. ing the cross." 3. Humility in "despising the shame." 4. Perseverance, in that it was nothing for Him to be "Author," unless He were "Finisher" too. These four. But above these and all, that which is the 5. *ratio idealis* of all, the band and perfection of all, love, in the signature of love, in the joy which He found in all this; love, *majorem quâ nemo,* to lay down His life; nay, *parem cui nemo,* in such Joh. 15. 13. sort to lay it down. *Majorem quâ nemo,* to do this for His friends; *Parem cui nemo,* to do it for His enemies. Notwithstanding their unworthiness antecedent to do it, and notwithstanding their unkindness consequent, yet to do it. This is the chief theory of all, but of love, chiefly, the most perfect of all. For sure, if ever aught were truly said of our Saviour, this was: that being spread and laid wide open on the cross, He is *Liber charitatis,* wherein he that runneth Hab. 2. 2. by may read, *Sic dilexit,* and *Propter nimiam charitatem,* Joh. 3. 16. Eph. 2. 4. and *Ecce quantam charitatem;* love all over, from one end 1 Joh. 3. 1. to the other. Every stripe as a letter, every nail as a capital Isa. 53. 5. letter. His *livores* as black letters, His bleeding wounds as so many rubrics, to shew upon record His love toward us.

Of which love the Apostle when he speaketh, he setteth it out with "height and depth, length and breadth," the four Eph. 3. 18. dimensions of the cross, to put us in mind, say the ancient writers, that upon the extent of the tree was the most exact love, with all the dimensions in this kind represented that ever was.

Having seen all these, what is the end and use of this 2. That we sight? Having had the theory, what is the *praxis* of this may run. theory? what the conclusion of our contemplation? "Looking into" is a participle; it maketh no sentence, but suspendeth it only till we come to a verb to which it relateth. That verb must be either the verb in the verse before, *ut curramus,* or the verb in the verse following, *ut ne fatigemur;* that thus looking we run, or that thus looking we tire not. This is the practice of our theory.

We said the use was, and so we see it is, to move us, or to make us move; to work in our feet, to work in them a motion; not any slow but a swift motion, the motion of running, to "run the race that is set before us." The operation it hath, this sight, is in our faculty motive; if we stand still, to cause us stir, if we move but slowly, to make us run apace; if we run already, never to tire or give over till we do attain. And by this we may know, whether our theory be a true one: if this *praxis* follow of it, it is; if not, a gaze it may be, a true Christian "theory" it is not.

And here first our ἀφορᾶν, that is, our "looking from," is to work a turning from sin. Sure this spectacle, if it be well looked into, will make sin shall not look so well-favoured in our eyes as it did; it will make us while we live have a less liking to look toward it, as being the only procurer and cause of this cross and this shame. Nay, not only ἀποτρέπειν, 'to turn our eye from it,' but ἀποτρέχειν, 'to turn our feet from it' too; and to run from, yea, to fly from it, *quasi a facie colubri,* 'as from the face of a serpent.'

At leastwise, if not to run from it, not to run to it as we have; to nail down our feet from running to sin, and our hands from committing sin, and in a word have St. Peter's 1 Pet. 4. 1. practice of the Passion, "to cease from sin." This abstractive force we shall find and feel; it will draw us from the delights of sin. And not only draw us from that, but draw from us too something, make some tears to run from us, or, if we be dry-eyed that not them, yet make some sighs of devotion, some thoughts of grace, some kind of thankful acknowledgments to issue from our souls. · Either by way of compassion as feeling that He then felt, or by way of compunction as finding ourselves in the number of the parties for whom He felt them. It is a proper effect of our view of the Passion, this, as St. Luke sets it down at the very place Lu. 23. 48. where he terms it θεωρίαν, that they return from it "smiting their breasts" as having seen a doleful spectacle, themselves the cause of it.

Now as the looking *from* worketh a moving from, so doth the looking *to* a moving to.

For first, who is there that can look unto those hands and feet, that head and that heart of His that endured all this, but must *primâ facie,* 'at the first sight' see and say, *Ecce quomodo dilexit nos?* If the Jews that stood by said truly of Him at Lazarus' grave, *Ecce quomodo dilexit eum!* when Joh. 11. 36. He shed but a few tears out of His eyes, how much more truly may it be said of us, *Ecce quomodo dilexit eos!* for whom He hath "shed both water and blood," yea even from His heart, and that in such plenty? And He loving us so, if our hearts be not iron, yea if they be iron, they cannot choose but feel the magnetical force of this loadstone. For to a loadstone doth He resemble Himself, when He saith of Himself, "Were I once lift up," *omnia traham ad Me.* This Joh. 12. 32. virtue attractive is in this sight to draw our love to it.

With which, as it were the needle, our faith being but touched, will stir straight. We cannot but turn to Him and trust in Him, that so many ways hath shewed Himself so true to us. *Quando amor confirmatur, fides inchoatur,* saith St. Ambrose, 'Prove to us of any that he loves us indeed, and we shall trust him straight without any more ado,' we shall believe any good affirmed of him. And what is there, tell me, any where affirmed of Christ to usward, but this love of His, being believed, will make it credible.

Now our faith is made perfect by "works," or "well-doing," Jas. 2. 22. saith St. James; it will therefore set us in a course of them. Of which, every virtue is a *stadium,* and every act a step toward the end of our race. Beginning at humility, the virtue of the first setting out,—"let the same mind be in Phil. 2. 5. you, that was in Christ Jesus, Who humbled Himself,"—and so proceeding from virtue to virtue, till we come to patience and perseverance, that keep the goal end. So saith St. Peter, *Modicum passos perficiet,* "suffering somewhat, more or less; 1 Pet. 5. 10. some crossing, if not the cross; some evil report, though not shame; so and no otherwise we shall come to our race end, our final perfection."

And as the rest move us if we stand still to run, so if we run already, these two, patience and perseverance—patience will make us for all our encounters, μὴ κάμνειν, saith the

SERM.
III.
Heb. 12. 3.

Apostle in the next verse, "not to be weary." Not in our minds, though in our bodies we be; and perseverance will make us, μὴ ἐκλύεσθαι, "not to faint or tire," though the time seem long and never so tedious; both these in the verse following. But hold on our course till we finish it, even till we come to Him, Who was not only "Author," but "Finisher;" Who held out till He came to *consummatum*

[¹ Curriculum omnium maximum. Jul. Poll.]

Gal. 5. 7.
2 Tim. 4. 7.

est. And so must we finish, not *stadium,* but *dolichum*¹; not like those, of whom it was said, *currebatis bene,* "ye did well for a start," but like our Apostle that said, and said truly, of himself, *cursum consummavi,* "I have finished my course, I have held out to the very end."

3. That we
faint not.

And in this is the *praxis* of our first theory or sight of our love. But our love without hope is but faint: that then with better heart we may thus do and bestir ourselves, it will not be amiss once more to lift up our eyes, and the second time to look on Him. We have not yet seen the end, the cross is not the end; there is a better end than so, "and is set down in the throne." As the Prophet saw Him, we have seen Him, in such case as we were ready to hide our faces at Him and His sight. Here is a new sight; as the Evangelist saw Him,

Joh. 1. 14.
Joh. 19. 5.
Joh. 20. 28.

so we now may; even His glory as the glory "of the only-begotten Son of God." *Ecce homo!* Pilate's sight we have seen. *Ecce Dominus et Deus meus!* St. Thomas' sight we now shall. The former in His hanging on the cross, the beginning of our faith. This latter sitting on the throne, the consummation of it.

Wherein there is an ample matter of hope, as before of love, all being turned in and out. He sits now at ease That before hung in pain. Now on a throne, That before on the cross. Now at God's right hand, That before at Satan's left.

Zech. 3. 1.

So Zachary saw Him; "Satan on His right hand," and then must He be on Satan's left. All changed; His cross into ease, His shame into glory.

Glory and rest, rest and glory, are two things that meet not here in our world. The glorious life hath not the most quiet, and the quiet life is for the most part inglorious. He that will have glory must make account to be despised oft and broken of his rest; and he that loveth his ease better, must be content with a mean condition far short of glory. Here then

these meet not; there our hope is they shall, even both meet
together, and glory and rest kiss each the other; so the
Prophet calleth it a " glorious rest." Isa. 11. 10.

And the right hand addeth yet a degree farther, for
dextera est pars potior. So that if there be any rest more
easy, or any glory more glorious than other, there it is on
that hand, on that side; and He placed in it in the best, in
the chiefest, the fulness of them both. At God's right hand
is not only power, power while we be here to protect us with
His might outward, and to support us with His grace inward;
but at " His right hand also is the fulness of joy for ever," Ps. 16. 11.
saith the Psalm; joy, and the fulness of joy, and the fulness
of it for evermore.

This is meant by His seat at the right hand on the throne.
And the same is our blessed hope also, that it is not His
place only, and none but His, but even ours in expectation
also. The love of His cross is to us a pledge of the hope of
His throne, or whatsoever else He hath or is worth. For if
God have given us Christ, and Christ thus given Himself,
what hath God or Christ They will deny us? It is the
Apostle's own deduction. Rom. 8. 32.

To put it out of all doubt, hear we His own promise That
never brake His word. " To him that overcometh will I give Rev. 3. 21.
to sit with Me in My throne." Where to sit is the fulness of
our desire, the end of our race, *omnia in omnibus;* and farther
we cannot go. Of a joy set before Him we spoke ere-while:
here is now a joy set before us, another manner joy than was
before Him; the worse was set before Him, the better before
us, and this we are to run to.

Thus do these two theories or sights, the one work to love,
the other to hope, both to the well performing of our course;
that in this theatre, between the Saints joyfully beholding us
in our race, and Christ at our end ready to receive us, we
may fulfil our " course with joy," and be partakers of the
blessed rest of His most glorious throne.

Let us now turn to Him and beseech Him, by the sight of
this day, by Himself first, and by His cross and throne both
—both which He hath set before us, the one to awake our
love, the other to quicken our hope—that we may this day
and ever lift up our eyes and heads, that we may this day

and ever carry them in our eyes and hearts, look up to them both; so look that we may love the one, and wait and hope for the other; so love and so hope that by them both we may move and that swiftly, even run to Him; and running not faint, but so constantly run, that we fail not finally to attain the happy fruition of Himself, and of the joy and glory of His blessed throne; that so we may find and feel Him as this day here, the "Author;" so in that day there, the "Finisher of our faith," by the same our Lord Jesus Christ! *Amen.*

SERMONS

OF THE RESURRECTION,

PREACHED ON EASTER-DAY.

A SERMON

PREACHED BEFORE

THE KING'S MAJESTY AT WHITEHALL,

ON THE SIXTH OF APRIL, A.D. MDCVI., BEING EASTER-DAY.

ROMANS vi. 9—11.

*Knowing that Christ, being raised from the dead, dieth no more;
death hath no more dominion over Him.*

*For, in that He died, He died once to sin; but in that He liveth,
He liveth to God.*

Likewise think (or account) *ye also, that ye are dead to sin, but
are alive to God in Jesus Christ our Lord.*

[*Scientes quod Christus resurgens ex mortuis jam non moritur, mors
Illi ultra non dominabitur.*

*Quod enim mortuus est peccato, mortuus est semel; quod autem vivit,
vivit Deo.*

*Ita et vos existimate, vos mortuos quidem esse peccato, viventes autem
Deo, in Christo Jesu Domino nostro.* Latin Vulg.]

[*Knowing that Christ, being raised from the dead, dieth no more;
death hath no more dominion over Him.*

*For in that He died, He died unto sin once; but in that He liveth,
He liveth unto God.*

*Likewise reckon ye also yourselves to be dead indeed unto sin, but
alive unto God through Jesus Christ our Lord.* Engl. Trans.]

THE Scripture is as the feast is, both of them of the Resurrection. And this we may safely say of it, it is thought by
the Church so pertinent to the feast, as it hath ever been and
is appointed to be the very entry of this day's service; to be
sounded forth and sung, first of all, and before all, upon this
day, as if there were some special correspondence between the
day and it.

Two principal points are set down to us, out of the two principal words in it: one, *scientes*, in the first verse, "knowing;" the other, *reputate*, in the last verse, "count yourselves;"—knowing and counting, knowledge and calling ourselves to account for our knowledge.

Two points very needful to be ever jointly called upon, and more than needful for our times, being that much we know, and little we count; oft we hear, and when we have heard, small reckoning we make of it. What Christ did on Easter-day we know well; what we are then to do, we give no great regard: our *scientes* is without a *reputantes*.

Now this Scripture, *ex totâ substantiâ*, 'out of the whole frame of it' teacheth us otherwise; that Christian knowledge is not a knowledge without all manner of account, but that we are accountants for it; that we are to keep an audit of what we hear, and take account of ourselves of what we have learned. Λογίζεσθε is an auditor's term: thence the Holy Ghost hath taken it, and would have us to be auditors in both senses.

And this to be general in whatsoever we know, but specially in our knowledge touching this feast of Christ's Resurrection, where there are special words for it in the text, where in express terms an account is called for at our hands as an essential duty of the day. The benefit we remember is so great, the feast we hold so high, as though at other times we might be forborne, yet on this day we may not.

Rom. 6. 11.
Now the sum of our account is set down in these words, *similiter et vos*; that we fashion ourselves like to Christ, dying and rising, cast ourselves in the same moulds, express Him in both as near as we can.

To account of these first, that is, to account ourselves bound so to do.

To account of these second, that is, to account with ourselves whether we do so.

First, to account ourselves bound thus to do, resolving thus within ourselves, that to hear a Sermon of the Resurrection is nothing; to keep a feast of the Resurrection is as much, except it end in *similiter et vos*. *Nisi*, saith St. Gregory, *quod de more celebratur etiam quoad mores exprimatur*, 'unless we express the matter of the feast in the form of our lives;' unless as He from the grave so we from sin, and live to godliness as He unto God.

Then to account with ourselves, whether we do thus; that is, to sit down and reflect upon the sermons we hear, and the feasts we keep; how, by knowing Christ's death, we die to sin; how, by knowing His resurrection, we live to God; how our estate in soul is bettered; how the fruit of the words we hear, and the feasts we keep, do abound daily toward our account against the great audit. And this to be our account, every Easter-day.

Of these two points, the former is in the two first verses, what we must know; the latter is in the last, what we must account for. And they be joined with *similiter*, to shew us they be and must be of equal and like regard; and as we know, so account. The division.

But because our knowing is the ground of our account, the Apostle beginneth with knowledge. And so must we.

Knowledge, in all learning, is of two sorts. 1. *rerum*, or 2. *causarum*, ὅτι, or διότι, 'that,' or 'in that.' The former is in the first verse: "knowing that Christ," &c. The latter, in the second; "for, in that," &c. And because we cannot cast up a sum, except we have a particular, the Apostle giveth us a particular of either. A particular of our knowledge *quoad res*, which consisteth of these three: that "Christ is risen from the dead." 2. That now "He dieth not." 3. That "from henceforth death hath no dominion over Him." All in the first verse. Then a particular of our knowledge *quoad causas*. The cause 1. of His death, sin; "He died to sin." 2. Of His life, God; "He liveth to God." And both these but once for all. All in the second verse. 1. 1. 2.

Then followeth our account, in the third verse. Wherein we consider, first, 1. the charge; 2. and then the discharge. 1. The charge first, *similiter et vos;* that we be like to Christ. And then wherein; 1. like, in dying to sin; 2. like, in living to God. Which are the two moulds wherein we are to be cast, that we may come forth like Him. This is the charge. 2. And last of all, the means we have to help us to discharge it, in the last words, "in Christ Jesus our Lord." II. 1. 2.

Before we take view of the two particulars, it will not be amiss to make a little stay at *scientes*, the first word, because I. Our knowing: The means of it.

SERM.
I.

it is the ground of all the rest. "Knowing that Christ is risen." This the Apostle saith, the Romans did;—"knowing." Did know himself indeed, that Christ was risen, for he saw Him. But how knew the Romans, or how know we? No other way than by relation, either they or we, but yet we much better than they. I say by relation, in the nature of a verdict, of them that had seen Him, even Cephas and the twelve; which is a full jury, able to find any matter of fact, and to give up a verdict in it. And that Christ is risen, is matter of fact. But if twelve will not serve in this matter of fact, which in all other matters with us will, if a greater inquest far, if five hundred will serve, you may have so many;

1 Cor. 15. 6. for "of more than five hundred at once was He seen," many of them then living ready to give up the same verdict, and to say the same upon their oaths.

But to settle a knowledge, the number moveth not so much as the quality of the parties. If they were persons credulous, light of belief, they may well be challenged, if they took not the way to ground their knowledge aright. That is ever best known that is most doubted of; and never was matter carried with more scruple and slowness of belief, with more doubts and difficulties, than was this of Christ's

Mark 16. 11.
Lu. 24. 13. 41.

rising. Mary Magdalene saw it first, and reported it. "They believed her not." The two that went to Emmaus, they also reported it. They believed them not. Divers women to-

Lu. 24. 11. gether saw Him, and came and told them; "their words seemed to them λῆρος, an idle, feigned, fond tale." They all

Mat. 28. 17. saw Him, and even seeing Him, yet they "doubted." When they were put out of doubt, and told it but to one that happened to be absent, it was St. Thomas, you know how pe-

Joh. 20. 25. remptory he was; "not he, unless he might not only see with his eyes, but feel with his fingers, and put in his hand into His side." And all this he did. St. Augustine saith well: *Profecto valde dubitatum est ab illis, ne dubitaretur a nobis;* 'all this doubting was by them made, that we might be out of doubt, and know that Christ is risen.'

Sure, they took the right course to know it certainly; and certainly they did know it, as appeareth. For never was any thing known in this world, so confidently, constantly, certainly testified as was this, that Christ is risen. By testifying it, they got nothing in the earth. Got nothing? Nay, they lost by it their living, their life, all they had to lose. They might have saved all, and but said nothing. So certain they were, so certainly they did account of their knowing, they could not be got from it, but to their very last breath, to the very last drop of their blood, bare witness to the truth of this article; and chose rather to lay down their lives and to take their death, than to deny, nay than not to affirm His rising from death. And thus did they know, and knowing testify, and by their testimony came the Romans to their knowing, and so do we. But, as I said before, we to a much surer knowing than they. For when this was written, the whole world stopped their ears at this report, would not endure to hear them, stood out mainly against them. The Resurrection! why it was with the Grecians at Athens, χλευ-ασμὸς, a very 'scorn.' The Resurrection! why it was with Acts 17. 32. Festus the great Roman, μανία, 'a sickness of the brain, Acts 26. 24. a plain frenzy.' That world that then was and long after in such opposition, is since come in; and upon better examination of the matter so strangely testified, with so many thousand lives of men, to say the least of them, sad and sober, hath taken notice of it, and both known and acknowledged the truth of it. It was well foretold by St. John, *hæc est* 1 Joh. 5. 4. *victoria quæ vincit mundum, fides vestra.* It is proved true since, that this faith of Christ's rising hath made a conquest of the whole world. So that, after all the world hath taken knowledge of it, we come to know it. And so more full to us, than to them, is this *scientes,* "knowing." Now to our particulars, what we know.

Our first particular is, That Christ is risen from the dead. 2. Properly, we are said to rise from a fall, and from death The particulars rather to revive. Yet the Apostle rather useth the term *quoad nos.* of rising than reviving, as serving better to set forth his Christ is risen from purpose. That death is a fall we doubt not, that it came the dead. with a fall, the fall of Adam. But what manner of fall? for it hath been holden a fall, from whence is no rising. But by Christ's rising it falls out to be a fall, that we may fall and yet get up again. For if Christ be risen from it, then is there a rising; if a rising of one, then may there be of another; if He be risen in our nature, then is our nature

SE R M. risen; and if our nature be, our persons may be. Especially
I.
————— seeing, as the Apostle in the fourth verse before hath told us,
[Rom.6.5.] He and we are σύμφυτοι, that is, so "grafted" one into the
other, that He is part of us, and we of Him; so that as
St. Bernard well observeth, *Christus etsi solus resurrexit,
tamen non totus,* 'that Christ, though He be risen only, yet
He is not risen wholly,' or all, till we be risen too. He is
but risen in part, and that He may rise all, we must rise
from death also.

This then we know first : that death is not a fall like that
Ex. 15. 10. of Pharaoh into the sea, that "sunk down like a lump of
Jonah 1.17.
Jonah 2.10. lead" into the bottom, and never came up more; but a fall
Mat. 12. 40. like that of Jonas into the sea, who was received by a fish,
and after cast up again. It is our Saviour Christ's own
Mat. 25.41. simile. A fall, not like that of the Angels into the bottom-
less pit, there to stay for ever; but like to that of men into
their beds, when they make account to stand up again. A
fall, not as of a log or stone to the ground, which, where
Isa. 26. 19. it falleth there it lieth still; but as of a wheat-corn into the
1Cor.15.36. ground, which is quickened and springeth up again.

The very word which the Apostle useth, ἐγερθεὶς, implieth
the two latter : 1. either of a fall into a bed in our chamber,
where, though we lie to see to little better than dead for
a time, yet in the morning we awake and stand up notwithstanding; 2. or of a fall into a bed in our garden, where,
though the seed putrify and come to nothing, yet we look to
see it shoot forth anew in the spring. Which spring is, as
[Vid. Ter- Tertullian well calleth it, the very resurrection of the year;
tull. de
Resurrect. and Christ's Resurrection falleth well with it; and it is, saith
Carn. 12.] he, no way consonant to reason, that man for whom all things
spring and rise again, should not have his spring and rising
too. But he shall have them, we doubt not, by this day's
work. He That this day did rise, and rising was seen of
Joh. 20. 15. Mary Magdalene in the likeness of a gardener, this Gardener
will look to it, that man shall have his spring. He will, saith
Isa. 26. 19. the Prophet, "drop upon us a dew like the dew of herbs, and
the earth shall yield forth her dead." And so, as Christ is
risen from the dead, even so shall we.

1. That Our second particular is, That as He is risen, so now He
Christ now
dieth not. dieth not. Which is no idle addition, but hath his force

and emphasis. For one thing it is to rise from the dead, and
another, not to die any more. The widow's son of Nain, Lu. 7. 14.--
the ruler's daughter of the synagogue, Lazarus,—all these Lu. 8. 54.
rose again from death, yet they died afterward; but "Christ Joh. 11. 43.
rising from the dead, dieth no more." These two are sensibly different, Lazarus' resurrection, and Christ's; and this
second is sure a higher degree than the former. If we rise
as they did, that we return to this same mortal life of ours
again, this very mortality of ours will be to us as the
prisoner's chain he escapes away withal; by it we shall be
pulled back again, though we should rise a thousand times.
We must therefore so rise as Christ, that our resurrection
be not *reditus,* but *transitus;* not a returning back to the
same life, but a passing over to a new. *Transivit de morte* Joh. 5. 24.
ad vitam, saith He. The very feast itself puts us in mind
of as much; it is *Pascha,* that is, the Passover, not a Deu. 17. 16.
coming back to the same land of Egypt, but a passing over
to a better, the Land of Promise, whither "Christ our 1 Cor. 5. 7.
Passover" is passed before us, and shall in His good time
give us passage after Him. The Apostle expresseth it
best where he saith, that Christ by His rising hath "abo-
lished death, and brought to light life and immortality;" 2 Tim.1.10.
not life alone, but life and immortality, which is this our
second particular. Risen, and risen to die no more, because
risen to life, to life immortal.

But the third is yet beyond both these, more worth the 3. That
knowing, more worthy our account; "death hath no do- from
henceforth
minion over Him." Where, as we before said, one thing "death
hath no
it was to rise again, another to die no more, so say we now; more dominion
it is one thing not to die, another not to be under the do- over Him."
minion of death. For death, and death's dominion are two
different things. Death itself is nothing else but the very
separation of the life from the body, death's dominion a
thing of far larger extent. By which word of "dominion,"
the Apostle would have us to conceive of death, as of some
great lord having some large signory. Even as three several
times in the chapter before he saith, *regnavit mors,* "death Rom. 5. 14.
reigned," as if death were some mighty monarch, having 17. 21.
some great dominions under him. And so it is; for look
how many dangers, how many diseases, sorrows, calamities,

SERM. miseries there be of this mortal life; how many pains, perils,
I.
snares of death; so many several provinces are there of this
dominion. In all which, or some of them, while we live,
we still are under the jurisdiction and arrest of death all
the days of our life. And say that we escape them all, and
none of them happen to us, yet live we still under fear of
them, and that is death's dominion too. For he is, as Job
Job 18. 14. calleth him, *Rex pavoris*, "King of fear." And when we
are out of this life too, unless we pertain to Christ and His
Resurrection, we are not out of his dominion neither. For
Rev. 20. 14. hell itself is *secunda mors*, so termed by St. John, "the
Rev. 21. 8. second death," or second part of death's dominion.

Now, who is there that would desire to rise again to this
life, yea, though it were immortal, to be still under this
dominion of death here; still subject, still liable to the
aches and pains, to the griefs and gripings, to the manifold
miseries of this vale of the shadow of death? But then the
other, the second region of death, the second part of his
dominion, who can endure once to be there? There they
seek and wish for death, and death flieth from them.

Verily, rising is not enough; rising, not to die again is
not enough, except we may be quit of this dominion, and
rid of that which we either feel or fear all our life long.
Therefore doth the Apostle add, and so it was needful he
should, "death hath no dominion over Him." "No dominion over Him?" No; for He, dominion over it. For
lest any might surmise He might break through some wall,
or get out at some window, and so steal a resurrection, or
Rev. 1. 18. casually come to it, he tells them—No, it is not so. *Ecce
claves mortis et inferni;* see here, the keys both of the first
and second death. Which is a plain proof He hath mas-
[Heb.2.14.] tered, and got the dominion over both "death and him
that hath the power of death, that is the devil." Both are
swallowed up in victory, and neither death any more sting,
1 Cor.15.55. nor hell any more dominion. *Sed ad Dominum Deum nos-
Ps. 68. 20. trum spectant exitus mortis;* "but now unto God our Lord
belong the issues of death;" the keys are at His girdle, He
can let out as many as He list.

Rev. 2. 10. This estate is it, which he calleth *coronam vitæ;* not life
alone, but "the crown of life," or a life crowned with im-

munity of fear of any evil, ever to befal us. This is it which
in the next verse he calleth "living unto God," the estate Rom. 6. 11.
of the children of the resurrection, to be the sons of God,
equal to the Angels, subject to no part of death's dominion,
but living in security, joy, and bliss for ever.

And now is our particular full. 1. Rising to life first;
2. and life freed from death, and so immortal; 3. and then
exempt from the dominion of death, and every part of it;
and so happy and blessed. Rise again? so may Lazarus,
or any mortal man do; that is not it. Rise again to life
immortal? so shall all do in the end, as well the unjust as
the just; that is not it. But rise again to life immortal,
with freedom from all misery, to live to, and with God, in
all joy and glory evermore;—that is it, that is Christ's resurrection. *Et tu,* saith St. Augustine, *spera talem resurrectionem, et propter hoc esto Christianus,* 'live in hope of such
a resurrection, and for this hope's sake carry thyself as a
Christian.' Thus have we our particular of that we are to
know touching Christ risen.

And now we know all these, yet do we not account ourselves to know them perfectly until we also know the reason
of them. And the Romans were a people that loved to see **2.**
the ground of that they received, and not the bare articles
alone. Indeed it might trouble them why Christ should
need thus to rise again, because they saw no reason why
He should need die. The truth is, we cannot speak of
rising well without mention of the *terminus a quo,* from
whence He rose. By means whereof these two, 1. Christ's
dying, and 2. His rising, are so linked together, and their
audits so entangled one with another, as it is very hard to
sever them. And this you shall observe, the Apostle never
goeth about to do it, but still as it were of purpose suffers
one to draw in the other continually. It is not here alone,
but all over his Epistles; ever they run together, as if he
were loath to mention one without the other.

And it cannot be denied but that their joining serveth to **1.**
many great good purposes. These two, 1. His death, and
2. His rising, they shew His two natures, human and Divine;
1. His human nature and weakness in dying, 2. His Divine
nature and power in rising again. 2. These shew His two **2.**

offices; His Priesthood and His Kingdom. 1. His Priesthood in the sacrifice of His death; 2. His Kingdom in the
3. glory of His resurrection. 3. They set before us His two
main benefits, 1. *interitum mortis*, and 2. *principium vitæ.*
1. His death, the death of death; 2. His rising, the reviving of life again; the one what He had ransomed us
4. from, the other what He had purchased for us. 4. They
serve as two moulds, wherein our lives are to be cast, that
the days of our vanity may be fashioned to the likeness of
the Son of God; which are our two duties, that we are to
render for those two benefits, proceeding from the two offices
of His two natures conjoined. In a word, they are not well
to be sundered; for when they are thus joined, they are the
very abridgment of the whole Gospel.

1. The
cause of
His dying.
1. His
dying
once.
Of them both then briefly. Of His dying first: "In that
He died, He died once to sin." Why died He once, and
why but once? Once He died to sin, that is, sin was the
cause He was to die once. As in saying "He liveth to
God," we say God is the cause of His life, so in saying
"He died to sin" we say sin was the cause of His death.
God of His rising, sin of His fall. And look, how the
Resurrection leadeth us to death, even as naturally doth
death unto sin, the sting of death.

To sin then He died; not simply to sin, but with reference to us. For as death leadeth us to sin, so doth sin to
sinners, that is, to ourselves; and so will the opposition be
more clear and full: "He liveth unto God," "He died unto
man." With reference, I say, to us. For first He died
Isa. 9. 6. unto us; and if it be true that *Puer natus est nobis*, it is as
true that *Vir mortuus est nobis;* if being a Child He was
born to us, becoming a Man He died to us. Both are true.

To us then first He died because He would save us. To
sin secondly, because else He could not save us. Yes He
could have saved us and never died for us, *ex plenitudine
potestatis,* 'by His absolute power,' if He would have taken
that way. That way He would not, but proceed by way of
justice, do all by way of justice. And by justice sin must
have death,—death, our death, for the sin was ours. It was
we that were to die to sin. But if we had died to sin, we
had perished in sin; perished here, and perished everlast-

ingly. That His love to us could not endure, that we should
so perish. Therefore, as in justice He justly might, He took
upon Him our debt of sin, and said, as the Fathers apply that
speech of His, *Sinite abire hos,* "Let these go their ways." Joh. 18. 8.
And so that we might not die to sin He did. We see why
He died once.

Why but once? because once was enough, *ad auferenda,* 2. And but
saith St. John; *ad abolenda,* saith St. Peter; *ad exhaurienda,* $\substack{\text{once.}\\ \text{Joh. 1. 29.}}$
saith St. Paul; 'to take away, to abolish, to draw dry,' and Acts 3. 19.
utterly to exhaust all the sins, of all the sinners, of all the Heb. 9. 28.
world. The excellency of His Person That performed it was
such; the excellency of the obedience that He performed,
such; the excellency of His humility and charity wherewith
He performed it, such; and of such value every of them, and
all of them much more; as made that His once dying was
satis superque, 'enough, and enough again;' which made the
Prophet call it *copiosam redemptionem,* "a plenteous redemp- [Ps. 130. 7.]
tion." But the Apostle, he goeth beyond all in expressing Eph. 2. 7.
this; in one place terming it ὑπερβάλλων, in another ὑπερ- $\substack{\text{Eph. 3. 20.}\\ \text{1 Tim. 1. 14.}}$
εκπερισσεύων[1], in another πλεονάζων[2],—mercy, rich, ex- [1 ὑπὲρ ἐκ
ceeding; grace over-abounding, nay, grace superfluous, for so περισσοῦ.
is πλεονάζων, and superfluous is enough and to spare; super- $\substack{\text{G. V.]}\\ \text{[}^2\text{ ὑπερ-}}$
fluous is clearly enough and more than enough. Once dying πλεονά-
then being more than enough, no reason He should die more $\substack{\text{ζων. G. V.]}}$
than once. That of His death.

Now of His life: "He liveth unto God." The rigour of 2. The
the law being fully satisfied by His death, then was He no $\substack{\text{cause of}\\ \text{His living.}}$
longer justly, but wrongfully detained by death. As there-
fore by the power He had, He laid down His life, so He took
it again, and rose again from the dead. And not only rose
Himself, but in one concurrent action, God, Who had by His
death received full satisfaction, reached Him as it were His
hand, and raised Him to life. The Apostle's word ἐγερθεὶς,
in the native force doth more properly signify, "raised by
another," than risen by himself, and is so used, to shew it
was done, not only by the power of the Son, but by the will,
consent, and co-operation of the Father; and He the cause
of it, Who for the over-abundant merit of His death, and His
humbling Himself, and "becoming obedient to death, even
the death of the cross," not only raised Him, but *propter hoc,* Phil. 2. 8, 9.

SERM.
I.

Ps. 36. 9.

II.
Our ac-
count.
1. Of our
comings
in: the
benefit.

1 Pet. 1. 3.

1 Thes. 4.
18.

Joh. 11. 23.

"even for that cause," exalted Him also, to live with Him, in joy and glory for ever. For, as when He lived to man He lived to much misery, so now He liveth to God He liveth in all felicity. This part being oppositely set down to the former; living, to exclude dying again; living to God, to exclude death's dominion, and all things pertaining to it. For, as with "God is life and the fountain of life" against death, even the fountain of life never failing, but ever renewing to all eternity; so with Him also is *torrens deliciarum*, "a main river of pleasures," even pleasures for evermore; never ebbing, but ever flowing to all contentment, against the miseries belonging to death's dominion. And there He liveth thus: not now, as the Son of God, as He lived before all worlds, but as the Son of man, in the right of our nature; to estate us in this life in the hope of a reversion, and in the life to come in the perfect and full possession of His own and His Father's bliss and happiness; when we shall also live to God, and God be all in all, which is the highest pitch of all our hope. We see then His dying and rising, and the grounds of both, and thus have we the total of our *scientes*.

Now followeth our account. An account is either of what is coming to us, and that we like well, or what is going from us, and that is not so pleasing. Coming to us I call matter of benefit, going from us matter of duty; where I doubt many an expectation will be deceived, making account to hear from the Resurrection matter of benefit only to come in, where the Apostle calleth us to account for matter of duty which is to go from us.

An account there is growing to us by Christ's rising, of matter of benefit and comfort; such an one there is, and we have touched it before. The hope of gaining a better life, which groweth from Christ's rising, is our comfort against the fear of losing this. Thus do we comfort ourselves against our deaths: "Now blessed be God that hath regenerated us to a lively hope, by the resurrection of Jesus Christ." Thus do we comfort ourselves against our friends' death; "Comfort yourselves one another," saith the Apostle, "with these words." What words be they? Even those of our Saviour in the Gospel, *Resurget frater tuus*, "Thy brother" or thy father, or thy friend, "shall rise again." And not only

against death, but even against all the miseries of this life.
It was Job's comfort on the dunghill: well yet, *videbo Deum in* Job 19. 25.
carne meâ; "I shall see God in my flesh." And not in our
miseries alone, but when we do well, and no man respecteth
us for it. It is the Apostle's conclusion of the chapter of the
Resurrection: Be of good cheer yet, *labor vester non erit in-*
anis in Domino, your "labour is not in vain in the Lord," 1Cor.15.58.
you shall have your reward at the resurrection of the just.
All these ways comfort cometh unto us by it.

But this of ours is another manner of account, of duty to 2. Of our
go from us, and to be answered by us. And such an one goings out.
there is too, and we must reckon of it. I add that this here duty or
is our first account, you see it here called for in the Epistle charge.
to the Romans; the other cometh after, in the Epistle to the
Corinthians.

In very deed, this of ours is the key to the other, and we
shall never find sound comfort of that, unless we do first well
pass this account here. It is I say, first, because it is present, and concerneth our souls, even here in this life. The
other is future, and toucheth but our bodies, and that in the
life to come. It is an error certainly, which runneth in
men's heads when they hear of the Resurrection, to conceive
of it as of a matter merely future, and not to take place till
the latter day. Not only "Christ is risen," but if all be as it
should be, "We are already risen with Him," saith the Colos. 3. 1.
Apostle, in the Epistle this day, the very first words of it;
and even here now, saith St. John, is there a "first resurrec- Rev. 20. 6.
tion," and happy is he that "hath his part in it." A like
error it is to conceit the Resurrection as a thing merely
corporal, and no ways to be incident into the spirit or soul at
all. The Apostle hath already given us an item to the contrary, in the end of the fourth chapter before, where he saith:
"He rose again for our justification," and justification is a Rom. 4. 25.
matter spiritual; *Justificatus est Spiritu,* saith the Apostle, 1 Tim. 3.16.
of Christ Himself. Verily, here must the spirit rise to grace,
or else neither the body nor it shall there rise to glory. This
then is our first account, that account of ours, which presently is to be passed, and out of hand; this is it which first
we must take order for.

The sum or charge of which account is set down in these 1.
To be like
Christ.

SERM.
I.

words, *similiter et vos;* that we be like Christ, carry His image Who is heavenly, as we have carried the image of the earthly, "be conformed to His likeness;" that what Christ hath wrought for us, the like be wrought in us; what wrought for us by His flesh, the like wrought in us by His Spirit. It is a maxim or main ground in all the Fathers, that such an account must be: the former, what Christ hath wrought for us, *Deus reputat nobis,* 'God accounteth to us;' for the latter, what Christ hath wrought in us, *reputate vos,* we must account to God. And that is, *similiter et vos,* that we fashion ourselves like Him.

Like Him in as many points as we may, but namely and expressly, in these two here set down: 1. "In dying to sin," 2. "In living unto God." In these two first; then secondly, in doing both these, ἐφάπαξ, but "once for all."

1. In dying to sin.
Eph. 5. 2.
1 Pet. 2. 21.

Like Him in these two: 1. In His dying. For He died not only to offer "a sacrifice" for us, saith St. Paul, but also to leave "an example" to us, saith St. Peter. That example are we to be like. 2. In His rising: for He arose not only

1 Pet. 1. 3.

that we might be "regenerated to a lively hope," saith St. Peter, but also that we might be "grafted into the similitude of His resurrection," saith St. Paul, a little before, in the fifth verse of this very chapter. That similitude are we to resemble. So have we the exemplary part of both these, whereunto we are to frame our *similiter et vos.*

"He died to sin:"—there is our pattern. Our first account must be, "count yourselves dead to sin." And that we do when there is neither action, nor affection, nor any sign of life in us toward sin, no more than in a dead body; when, as men crucified, which is not only His death, but the kind of His death too, we neither move hand, nor stir foot toward it, both are nailed down fast. In a word, to

1 Pet. 4. 1.

"die to sin," with St. Paul here, is to "cease from sin," with St. Peter.

To "cease from sin" I say, understanding by sin, not from sin altogether—that is a higher perfection than this life will bear, but as the Apostle expoundeth himself in the very next

Rom. 6. 12.

words, *Ne regnet peccatum,* that is, from the "dominion of sin" to cease. For till we be free from death itself, which in this life we are not, we shall not be free from sin altogether;

only we may come thus far, *ne regnet*, that sin "reign not," wear not a crown, sit not in a throne, hold no parliaments within us, give us no laws; in a word, as in the fourth verse before, that we serve it not. To die to the dominion of sin, [Rom. 6. 6.] —that by the grace of God we may, and that we must account for.

" He liveth to God." There is our similitude of His re- 2. In living surrection: our second account must be, count yourselves to God. "living unto God." Now how that is, he hath already told us in the fourth verse, even "to walk in newness of life." To walk is to move; moving is a vital action, and argueth life. But it must not be any life, our old will not serve; it must be a new life, we must not return back to our former course, but pass over to another new conversation. And in a word as before, to live to God with St. Paul here, is to live *secundum Deum,* "according to God in the Spirit," with 1 Pet. 4. 6. St. Peter. And then live we according to Him, when His will is our law, His word our rule, His Son's life our example, His Spirit rather than our own soul the guide of our actions. Thus shall we be grafted into the similitude of His resurrection.

Now this similitude of the Resurrection calleth to my mind another similitude of the Resurrection in this life too, which I find in Scripture mentioned; it fitteth us well, it will not be amiss to remember you of it by the way, it will make us the better willing to enter into this account.

At the time that Isaac should have been offered by his father, Isaac was not slain: very near it he was, there was Gen. 22. 7. fire, and there was a knife, and he was appointed ready to be a sacrifice. Of which case of his, the Apostle in the mention of his father Abraham's faith,—"Abraham," saith he, "by Heb. 11. 17- faith," λογισάμενος, " made full account," if Isaac had been 19. slain, " God was able to raise him from the dead." And even from the dead God raised him, and his father received him, ἐν παραβολῇ, "in a certain similitude," or after a sort. Mark that well: Raising Isaac from imminent danger of present death, is with the Apostle a kind of resurrection. And if it be so, and if the Holy Ghost warrant us to call that a kind of resurrection, how can we but on this day, the day of the Resurrection, call to mind, and withal render unto God our unfeigned thanks and praise, for our late resurrection¹ ἐν παρα-βολῇ, for our kind of resurrection, He not long since vouchsafed us. Our case was Isaac's case without doubt: there was fire, and instead of a knife, there was powder enough, and we were designed all of us, and even ready, to be sacrificed, even Abraham, Isaac, and all. Certainly if Isaac's were, ours was a kind of resurrection, and we so to acknowledge it. We were as near as he; we were not only within the dominion, but within the verge, nay even within the very gates of death. From thence hath God raised us, and given us this year this similitude of the Resurrection, that we might this day of the resurrection of His Son, present Him with this, in the text, of " rising to a new course of life."

And now to return to our fashioning ourselves like to Him, in these: As there is a death natural, and a death civil, so is there a death moral, both in philosophy and in divinity; and if a death, then consequently a resurrection too. Every great and notable change of our course of life, whereby we are not now any longer the same men that before we were, be it from worse to better, or from better to worse, is a moral death; a moral death to that we change from, and a moral resurrection to that we change to. If we change to the better, that is sin's death; if we alter to the worse, that is sin's resurrection. When we commit sin, we die, we are dead in sin; when we repent, we revive again; when we repent ourselves of our repenting and relapse back, then sin riseth again from the dead: and so *toties quoties.* And even upon these two, as two hinges, turneth our whole life. All our life is spent in one of them.

3. And that "once for all."
Now then that we be not all our life long thus off and on, fast or loose, in dock out nettle, and in nettle out dock, it will behove us once more yet to look back upon our *similiter et vos,* even upon the word ἐφάπαξ, *semel,* " once." That is, that we not only " die to sin," and " live to God," but die and live as He did, that is, " once for all;" which is an utter abandoning " once" of sin's dominion, and a continual, constant, persisting in a good course " once" begun. Sin's dominion, it languisheth sometimes in us, and falleth haply into a swoon, but it dieth not quite " once for all." Grace lifteth up the eye, and looketh up a little, and giveth some sign of

life, but never perfectly receiveth. O that once we might
come to this! no more deaths, no more resurrections, but
one! that we might once make an end of our daily continual
recidivations to which we are so subject, and once get past
these pangs and qualms of godliness, this righteousness like
the morning cloud, which is all we perform; that we might
grow habituate in grace, *radicati et fundati*, "rooted and
founded in it;" ἐῤῥιζωμένοι, "steady," and ἐδραῖοι, "never
to be removed;" that so we might enter into, and pass a
good account of this our *similiter et vos!*

Eph. 3. 17.
1 Cor. 15.
ult.

And thus are we come to the foot of our account, which is
our *onus*, or 'charge.' Now we must think of our discharge,
to go about it; which maketh the last words no less necessary for us to consider, than all the rest. For what? is it in
us, or can we, by our own power and virtue, make up this
account? We cannot, saith the Apostle; nay we cannot,
saith he, λογίσασθαι, "make account of any thing," no not
so much as of a good thought toward it, as of ourselves. If
any think otherwise, let him but prove his own strength
a little, what he can do, he shall be so confounded in it, as he
shall change his mind, saith St. Augustine, and see plainly,
the Apostle had reason to shut up all with *in Christo Jesu
Domino nostro :* otherwise our account will stick in our hands.
Verily, to raise a soul from the death of sin, is harder,
far harder, than to raise a dead body out of the dust of death.
St. Augustine hath long since defined it, that Mary Magdalene's resurrection in soul, from her long lying dead in
sin, was a greater miracle than her brother Lazarus' resurrection, that had lain four days in his grave. If Lazarus lay
dead before us, we would never assay to raise him ourselves;
we know we cannot do it. If we cannot raise Lazarus that
is the easier of the twain, we shall never Mary Magdalene
which is the harder by far, out of Him, or without Him, That
raised them both.

2.
The dis-
charge
and means
of it.
"In Jesus
Christ our
Lord."

2 Cor. 3. 5.

But as out of Christ, or without Christ, we can do nothing
toward this account; not accomplish or bring to perfection,
but not do—not any great or notable sum of it, but nothing
at all; as saith St. Augustine, upon *sine Me nihil potestis
facere*. So, in Him and with Him enabling us to it, we can

Joh. 15. 5.
[S. Aug.
Tract. in
Joann.
81. 3.]

SERM. think good thoughts, speak good words, and do good works,
I.   and die to sin, and live to God, and all.   *Omnia possum,*
Phil. 4. 13. saith the Apostle.   And enable us He will, and can, as not
only having passed the resurrection, but being the Resurrection itself; not only had the effect of it in Himself, but being
Joh. 11. 25. the cause of it to us.   So He saith Himself: " I am the Resurrection and the Life;" the Resurrection to them that are
dead in sin, to raise them from it; and the Life to them that
live unto God, to preserve them in it.

Where, besides the two former, 1. the article of the Resurrection, which we are to know; 2. and the example of the
Resurrection, which we are to be like; we come to the notice
of a third thing, even a virtue or power flowing from Christ's
resurrection, whereby we are made able to express our *si-*
militer et vos, and to pass this our account of " dying to sin,"
and " living to God."   It is in plain words called by the
Phil. 3. 10. Apostle himself, *virtus resurrectionis,* " the virtue of Christ's
resurrection," issuing from it to us; and he prayeth that as
he had a faith of the former, so he may have a feeling of this;
and as of them he had a contemplative, so he may of this
have an experimental knowledge.   This enabling virtue proceedeth from Christ's resurrection.   For never let us think,
if in the days of His flesh there " went virtue out" from even
Lu. 8. 46. the very edge of His garment to do great cures, as in the
case of the woman with the bloody issue we read, but that
from His Ownself, and from those two most principal and
powerful actions of His Ownself, His 1. death and 2. resurrection, there issueth a divine power; from His death a power
working on the old man or flesh to mortify it; from His
resurrection a power working on the new man, the spirit, to
quicken it.   A power able to roll back any stone of an evil
custom, lie it never so heavy on us; a power able to dry up
any issue, though it have run upon us twelve years long.

And this power is nothing else but that divine quality of
grace, which we receive from Him.   Receive it from Him we
do certainly : only let us pray, and endeavour ourselves, that
2 Cor. 6. 1. we " receive it not in vain," the Holy Ghost by ways to flesh
and blood unknown inspiring it as a breath, distilling it as
a dew, deriving it as a secret influence into the soul.   For

if philosophy grant an invisible operation in us to the celestial bodies, much better may we yield it to His eternal Spirit, whereby such a virtue or breath may proceed from it, and be received of us.

Which breath, or spirit, is drawn in by prayer, and such other exercises of devotion on our parts; and, on God's part, breathed in, by, and with, the word, well therefore termed by the Apostle, "the word of grace." And I may safely say it Acts 20. 32. with good warrant, from those words especially and chiefly; which, as He Himself saith of them, are "spirit and life," Joh. 6. 63. even those words, which joined to the element make the blessed Sacrament.

There was good proof made of it this day. All the way did He preach to them, even till they came to Emmaus, and their hearts were hot within them, which was a good sign; but their eyes were not opened but "at the breaking of Lu. 24. 31. bread," and then they were. That is the best and surest sense we know, and therefore most to be accounted of. There we taste, and there we see; "taste and see how Ps. 34. 8. gracious the Lord is." There we are made to "drink of the 1 Cor. 12. Spirit," there our "hearts are strengthened and stablished 13. with grace." There is the blood which shall "purge our Heb. 9. 14. consciences from dead works," whereby we may "die to sin." There the Bread of God, which shall endue our souls with much strength; yea, multiply strength in them, to live unto God; yea, to live to Him continually; for he that "eateth Joh. 6. 33. His flesh and drinketh His blood, dwelleth in Christ, and Joh. 6. 56. Christ in him;" not inneth, or sojourneth for a time, but dwelleth continually. And, never can we more truly, or properly say, *in Christo Jesu Domino nostro,* as when we come new from that holy action, for then He is in us, and we in Him, indeed. And so we to make full account of this service, as a special means to further us to make up our Easter-day's account, and to set off a good part of our charge. In Christ, dropping upon us the anointing of His grace. In Jesus, Who will be ready as our Saviour to succour and support us with His *auxilium speciale,* 'His special help.' Without which assisting us, even grace itself is many times faint and feeble in us; and both these, because He is our

SERM. Lord Who, having come to save that which was lost, will not
I.   suffer that to be lost which He hath saved.   Thus using His
own ordinance of Prayer, of the Word, and Sacrament, for
our better enabling to discharge this day's duty, we shall I
trust yield up a good account, and celebrate a good feast of
His resurrection.   Which Almighty God grant, &c.

A SERMON

PREACHED BEFORE

THE KING'S MAJESTY, AT WHITEHALL,

ON THE FIFTH OF APRIL, A.D. MDCVII., BEING EASTER-DAY.

---

1 CORINTHIANS XV. 20.

But now is Christ risen from the dead, and was made the first fruits of them that sleep.

Nunc autem Christus resurrexit a mortuis primitiæ dormientium.

[But now is Christ risen from the dead, and become the first fruits of them that slept. Engl. Trans.]

THE same Apostle that out of Christ's resurrection taught the Romans matter of duty, the same here out of the same resurrection teacheth the Corinthians matter of hope. There, *similiter et vos,* by way of pattern to conform ourselves Rom. 6. 4. to Him "in newness of life;" and here, *similiter et vos,* in another sense by way of promise; that so doing, He shall hereafter conform us to Himself, "change our vile bodies," Phil. 3. 21. and make them like "His glorious body." That former is our first resurrection from sin, this latter our second resurrection from the grave; this, the reward of that. In that, the work what to do; in this, our reward; what to hope for. These two, labour and hope, the Church joineth in one Anthem to-day, her first Anthem. They sort well, and being sung together make a good harmony. But that without this, labour without hope, is no good music.

To rise, and to reclaim ourselves from a sinful course of life we have long lived in, is labour sure, and great labour. Now labour of itself is a harsh unpleasant thing, unless it be seasoned with hope. *Debet qui arat in spe arare,* saith the 1 Cor. 9. 10. Apostle above at the ninth chapter, in the matter of the

P

SERM. II.

Clergy's maintenance, "He that plows must plow in hope;" his plough will not go deep else, his furrows will be but shallow. Men may frame to themselves what speculations they please, but the Apostle's saying will prove true: sever hope from labour, and you must look for labour and labourers accordingly, slight and shallow God knoweth. Labour then leads us to hope.

2. The Apostle saw this, and therefore is careful, whom he thus presseth to newness of life and the labour therefore, to raise for them, and to set before them, matter of hope. Hope here in this life he could set them none. They were, as he was himself, at *quotidie morior* every hour, in danger to be drawn to the block. It must therefore be from another, or at least as the text is, by a hope of being restored to life again. It was their case at Corinth, here in this chapter, plainly: If we must die to-morrow, if there be all that shall become of us, then "let us eat and drink" while we may. If we be not sure of another life, let us make sure of this. But when in the sequel of the chapter, he had shewed there was restoring, and that so sure he was of it that he falls to insult over them in these terms, they gird up their loins again, and fall to their labours afresh, as knowing their labour should not be "in vain in the Lord." This hope leads us to our restoring.

1 Cor. 15. 31.

1 Cor. 15. 32.

1 Cor.15.58.

3. Our restoring is but a promise—*shall be* restored: that necessarily refers to a party that is to make it good. Who is that? Christ. "Christ is our hope." Why, "hope is joined to the living," saith the Wise Man. Christ is dead; buried last Friday. If He be our hope, and He be dead, our hope is dead too; and if our hope be dead, our labour will not live long, nay both are buried with Christ in His grave. It was their case this day that went to Emmaus: say they, supposing Christ to be dead, *nos autem sperabamus*, "we were once in good hope" by Him, that is, while He lived; as much to say as 'Now He is in His grave, our hope is gone, we are even going to Emmaus.' But then after, as soon as they saw He was alive again, their hope revived, and with their hope their labour; and presently back again to Jerusalem to the Lord's work and bade Emmaus farewell. So He leads us to labour; labour, to hope; hope, to our restoring; our restoring to Christ's, Who, as He hath restored Himself, will restore us

[1Tim.1.1.]

Ecc. 9. 4.

Lu. 24. 21.

also to life. And this keeps us from going to Emmaus. It
is used proverbially. Emmaus signifieth ' a people forlorn:'
all that are at *sperabamus,* have lost their hopes, are said to
go thither; and thither we should all go, even to Emmaus,
but for the hope that breathes from this verse, without which
it were a cold occupation to be a Christian.

This then is the hope of this text, *spes viva, spes beata,*
worth all hopes else whatsoever. All hopes else are but *spes
spirantium,* ' hopes while we breathe;' this is *spes expiran-
tium,* ' the hope when we can fetch our breath no longer.'
The carnal man—all he can say is, *dum spiro spero,* ' his hope
is as long as his breath.' The Christian aspireth higher,
goeth farther by virtue of this verse and saith, *dum expiro
spero;* ' his hope fails him not when his breath fails him.'
Even then, saith Job, *reposita est mihi spes in sinu meo;* this Job 19. 27.
hope, and only this, is laid up in our bosom, that though our [Vide Vulg.]
life be taken from us, yet in Christ we to do it, and it to us
shall be restored again.

Our case is not as theirs then was: no persecution, nor
we at *quotidie morior,* and therefore not so sensible of this
doctrine. But yet to them that are daily falling toward
death, rising to life is a good text; peradventure not when
we are well and in good health, but the hour is coming,
when we shall leave catching at all other hopes, and must
hold only by this; *in horá mortis,* when all hope save the
hope of this verse shall forsake us. Sure it is, under these
very words are we laid into our graves, and these the last
words that are said over us, as the very last hold we have;
and we therefore to regard them with Job, and lay them up
in our bosom.

There is in this text, I. a text, and II. an exposition. The di-
I. The text, we may well call the Angel's text, for from vision.
them it came first. II. The exposition is St. Paul's. These
words, " Christ is risen," were first uttered by an Angel this Mat. 28. 6.
day in the sepulchre; all the Evangelists so testify. Mark 16. 6.
Lu. 24. 6.
This text is a good text, but reacheth not to us, unless it II.
be helped with the Apostle's exposition, and then it will.
The exposition is it that giveth us our hope, and the ground
of our hope. " Christ is risen," saith the Angel. " Christ
the first fruits," saith the Apostle. And mark well that word

S E R M.
II. "first fruits," for in that word is our hope. For if He be as the "first fruits" in His rising, His rising must reach to all that are of the heap whereof He is the "first fruits." This is our hope.

III. But our hope must have "a reason," saith St. Peter, and
1 Pet. 3. 15.
Heb. 11. 1.
Rom. 5. 5. we be ready with it. The hope that hath a ground, saith St. Paul, that is, *spes quæ non confundit.* Having then shewed us this hope, he sheweth us the ground of it. This: that in very equity we are to be allowed to be restored to life, the same way we lost it. But we lost it by man, or to speak in particular, by Adam we came by our attainder. Meet therefore, that by man, and to speak in particular, that by Christ, we come to our restoring. This is the ground or substance of our hope.

IV. And thus he hath set before us this day life and death, in themselves and their causes, two things that of all other do most concern us. Our last point shall be to apply it to the means, this day offered unto us toward the restoring us to life.

I.
The text.
"Christ is
risen."
Heb. 6. 1.
1 Cor. 10. 4. The doctrine of the Resurrection is one of the foundations, so called by the Apostle. It behoveth him therefore, as a skilful workman, to see it surely laid. That is surely laid that is laid on the rock, and "the rock is Christ." Therefore he laid it on Christ by saying first, "Christ is risen."

Of all that be Christians, Christ is the hope; but not Christ every way considered, but as risen. Even in Christ un-risen there is no hope. Well doth the Apostle begin
Hos. 2. 15. here; and when he would open to us "a gate of hope," carry us to Christ's sepulchre empty; to shew us, and to hear the Angel say, "He is risen." Thence after to deduce; if He were able to do thus much for Himself, He hath promised us as much, and will do as much for us. We shall be restored to life.

Thus had he proceeded in the four verses before, *destruc-*
1 Cor. 15.
19.
1 Cor. 15.
18. *tive.* 1. Miserable is that man, that either laboureth or suffereth in vain. 2. Christian men seem to do so, and do so, if there be no other life but this. 3. There is no other life but this, if there be no resurrection. 4. There is no
1 Cor. 15.
17. resurrection, "if Christ be not risen;" for ours dependeth on His. And now he turneth all about again. " But now,"

saith he, 1. "Christ is risen." 2. If He be, we shall. 3. If we shall, we have, as St. Paul calleth it, a " blessed hope," Tit. 2.13. and so a life yet behind. 4. If such hope we have, we of all men "labour not in vain." So there are four things : 1. Christ's rising; 2. our restoring; 3. our hope; and 4. our labour. All the doubt is of the two first, the two other will follow of themselves. If a restoring, we have good hope; if good hope, our labour is not lost. The two first are in the first; the other in the last words. The first are, " Christ is risen ;" the last, we shall be restored to life. Our endeavour is to bring these two together, but first to lay the corner-stone.

" Christ is risen," is the Angel's text, a part of the " great mystery of godliness," which, as the Apostle saith, was " seen 1 Tim.3.16. of Angels," by them " delivered," and " believed on by the world." *Quod credibile primum fecit illis videntium certitudo, post morientium fortitudo, jam credibile mihi facit credentium multitudo.* ' It became credible at first by the certainty of them that saw it, then by the constancy of them that died for confession of it, and to us now the huge multitude of them that have and do believe it, maketh it credible.' For if it be not credible, how is it credible that the world could believe it? the world, I say, being neither enjoined by au-thority, nor forced by fear, nor inveigled by allurements; but brought about by persons, by means less credible than the thing itself. Gamaliel said, "If it be of God, it will Acts 5. 39. prevail." And though we cannot argue, all that hath pre-vailed is of God, yet thus we can : that which hath been mightily impugned, and weakly pursued, and yet prevailed, that was of God certainly. That which all the powers of the earth fought but could not prevail against, was from Heaven certainly. Certainly, " Christ is risen ;" for many have risen, and lift up themselves against it, but all are fallen. But the Apostle saith, it is a "foundation," that he will not lay it again; no more will we, but go forward and raise upon it, and so let us do.

" Christ is risen :" suppose He be, what then? Though Christ's rising did no way concern us or we that, yet 1. first, In that a man, one of our own flesh and blood hath gotten such a victory, even for humanity's sake; 2. Then, in that

One that is innocent hath quit Himself so well for innocency's sake; 3. thirdly, In that He hath foiled a common
enemy, for amity's sake; 4. lastly, In that He hath wiped
away the ignominy of His fall with the glory of His rising
again, for virtue and valour's sake; for all these we have cause
to rejoice with Him, all are matter of gratulation.

II.
The Apo-
stle's ex-
position,
Christ as
" the first
fruits."
But the Apostle is about a farther matter; that text, the
Angel's text, he saw would not serve our turn, farther than
I have said. Well may we congratulate him, if that be
all, but otherwise it pertains to us, "Christ is risen." The
Apostle therefore enters farther, telling us that Christ did
thus rise, not as Christ only, but as "Christ the first fruits."
"Christ is risen," and in rising become the "first fruits;"
risen, and so risen; that is, to speak after the manner of
men, that there is in Christ a double capacity. 1. One as a
body natural, considered by Himself, without any relative
respect unto us, or to any; in which regard well may we
be glad, as one stranger is for another, but otherwise His
rising concerns us not at all. 2. Then that He hath a
second, as a body politic, or chief part of a company or cor-
poration, that have to Him, and He to them, a mutual and
reciprocal reference, in which respect His resurrection may
concern us no less than Himself; it is that He giveth us the
first item of in the word *primitiæ*, that Christ in His rising
cometh not to be considered as a *totum integrale*, or body
natural alone, as Christ only; but that which maketh for us,
He hath besides another capacity, that He is a part of a cor-
poration or body, of which body we are the members. This
being won, look what He hath suffered or done, it pertaineth
to us, and we have our part in it.

As a part
of the
whole.
Eph. 1. 22.
Rev. 22. 16.
You shall find, and ever when you find such words make
much of them, Christ called a "Head,"—a head is a part;
Christ called a "Root,"—a root is a part; and here Christ
called "first fruits," which we all know is but a part of the
fruits, but a handful of a heap or a sheaf, and referreth to
the rest of the fruits, as a part to the whole. So that there
is in the Apostle's conceit one mass or heap of all mankind,
of which Christ is the "first fruits," we the remainder. So as
by the law of the body all His concern us no less than they
do Him, whatsoever He did, He did to our behoof. Die

He, or rise, we have our part in His death and in His resurrection, and all: why? because He is but the "first fruits."

And if He were but *Primus,* and not *Primitiæ dormientium,* there were hope. For *primus* is an ordinal number, and draweth after a second, a third, and God knoweth how many. But if in that word there be any scruple, as sometime it is *ante quem non est* rather than *post quem est alius,* if no more come by one; all the world knows the first fruits is but a part of the fruits, there are fruits beside them, no man knoweth how many.

But that which is more, the "first fruits" is not every part, but such a part as representeth the whole, and hath an operative force over the whole. For the better understanding whereof, we are to have recourse to the Law, to the very institution or first beginning of them. Ever the legal ceremony is a good key to the evangelical mystery. Thereby we shall see why St. Paul made choice of the word "first fruits," to express himself by; that he useth *verbum vigilans,* 'a word that is awake,' as St. Augustine saith, or as Solomon, "a word upon his own wheel." The head or the root would have served, for if the head be above the water, there is hope for the whole body, and if the root hath life, the branches shall not long be without; yet he refuseth these and other that offered themselves, and chooseth rather the term of "first fruits." And why so? *As a part for the whole.*

Lev. 23. 10.

Pro. 25. 11.

[See the Marg.]

This very day, Easter-day, the day of Christ's rising, according to the Law, is the day or feast of the "first fruits;" the very feast carrieth him to the word, nothing could be more fit or seasonable for the time. The day of the Passion is the day of the Passover, and "Christ is our Passover;" the day of the Resurrection is the day of the first fruits, and Christ is our "first fruits." *1 Cor. 5. 7.*

And this term thus chosen, you shall see there is a very apt and proper resemblance between the Resurrection and it. The rite and manner of the first fruits, thus it was. Under the Law, they might not eat of the fruits of the earth so long as they were profane. Profane they were, until they were sacred, and on this wise were they sacred. All the sheaves in a field, for example's sake, were unholy. One sheaf is taken out of all the rest, which sheaf we call the first fruits. *Lev. 23. 10.*

SERM. That in the name of the rest is lift up aloft and shaken to
II.
——— and fro before the Lord, and so consecrated. That done,
Lev. 23. 11.
Lev. 23. 14. not only the sheaf so lifted up was holy, though that alone
was lift up, but all the sheaves in the field were holy, no less
Rom. 11.16. than it. The rule is, " If the first fruits be holy, all the lump
is so too."

And thus, for all the world, fareth it in the Resurrection.
2 Cor. 5. 14. " We were all dead," saith the Apostle, dead sheaves all.
One, and that is Christ, this day, the day of first fruits,
was in manner of a sheaf taken out of the number of the
dead, and in the name of the rest lift up from the grave, and
Mat. 28. 2. in His rising He shook, for there was a great earthquake, by
virtue whereof the first fruits being restored to life, all the
rest of the dead are in Him entitled to the same hope, in
that He was not so lift up for Himself alone, but for us and
in our names; and so the substance of this feast fulfilled in
Christ's resurrection.

Not of
the dead,
but "of
them that
sleep:"
Our hope.

Now upon this lifting up, there ensueth a very great alteration, if you please to mark it. It was even now, " Christ is
risen from the dead, the first fruits"—it should be of the
dead too, for from thence He rose; it is not so, but "the
first fruits"—" of them that sleep;" that you may see the
consecration hath wrought a change. A change and a great
change certainly, to change νεκροὶ into κεκοιμημένοι, a burial
place into a cemetery, that is a great *dortor*; graves into
beds, death into sleep, dead men into men laid down to take
Joh. 11. 12. their rest, a rest of hope, of hope to rise again. " If they
sleep, they shall do well."

And that which lieth open in the word, *dormientium*, the
very same is enfolded in the word " first fruits:" either word
affordeth comfort. For first fruits imply fruits, and so we, as
the fruits of the earth, falling as do the grains or kernels into
the ground, and there lying, to all men's seeming putrified
and past hope, yet on a sudden, against the great feast of
first fruits, shooting forth of the ground again. The other
of *dormientium* the Apostle letteth go, and fastens on this
of fruits, and followeth it hard through the rest of the
1 Cor. 15. chapter; shewing, that the rising again of the fruits sown
36.
would be no less incredible than the Resurrection, but that
we see it so every year.

These two words of 1. sleeping and 2. sowing would be laid up well. That which is sown riseth up in the spring, that which sleepeth in the morning. So conceive of the change wrought in our nature; that feast of first fruits, by "Christ our first fruits." Neither perish, neither that which is sown, though it rot, nor they that sleep, though they lie as dead for the time. Both that shall spring, and these wake well again. Therefore as men sow not grudgingly, nor lie down at night unwillingly, no more must we, seeing by virtue of this feast we are now *dormientes,* not *mortui;* now not as stones, but as fruits of the earth, whereof one hath an annual, the other a diurnal resurrection. This for the first fruits, and the change by them wrought.

There is a good analogy or correspondence between these, it cannot be denied. To this question, Can one man's resurrection work upon all the rest? it is a good answer, Why not as well as one sheaf upon the whole harvest? This simile serves well to shew it, to shew but not prove. Symbolical Divinity is good, but might we see it in the rational too? We may see it in the cause no less; in the substance, and let the ceremony go. This I called the ground of our hope.

III.
The ground of our hope.

Why, saith the Apostle, should this of the first fruits seem strange to you, that by one Man's resurrection we should rise all, seeing by one man's death we die all? " By one man," saith he, "sin entered into the world, and by sin death;" to which sin we were no parties, and yet we all die, because we are of the same nature whereof he the first person; death came so certainly, and it is good reason life should do so likewise. To this question, Can the resurrection of one, a thousand six hundred years ago, be the cause of our rising? it is a good answer, Why not, as well as the death of one, five thousand six hundred years ago, be the cause of our dying? The ground and reason is, that there is like ground and reason of both. The wisest way it is, if wisdom can contrive it, that a person be cured by mithridate made of the very flesh of the viper bruised, whence the poison came, that so that which brought the mischief might minister also the remedy; the most powerful way it is, if power can effect it, to make strength appear in weakness;

Rom. 5. 12.

and that he that overcame should by the nature which he overcame, be "swallowed up in victory." The best way it is, if goodness will admit of it, that as next to Sathan man to man oweth his destruction, so next to God man to man might be debtor of his recovery. So agreeable it is to the power, wisdom, and goodness of God this, the three attributes of the blessed and glorious Trinity.

And let justice weigh it in her balance, no just exception can be taken to it, no not by justice itself; that as death came, so should life too, the same way at least. More favour for life, if it may be, but in very rigour the same at the least. According then to the very exact rule of justice, both are to be alike; if by man one, by man the other.

We dwell too long in generalities; let us draw near to the persons themselves, in whom we shall see this better. In them all answer exactly, word for word. Adam is fallen, and become the first fruits of them that die. "Christ is risen, and became the first fruits of them" that live,—for they that sleep live. Or you may, if you please, keep the same term in both, thus: Adam is risen, as we use to call Gen. 3. 5. rebellions risings; he did rise against God by *eritis sicut Dii;* he had never fallen, if he had not thus risen; his rising was his fall.

We are now come to the two great persons, that are the two great authors of the two great matters in this world, life and death. Not either to themselves and none else, but as two heads, two roots, two first fruits, either of them in reference to his company whom they stand for. And of these two hold the two great corporations: 1. Of them that die, they are Adam's; 2. Of them that sleep and shall rise, that is Christ's.

To come then to the particular: no reason in the world that Adam's transgression should draw us all down to death, only for that we were of the same lump; and that Christ's righteousness should not be available to raise us up again to life, being of the same sheaves, whereof He the first fruits, no less than before of Adam. Look to the things, death and life; weakness is the cause of death, raising to life cometh of 2 Cor. 15. 4. power. Shall there be in weakness more strength to hurt, than in power to do us good? Look to the persons, Adam

and Christ: shall Adam, being but a "living soul," infect us 1Cor.15.45.
more strongly than Christ, "a quickening Spirit," can heal us
again? Nay then, Adam was but "from the earth, earthy, 1 Cor. 15.
Christ the Lord from Heaven." Shall earth do that which [47.]
Heaven cannot undo? Never. It cannot be; *sicut, sic,* 'as'
and 'so,'—so run the terms.

But the Apostle, in Rom. 5. where he handleth this very
point, tells us plainly, *non sicut delictum, ita et donum ;* "not Rom. 5. 15.
as the fault, so the grace;" nor as the fall, so the rising, but
the grace and the rising much more abundant. It seemeth
to be *a pari ;* it is not indeed, it is under value. Great
odds between the persons, the things, the powers, and the
means of them. Thus then meet it should be; let us see
how it was.

Here again the very terms give us great light. We are,
saith he, restored; restoring doth always presuppose an
attainder going before, and so the term significant; for the
nature of attainder is, one person maketh the fault, but it
taints his blood and all his posterity. The Apostle saith that
a statute there is, "all men should die;" but when we go to Heb. 9. 27.
search for it, we can find none, but *pulvis es,* wherein only Gen. 3. 19.
Adam is mentioned, and so none die but he. But even by
that statute, death goeth over all men; even "those," saith
St. Paul, "that have not sinned after the like manner of [Rom. 5.
transgression of Adam." By what law? By the law of [14.]
attainders.

The restoring then likewise was to come, and did come,
after the same manner as did the attainders; that by the
first, this by the second Adam, so He is called verse 45.
There was a statute concerning God's commandments, *qui
fecerit ea, vivet in eis ;* 'he that observed the commandments Lev. 18. 5.
should live by that his obedience,' death should not seize on
him. Christ did observe them exactly, therefore should not
have been seized on by death; should not but was, and
that seizure of his was death's forfeiture. The laying of the
former statute on Christ was the utter making it void; so
judgment was entered, and an act made, Christ should be
restored to life. And because He came not for Himself but
for us, and in our name and stead did represent us, and so
we virtually in Him, by His restoring we also were restored,

by the rule, *si primitiæ, et tota conspersio sic;* " as the first fruits go, so goeth the whole lump," as the root the branches. And thus we have gotten life again of mankind by passing this act of restitution, whereby we have hope to be restored to life.

But life is a term of latitude, and admitteth a broad difference, which it behoveth us much that we know. Two lives there be; in the holy tongue, the word which signifieth life is of the dual number, to shew us there is a duality of lives, that two there be, and that we to have an eye to both. It will help us to understand our text. For all restored to life; all to one, not all to both. The Apostle doth after, at the forty-fourth verse, expressly name them both. 1. One a natural life, or life by the " living soul;" the other, 2. a spiritual life, or life by the " quickening Spirit." Of these two, Adam at the time of his fall had the first, of a " living soul," was seized of it; and of him all mankind, Christ and we all, receive that life. But the other, the spiritual, which is the life chiefly to be accounted of, that he then had not, not actually; only a possibility he had, if he had held him in obedience, and " walked with God," to have been translated to that other life. For clear it is, the life which Angels now live with God, and which we have hope and promise to live with Him after our restoring, when we " shall be equal to the Angels," that life Adam at the time of his fall was not possessed of.

Now Adam by his fall fell from both, forfeited both estates. Not only that he had in reversion, by not fulfilling the conditions, but even that he had in *esse* too. For even on that also did death seize after *et mortuus est.*

Christ in His restitution, to all the sons of Adam, to all our whole nature, restoreth the former; therefore all have interest, all shall partake that life. What Adam actually had we shall actually have, we shall all be restored. To repair our nature He came, and repair it He did; all is given again really that in Adam really we lost touching nature. So that by his fall, no detriment at all that way.

The other, the second, that He restoreth too; but not *promiscue,* as the former, to all. Why? for Adam was never seized of it, performed not that whereunto the possibility was annexed, and so had in it but a defeasible estate. But then, by His special grace, by a second peculiar act, He hath enabled us to attain the second estate also which Adam had only a reversion of, and lost by breaking of the condition whereto it was limited. And so to this second restored so many as, to use the Apostle's words in the next verse, "are in Him;" that is, so many as are not only of that mass or lump whereof Adam was the first fruits, for they are interested in the former only, but that are besides of the *nova conspersio,* whereof Christ is the *primitiæ.*

"They that believe in Him," saith St. John, them He Joh. 1. 12. hath enabled, "to them He hath given power to become the sons of God," to whom therefore He saith, this day rising, *Vado ad Patrem vestrum;* in which respect the Apostle Joh. 20. 17. calleth Him *Primogenitum inter multos fratres.* Or, to make Rom. 8. 29. the comparison even, to those that are—to speak but as Esay speaketh of them — "His children;" "Behold, I and the Isa. 8. 18. children God hath given Me." The term He useth Himself to them after His resurrection, and calleth them "children;" [Joh. 21. 5.] and they as His family take denomination of Him—Christians, of Christ.

Of these two lives, the first we need take no thought for. It shall be of all, the unjust as well as the just. The life of the "living soul," shall be to all restored. All our thought is to be for the latter, how to have our part in that supernatural life, for that is indeed to be restored to life. For the former, though it carry the name of life, yet it may well be disputed and is, Whether it be rather a death than a life, or a life than a death? A life it is, and not a life, for it hath no living thing in it. A death it is, and not a death, for it is an immortal death. But most certain it is, call it life if you will, they that shall live that life shall wish for death rather than it, and, this is the misery—not have their wish, for death shall fly from them.

Out of this double life and double restoring, there grow two resurrections in the world to come, set down by our Saviour in express terms. Though both be to life, yet, 1. that is called "condemnation to judgment;" and 2. this [Rom. 5. only "to life." Of these the Apostle calleth one "the better 16.] resurrection," the better beyond all comparison. To attain Heb. 11. 35.

SERM. this then we bend all our endeavours, that seeing the other
II. will come of itself, without taking any thought for it at all,
we may make sure of this.

1.   To compass that then, we must be "in Christ:" so it is in
[1 Cor. 15. the next verse; to all, but to "every one in order, Christ"
23.] first, "the first fruits, and then, they that be in Him."

2.   Now He is in us by our flesh, and we in Him by His
Spirit; and it standeth with good reason, they that be restored to life, should be restored to the Spirit. For the
Spirit is the cause of all life, but specially of the spiritual
life which we seek for.

3.   His Spirit then we must possess ourselves of, and we must
do that here; for it is but one and the same Spirit That
Rom. 8. 11. raiseth our souls here from the death of sin, and the same
That shall raise our bodies there from the dust of death.

4.   Of which Spirit there is "first fruits," to retain the words
of the text, and "a fulness;" but the fulness in this life we
shall never attain; our highest degree here is but to be of
Rom. 8. 23. the number whereof he was that said, *Et nos habentes pri-
mitias Spiritus.*

5.   These first fruits we first receive in our Baptism, which
Tit. 3. 5. is to us our "laver of regeneration," and of our "renewing
by the Holy Spirit," where we are made and consecrate
primitiæ.

6.   But as we need be restored to life, so I doubt had we need
to be restored to the Spirit too. We are at many losses of it,
Heb. 12. 1. by this sin that "cleaveth so fast" to us. I doubt, it is with
us, as with the fields, that we need a feast of first fruits, a
day of consecration every year. By something or other we
grow unhallowed, and need to be consecrate anew, to re-seize
us of the first fruits of the Spirit again. At least to awake
it in us, as *primitiæ dormientium* at least. That which was
given us, and by the fraud of our enemy, or our own negli-
gence, or both, taken from us and lost, we need to have re-
1 Thes. 5. stored; that which we have quenched, to be lit anew; that
19.
Eph. 5. 14. which we have cast into a dead sleep, awaked up from it.

If such a new consecrating we need, what better time than
the feast of first fruits, the sacrificing time under the Law?
and in the Gospel, the day of Christ's rising, our first fruits,
by Whom we are thus consecrate? The day wherein He was

Himself restored to the perfection of His spiritual life, the life of glory, is the best for us to be restored in to the first fruits of that spiritual life, the life of grace.

And if we ask, what shall be our means of this conse- IV.
crating? The Apostle telleth us, we are sanctified by the The application of
"oblation of the body of Jesus." That is the best means to the Sacrament.
restore us to that life. He hath said it, and shewed it Him- Heb. 10.10.
self; "He that eateth Me shall live by Me." The words
spoken concerning that, are both "spirit and life," whether Joh. 6.
we seek for the spirit or seek for life. Such was the means 57. 63.
of our death, by eating the forbidden fruit, the first fruits
of death; and such is the means of our life, by eating the
flesh of Christ, the first fruits of life.

And herein we shall very fully fit, not the time only and the means, but also the manner. For as by partaking the flesh and blood, the substance of the first Adam, we came to our death, so to life we cannot come, unless we do partici-pate with the flesh and blood of the "second Adam," that is Christ. We drew death from the first, by partaking the substance; and so must we draw life from the second, by the same. This is the way; become branches of the Vine, and partakers of His nature, and so of His life and verdure both.

So the time, the means, the manner agree. What letteth then but that we, at this time, by this means, and in this manner, make ourselves of that conspersion whereof Christ is our first fruits; by these means obtaining the first fruits of His Spirit, of that quickening Spirit, Which being ob-tained and still kept, or in default thereof still recovered, shall here begin to initiate in us the first fruits of our resti-tution in this life, whereof the fulness we shall also be re- Acts 3. 21.
stored unto in the life to come; as St. Peter calleth that time, the "time of the restoring of all things." Then shall the fulness be restored us too, when God shall be "all in all;" not some in one, and some in another, but all in all. *Atque hic est vitæ finis, pervenire ad vitam cujus non est finis;* ‘this is the end of the text and of our life, to come to a life whereof there is no end.’ To which, &c.

A SERMON

PREACHED BEFORE

THE KING'S MAJESTY, AT WHITEHALL,

ON THE TWENTY-SEVENTH OF MARCH, A.D. MDCVIII., BEING EASTER-DAY.

MARK xvi. 1—7.

*And when the Sabbath day was past, Mary Magdalene, and
Mary the mother of James, and Salome, bought sweet ointments, that they might come and embalm Him.*

*Therefore early in the morning, the first day of the week, they
came unto the sepulchre, when the sun was yet rising.*

*And they said one to another, Who shall roll us away this
stone from the door of the sepulchre?*

*And when they looked, they saw that the stone was rolled
away; for it was a very great one.*

*So they went into the sepulchre, and saw a young man sitting
at the right side, clothed in a long white robe; and they
were afraid.*

*But he said unto them, Be not afraid: ye seek Jesus of Naza-
reth, Which hath been crucified; He is risen, He is not
here; Behold the place where they put Him.*

*But go your way and tell His disciples, and Peter, that He
will go before you into Galilee: there shall ye see Him, as
He said unto you.*

[*Et cum transîsset Sabbatum, Maria Magdalene, et Maria Jacobi, et
Salome emerunt aromata ut venientes ungerent Jesum.*

*Et valde mane unâ sabbatorum, veniunt ad monumentum, orto jam
sole.*

*Et dicebant ad invicem: Quis revolvet nobis lapidem ab ostio monu-
menti?*

*Et respicientes viderunt revolutum lapidem. Erat quippe magnus
valde.*

*Et introeuntes in monumentum viderunt juvenem sedentem in dextris,
coopertum stola candida, et obstupuerunt.*

*Qui dicit illis, Nolite expavescere: Jesum quæritis Nazarenum, cru-
cifixum; surrexit, non est hîc, ecce locus ubi posuerunt Eum.*

*Sed ite, dicite discipulis Ejus, et Petro quia præcedit vos in Gali-
læam: ibi Eum videbitis, sicut dixit vobis.* Lat. Vulg.]

[*And when the Sabbath was past, Mary Magdalene, and Mary the mother of James, and Salome, had bought sweet spices, that they might come and anoint Him.*

And very early in the morning, the first day of the week, they came unto the sepulchre at the rising of the sun.

And they said among themselves, Who shall roll away us the stone from the door of the sepulchre?

And when they looked, they saw that the stone was rolled away; for it was very great.

And entering into the sepulchre, they saw a young man sitting on the right side, clothed in a long white garment; and they were affrighted.

And he saith unto them, Be not affrighted. Ye seek Jesus of Nazareth, Which was crucified: He is risen, He is not here; behold the place where they laid Him.

But go your way, tell His disciples and Peter that He goeth before you into Galilee: there shall ye see Him, as He said unto you. Engl. Trans.]

THE sum of this Gospel is a gospel, that is, a message of good tidings. In a message these three points fall in naturally: I. the parties to whom it is brought; II. the party by whom; III. and the message itself. These three: 1. the parties to whom,—three women, the three Maries. 2. The party by whom,—an Angel. 3. The message itself, the first news of Christ's rising again. These three make the three parts in the text. 1. The women, 2. the Angel, 3. the message. *[margin: The sum. I. II. III.]*

Seven verses I have read ye. The first four concern the women, the fifth the Angel, the two last the Angel's message. In the women, we have to consider 1. themselves in the first; 2. their journey in the second and third; and 3. their success in the fourth. *[margin: The division.]*

In the Angel, 1. the manner of his appearing, 2. and of their affecting with it.

In the message, the news itself: 1. that Christ "is risen;" 2. that "He is gone before them to Galilee;" 3. that "there they shall see Him;" 4. Peter and all. 5. Then, the *Ite et dicite*, the commission *ad evangelizandum;* not to conceal these good news but publish it, these to His Disciples, they to others, and so to us; we to-day, and so to the world's end.

Q

SERM.
III.
——
I.
The par-
ties to
whom:
three
women.

Heb. 6. 10.

[M. T.
Cicer.
Off. 1. 18.]

Joh. 20. 19.

Joh. 21.
15. 20.

Mary Mag-
dalene
first.

Mark 16. 9.

Lu. 7. 37.

As the text lieth, the part that first offereth itself, is the parties to whom this message came. Which were three women. Where, finding that women were the first that had notice of Christ's resurrection, we stay. For it may seem strange that passing by all men, yea the Apostles themselves, Christ would have His resurrection first of all made known to that sex. Reasons are rendered, of divers diversely. We may be bold to allege that the Angel doth in the text, verse 5. *Vos enim quæritis*, for they sought Christ. And, Christ "is not unrighteous to forget the work and labour of their love" that seek Him. Verily there will appear more love and labour in these women, than in men, even the Apostles themselves. At this time, I know not how, men were then become women and did *animos gerere muliebres*, and women were men. Sure the more manly of the twain. The Apostles, they set mured up, all "the doors fast" about them; sought not, went not to the sepulchre. Neither Peter that loved Him, nor John whom He loved, till these women brought them word. But these women we see were last at His Passion, and first at His Resurrection; stayed longest at that, came soonest to this, even in this respect to be respected. Sure, as it is said of the Law, *Vigilantibus et non dormientibus succurrit Lex*, so may it no less truly be said of the Gospel. We see it here, it cometh not to sleepers, but to them that are awake, and up and about their business, as these women were. So that there was a capacity in them to receive this prerogative.

Before I leave this part of the parties, I may not omit to observe Mary Magdalene's place and precedence among the three. All the Fathers are careful to note it. That she standeth first of them, for it seemeth no good order. She had had seven devils in her, as we find, verse 9. She had had the blemish to be called *peccatrix*, as one famous and notorious in that kind. The other were of honest report, and never so stained, yet is she named with them. With them were much, but not only with them, but before them. With them;—and that is to shew Christ's resurrection, as well as His death, reacheth to sinners of both sexes; and that, to sinners of note, no less than those that seem not to have greatly gone astray;—but before them too, and that is indeed to be noted; that she is the first in the list of women, and St. Peter in that of men. These two, the two chief sinners, either of their sex. Yet they, the two whose lots came first forth *in sorte sanctorum,* in partaking this Col. 1. 12. news. And this to shew that chief sinners as these were, if they carry themselves as they did, shall be at no loss by their fall; shall not only be pardoned but honoured even as Lu. 15. 22. he was, like these, with *stolâ primâ,* "the first robe" in all the wardrobe, and stand foremost of all. And it is not without a touch of the former reason, in that the sinner, after his recovery, for the most part seeketh God more fervently, whereas they that have not greatly gone astray, are but even so so; if warm, it is all. And with God it is a rule, *plus valet hora fervens quam mensis tepens,* 'an hour of fervour more worth than a month of tepor.' Now such was Mary Magdalene, here and elsewhere vouchsafed therefore this degree of exaltation, to be "of the first three;" nay, to be 2 Sam. 23. the first of the three, that heard first of His rising; yea, as $^{19.}$ in the ninth verse, that first saw Him risen from the dead. This of the persons.

And now, because their endeavours were so well liked as Their they were for them counted worthy this so great honour, it journey: falleth next to consider what those were, that we being like in, their prepared may partake the like good hap. So seeking as love. they, we may find as they did. They were four in number. The first and third in the second, the second in the first, and the last in the third verse. All reduced, as Christ reduced them in Mary Magdalene, to *dilexit multum,* 'their great love,' of which these four be four demonstrations; or, if love be an "ensign" as it is termed Cant. 2., the four Cant. 2. 4. colours of it. 1. That they went to the sepulchre;—love to one dead. 2. That they bought precious odours;—love that is at charges. 3. That out they went early, before break of day;—love that will take pains. 4. That for all the stone, still they went on;—love that will wrestle with impediments. The first is constant as to the dead; the second bounteous, as at expense; the third diligent, as up betimes; the last resolute, be the stone never so great. According to which four, are the four denominations of love: 1. *Amor, a mor-te,* when it surviveth death. 2. When it buyeth dearly, it is

SERM. *charitas;* 3. When it sheweth all diligence, it is *dilectio;*
III. 4. When it goeth *per saxa,* when stones cannot stay it, it is
zelus, which is specially seen in encountering difficulties.
It shall not be amiss to touch them severally; it will serve
to touch our love, whether ours be of the same assay.

1. Love to   The first riseth out of these words, "They went to the
the dead:
Amor.   sepulchre;" and indeed, *ex totâ substantiâ,* 'out of the whole
text.' For, for whom is all this ado, is it not for Christ?
But Christ is dead, and buried three days since, and this
is now the third day. What then, though He be dead, to
their love He liveth still: death may take His body from
their eyes, but shall never take His remembrance from their
hearts. Herein is love, this is the first colour, saith a great
Cant. 8. 6.   master in that faculty, *fortis sicut mors,* "love, that death
cannot foil," but continueth to the dead, as if they still
were alive. And when I say the dead, I mean not such as
the dead hath left behind them, though that be a virtue,
Ruth 2. 20.   and Booz worthily blessed for it that shewed mercy to the
living for the dead's sake; but I mean performing offices of
love to the dead himself; to see he have a sepulchre to go
to; not so to bury his friend, as he would bury his ass being
dead. To see he have one, and not thither to bring him,
and there to leave him, and bury him and his memory both
Ecc. 9. 4.   in a grave. Such is the world's love. Solomon sheweth it
by the lion and the dog. All after Christ living, but go to
His sepulchre who will, not we. The love that goeth thither,
that burieth not the memory of Him that is buried, is love
indeed.

2. Love   The journey to the sepulchre is *iter amoris;* had it been
that was
at charges: but to lament, as Mary Magdalene to Lazarus:—but then
Charitas.   here is a farther matter, they went to anoint Him. That is
Joh. 11. 31.   set for another sign, that they spared for no cost, but bought
precious odours wherewith to embalm Him.

1. To go to anoint Christ, is kindly; it is to make Him
Christ, that is, "Anointed." That term referreth principally
to His Father's anointing, I grant; but what, if we also
anoint Him, will He take it in evil part? Clearly not,
neither quick, nor dead. Not quick, Luke 7. Mark 14.
Lu. 7. 46.   Not dead; this place is pregnant, it is the end of their
Mark 14. 3.
&c.   journey to do this. He is well content to be their, and

òur Anointed, not His Father's only; yea, it is a way to make Him *Christum nostrum,* 'our Christ,' if we break our boxes, and bestow our odours upon Him.

2. To anoint Him, ánd not with some odd cast ointment, lying by them, kept a little too long, to throw away upon Him; but to buy, to be at cost, to do it *emptis odoribus,* 'with bought odours.'

3. This to do to Him alive, that would they with all their hearts; but if that cannot be, to do it to Him dead, rather than not at all. To do it to whatsoever is left us of Christ, to that to do it.

4. To embalm Christ, Christ dead, yea though others had done it before, for so is the case. Joseph and Nicodemus Joh. 19. 39. had bestowed myrrh and aloes to that end already. What then? though they had done it, it is not enough, nay, it is nothing. Nay, if all the world should have done it, unless they might come with their odours and do it too, all were nothing. *In hoc est charitas,* 'herein is love,' and this a sign of it. A sign of it every where else, and to Christ a sign it was. Indeed, such a sign there was, but it is beaten down now. We can love Christ *absque hoc,* and shew it some other way well enough. It sheweth our love is not *charitas,* no dear love; but *vilitas,* love that loves to be at as little charges with Christ as may be, faint love. You shall know it thus: *Ad hoc signum se contrahit,* 'at this sign it shrinks,' at every word of it. 1. "They bought,"—that is charge; we like it not, we had rather hear *potuit vendi.* 2. "Odours." What Mark 14. 5. need odours? An unnecessary charge. We like no odour but *odor lucri.* 3. To Christ. Nay, seeing it is unnecessary, we trust Christ will not require it. 4. Not alive, but especially, not dead. There was much ado while He lived to get allowance for it; there was one of His own Apostles, a good charitable man, *pater pauperum,* held it to be plain Mark 14. 4. *perditio.* Yet, to anoint the living, that many do, they can anoint us again; but to the dead, it is quite cast away. But then, if it had been told us, He is embalmed already, why then, take away their odours, that at no hand would have been endured. This sheweth our love is not *charitas.* But so long as this is a Gospel, it shall sound every Easter-day in our ear, That the buying of odours, the embalming of

whatsoever is left us of Christ, is and will be still a sign of
our loving and seeking Him, as we should; though not heretofore, yet now; now especially, when that objection ceaseth,
He is embalmed enough already. He was indeed then, but
most of the myrrh and aloes is now gone. That there is
good occasion left, if any be disposed *in hoc signo signari,*
'with this sign to seal his love to Christ anew again.'

3. Love,
that takes
pains:
Dilectio.
From this of their expense, *charitas,* we pass to the third,
of their diligence, *dilectio,* set down in the second verse in
these words "very early," &c. And but mark how diligent
the Holy Ghost is in describing their diligence. "The very
first day of the week," the very first part of that first day,
"in the morning;" the very first hour of that first part,
"very early, before the sun was up," they were up. Why
good Lord, what need all this haste? Christ is fast enough
under His stone. He will not run away ye may be sure; ye
need never break your sleep, and yet come to the sepulchre
time enough. No, if they do it not as soon as it may be
done, it is nothing worth. Herein is love, *dilectio,* whose
proper sign is *diligentia,* in not slipping the first opportunity
of shewing it. They did it not at their leisure, they could
not rest, they were not well, till they were about it. Which
very speed of theirs doubleth all the former. For *cito* we
know is esteemed as much as *bis.* To do it at once is to do
it more than once, is to do it twice over.

Yet this we must take with us, Διαγενομένου σαββάτου.
Where falleth a very strange thing, that as we have commended them for their quickness, so must we now also for
their slowness, out of the very first words of all. "When
the Sabbath was past," then, and not till then, they did it.
This diligence of theirs, as great haste as it made, stayed yet
till the Sabbath were past, and by this means hath two contrary commendations: 1. One, for the speed; 2. another for
the stay of it. Though they fain would have been embalming Him as soon as might be, yet not with breach of the
Sabbath. Their diligence leapt over none of God's commandments for haste. No, not this commandment, which
of all other the world is boldest with; and if they have
haste, somewhat else may, but sure the Sabbath shall never
stay them. The Sabbath they stayed, for then God stayed

them. But that was no sooner over, but their diligence appeared straight. No other thing could stay them. Not their own sabbath, sleep—but "before day-light" they were well onward on their way.

The last is in the third verse, in these words, "As they went, they said," &c. There was a stone, a very great one, to be rolled away ere they could come at Him. They were so rapt with love, in a kind of ecstacy, they never thought of the stone; they were well on their way before they remembered it. And then, when it came to their minds, they went not back though, but on still, the stone *non obstante.* And herein is love, the very fervor of it, zeal; that word hath fire in it. Not only diligence as lightness to carry it upward, but zeal as fire to burn a hole and eat itself a way, through whatsoever shall oppose to it. No stone so heavy as to stay them, or turn them back. And this is St. John's sign: *foras pellit timorem,* "love, if it be perfect, casts out fear;" *et erubescit nomen difficultatis,* 'shames to confess any thing too hard for it.' Ours is not so; we must have, not great stones, God wot, but every scruple removed out of our way, or we will not stir. But as, if you see one *qui laborem fingit in præcepto,* 'that makes a great deal more labour in a precept' than needs, that is afraid where no fear is; of *leo in viâ,* "a lion" or I wot not what perilous beast "in the way," and no such matter; it is a certain sign his love is small, his affection cold to the business in hand; so, on the other side, when we see, as in these here, such zeal to that they went about, as first they forgot there was any stone at all, and when they bethought them of it, they brake not off, but went on though; ye may be bold to say of them, *dilexerunt multum,* 'their love was great' that *per saxa,* 'through stones' and all, yet goeth forward; that neither cost nor pains nor peril can divert. Tell them the party is dead they go to; it skills not, their love is not dead; that will go on. Tell them He is embalmed already, they may save their cost; it is not enough for them except they do it too, they will do it nevertheless for all that. Tell them they may take time then, and do it; nay, unless it be done the first day, hour, and minute, it contents them not. Tell them there is a stone, more than they remember, and more than they can

4. Love that wrestles with impediments: *Zelus.*

1 Joh. 4. 18.

Prov. 26. 13.

remove; no matter, they will try their strength and lift at it, though they take the foil. Of these thus qualified we may truly say, They that are at all this cost, labour, pains, to anoint Him dead, shew plainly, if it lay in them to raise Him again, they would not fail but do it; consequently would be glad to hear He were risen, and so are fit hearers of this Gospel; hearers well disposed, and every way meet to receive this Messenger, and this message. Now to the success.

We see what they sought, we long to see what they found. Such love and such labour would not be lost. This we may be sure of, there is none shall anoint Him alive or dead, without some recompense or consideration; which is set down of two sorts. 1. "They found the stone rolled away," as great as it was. That which troubled them most, how it might be removed, that found they removed ere they came. They need never take pains with it, the Angel had done it to their hands. 2. They found not indeed Whom they sought, Christ; but His Angel they found, and heard such a gospel of Him, so good news, as pleased them better than if they had found His body to embalm it. That news which of all other they most longed to hear, that He they came to anoint needed no such office to be done to Him, as being alive again. This was the success.

And from this success of theirs our lesson is. 1. That as there is no virtue, no good work, but hath some impediment, as it were some great stone to be lifted at,—*Quis revolvet?* so that it is ofttimes the lot of them that seek to do good, to find many imaginary stones removed to their hands; God so providing, *ut quod admovit Satanas, amoveat Angelus,* 'what Satan lays in the way, a good Angel takes out of the way;' that it may in the like case be a good answer to *Quis revolvet?* to say, *Angelus Domini,* "the Angel of the Lord," he shall do it, done it shall be: so did these here, and as they did, others shall find it.

2. Again, it is the hope that all may have that set themselves to do Christ any service, to find His Angel at least, though not Himself; to hear some good news of Him, though not see Him at the first. Certain it is with *ungentes ungentur,* 'none shall seek ever to anoint Him, but they shall be

anointed by Him again,' one way or other; and find, though
not always what they seek, yet some supply that shall be
worth the while. And this we may reckon of, it shall never
fail us.

To follow this farther. Leave we these good women, and
come first to the Angel, the messenger, and after to his message. An Angel was the messenger, for none other messenger was meet for this message. For if His birth were
tidings of so great joy as none but an Angel was meet to report it, His Resurrection is as much. As much? nay, much
more. As much; for His resurrection is itself a birth too.
To it doth the Apostle apply the verse in the Psalm, "This
day have I begotten Thee." Even this day when He was
born anew, *tanquam ex utero sepulchri,* 'from the womb of
the grave.' As much then, yea much more. For the news of
His birth might well have been brought by a mortal, it was
but His entry into a mortal life; but this here not properly
but by an Angel, for that in the Resurrection we shall be
"like the Angels," and shall die no more; and therefore an
immortal messenger was meetest for it.

We first begin with what they saw—the vision. They
saw an Angel in the sepulchre. An Angel in a sepulchre is
a very strange sight. A sepulchre is but an homely place—
neither savoury, nor sightly, for an Angel to come in. The
place of dead men's bones, of stench, of worms, and of rottenness;—What doth an Angel there? Indeed, no Angel ever
came there till this morning. Not till Christ had been there;
but, since His body was there, a great change hath ensued.
He hath left there *odorem vitæ,* and changed the grave into a
place of rest. That not only this Angel here now, but after
this, two more, yea divers Angels upon divers occasions, this
day did visit and frequent this place. Which very finding of
the Angels thus, in the place of dead bodies, may be and is
to us a pledge, that there is a possibility and hope, that the
dead bodies may come also into the place of Angels. Why
not the bodies in the grave to be in Heaven one day, as well
as the Angels of Heaven to be in the grave this day?

This for the vision. The next for the manner of his appearing, in what form he shewed himself. A matter worth
our stay a little as a good introduction to us, in him as in a

II.
The party
by whom:
the Angel.

Lu. 2. 10.

Acts 13. 33.

Mat. 22. 30.

1.
The vision.

Joh. 20. 12.

The man-
ner of his
appearing.

SERM. mirror to see what shall be the state of us and our bodies
III.   in the Resurrection, inasmuch as it is expressly promised
Mat. 22. 30. we shall then be ἰσάγγελοι, "like and equal to the Angels
themselves."

1. As "a   2. They saw "a young man," one in the vigour and
young
man."   strength of his years, and such shall be our estate then; all
age, sickness, infirmity removed clean away. Therefore it
was also that the Resurrection fell in the spring, the freshest
time of the year; and in the morning, the freshest time of
Isa. 26. 19. the day, when saith Esay "the dew is on the herbs." Therefore, that it was in a garden, (so it was in Joseph of Arimathea's
garden) that look, as that garden was at that time of the year,
the spring, so shall our estate then be in the very flower and
prime of it.

2. "Sit-   They saw him "sitting," which is we know the site of rest
ting."   and quietness, of them that are at ease. To shew us a second
quality of our estate then; that in it all labour shall cease, all
motions rest, all troubles come utterly to an end for ever, and
the state of it a quiet, a restful state.

3. "On the   They saw him sit "on the right side." And that side is
right side." the side of pre-eminence and honour, to shew that those also
shall accompany us rising again. That we may fall on the
1 Cor. 15. 43. left side, but we shall rise on the right; be "sown in dishonour," but shall "rise again in honour," that honour which
His Saints and Angels have and shall have for ever.

4. "Clothed   Lastly, they saw him "clothed all in white." And white is
in white."
Ecc. 9. 8. the colour of gladness, as we find Eccles. 9. 8. All to shew
still, that it shall be a state, as of strength, rest, and honour,
so of joy likewise. And that, robe-wise; not short or scant,
but as his stole, all over, down to the ground.

Neither serves it alone to shew us, what then we shall be,
but withal what now we ought to be this day, the day of His
Mat. 27. 45. rising. In that we see, that as the heavens at the time of
His Passion were in black, by the great eclipse shewing us it
was then a time of mourning; so this day the Angels were all
in white, to teach us thereby with what affection, with how
great joy and gladness, we are to celebrate and solemnize this
feast of our Saviour's rising.

3.   Their affection here was otherwise, and that is somewhat
Their
affecting strange. In the apparition there was nothing fearful as ye
therewith.

see, yet it is said, "they were afraid." Even now they feared nothing, and now they fall to be afraid at this so comfortable a sight. Had they been guilty to themselves of any evil they came to do, well might they then have feared, God first, as the malefactor doth the judge, and then His Angel, as the executioner of His wrath. But their coming was for good. But I find it is not the sinner's case only, but even of the best of our nature. Look the Scripture; Abra- Gen. 15.12. ham and Jacob in the Old, Zachary and the Blessed Virgin Gen. 28. 17. Lu. 1. 12. in the New, all strucken with fear still, at the sight of good Lu. 1. 29. Angels; yea even then, when they came for their good.

It fareth with the Angels of light, as it doth with the light itself. Sore eyes and weak cannot endure it, no more can sinners them. No more can the strongest sight neither bear the light, if the object be too excellent, if it be not tempered to a certain proportion; otherwise, even to the best that is, is the light offensive. And that is their case. Afraid they are, not for any evil they were about, but for that our very nature is now so decayed, *ut lucem ad quam nata est sustinere nequeat,* as the Angels' brightness, for whose society we were created, yet as now we are, bear it we cannot, but need to be comforted at the sight of a comfortable Angel. It is not the messenger angelical, but the message evangelical that must do it.

Which leadeth us along from the vision that feared them, III. to the message itself that relieved them; which is the third The mes- sage. part. The stone lay not more heavy on the grave, than did that fear on their hearts, pressing them down hard. And no less needful was it, the Angel should roll it away, this spiritual great stone from their hearts, than he did that other material from the sepulchre itself. With that he begins.

1. "Fear not." A meet text for him, that maketh a ser- 1. "Fear not." mon at a sepulchre. For the fear of that place maketh us out of quiet all our life long. It lieth at our heart like a Heb. 2. 15. stone, and no way there is to make us willing to go thither, but by putting us out of fear; by putting us in hope, that the great stones shall be rolled away again from our sepulchres, and we from thence rise to a better life. It is a right beginning for an Easter-day's sermon, *nolite timere.*

2. And a good reason he yields, why not. For it is not

every body's case, this *nolite timere vos*, " fear not you." Why
not ? For " you seek Jesus of Nazareth Which hath been
crucified." " Nazareth" might keep you back, the meanness
of His birth, and "crucified" more, the reproach of His
death. Inasmuch as these cannot let you, but ye seek
Him; are ashamed neither of His poor birth, nor of His
shameful death, but seek Him; and seek Him, not as some
did when He was alive, when good was to be done by Him,
but even now, dead, when nothing is to be gotten; and not
to rob or rifle Him, but to embalm Him, an office of love
and kindness, (this touched before) "fear not you," nor
let any fear that so seek Him.

Now, that they may not fear, He imparts them His
message full of comfort. And it containeth four comforts
of hope, answerable to the four former proofs of their love :
1. " He is risen ;" 2. But " gone before you ;" 3. " Ye shall
see Him ;" 4. "All His Disciples," " Peter" and all; " Go
tell them so."

1. "He is
risen."
In that you thus testify your love in seeking Him, I dare
say ye had rather He ye thus come to embalm, that He were
alive again ; and no more joyful tidings could come to you
than that He were so. Ye could I dare say with all your
hearts be content to lose all your charge you have been at,
in buying your odours, on condition it were so. Therefore I
certify you that He is alive, He is risen. No more than

Judg. 16. 3.
Jonah 2. 10.
Gaza gates could hold Samson, or the whale Jonas, no more
could this stone keep Him in the sepulchre, but risen He is.

First, of this ye were sure, here He was : ye were at His
laying in, ye saw the stone sealed, and the watch set, so that
here He was. But here He is not now ; come see the place,
trust your own eyes, *non est hîc.*

But what of that, this is but a lame consequence for all
that ; He is not here, therefore He is risen. For may it not
be, He hath been taken away ? Not with any likelihood ;

Mat. 28.13.
though such a thing will be given out, that the Disciples
stole Him away while the watch was asleep. But your
reason will give you ; 1. small probability there is, they
could be asleep, all the ground shaking and tottering under

Mat. 28. 2.
them by means of the earthquake. 2. And secondly, if they
did sleep for all that, yet then could they not tell sleeping,

how, or by whom, He was taken away. 3. And thirdly, that
His Disciples should do it; they you know of all other were
utterly unlike to do any such thing; so fearful as miserably
they forsook Him yet alive, and have ever since shut themselves up since He was dead. 4. And fourthly, if they durst
have done such a thing, they would have taken Him away,
linen, clothes, and all, as fearful men will make all the haste
they can possibly, and not stood stripping Him and wrapping
up the clothes, and laying them every parcel, one by one in
order, as men use to do that have time enough and take
deliberation, as being in no haste, or fear at all. To you
therefore, as we say, *ad hominem*, this consequence is good;
not taken away, and not here, therefore risen He is.

But to put all out of doubt, you shall trust your own "He is
eyes; *videbitis*, 'you shall see' it is so; you shall see Him. gone be-
Indeed, *non hîc* would not serve their turns; He knew their
question would be, Where is He? Gone He is; not quite
gone, but only gone before, which is the second comfort;
for if He be but gone before, we have hope to follow after;
I præ, sequar; so is the nature of relatives. But that we
may follow then, whither is He gone? Whither He told
ye Himself, a little before His Passion, chap. 14. 28. "into
Galilee."

1. No meeter place for Jesus of Nazareth to go, than to
"Galilee:" there He is best known, there in Nazareth He Mat. 2. 23.
was brought up, there in Cana He did His first miracle, Joh. 2. 1.
shewed His first glory—meet therefore to see His last; there
in Capernaum, and the coasts about, preached most, bestowed most of His labour.

2. "Galilee;" it was called "Galilee of the Gentiles," for Mat. 4. 15.
it was in the confines of them; to shew, His Resurrection,
tanquam in meditullio, 'as in a middle indifferent place,'
reacheth to both; concerneth and benefiteth both alike. As
Jonas after his resurrection went to Nineveh, so Christ after Jonah 3. 3.
His to Galilee of the Gentiles.

3. "Galilee;" that from Galilee, the place from whence
they said, No good thing could ever come, He might bring
one of the best things, and of most comfort that ever was;
the sight and comfort of His Resurrection.

4. "Galilee" last, for Galilee signifieth a revolution or

SERM.
III.
turning about to the first point, whither they must go that shall see Him, or have any part or fellowship in this feast of His Resurrection. Thither is He gone before, and thither if ye follow, there ye shall see Him.

3. "Ye shall see Him." This is the third comfort, and it is one indeed. For sight is the sense of certainty, and all that they can desire, and there they did see Him. Not these here only, or the twelve only, or the one hundred and twenty names, in Acts 1. only, Acts 1. 15.
1 Cor. 15. 6. but even five hundred of them at once, saith the Apostle; a [Heb.12.1.] whole "cloud of witnesses," to put it clean out of question. And of purpose doth the Angel point to that apparition, which was the most famous and public of all the ten.

4. And "His Disciples, Peter" and all. This was good news for those here, and they were worthy of it, seeking Him as they did. But what shall become of the rest, namely of His Disciples that lost Him alive, and seek Him not dead? They shall never see Him more? Yes (which is *evangelicum*, 'good tidings' indeed, the chief comfort of all) they too that left Him so shamefully but three days ago, them He casts not off, but will be glad to see them in Galilee. Well, whatsoever become of other, Peter that so foully forsook, and forsware Him both, he shall never see Him more? Yes, Peter too, and Peter by name. And indeed, it is more than needful He should name him, he had greatest cause of doubt; the greatest stone upon him to be Mark 14. 71. rolled away of any, that had so often with oaths and execrations so utterly renounced Him. This is a good message for him, and Mary Magdalene as fit a messenger as can be to carry it, one great sinner to another. That not only Christ is risen, but content that His forsakers, deniers, forswearers, Peter and all, should repair to Him the day of His Resurrection; that all the deadly wounds of His Passion have not killed His compassion over sinners; that though they have made wrack of their duty, yet He hath not lost His mercy, not left it in the grave, but is as ready to receive them as ever. His Resurrection hath made no change in Him. Dying and rising, He is to sinners still one and the same, still like Himself, a kind, loving, and merciful Saviour. This is the last; Peter and all may see Him.

2. Their commission. And with this He dismisseth them, with *ite et dicite*, with a commission and precept, by virtue whereof He maketh

these women *Apostolos Apostolorum,* 'Apostles to the Apostles themselves,'—for this article of the Resurrection did they first learn of these women, and they were the first of all that preached this Gospel—giving them in charge, that seeing this day is a day of glad tidings, they would not conceal it, but impart it to others, even to so many as then were, or would ever after be Christ's disciples.

They came to embalm Christ's body natural; that needs it not, it is past embalming now. But another Body He hath, a mystical body, a company of those that had believed in Him, though weakly; that they would go and anoint them, for they need it. They sit drying away, what with fear, what with remorse of their unkind dealing with Him; they need to have some oil, some balm to supple them. That they do with this Gospel, with these four; of which four ingredients is made the balm of this day.

Thus we see, these that were at cost to anoint Christ were fully recompensed for the costs they had been at; themselves anointed with oil and odours of a higher nature, and far more precious than those they brought with them, *Oleum* Ps. 45. 7. *lætitiæ,* saith the Psalm, *Odor vitæ,* saith the Apostle. And 2 Cor. 2. 16. that so plenteously, as there is enough for themselves, enough too for others, for His Disciples, for Peter and all.

But what is this to us? Sure, as we learned by way of The application. duty how to seek Christ after their example, so seeking Him in that manner, by way of reward we hope to have our part in this good news no less than they.

1. "Christ is risen." That concerneth us alike. "The Eph. 4. 15. head" is got above the water, "the root" hath received life Rom. 11. 16. and sap, "the first fruits" are lift up and consecrate; we no 1 Cor. 15. less than they, as His members, His branches, His field, 23. recover to this hope.

2. And for His going before, that which the Angel said here once, is ever true. He is not gone quite away, He is but gone before us; He is but the antecedent, we as the consequent to be inferred after. Yea, though He be gone to *Galilæa superior,* 'the Galilee that is above,' Heaven, the place of the celestial spheres and revolutions, even thither is He gone, not as a party absolute, of or for Himself, but as "a Harbinger," saith the Apostle, with relation to others Heb. 6. 20.

SERM. III.

Joh. 14. 2.

[Rev. 1. 7.]

Joh. 19. 37.

Rev. 20. 6.

that are coming after, for whom He goeth before to take up a place. So the Apostle there, so the Angel here. So He Himself, *Vado;* not *Vado* alone, but *Vado parare locum vobis,* "I go to prepare a place wherein to receive you," when the number of you and your brethren shall be full.

3. To us likewise pertaineth the third *videbitis,* that is, the Gospel indeed. "He is risen." Rising of itself is no Gospel, but He is risen and we shall see Him; that is it. That the time will come also, that we shall see Him in the Galilee celestial that is above; yea, that all shall see Him, even "they that pierced Him." But they that came to embalm Him, with joy and lifting up their heads they shall see Him; with that sight shall they see Him, That shall evermore make them blessed.

4. Lastly, which is worth all the rest, That we shall not need to be dismayed with our unworthiness, in that willing He is Peter should have word of this, and Mary Magdalene should carry it. That such as they were, sinners, and chief sinners, should have these tidings told them, this Gospel preached them; that He is as ready to receive them to grace as any of the rest, and will be as glad to see them as any others in Galilee.

But then are we to remember the condition, that here we get us into Galilee, or else it will not be. And Galilee is 'a revolution, or turning' *ad principia* 'to the first point,' as doth the Zodiac at this time of the year. The time of His resurrection is *pascha,* 'a passing over;' the place Galilee, 'a turning about.' It remaineth then that we pass over as the time, and turn as the place, putteth us in mind. Reuniting ourselves to His Body and Blood in this time of His rising, of the dissolving and renting whereof our sins were the cause. The time of His suffering, keeping the feast of Christ our new Passover offered for us; leaving whatsoever formerly hath been amiss in Christ's grave as the weeds of our dead estate, and rising to newness of life, that so we may have our parts "in the first resurrection;" which they are happy and blessed that shall have, for by it they are sure of the second. Of which blessing and happiness, He vouchsafe to make us all partakers, That this day rose for us, Jesus Christ the righteous!

A SERMON

PREACHED BEFORE

THE KING'S MAJESTY AT WHITEHALL,

ON THE SIXTEENTH OF APRIL, A.D. MDCIX., BEING EASTER-DAY.

JOHN xx. 19.

The same day then, at night, which was the first day of the
week, and when the doors were shut where the Disciples
were assembled for fear of the Jews, came Jesus, and stood
in the midst, and said to them, Peace be unto you.

Cum ergo sero esset die illo, una sabbatorum, et fores essent clausæ,
ubi erant Discipuli congregati propter metum Judæorum, venit
Jesus, et stetit in medio, et dixit eis, Pax vobis.

[*Then the same day at evening, being the first day of the week, when*
the doors were shut where the Disciples were assembled for fear of
the Jews, came Jesus and stood in the midst, and saith unto them,
Peace be unto you. Engl. Trans.]

THIS is the interview of Christ and His Disciples, and this
His first speech at His first interview; both this day, the
very first day of His rising.

Five sundry times appeared He this day. To Mary Mag- Mark 16. 9.
dalene, to the women coming from the sepulchre, to the Mat. 28. 9.
two that went to Emmaus, to St. Peter, and here now to Lu. 24. 15.
Lu. 24. 34.
the Eleven and those that were with them. The two first to In text.
women, the three last to men; so both sexes. To Peter
and to Mary Magdalene, so to sinners of both sexes. To
the Eleven as the Clergy, to those with them, as the Laity:
so, to both estates. Abroad at Emmaus, at home here.
Betimes, and now late. When they were scattered severally,
and now jointly when they were gathered together. That
no sex, sort, estate, place or time excepted, but as *visitavit* Lu. 1. 78.
nos oriens ab alto, so *visitavit occidens ab imo;* 'rising from

R

S E R M.
IV. above at His birth, rising from beneath at His resurrection, He visited all.'

But of all the five, this is the chief. Those were to one, as Peter; or two, as those of Emmaus; or three, as the women. This to all; the more, the more witnesses, the better for faith. Those when they were scattered; this here when they were all together. The more together, the more meet for this salutation here, Peace be to you.

The division.
I.

Which salutation is the very substance of the text, the rest but appendant all.

In it, two things give forth themselves: 1. The persons to whom, *vobis.* 2. The matter of the wish itself, "peace." The persons are thus set down: *Discipuli, congregati, conclusi.* 1. His "Disciples" they were, 2. "gathered," 3. and "the doors shut" on them "for fear of the Jews."

There will fall out besides four other points. 1. Christ's site; that He stood, when He wished it. 2. His place; that in the midst He stood. 3. The time; all this, the same day, the first day of the week, Sunday, Easter-day: 4. and the very time of the day, that it was late.

II.

The speech of itself is a salutation; any will so conceive it at the first hearing. And if it were but so, and no more, that were enough. Christ's salutations are not, as ours be, formal, but good matter in them.

But it is more than a salutation, say the Fathers, for this reason. At meeting men use to salute but once: within a verse, he repeateth it again. So it keeps not the law of a salutation, but it is certainly somewhat besides. *Votum Christi,* they call it. *Votum pacis, votum Christi;* 'Christ's vow, or wish;' His vow, and His first vow.

Now every vow implieth an advice at the least. What Christ wisheth to us, He wisheth us to. Every wish so. But if it be the wish of a superior in His optative, there is an imperative; His wish is a command, if he have wit that hears it. So that these words, rightly understood, are both an advice, and an injunction to it, of the nature of an edict.

Mark 9. 50. *Pax vobis* is as much as *Pacem habete in vobis,* "be at peace among yourselves."

We are then to join with Christ, to follow Him in His wish. To whom He wisheth it; to all Christ's Disciples

together, even to His whole Christian Church; and even to
them that, it may be, as little deserve it, as these here did.
1. To make it *caput voti*, 'our first vow;' yea, first and
second, as Christ here did. 2. *Oportet stantem optare*, 'to
wish it standing.' 3. And standing where Christ stood, that
is material, "in the midst." 4. This day to do it, and
think it pertinent to the time; it is *votum paschale*. As for
sero, we shall never need to take thought for it, it is never
too soon; late enough always if it be not too late, that is
all the fear.

The chief point first: *Pax vobis.* The words are but two, _{1.}
yet even between them there seemeth to be no peace, but ^{The per-}
one in a manner opposite to the other. Looking to *vobis*, ^{sonal part of Christ's salutation.}
the persons, this should not be a salutation for them, *pax.* ^{Pax and vobis,}
Looking to the salutation, "peace," it should not be to ^{reconciled.}
those persons, *vobis*, "to you." So that our first work will
be, to make peace between the two words.

Vobis, "to you." Will you know who they be? "To
you," Peter, and John, and the rest. "To you," of whom
none stood by Me. "To you," of whom some ran away, ^{Mat. 26. 56.}
some denied, yea forsware Me. "To you," of whom all, ^{Mat. 26. 72.}
every one shrunk away and forsook Me. How evil doth this ^{Mark 14. 50.}
greeting agree with this *vobis!* Yet even to these, *venit, et
stetit, et dixit;* "He came, stood, and said, Peace be to you." ^[Joh. 20. 19.]

Used by them as He had been, no cause He should come,
or stand, or speak at all; or if speak, not thus. Not come
to them that went from Him, nor stand amongst them that
had not stood to Him, nor speak to them that had renounced
Him. It is said, "they feared the Jews." All things con- ^{Joh. 9. 22.}
sidered, they had more cause to fear Him, and to look for
some real revenge at His hands. If not that, some verbal
reproof, a salutation of another style or tenor; and well, if
they might scape so. *Confitemini Domino, quia bonus :*—it is ^{Ps. 107. 1.}
not so, no evil deed for all this, no, not so much as an unkind
word. Above that they could look for, far above that they
deserved it is; *Pax vobis.* You and I are at peace, you
and I are friends; "Peace be unto you." This is His first
goodness, His making a peace between *pax* and *vobis*.

This speech to these persons is much mended by adding ^{Illo die,}
the time in the text, that it was *illo die,* the day of His ^{that is, Primo die.}

rising. *Pax vobis* is a good speech for Good-Friday; then men grow charitable, when ready to die. But on their Easter-day, at their rising, the day when *exultavit Eum Deus,*

Phil. 2. 9. 'the day of their exaltation,' they use to take other manner spirits, and remember former disgraces, with a far other congie. *Hæc est lex hominis;* men do thus, but not Christ. Neither their indignity, *vobis;* nor His own dignity changeth Him. Rising, exalted, the very day of His exaltation, *illo die,* He saith, "Peace be unto you."

Prima sabbati.
Lu. 24. 1.
Another yet: that it was *primâ sabbati,* the very "first day of the week;" took no long day for it, nay, no day at all, but the very first day. Joseph exalted dealt well with his brethren, but not the first day; it was some time first. He kept them in fear a while, but shewed himself at the last. Christ doth not so hold them in suspense: *illo die, primo die,* "the same day, the first day," He came, and shewed Himself and said, "Peace be unto you."

Dixit, not *respondit.*
Yea, not so much as *dixit* here but, as it falls out, will bear a note. Even that it is *dixit,* and not *respondit;* a speech not an answer. That He spake it, unspoken to; He to them first, ere they to Him. He might well have stayed till then, and reason would they should first have sued for it.

Ps. 21. 3.
Ere they ask it He giveth it, and "prevents them with the blessing of peace." They first in falling out, He first at making friends.

A great comfort for poor sinners, when the many indignities we have offered Christ shall present themselves before us, to think of this *vobis.* That when the Disciples had done the like, yet He forgat all, and spake thus kindly to them this day; that He will vouchsafe us the like, specially if we seek it He will, and say to us, *Pax vobis.*

Will ye remember now to extend your wish of peace 1. to them that, it may be, deserve it as evil as these here, even *his qui longe?* 2. To do it at our rising, at our high day, when it is Easter with us; 3. not to make their hearts to pant, and eyes to fail first, but even *primâ sabbati* to do it. 4. And not to take state upon us, and be content to answer, Peace, and not speak; be moved for it, but not move it; yes, even move it first? If we do, we join with Christ in His first part, the personal part of the wish.

Illis, and *illo die,* and *primo die,* what they were we see, and in what sort. Yet not to grate on this point altogether, some smoke yet was there in the flax, some small remainders, *illices misericordiæ,* as Tertullian, to move His mercy. In these words, 1. *Discipuli,* 2. *congregati,* 3. *conclusi,* 4. *propter timorem Judæorum :* that His "Disciples" yet they were; and "together" they were; and "in fear of the Jews" they were "shut up."

2. The persons to whom.

[Tertull. de Pœnit. c. 9.]

Whatsoever, or howsoever they were else, yet they were His Disciples; "unprofitable servants," yet servants : "lost" sons, yet sons : forgetful Disciples, yet Disciples. His Disciples they were, and howsoever they had made a fault, as it seemeth, so meant to hold themselves still, and hereafter to learn their lesson better.

1. His "Disciples."

Lu. 17. 10. Lu. 15. 24.

And I like well their fear, that they were afraid of the Jews. It shews there were no good terms betwixt them, and that they shut their doors upon them; therefore they meant not to go out to them, or seek *Pax vobis* of the Jews. They had no meaning it seemeth to give over Christ. If they had, what need they fear the Jews? The Jews would have done them no harm, they might have set open their doors well enough.

2. "For fear of the Jews."

And *congregatis,* I take it well, is no evil sign. It would have been *ex aliâ causâ,* for love rather than fear; and again, for fear of God, rather than of the Jews. Yet even thus I mislike it not, and much better this fear, than that at the Passion. That scattered them one from another, every man shift for one. This makes them draw together, and keep together, as if they meant to stand out afresh. Which very *congregatis* makes them fit for this salutation. It cannot well be said, *disgregatis,* 'to them that are in sunder.' *Una* is a disposition to unity; and gathering, to the binding up in the band of peace. Christ that said, *Quoties volui congregare?* liked it well to find them thus together; and His coming was, as to take away their fear, so to continue their gathering still.

3. "Assembled."

Mat. 23. 37.

And shall we learn this of the Disciples? 1. If a fault fall out, not to give over school, but to continue our discipleship still. 2. And not to go over, to seek our *Pax vobis* at the hands of His enemies; to shut out both them, and their

SERM.
IV.
peace too. 3. And lastly, not to forsake the fellowship, to keep together still. For being so together, we are nearer our peace. This shall make Christ come and say it to us the sooner, and the more willingly.

II.
The real
part.
The real part, *voti summa,* that which He wisheth, is "peace." First, Why peace? then, What peace?

1.
Why
"peace?"
Why peace? Is there nothing more worth the wishing? Nothing more, of itself; nothing more fit for these persons, this place, and this time?

Of itself, *votum pacis summa votorum.* 'It is all wishes in one,' nothing more to be wished. For *in brevi voce breviarium,* 'this little word is a breviary of all' that good is.

1. As good.
Ps. 133. 1.
Prov. 15.
16, 17.
Prov. 17. 1.
To shew how, a little; *quam bonum,* "how good," how worth the wishing it is. It is *tam bonum,* 'so good,' as without it nothing is good. With it, saith Solomon, "an handful of herbs;" without it, "an house full of sacrifices is not good." With trouble and vexation nothing is good, nothing is to be wished.

And as without it nothing is to be wished, so all that is to be wished, all good, is within it. *Evangelizantium pacem,*
Rom.10.15.
evangelizantium bona, quia in pace omnia bona: "to bring news of peace, is to bring news of all good things," 'for all good things are in peace.' *Bona* is the true gloss or exposition of peace.

2. Pleasant.
Ps. 133. 1.
3. Profitable.
Ps. 72. 7.
Quam bonum, you know, and *quam jucundum* too. But good and pleasant; and pleasant, not only as Aaron's ointment which was only pleasant, but as Hermon dew which brings profit with it. *Abundantia pacis,* saith the Psalm, "peace and plenty" go together.

4. Wished
by all.
Lu. 2. 14.
2 Cor. 13.
11.
Phil. 4. 7.
And yet, how much it is to be wished, this sheweth, *pacem te poscimus omnes.* All wish it. Angels wish it, Heaven to earth, *pax in terris;* and men wish it, earth to Heaven, *pax in Cœlis.* God wisheth it, most kindly for Him; *Deus pacis, pacem Dei;* "the God of peace," "the peace of God."

Lu. 4. 34.
Yea the enemy of all peace wisheth it, for he complains, *Venisti nos inquietare,* "Are ye come to trouble us?" So he would not be troubled that troubles all, but set all together by the ears, and sit quiet himself.

But it is much for the honour of peace, that *cum bellum geritur, pax quæritur.* Even military persons, with sword in one hand and fire in the other, give this for their emblem, *sic quærimus pacem,* 'thus, with sword and fire, seek we peace.' As seek it at last they must; we must all. Best *primâ sabbati,* but *sero,* 'sooner or later,' come to it we must: if it be not the first, it must be our last.

But if there were nothing else, this only were enough, and though there be many, this chiefly doth shew it; that our Saviour Christ so often, so divers ways, so earnestly wisheth it. Going He did it, *Pacem Meam do vobis.* And now coming, He doth it. Sitting, He did it; and now, standing. Living, when He was born, *Pax in terris, Xenium Christi,* 'it was Christ's New-year's gift.' Dying, when He was to suffer, *Pacem Meam relinquo vobis,* it was *legatum Christi,* 'Christ's legacy.' And now here rising again, it is His wish still. To shew, not only the good of this life, but of the next, to be in peace. Prayed for it, paid for it, wept for it; "O if thou hadst known the things that pertain to thy peace!" Wept for it, and bled for it: therefore immediately, the very next words, He sheweth them His hands and His side, as much to say, See what I have suffered to procure your peace. Your peace cost Me this, *Pax vobis* cost *Crux Mihi;*—see you hold it dear. Now sure, if there were any one thing better than other, those hands would not have withheld it, and that heart would wish it. And peace it doth wish, therefore nothing more to be wished. Complete it is, *Votum pacis summa votorum.*

There need no other sign be given but that of the Prophet Jonas, that Christ wished His wish: so the tempest may cease, and peace as a calm ensue, spare me not, "take me, cast me into the sea," make me a peace-offering and kill me. This is enough to shew it is to be wished, to make it precious in our eyes. For we undervalue it at too low a rate, when that which cost so dear, for every trifling ceremony we are ready to lose it. Our faint persuasion in this point is the cause we are faint in all the rest.

Well, though this be thus good, yet good itself is not good, unless it be in season, come fitly. Doth this so? Every way fitly. 1. For the persons; 2. For the place; 3. and for the time.

Marginal notes:

2. And by Christ often.

Joh. 14. 27.

Joh. 16. 33.

Lu. 2. 14.

Joh. 14. 27.

Joh. 17. 21.

Lu. 19. 42.

Joh. 18. passim.

Jonah 1. 12.

SERM.
IV.
—
I.
And now
fitly for
the per-
sons.
1. By
whom:
Christ.
Eph. 2. 14.
2. To
whom:
the Dis-
ciples.
[Cyril.
Alex. in
loc.]

The persons; both 1. Christ by Whom, and 2. they to whom it is wished. 1. Christ, by Whom; *decet largitorem pacis hæc salutatio,* saith Cyril. 'It is meet for Him to give peace That made peace;' nay, *Ipse est pax nostra,* saith the Apostle, and for peace, what fitter salutation than peace?

2. They to whom, for they needed it. With God they had no peace, Whom they had provoked; nor peace with men, nor with the Jews about them; nor peace with themselves, for they were in fear, and night-fear, which is the worst of all others. Fit for them, and they for it, for together they were, and so not unfit to entertain it.

2.
For the
place.

And with the place it suiteth well. For they were shut up, as men environed and beleaguered with their enemies, *conclusi et derelicti,* 'shut up and forsaken;' and to such peace is ever welcome.

3.
For the
time.

1Cor.15.26.

And for the time, seasonable. For after a falling out, peace is so; and after a victory, peace is so. Fit therefore for this day, the day of the Resurrection; for till then it was not in kind. The great battle was not fought, "the last enemy, death," was not overcome. Never till now, but now the last enemy is conquered, now it is in season.

4.
For the
thing
itself:
peace, a
resurrec-
tion.
Gen. 45. 27.

And for the thing itself, peace is a kind of resurrection. When Christ was risen, His Disciples were dead. Those dead affections of sorrow and fear, when they seize throughly upon men, what are they but *mors ante mortem?* Upon good news of Joseph, Jacob is said to "revive," as if before he had been given for dead. It was their case here. The house was to them as their grave, and the door as the gravestone, and they buried in fear. When they saw Him, in the next verse, and were thus saluted by Him, they gat hope, were glad, that is, revived again. For if those were the pangs of death, peace after a sort is a resurrection; and so a fit wish for the time.

Never
kindly till
then.

And to say truth, peace is never kindly till then. They define felicity shortly, to be nothing else but *pax desiderii.* For give the desire perfect peace, and no more needs to make us happy. Desire hath no rest, and will let us have none, till it have what it would, and till the Resurrection that will not be.

1. *Pax et pressura,* our Saviour opposeth. If we be Joh. 16. 33.
pinched with any want, desire hath no peace. 2. Let us
want nothing if it were possible. No peace yet; *pax et* Ps. 119.
scandalum the Psalmist opposeth. When we have what we 165.
would, somewhat cometh to us we would not, somewhat
thwarts us. Till *non est eis scandalum,* till that be had
away, desire hath no peace. 3. Let that be had away, yet a
new war there cometh. Peace and fear are here opposed.
We are well; neither *pressura* nor *scandalum,* but we fear
tolletur a vobis, that it will not hold, or we shall not hold.
"The last enemy" will not let us be quiet. Till he "be
overcome," our desire hath no perfect peace. That will not
be till the Resurrection. But then it is *pax plena, pura,
perpetua;* 'full' without want, 'pure' without mixture of
offensive matter, and 'perpetual' without all fear of foregoing, of *tolletur a vobis.* And that is *pax desiderii,* and
that is perfect felicity; the state of the Resurrection, and
the wish of the Resurrection day.

Thus we see good it is, and fit it is. It remains we see 2. What
what it is, what peace. When we speak of peace, the na- peace.
ture of the word leadeth us to ask, With whom? And
they be diverse. But as diverse as they be, it must be
understood of all, though of some one more especially than
the rest.

There is a peace above us in Heaven with God; that first. 1. Peace
They were wrong here, their fear ran all upon the Jews, it with God.
should have looked higher. The Jews they kept out with
shutting their doors; against God no door can be shut.
First, peace with Him; and with Him they have peace, to
whom Christ saith *Pax vobis.*

There is another peace within us, *in sinu,* 'with our 2. With
heart.' For between our spirit and our flesh there is in our own
hearts.
manner of a war. "The lusts of the flesh" even militant, [Gal. 5. 17.]
"wage war," saith St. Peter, "against the soul;" and where 1 Pet. 2. 11.
there is a war, there is a peace too. This is peace with fear,
here. Which war is sometime so fearful, as men to rid
themselves of it, rid themselves of life and all, conclude
a peace there. This followeth of the first; if all be well
above, all is well within.

There is a peace without us, in earth with men, with all 3. With all
men.

SERM.
IV.
[Heb. 12.
14.]
Mat. 5. 9.

Tertul.
Apolog.
[c. 30.]
men. The Apostle warrants it; peace with the Jews here and all. I will never fear to make civil peace a part of Christ's wish, nor of His *beati pacifici* neither. He will be no worse at Easter, than at Christmas He was; at this His second, than at that His first birth. Then Janus was shut, and peace over all the world. *Orbem pacatum* was ever a clause in the prayers of the Primitive Church, that the world might be quiet.

4. Among themselves.

Ps. 133. 2, 3.

Ps. 122. 3.

Acts 4. 32.

Mark 9. 50.
Phil. 4. 9.
Ps. 122. 6.
Prov. 12. 20.
Mat. 5. 9.

Yet is not this the peace of Christ's principal intendment, but their peace to whom Christ spake, *Pax discipulorum, Pax vobis inter vos;* ' Peace among them, or between themselves,' it was " the ointment on Aaron's head," Aaron that had the care of the Church. It was " the dew" that fell upon Sion, Sion the place where the Temple stood. "The peace of Jerusalem," that it may be once " as a city at unity within itself." The primitive peace, that " the multitude of believers" may be " of one heart and one mind." All the rest depend upon our peace with God, and our peace with Him upon this; *pacem habete inter vos,* and *Deus pacis erit vobiscum.* "The peace of Jerusalem," "they shall prosper that love it," saith David. " Joy shall be to them that counsel it," saith Solomon. " Blessed" shall they be that make it, saith Christ. How great a reward should he find in Heaven, how glorious a name should he leave on earth, that could bring this to pass !

1. Peace, Christ's wish.

Mat. 12. 42.
Mark 9. 50.

This is Christ's wish, and what is become of it ? If we look upon the Christian world, we see it not, it is gone as if Christ had never wished it. Between Jehu and Jeroboam, Solomon's seed went to rack. Jehu's proceedings, like his chariot-wheels, headlong and violent. But Jehu is but a brunt, too violent to last long. Jeroboam is more dangerous, who makes it his wisdom to keep up a schism in religion; they shall sway both parts more easily. God forbid we should ever think Jeroboam wiser than Solomon ! If peace were not a wise thing, the wisest man's name should not have been Solomon. " A greater than Solomon" would never have said *Habete salem et pacem;* " if you have any salt, you will have peace." Sure, when the Disciples lost their peace, they lost their wisdom; their wisdom and their strength both. They were stronger by *congregatis,* than by *clausis foribus;* 'more safe by their being together, than any door could make them.'

It is as Christ told us Luke x., where He prescribes this form of salutation: it speeds or it misses thereafter, as it meets with "the Son of peace;" speeds if it find him, if not, Lu. 10. 5, 6. comes back again, and takes no place.

Well, though it do not, we must still hold us to Christ's wish, and when all fails, still there must be *Votum pacis in corde;* though enmity in the act, yet "peace in the heart still." Still it must hold, *amicus ut non alter, inimicus ut non idem;* 'friends as if never otherwise, enemies as if not ever so.' *Quasi torrens, bellum;* 'war, like a land-flood,' that will be dry again. *Quasi fluvius, pax;* "peace, as a [Isa.48.18.] river," never dry, but to run still and ever.

But yet, many times "we ask and have not, because we Jas. 4. 3. ask not aright," saith St. James; "we know not the things that belong to our peace;" we err in the order, manner, site, place, or time.

The order, which helpeth much, first it is; first, *primum*   1.
et ante omnia, caput fidei, 'the prime of His wishes.' No The order
of it : first
sooner born, but *pax in terris;* no sooner risen, but *pax* wished.
vobis. Apertio labiorum, 'the very opening of His lips' was with these words; the first words at the first meeting, on the very first day. It is a sign it is so in His heart. That which most grieveth us, we first complain of; and that which most affecteth us, ever soonest speak of. This is the first error. That which was first with Christ, is last with Christians, and I would it were so last; for then it were some, now scarce any at all as it seemeth.

In the manner; for first is but first, that is but once.   2.
This is first and second. Here He saith it, and within a The manner: thrice
verse He is at it again. Nay first, second, and third, 1. in wished.
this, 2. the twenty-first, and 3. the twenty-sixth verses; as if like *actio* in Rhetoric, all in all.

All Christ's vows are to be esteemed, specially His solemn vows; and His speeches, chiefly those He goeth over and over again. That which by Him is double and treble said, would not by us be singly regarded. He would have it better marked; therefore He speaketh it the second time. He would have it yet sink deeper; therefore the third also. We

faulty in the manner. Once we do it, it may be, but upon any repulse we give over; if it come not at first, we go not to it *secundo et tertio, repetitis vicibus.* We must not leave at once that Christ did so oft.

2. His site in wishing it: *Stetit.*

The second error is; we ask it sitting, I fear, and Christ stood; His standing imports something. Standing is the site of them that are ready to go about a matter, as they to Ex. 12. 11. take their journey in the twelfth of Exodus. That site is the site of them that wish for peace; *oportet stantem optare.* A sedentary desire it may be we have, but loathe to leave our cushion. We would it were well, but not willing to dis- [¹ *i. e.* trou- ease ¹ ourselves. *Utinam hoc esset laborare,* said he, that ble, or put ourselves to lay along and stretched himself. So say we; peace we pain.] would, but standing is painful. Our wish hath lips but no legs.

Isa. 52. 7.
Rom. 10.15.
But it could not be said, "beautiful are the feet of them that bring peace," if the feet had nothing to do in this business. With sitting and wishing it will not be had. Ps. 34. 14. Peace will hide itself, it must be sought out; it will fly away, it must be pursued. This then is a point wherein we are to conform ourselves to Christ; as well to use our legs, as to open our lips for it. To stand is *situs voventis;* to hold up the hands, *habitus orantis.* The meaning of which ceremony of lifting up the hands with prayer is, *ut pro quo quis orat pro eo laboret,* 'what we pray for we should labour for;' what we wish for, stand for. We see Christ sheweth His hands and His feet, to shew what must be done with both for it. If we should be put to do the like, I doubt our wish hath never a good leg to stand on.

3. His place: *In medio.*
Lu. 1. 79.
To stand then, but to stand in a certain place. Every where to stand will not serve the turn. *Stetit in medio,* that standing place is assigned for it, thus "guiding our feet into the way of peace." And the place is material for peace. All bodies natural never leave moving, are never quiet, till they recover their proper places; and there they find peace. The By nature. midst is Christ's place by nature; He is the second Person *in Divinis,* and so the middlemost of the other two. And on earth, follow Him if you will, you shall not lightly find Him out of it; not according to the letter, speaking of the Lu. 2. 7. material place. At His birth, *in medio animalium,* in the

stable. After, a child, *in medio doctorum*, in the Temple. Lu. 2. 46.
After, a man, *medius vestrûm stetit*, saith John Baptist, " in Joh. 1. 26.
the midst of the people;" saith He of ' Himself,' *Ecce ego in
medio vestrî,* " in the midst of His Apostles." At His death Lu. 22. 27.
it fell to His turn likewise, that place : even then, He was in Lu. 23. 33.
the midst. And now rising, there He is, we see. They in
the midst of the Jews, and He in the midst of them. After
this, in Patmos, St. John saw Him in Heaven, " in the midst Rev. 7. 17.
of the Throne;" in earth, walking " in the midst of the Rev. 1. 13.
candlesticks." And at the last day He shall be in the midst
of " the sheep on His right hand, and the goats on His left." Mat. 25. 33.
All which shew, the place and He sort very well.

But were it not natural for Him, as the case standeth, By office,
there He is to stand, being to give peace? No place so fit for as a Mediator.
that purpose, none so kindly as it. His office being to be
" a Mediator," *Medius* " between God and man," where 1 Tim. 2. 5.
should a Mediator stand but *in Medio ?*

Besides, the two qualities of good, being to be *diffusivum* The reason
and *unitivum*, that is the fittest place for both. To distribute of it.
best done from the centre. To unite likewise, soonest meet
there. The place itself hath a virtue specially to unite, which
is never done but by some middle thing. If we will conclude, we must have a *medius terminus ;* else we shall never
get *majus* and *minus extremum* to come together. Nor in
things natural either combine two elements disagreeing in
both qualities, without a middle symbolizing with both ; nor
flesh and bone, without a cartilage between both. As for
things moral, there the middle is all in all. No virtue without it. In justice, incline the balance one way or the other,
the even poise is lost, *et opus justitiæ pax*, ' peace is the very
work of justice.' And the way to peace is the mid-way ;
neither to the right hand too much, nor to the left hand too
little. In a word, all analogy, symmetry, harmony, in the
world, goeth by it.

It cometh all to this ; the manner of the place doth teach
us what manner of affection is to be in them, that wish for
or stand for peace. The place is indifferent, equally distant,
alike near to all. There pitch the ark, that is the place for
it. Indifferency in carriage preserveth peace ; by foregoing
that, and leaning to extremities, it is lost. Thither we must

SERM.
IV.

get again, and there stand, if ever we shall recover it. *Discessit a medio* lost it, *stetit in medio* must restore it.

Therefore, when you hear men talk of peace, mark whether they stand where they should. If with the Pharisee to the corners, either by partiality one way, or prejudice another, no good will be done. When God will have it brought to pass, such minds He will give unto men, and make them meet to wish it, seek it, and find it.

4. The
time:
In illo die.

A little now of the time. This was Christ's wish at this time, and Christ never speaks out of season. Therefore a special interest hath this feast in it. It is *votum paschale*, and this is *festum pacis*.

1 Cor. 11. 16.

And sure, *Habemus talem consuetudinem, et Ecclesia Dei*; 'such a custom we have, and so the Church of God hath used it,' to take these words of Christ in the nature of an edict for pacification, ever at this time. That whatsoever become of it all the year beside, this time should be kept a time of peace; we should seek it and offer it—seek it of God, and offer it, each to other.

There hath not, these sixteen hundred years, this day passed without a peace-offering. And the law of a peace-offering is; he that offers it must take his part of it, eat of it, or it doth him no good. This day therefore the Church never fails, but sets forth her peace-offering;—the Body Whose hands were here shewed, and the side whence issued

Col. 1. 20.

Sanguis crucis, "the Blood that pacifieth all things in earth and Heaven," that we, in it and by it, may this day renew the covenant of our peace. Then can it not be but a great grief to a Christian heart, to see many this day give Christ's peace the hearing, and there is all; hear it, and then turn their backs on it; every man go his way, and forsake his peace; instead of seeking it shun it, and of pursuing, turn away from it.

Eph. 4. 20.
1 Cor. 5. 7, 8.

We "have not so learned Christ," St. Paul hath not so taught us. His rule it is; "Is Christ our Passover offered for us" as now He was? *Epulemur itaque*—that is his conclusion, "Let us then keep a feast," a feast of sweet bread without any sour leaven, that is, of peace without any malice.

So to do, and even then this day when we have the peace-offering in our hands, then, then, to remember always, but then specially to join with Christ in His wish; to put into our hearts, and the hearts of all that profess His Name, theirs specially that are of all others most likely to effect it, that Christ may have His wish, and there may be peace through the Christian world; that we may once all partake together of one peace-offering, and "with one mouth [Rom. 15. and one mind glorify God, the Father of our Lord Jesus 6.] Christ."

A SERMON

THE KING'S MAJESTY, AT WHITEHALL,

ON THE EIGHTH OF APRIL, A.D. MDCX., BEING EASTER-DAY.

JOB xix. 23—27.

Oh that my words were now written! Oh that they were written even in a book!

And graven with an iron pen in lead, or in stone for ever!

For I am sure that my Redeemer liveth, and He shall stand the last on the earth (or, and I shall rise again in the last day from the earth.)

And though after my skin worms destroy this body, I shall see God in my flesh.

Or, And I shall be compassed again with my skin.

Whom I myself shall see, and mine eyes shall behold, and none other for me, though my reins are consumed within me. (Or, and this hope is laid up in my bosom.)

[*Quis mihi tribuat ut scribantur sermones mei? quis mihi det ut exarentur in libro*

Stylo ferreo, et plumbi laminá, vel celte sculpantur in silice?

Scio enim quod Redemptor meus vivit, et in novissimo die de terra surrecturus sum:

Et rursum circumdabor pelle meá, et in carne mea videbo Deum meum.

Quem visurus sum ego ipse, et oculi mei conspecturi sunt, et non alius: reposita est hæc spes mea in sinu meo. Latin Vulg.]

[*Oh that my words were now written! Oh that they were printed in a book!*

That they were graven with an iron pen and lead in the rock for ever!

For I know that my Redeemer liveth, and that He shall stand at the latter day upon the earth:

And though, after my skin, worms destroy this body, yet in my flesh shall I see God:

Whom I shall see for myself, and mine eyes shall behold, and not another; though my reins be consumed within me. Engl. Trans.]

THIS day calleth us to say somewhat of Christ's resurrection. To find Christ's resurrection in the New Testament, is no mastery. Out of many places you have thence heard of it heretofore many times, and many times may hereafter out of many places more. If it be but for variety, it will do well not to dwell still on the New, but otherwhiles to see if we can find it in the Old. It will give us good satisfaction to see "Jesus Christ to-day and yesterday the same;" Heb. 13. 8. "yesterday" to them, "to-day" to us; to read *resurget* in Job, "He shall rise," as we read *resurrexit* in John, "He is risen;" to see their creed and ours differ but in tense, "shall rise," and "is risen," "shall" and "is," but the Redeemer all one in both. Much ado is made by your antiquaries, if an old stone be digged up with any dim letters on it. In this text I find mention of a stone to be graven, so that I shall present you this day with an antiquity, an old stone digged up in the land of Uz, as old as Job's time, and that as old as Moses; with a fair inscription, the characters of it yet legible, to prove the faith of this feast, so ancient that it began not with the Christians, the patriarchs had it as many hundred years before Christ as we are after. This text is a monument of it. And it will be never the worse welcome to us that are Gentiles, that it cometh from one that is a Gentile as Job was, and not of Jacob's line. It is the stronger for that Moses and Job, the Jew and Gentile believed it; Moses put it in his ordinary prayer, the nineteenth Psalm, as it were his *Pater noster*, and Job here in his creed.

St. Hierome saith of Job: *Nullum tam aperte post Christum,* [S. Hieron, *quam iste hîc ante Christum de Resurrectione loquitur Christi* Epist. 38. *et suâ:* 'No man ever since Christ did so clearly speak of mach.] Christ's resurrection and his own, as Job did here before Christ,' "That his Redeemer liveth and shall rise again." Which is as much to say as, "He is the Resurrection and Joh. 11. 25. the Life;"—St. John could say no more. It is his hope, he is by it "regenerate to a lively hope;"—St. Peter could say 1 Pet. 1. 3. no more. Enters into such particulars, "this flesh," and 'these eyes;"—St. Paul could do no more. There is not 1Cor.15.53. in all the Old, nay there is not in all the New, a more pregnant direct place.

There is then in this monument of antiquity, a direct prophecy; or, if you will, a plain creed, of the substance of this feast, of his Redeemer's rising, and of his hope to rise by Him; the one *positive*, the other *illative*. There is a pathetical poem set before it; and there is a close or farewell by way of *epiphonema* after it, no less pathetical.

The two first verses we may well call the *parasceue*, or "preparation to the feast of passover," which serve to stir

I. up our regard, as to a mystery or matter of great moment, worthy not only to be written or enrolled in a book, but to be cut in stone; a monument to be made of it, *ad perpetuam rei memoriam,* "Oh that," &c.

II. Then followeth in the third, his Redeemer and His rising, His passing over from death to life : "I know," &c., and out of it in the last, by way of inference, his own, *Et quod ego, &c.* set down with words so clear, and so full of caution, as in the Epistle to the Corinthians it is not fuller expressed.

III. Upon these two, there be two acts here set down, 1. *Scio*, and 2. *Spero.* He begins with *scio*, for the truth, and ends with *hæc mihi spes* for the comfort or use of this knowledge. Graven, that it may be known; known, that it may be our hope. His it was, and ours it must be; *reposita* with him, *reponenda* with us, to be lodged and laid up in our bosoms, against we be laid into the bosom of the earth. Indeed, *sculpsit in lapide* is nothing without *reponi in sinu,* 'Graving in stone will do no good, without laying it up in the bosom.'

I.
The *parasceue* or
"prepara-
tion."
Job's wish.
Job fearing it should seem, if he had but barely propounded the point following, it would have been but slenderly regarded, doth enforce himself to set it down with some solemnity, to make the deeper impression, which I call the *parasceue;* that we might not reckon of it as a light holyday, but as a high feast. He would have the *scio* of it stamped in stone, as worthy everlasting remembrance, and the *spero* of it carefully laid up, as worthy precious

account. It is as much as St. Paul had said; "It is a faithful saying, and by all means worthy to be received;" for the *scio*, "faithful," for the *spero*, "worthy all receiving;" for the truth, to be graven in marble, for the comfort to be lodged in the bosom.

For the first, thus he proceedeth. He was dying now,

and seeing he must die, one thing he had he would not have die with him. It was that when he had lost all, he kept in his bosom still; when all comforters, and comforts forsook him, and, as he saith, his physicians grew of no value, he found comfort in. This he thought it was pity should perish, but though he die, it live. It was certain words; and because they had been cordial to him—had been to him, and might be to others—he desires they might remain to memory; and because writing serves to that end, they might be written.

Which his wish of writing consists of three degrees, is as it were three wishes in one.

1. They be words; and because words be but wind his own proverb—that they might not blow away with the wind, he wisheth they were written. *Quis mihi tribuat,* 'who will help him to a clerk, to set them down in writing?' 1. That it were ".written." Job 6. 26.

But then, he bethinks himself better. They were no common ordinary matter, therefore not to be committed to common ordinary writing. So, they might be rent or lost: they be more worth than so. Therefore now secondly, he mends his wish; he would not have them to be barely written, but registered in a book, enrolled upon record, as public instruments, men's deeds, judicial proceeding; or, as the very word gives it, Acts of Parliament, or whatsoever is most authentical. 2. "Written in a book."

And yet, upon farther advice, he calls back that too, by a third wish. If they were upon record, records will last long, yet even them time will injure. No ink, no parchment, but will decay with time. Now these he would have last for ever: therefore he gives over his scribe, and instead of him ♦wisheth for a graver; no paper or parchment will serve, it must be stone, and the hardest stone, the rock. For this paper he must have "a pen of iron;"—that he wisheth too. But here is mention of lead; what is to be done with that? If we believe the Hebrews, that best knew the fashion of their country monuments, when it is graven, the graving may be choked with soil, and the edges of the letters being rough and uneven, may be worn in, or broken and so defaced; to provide for that, the graving he would have filled with lead, that so it might keep smooth and even from de- 3. "Written in stone, with a pen of iron for ever."

SERM.
V.
facing, and full from choking up. That it be לְעַד, the last word, that is, last "for ever," to the last ages and generations to come, never to be worn, but to hold for ever. If it were the best in the world, more cannot be done or wished than this, and this he wisheth, and not coldly, but earnestly. "Oh that it were, would God it were!" *Quis mihi tribuat?* Who will do so much? Who? as if he were earnest begging of God and man to have it done.

Why "in stone," &c.
Now in the name of God, what may this be that all this work is kept about? It is the work of this day. And why would not a book serve for this? Why no remedy but it must be in stone? There want not reasons; let me touch

1. Reason.
Exod. 34. 1.
1 Cor. 15. 14.
some few. Moses and Job are holden to have lived at one time. Moses' law was graven in stone, we know. This of Job here is Gospel, the substance, the chief article of it. No reason the Law in tables of stone, and the Gospel in sheets of paper. Good reason Job as zealous for the Gospel, as Moses for the Law. If that wrought in stone, this no less; as firm and durable as it every way. And the same reason is for the iron pen. As the stone for the Law, so the pen for the Prophets. If in the Prophet men's sins be

Jer. 17. 1.
"written with a pen of iron," meet the discharge should be written no less deep, with as hard a pen as it; that so the characters of one may match the other at each point.

2. Reason.
1 Cor. 10. 4.
Ps. 19. 14.
This for Moses, now for our Redeemer. There it was meet, *ut de Petrâ, in petrâ. Petra autem Christus,* our Redeemer is "a Rock;" "O Lord my Rock and my Redeemer," saith David, or "my Redeemer of the Rock," alluding to this of Job. Kindly it is it should be wrought in the Rock, that is, of the Redeemer Who is the Rock.

1 Cor. 15. 54.
And so the Resurrection, being a putting on incorruption, would not be written in corruptible stuff, but in that cometh nearest to incorruption, and is least of all subject to corrupt and decay. The words would be immortal, that treat of immortality.

3. Reason.
Hos. 13. 14.
1 Cor. 15. 54, 55.
A third, in respect of those works, that are usually wrought of stone, as gravestones, as arches triumphal. The Resurrection is *mors mortis,* saith Osee, "O death I will be thy death:" for the death of him that is the death of us all, here is a gravestone allowed, and an epitaph graven on it.

Here it is, and so doth Nazianzen call this Scripture, death's
epitaph. Either—if as Esay saith, "death" by Christ's rising Isa. 25. 8.
be "swallowed up in victory,"—a trophy of this victory would 1 Cor. 15.
remain, and that, as all victories, in a *pyramis* of stone; and ^{54.}
that, arch-wise on two pillars, 1. one for Christ's, 2. one for
our resurrection.

One more: That Job needeth this wish in regard of those 4. Reason.
that were to receive this doctrine. It will not well be
written, there is such unbelief and hardness of heart, yea
even in the Disciples, and so generally in our nature, as
enough to do to *grave* it in us; yet so necessary withal, as
where it will not be written, he wishes it graven. Written
where it may, but graven where it must. But written or
graven, one of them in us all.

This for Job's wish. Shall we now pass to the third verse, II.
and see what these words be, that no paper will serve, but The object:
stone; nor pen, but iron; nor ink, but lead? Great expec- Job's Redeemer,
tation is raised with this so stately an entry. The words be and His
resurrec-
Job's, his *scio* and his *spero*, touching the two articles of this tion.
day, 1. his Redeemer, and His rising; 2. and the train of it,
his own rising, and his seeing God. They begin with *scio*
the pillar of this faith, and end with *hæc mihi spes*, the arch
of his hope, ever hope giving the assumption to faith's pro-
position.

Let us begin with the object of his knowledge. The first 1. *Quod*
Redemp-
is news of a Redeemer. We owe this word to Job, he the *tor.*
first in the Bible that ever named Him so. Of the creation
we read in Moses, and God provided well for us that we
should no sooner hear of a Creator by Moses, but we should
of a Redeemer by Job. For though God by right of creation
were, as saith Melchisedek, "owner of heaven and earth," Gen. 14. 19.
yet "the creature being subject to vanity" shewed they Rom. 8. 20.
were gone, aliened from God. But this is good news, that
seeing we were God's and not our own, He would not see
that carried away that was His own, but would be content
one should redeem it back.

But it is news to hear that Job is at his Redeemer, Job
with all his innocency, with his so just and holy life, as God Job 1. 8, 9.
Himself bare witness unto it, as Satan himself could not Job 2. 3, 4.
except against it; yet he is not at *scio quod Judex,* but *scio*

S E R M.
V.
quod Redemptor, doth *deprecari Judicem*, and for all his virtues, a Redeemer will do well though; and he in the number
of those that are glad to say *scio*, to take notice of Him.

From which his *scio*, his notice taking, we take a true
estimate of Job's estate. For if he look after a Redeemer,
then is he either sold for a servant, or carried away for a
captive; one of these. For these two only we read of; redeemed from Egypt the house of bondage, or redeemed from
Babylon, the land of their captivity. St. Paul confesseth
Rom. 7. 14. both by himself; "sold under sin," and "led away captive
Rom. 7. 23. under the law of sin." Job confesseth as much. *Peccavi,*
Job 7. 20. *quid faciam?* sinned he had, and by committing of sin was
become *servus peccati*. Sold by himself, and made subject
by sin; and sold by God, and made subject to corruption,
from both of which he needed a Redeemer. Whether servant or captive, one or both, it falleth out well that both
states are redeemable, neither past redemption. " Sinned,"
that he needs a Redeemer; not so sinned, but a Redeemer
Job 33. 24. will serve. God is willing, saith Elihu, to receive a recon-
Job 34. 31. ciliation, to admit of a Redeemer; if we can get us one to
lay down the price, there is hope we may be restored, to see
God again. A Redeemer will do it.

Why then, *scio quod*, he knows of one. Good tidings to
all that need to know, there is one presently in being. For
[Lu. 2. 29.] then, *nunc dimittis* may Job say; he may " depart in peace,"
die when he will, his Redeemer lives Who will never see
that perish He hath paid the price for, but since He came to
redeem that which was lost, will not suffer that to be lost
which He hath redeemed.

2.　　　This of his Redeemer. Now, what he believes of Him.
Quod vivit. First, live He must, be a living, quick thing; not dead, or
[1Pet.1.18.] without life. Silver, gold, will not do it; our redemption is
personal, not real, to give somewhat and save himself. But
such a Redeemer as must answer body for body, and life for
life; give Himself for Job, and those He redeems;—so is
the nature of the word, so the condition of our redeeming.
There is His person.

Of what nature, out of the word Redeemer. Sure if a
His na-　Redeemer, God. The Psalm deduceth at large: " Man can-
tures:
God.　not redeem his brother, nor give an atonement unto God
Ps. 49. 7, 8.

for him. It cost more to redeem souls, so that he must let
that alone for ever." Then tells he us plainly, "It is God
shall redeem our souls from the hand of hell." Job saith
the same in effect: "In His Saints He found folly, and in _{Job 4. 18.}
His Angels *pravitatem,* somewhat awry;" they both need _{Job 15. 15.}
_{Job 25. 4, 5.}
a Redeemer, themselves. That they want themselves, they
cannot perform to others; and if neither Saint nor Angel,
then no Redeemer but God.

On the other side, if a Redeemer, man He is to be of _{And man.}
necessity. So is the flat law of redemption of persons. He
must be *frater,* or *propinquus,* "a brother or next of blood;" _{Lev. 25. 25.}
else not admitted to redeem a person. That He may be _{Ruth 3. 12.}
admitted then, He must be flesh of our flesh, and then
He may. The very word sheweth it which doth as properly
signify, to be "next of kin," as "to redeem." Upon the אל
point then, both He must be. Man cannot, God may not;
but God and man both, may and can.

But what stand we straining the word Redeemer, or the _{*Deum in*}
conditions of it, when we have both twain His natures in _{*carne.*}
formal terms, immediately in the verse following, *videbo*
Deum in carne? There is God in plain terms, and His flesh
is human flesh, and that is man. I know, *in carne* there
may be construed two ways, but I know both ways well, and
both ways it is taken by the Fathers: 1. "I, in my flesh,
shall see God;" or, 2. "I shall see" *Deum in carne,* that is,
Deum incarnatum, "God having taken flesh upon Him."
This latter way, I find, St. Augustine taketh it: *videbo Deum* _{[Vid. S.}
in carne; quod ad id tempus pertinet cum Christi Deitas _{August. de}
_{Civ. Dei,}
habitu carnis induta est. 'I shall see God in my flesh: this _{18. 47. et}
_{22. 29.]}
pertains to the time, when the Godhead of Christ was
clothed with the habit of flesh.' And well both, for one
depends on the other; our seeing God in the flesh, upon
God's being seen in our flesh. But *Deus in carne,* are the
two natures.

Now His office is redeeming. How discharges He that? _{*Quod re-*}
How brings He the work of our redemption to pass? Many _{*surget.*}
_{His office.}
were His works concurring to it. Job singles out, and
makes choice of one among them all, which is the chief of
all, the accomplishment of all, and where He shewed Himself
a complete Redeemer. For then a Redeemer right, when

SERM.　He had brought His work to perfection, and that He did
V.　　when He rose again.

So I read, "rise again," and not "stand." It is well
known, it is the proper word for rising, and not standing.
The Seventy so turn it, not στήσεται, "shall stand," but
ἀναστήσεται, "shall rise again." The Fathers so read it:

[S. Hieron.　*Nec dum natus erat Dominus,* saith St. Hierome, *et Athleta*
Epist. 38.
ad Pam-　*Ecclesiæ Redemptorem suum vidit a mortuis resurgentem,* 'He
mach.]　was not yet born, and the Church's champion, Job, saw his

[S. Gregor.　Redeemer rising from the dead.' *Victurum me certâ fide*
lib. 14. in
cap. 19.　*credo, liberâ voce profiteor, quia Redemptor meus resurget,*
Beat. Job.　*Qui inter impiorum manus occubuit;* 'With assured faith I
67.]
believe, and with free courage confess, that rise I shall, inasmuch as my Redeemer shall rise, Who is to die by the hands
of wicked men,' saith Gregory upon these very words.

"Rise again" then shall our Redeemer from the dead.
There He was then, or He could not rise thence. How
came He there? So that here is His death implied evidently, that brought Him thither. Rise He cannot, except
first He fall. Fall therefore He must, and be laid up in
the earth, before He can rise from thence again. Specially,
seeing we find Him first alive in the fore-part of the verse,
and then rise again in the latter. For how can that be,
unless death come between?

Yea, the Fathers go farther, and from the words, *carne*
meâ, set down the very state of His death. In my flesh,
that is, say they, such flesh as mine, rent and torn. As
to say true, between Christ's flesh when Pilate shewed Him

Joh. 19. 5.　with *Ecce Homo,* and Job's, no great odds. *Unum in toto*
corpore vulnus, 'one resembled somewhat the other,' scarce
any skin left on Him no more than Job; *postquam pellem*
Meam contriverunt, might Christ as truly say.

In this case he saw Him brought to the dust, and thence
he seeth Him rising again; and so now it is Easter-day
with Job. For this text this day was fulfilled. Then He
rose again, and rising shewed Himself a perfect Redeemer.
Then, for till then, though the price were paid, nothing was

Ps. 16. 10.　seen to come back. Now, "His soul was not left in hell,"
Acts 2. 31.　and so that came back; nor "His flesh to see corruption,"
Acts 13. 35.　and so that came back. And having thus with a mighty

hand redeemed and raised Himself, He is able to do as much for us. *Quam in Se ostendit, et in me facturus est,* [S. Greg. lib. 14. in saith Gregory; *Exemplo hîc monstravit, quod promisit in* cap. 19. *præmio;* 'what He shewed in Himself, He will perform in Beat. Job. us; and what we see now in this example, then we shall 68.] feel in our own reward.'

But thus have we in this verse comprised His person, His two natures, Godhead and manhood, His office, His death and His resurrection, and His second coming; for at His first Job saw Him not as Simeon, but at His second shall. What would we more? with a little help, one might make up a full creed.

Very well then, on he goeth, and out of this *Scio quod* Job's own *Redemptor* he inferreth *Scio quod ego,* arguing from his tion. resurrection. Redeemer to himself. *Eâdem catenâ revincta est Christi resurrectio, et nostra,* 'One chain they are linked with, His and ours;' you cannot stir one end, but the other moveth with it. The sinews of which reason are in this, that the Redeemer doth but represent the person of the redeemed. For a Redeemer is *res propter alium,* 'all He doth is for another;' lives not, dies not, rises not, to or for Himself, but to or for others; him or them, He undertakes for. His life, death, resurrection, theirs, and the consequence so good; *Scio quod Ille, et quod ego.* So there is no error in reading as we do, in our Office of the Dead, "I shall rise again at the last." Though it be the third person in the text, the first is as infallibly deduced by consequence, as if it were there expressly set down; as sure as He shall rise, so sure He shall raise, for to that is He a Redeemer.

We see the coherence; let us see the benefit, which The bene- standeth of these four points. First, he shall see God; fit. secondly, see Him in his "flesh," and with his "eyes;" thirdly, in the same flesh, and with "the same eyes and no other;" fourthly, and he shall see Him, *sibi,* "for his own good and benefit;" and all this, *non obstante* the case he was in, which gave but small likelihood of it.

The first and main benefit his Redeemer will raise him to, *Videbo* is to see God. That he lost when he became aliened; that *Deum.* he recovers, being redeemed. Here begins all misery, to be see God." cast out of His presence; here all happiness, to be restored

SERM.
V.
Ps. 16. 11.
Joh. 14. 8.

to the light of His countenance. *Visio Dei,* all along the Scriptures, is made our chief good ; and our felicity still set forth under that term. "In Thy presence is the fulness of joy," saith the Psalm. *Ostende nobis Patrem et sufficit,* and we will never desire more. A conjecture we may have of the glory of this sight, from Moses. He saw Him, and not

Exod. 33.
22, 23.

His face neither, and that but a glimpse, and but as He passed by, yet got he so glorious a brightness in his countenance, he was fain to be veiled; no eye could endure to

Mat.17.2,4.

behold him. And a like conjecture of the joy, by the transfiguration. They did but look up at it, they desired never to be any where but there, never to see any sight but that ; so were they ravished with the beholding of it.

2. *Videbo in carne.*
"See Him in my flesh."
[Jam. 4. 6.]

"See God," and so he may in spirit, as do the souls of the righteous departed, it skills not for the flesh. Yes, see Him " in the flesh." That as proper to this text, and this day, which "offers more grace." This day Christ rose in the flesh, and this text is, "we shall see Him in the flesh." It is meet the flesh partake the redemption wrought in the flesh, and He be seen of flesh, That was seen in the flesh. He will do it for the flesh, it is now His nature, no less than the Godhead; He will not forget it, we may be sure. It was hard the Redeemer should be in the flesh, and the flesh never the better for it.

1. Reason.

For the soul is but half: though the better half, yet but half, and the redeeming it is but a half redemption; and if but half, then imperfect. And our Redeemer is God, and God's works are all perfect; if He redeem, He doth it not by halves. His redemption is a complete redemption, certainly. But so it is not, except He redeem the whole man, soul, flesh and all; his soul from Hell, his flesh from the grave, both to see God. His redemption is imperfect, till it extend so far. Therefore, at His coming again, they are

Lu. 21. 28.

willed to "lift up their heads, their redemption is at hand," their full redemption; then full, when both soul and body shall enjoy the presence of God.

2. Reason.

And what we say of God's work, the same we say of the soul's desire; it is not full neither, without this. Every

2 Cor. 5. 4.

man, yea the Saints, St. Paul by name, professeth all our desire, *Nolumus exspoliari sed supervestiri,* "we would not be stripped of this flesh, but be clothed with glory immortal, upon soul and flesh both;" which desire, being both natural, and having with it the concurrence of God's Spirit, cannot finally be disappointed.

I add farther that it is agreeable, not only to the perfec- 3. Reason. tion of His work, but even to His justice, that Job's flesh should be admitted, upon the Septuagint's reason in the forepart of the verse, τὸ ἀναντλοῦν ταῦτα, that it hath gone through, joined in the good, endured all the evil, as well as the soul. "For God is not unrighteous, to deprive the Heb. 6. 10. labourer of his hire," but with Him it is a righteous thing to reward them jointly that have jointly done service, and not sever them in the reward that in the labour were not severed. But the flesh hath done her part, either in good or evil; her "members" have been members either ways. In the good, Rom. 6. 13. the flesh hath kneeled, prayed, watched, fasted, wasted, and wearied itself, to and for God. In evil it hath done, I need not tell you what; and that, to and for sin. Therefore, even justice would they should share in the reward of the good; and in the evil, take like part of the punishment. This may serve for the flesh.

And sure, the very same may be said, and is no less 3. *In carne* strong for the third degree; as for the flesh and the eyes, so *mea, &c.* "In my that the same flesh should participate, and the same eyes, own flesh, and with the same and no other for them. No justice, one flesh should labour, the same eyes." and another reap that it never laboured for. What comfort can it be for the poor body to abridge itself of much pleasure, and to devour much tediousness and many afflictions; and another strange body shall step up, come between, and carry away the reward? Nay, if these eyes of Job's have dropped many a tear, it is reason the tears be wiped from Job 16. 20. them, not from another pair of new-made eyes. If they have restrained themselves, even by "covenant," from stray- Job 31. 1. ing after objects of lust, it is meet they be rewarded with the view of a better object.

But to say true, so should there be no resurrection indeed, a rising up rather of a new, than a rising again of the old. Job should not rise again, this Job, but another new Job in his place and stead. Therefore is this point ever most stood on, of the rest. St. Paul—not a corruptible or a mortal at

SERM.
V.
1Cor. 15. 53.
Joh. 2. 19.
large, but *hoc*, "this corruptible, this mortal." Yea, our
Saviour Himself, *solvite Templum hoc*, "this very Temple ;"
and to shew, it was that very one indeed, it pleased Him to
retain the print, both of the nails and spear. And Job
most plain of all, using not only the word *his*, as it were
pointing to it with his finger, *positive*, but by adding "this
and no other," *exclusive* too, to express it the more fully
above exception.

4. *Videbo*
mihi.
" I myself
shall," &c.
But now these all, 1. seeing God, and 2. in the flesh,
and 3. in the same flesh, all are as good as nothing without
the fourth. *Videbo mihi*, a little word, but not to be little
regarded. In the translation it is left out sometimes,
never in the treaty. To see Him for our good, else all
the rest is little worth. For all shall see Him, and in the
flesh, and in the same flesh, but all not *sibi* but many
contra se; not to their good all, but many to their utter
destruction.

This very word is it which draweth the diameter between
the resurrection of life and the resurrection of condemnation,
the right hand and the left, the sheep and the goats. They
Isa. 26. 19. that see Him *sibi*, to them Esay, "Arise and sing." They
Rev. 1. 7. that *contra se*, of them St. John, *Videbunt et plangent*, "See
Lu. 17. 37. they shall and mourn." Those shall fly as eagles with all
speed to the body; these other draw back and shrink into
their graves, creep into the clefts and holes to avoid the
Lu. 23. 30. sight, cry to the hills to fall upon them, and hide them from
1 Thes. 4.
17.
Ps. 9. 17. that sight. One shall *rapi in occursum*, "be caught up to
meet;" the other shall *converti retrorsum*, "be tumbled
backward into hell, with all the people that forget God."
So that this word is all in all; which God after expounds,
Job 33. 26. *videbit faciem Meam in jubilo*, "with joy and jubilee shall he
behold My face," as a Redeemer, not as a Revenger; and as
it followeth, with hope and not with fear in his bosom.

And the very next point was it that revived him, and in
very deed the tenor of his speech, so often iterating the same
thing, and dwelling so upon it, sheweth as much. Once
had been enough, "I shall see God." He comes over it
again and again, as if he felt some special comfort even by
speaking it. Three several times he repeats this seeing, and
three other, his person—I, and I myself, and I, and none

other but I. And as if he were not enough, he reckons up three parts, his skin, flesh, and eyes; as if being once in, he could not tell how to get out. Blame him not: it seems, he felt some ease of his pains, at least forgat them all the while he was but talking. It did so ravish him; having begun, he knew not how to make an end.

Thus much for the object. Now to his *scio*, his knowledge first, and then his *spero*, his hope after. For his knowledge, there be four things I would note out of four words. 1. his certainty out of *scio*; 2. his propriety out of *meus*; 3. his patient waiting out of *tandem*; 4. and his valour or constancy in *non obstante*. III.
The two acts. *Scio.*
His knowledge.

Scio, his certainty; that he did not imagine or conceive it might be, but knew it for certain, even for a principle. *Quis scit,* 'Who knows,' saith one. 'Who knoweth, whether men die as beasts?' *Quis scit? Scio.* 'Who knows?' "I know," saith Job. *Putasne*, saith he, chapter 14. "Think you, one that is dead may rise again?" Think? "I know it," saith Job. It was *res facta*, even this day to His Disciples. It was *res certa* to Him, many hundred years before. It is much to the praise of his faith; " so much was not found, no not in Israel." And we shall not need to trouble ourselves to know how he knew it. Not by any Scripture, he had it not from Moses, but the same way that Moses had it; he looked in the same mirror Abraham did, when he saw the same Person, and the same day, and rejoiced to see it. 1.
His certainty.
Scio.

Mat. 8. 10.

Joh. 8. 56.

Out of *scio* his certainty, and out of *meus* his peculiar, as it were. The Redeemer of the world would not serve him, nor St. Paul's *maxime fidelium*, " of the faithful chiefly." This of the Ephesians would not content him, "That loved us and gave Himself for us:" none but the second of Galatians, "That loved me, and gave Himself for me." "My Redeemer;" which they call faith's possessive. 2.
His propriety.
Meus.
1 Tim. 4. 10.
Eph. 5. 2.

Gal. 2. 20.

In *tandem*, the third word, his " patient enduring." For patience is not only shewed in suffering the cross, but in waiting also for the promise. It will not be done by and by, this; but *tandem*, " at the last" it will. " He shall rise again at the last:" he shall, and we shall. *Qui crediderit ne festinet,* " He that believeth, let him not be in all haste." No: 3.
His patient waiting.
Tandem.
Heb. 6. 15.
Tit. 2. 13.
Isa. 28. 16.
Hab. 2. 3.

SERM. *Si moram fecerit, expecta Eum,* "If He stay, stay His
V.
leisure." Tarry His *tandem.*

4.
His cou-
rage.
Tametsi.

And last, all these, *Non obstante* or *tametsi,* the resolute
courage or valour of his faith; that this he saith being in
case he was, small likelihood of it in appearance, seeing and
feeling that he saw and felt. There sat he falling away by
piecemeal, *vivum cadaver.* For him then to talk of *scio* and
meus thus, having no better signs and arguments than he
had; in the sense of his anger, to believe his favour;
brought to the day of death, to promise himself so glorious

Rom. 4. 18. an estate;—this is Abraham's faith, *contra spem in spe cre-*
dere, faith without, nay faith against feeling. His state in
sense of misery, want of comfort, his friends dismaying him,
for all that he keeps to his *scio,* and to his *meus* still. All
else, even all he hath, his righteousness too, they may take
from him; *salutem non auferent,* 'his Redeemer they should
never get;' *non obstante,* he would hold him fast.

2. Act,
Spero :
His hope.

This for his *scio,* and now to his *spero,* which word leadeth
us to the use he did, and we are to make of this knowledge.
Not, know to know; or to be known, to know; but know,
to lodge in our bosoms true hope. It is the general use of

Rom. 15. 4. all our knowledge of the Scriptures, "Whatsoever is written
for our learning, that we by patience and comfort in the
Scriptures may have hope." Generally of all, but above all
of these, of Christ our Redeemer. He is our hope, and His
rising, that is *caput bonæ spei,* 'our cape of good hope,' the
most hopeful of all other.

Spes re-
posita.
"Hope
laid up."

The use of hope is to expel fear. No fear, to the fear of
death, what shall become of us after our short time here,
which makes us never quiet, but in "the valley of Achor" all

Hos. 2. 15. our life long: the Resurrection opens us "a gate of hope."

Mark 16. 6. Therefore this day, *Noli timere,* say the Angels; *Nolite ti-*

Lu. 24. 38. *mere,* saith Christ. That our proper salutation of the day.

Ps. 16. 9. This, a day of hope. And this use made David of it: "My
flesh shall rest in hope," though we were not in Job's case,
but in all his royalty. For even Kings, in all their royalty,
sometimes have before them the hand-writing on the wall;

Dan. 5. 5, *Numeravit,* "He hath numbered thy days," and even then
26.
they rest on this hope, and read this inscription not un-

[1 Pet. 1.3.] willingly. The same use do the Apostles: "Who hath regenerated us," *in spe*, "to a lively hope, by the resurrection of Christ"—it is St. Peter. "Rest in hope," saith David; "a lively hope"—Peter; rest in hope of rising and living again.

And the term, that Job here gives hope, is worth a note; he calls it "the kidneys" of the soul. It made the translator כליות miss, that knew not this idiom. For as in that part of the body is bred, and from thence doth issue, the same *generativus humor*, whereby we propagate our kind, and live here in a sort after we be dead; in like manner by this hope, saith Job, and so saith St. Peter, "we are begotten anew;" 1 Pet. 1. 3. "we are sown," saith St. Paul, and of that seed, rise again 1 Cor. 15. "in power, honour, and immortality." 42, &c.

And this is *hæc spes*, "this hope." For hope at large heareth evil, hath no good name. Many our hopes prove *vigilantis somnia*, 'waking dreams,' we cannot lay them up: and if we would, they are not worth the laying up, no more than our dreams be. That the heathen man made it his happiness, to say; *vale spes*, 'farewell all hoping.' This is true, where the rest of our hope is vanishing as man, whose breath is in his nostrils; and when that goeth, "all his Ps. 146. 4. thoughts perish." But this hope is of another nature; *non* Rom. 5. 5. *confundet*, "it will not make you ashamed." There is a reality in it, "an anchor-hold;" "it is built on the rock," it Heb. 6. 19. will endure as the rock on which it is built, and on which it is Lu. 6. 48. graven here. There will come an end, and his hope will not be cut off, of all other; you may make a *depositum* of it, lay it up, *repone illam, et repone te in illâ*; you may rest on it, it is, *spes viva*, "a living hope" in Him That liveth, and shall 1 Pet. 1. 3. restore us all to life.

Now, the place is much, where we lay it; every thing is *Reposita* best kept in his proper place. Job saith, he bestowed it in *in sinu.* his bosom, and would have us to do the like. Of that place "In my bosom." he made choice, of none without us, behind us. That we might ever carry it about us, ever have it before us and in our sight, ever at hand; not to seek, but ready and easy to be had, when we call for it; and these, for the continual use we are to have of it, in all the dismays and discomforts of our life. Beside, there it will be safely, that being the surest place, as being within the fold of our arms where our strength

S E R M. lieth, and whence hardest to take it from us.   And there it
    V.
———— will be best cherished in the warmth, and vital heat of the
bosom.   There the nurse carrieth her child, and the wife is
Deu. 13. 6. called "the wife of the bosom."   And what is dearer to us
than these two?   But above all, there it will be next the
heart, for the bosom is but the coffer of the heart, and there
Job would have it.   As well for that that place is the best
place, and so best for the best hope, as that there is in this
hope a special cordial virtue against the fainting of the heart;
as indeed it is *cor cordis*, 'the very heart of the heart,' and
whereby the heart itself is more heartened.   Job found it so.
So did St. Paul, when he grew out of heart.   Put his hand
in his bosom, took out this hope, looks upon it, presently
2 Cor. 4. 16. saith, *propter quod non deficimus*.   And when Timothy was
in the like *deliquium*, he applies to him—What man!   *Me-*
2 Tim. 2. 8. *mento*, "Remember, Christ is risen," and we shall rise and
see God; an amends for all we can suffer—as a special receipt against all cardiack passions.

But, in choosing this place, Job's mind was specially to
except to the brain, where commonly men lodge it, and are
mistaken; it is not the right place.   *Scio* there if you will,
in the brain, it is the place of memory; but *spero* in the
heart, the place of affection, namely fear, and till the heart
be the less fearful, and the more cheerful for it, it is not
where it should be, not laid in the right place.   Nay, not
scientia cerebri, knowledge is not the best neither, not in the
brain.   *Scientia sinus*, and *corde creditur :* best, when it hath
his rest there, when knowledge in the heart, and hope in the
reins, and He that searcheth heart and reins may there find
them.   Err not then in laying it up in the head, or any
where, but whither Job carried it, and where he laid it, "in
the bosom."

To end; because we be speaking of a hope to be laid up
in our bosom, it falleth out very fitly, that even at this time,
festum spei, the Church offereth us a notable pledge and earnest of this hope there to bestow; even the holy Eucharist,
Joh. 6. 24. the flesh wherein our Redeemer was seen and suffered, and
Eph. 4. 30. paid the price of our redemption; and together with it "the
Holy Spirit, whereby we are sealed to the great day of our
redemption."   To the laying up of which earnest of our hope,

and interest in all these, we are invited at this time, even literally to lodge and lay it up in our bosom. We shall be the nearer our *scio*, if "we taste and see by it, how gracious [Ps. 34. &. the Lord is;" the nearer our *spero*, if an earnest or pledge of it be laid up within us; the nearer our redemption, if we have within us the price of it; and the nearer our resurrection—they be His own words, "He that eateth My flesh Joh. 6. 54. and drinketh, &c. hath eternal life, and I will raise him up at the last day." So dwell we in Him, and He in us; we in Him by our flesh in Him, and He in us by His flesh in us. Thereby drawing life from Him the second, as we do death from the first Adam.

But this hope hath this property, saith St. John, it will mundify the place where it lieth, "Every one that hath this 1 John 3. 3. hope cleanseth himself;" which place by virtue of it we shall so cleanse, *ut videatur in carne nostrâ Deus*, "that the life of [2 Cor. 4. Jesus may be manifest in our flesh;" and all men see the 10.] virtue of His resurrection to have His work in us, by our rising out of the old dusty conversation to newness of life. His resurrection and the power of it being exemplarily seen in our flesh, our end shall be to "see Him in our flesh," and that *nobis*, not *contra nos*, for our eternal joy and comfort. And then have we the feast in kind, and as much fruit of it, as either Patriarch or Apostle can wish us. Which that we may, pray we to Him, &c.

T

A SERMON

PREACHED BEFORE

THE KING'S MAJESTY, AT WHITEHALL,

ON THE TWENTY-FOURTH OF MARCH, A.D. MDCXI. BEING EASTER-DAY, AND
BEING ALSO THE DAY OF THE BEGINNING OF HIS MAJESTY'S MOST
GRACIOUS REIGN.

PSALM cxviii. 22.

The Stone Which the builders refused, the same Stone is become
(*or* made) *the Head of the corner.*

[*Lapidem, Quem reprobaverunt ædificantes, Hic factus est in Caput
anguli.* Latin Vulg.]

[*The Stone Which the builders refused is become the Head-stone of
the corner.* Engl. Trans.]

SERM. "THE Stone which the builders refused," saith the Pro-
VI. phet David. "This is the Stone which ye builders refused,"
1.
Acts 4. 11. saith the Apostle Peter. And saith it of Christ our Saviour,
Hic est Lapis, "He is the Stone." And saith it to Caiaphas
and the rest that went for builders. We know then who
this Stone is, and who these builders be, to begin with.

And in the very same place, the same Apostle telleth us
farther what is meant by "refused," and what by "made
Acts 4. 10. head of the corner." *Quem vos,* "whom ye" denied and
"crucified;"—that was His refusing. And then, *Quem Deus,*
"whom God" hath raised again from the dead;—that was
His making *Caput anguli.* "Refused" when? Three days
ago. "Made Head," when? This very day, for *Hic est dies*
Ps. 118. 24. followeth straight within a verse, "This is the day." Which
day? there is not one of the Fathers that I have read, but
interpret it of Easter-day.

. And so we have brought the text, and the time together. We know who is " the Stone ;" Christ. Who " the builders ;" Caiaphas and those with him. When " refused ?" In His Passion. When " made head ?" at His Resurrection, that is this day, which day is therefore at the twenty-seventh verse said to be, *constitutus dies solennis,* " made a solemn feast-day," *in condensis,* on which the Church to stand " thick and full," *usque ad cornua altaris,* "even up to the very corners of the altar."

This I take it is a good warrant for our Church, to make this Psalm a select choice Psalm for this day, as peculiar and pertinent to the feast itself. And a good warrant for us so to apply it. It is the Holy Ghost's own application by the mouth of St. Peter, we may boldly make it ours.

But though this be the chief sense, yet it is not the only. 2. The chief it is, for " the spirit of prophecy" is in it, which 'Rev. 19.10. " is the testimony of Jesus." Yet not the only, for according to the letter we cannot deny, but that originally it was meant of David. He was a stone too, and in his time refused, yet after raised by God to the highest place, even to be King over His people. The Chaldee Paraphrast, the oldest we have, is enough for this; thus he turneth the verse. סלא &c. " The Child Whom the chiefest men oppugned, He of all the sons of Ishai, was made Ruler of Israel." A second sense then it hath, of David.

And by analogy it will bear a third, and it will sort with 3. ours, or with any Prince, in like manner banded against, and sought to be put by as he ; and yet after brought by God to the same place that David was. To any such it will well agree, and be truly verified of him, and rightly applied to him. And I confess, I chose it the rather for this third. Because, as this year falleth out, upon one day, and *Hic est dies,* "this is the day," we have in one a memorial of two benefits ; 1. of our Saviour's exalting, by His Resurrection, 2. and of our Sovereign's exalting, and making head of this kingdom. Both lighting together, we were, as we thought, so to remember the one, that we left not the other out. And this text will serve for both. Both may in one be set before us, and so we rejoice and render thanks to God for both ; for the Lord Christ, and for the Lord's christ under one.

Three senses then there are in the text, and to do it right, we to touch them all three. 1. Christ in prophecy; 2. David in history; 3. Our own in analogy. But we will give Christ the precedence. Both for His person—He "is David's Lord,"

Col. 1. 18. and the Head of all Head-stones; it is meet He have *primatum in omnibus*, "He in all things have the pre-eminence"— and, for that the truth of the text never was so verified in any as in Him. We may truly say, none ever so low cast down, none ever so high lift up again as He. Others refused, but none like Him; and their heads exalted, but nothing in comparison of His. 1. First then of Christ's; 2. after, of David's briefly; 3. and last, of our own.

I. To apply it to Christ. "The stone" is the ground of all. Two things befal it, two things as contrary as may be. 1. "Refused," cast away; 2. then, called for again, and "made Head of the building." So two parts there are, to the eye. 1. The refusing, 2. and the raising, which are His two estates, His humiliation, and His exaltation.

1. In either of these ye may observe two degrees. *A quibus*, and *quousque;* 'by whom,' and 'how far.' By whom "refused?" We weigh the word *ædificantes;* not by men unskilful, but by workmen, "builders" professed; it is so much the more.

2. How far? We weigh the word *reprobaverunt, usque ad reprobari,* 'even to a reprobation.' It is not *improbaverunt,* 'disliked,' as not fit for some eminent place, but *reprobaverunt,* 'utterly reprobate' for any place at all.

II. Again, exalted by whom? The next words are, *a Domino,*

1. "by God," as good a Builder, nay better than the best of them; which makes amends for the former.

2. And how far? Placed by Him, not in any part of the building, but in the part most in the eye, "the corner," and in the highest place of it, "the very Head."

So rejected, and that by the builders, and to the lowest estate; and from the lowest estate exalted *in Caput anguli,* to the chiefest place of all, and that by God Himself. This for Christ.

3. And David is a stone, and so is ours, and so is every good

Gen. 49. 24. prince, *lapis Israel,* as Jacob in his testament calleth them. And builders there be, such as by office should, but many times do not their office, no more than Caiaphas here. *Re-probaverunt* is, when "they devise to put Him by, whom Ps. 62. 4. God would exalt;" and *factus Caput,* when God for all that doth them right, and brings them to their place, the Throne Royal. And this was the day when God so brought David, as appeareth by the twenty-fourth verse. And *hic est dies,* "this is the day" when He brought his Majesty to be head of this kingdom. Of these in their order.

"The Stone which the builders refused, &c." The estate I. of mankind, as they are in society, either of Church or king-dom, is in divers terms set forth to us in Scripture; some-times of a flock, sometimes of husbandry, otherwhile of a [See Ps 74. building. Ye are "His flock"—divers times in the Psalms. 1. 77. 20. "You are God's husbandry, you are God's building"—both 13. 80. 1. in one verse. Now, the style of this text runs in terms of 41.] this last, of Building or Architecture. For here are builders, and here is stone, and a coin or corner, and a top or turret 1 Cor. 3. 9. over it.

Of this spiritual building we all are stones, and which is strange, we all are builders too. To be built, and to build, both stones, in regard of them whom God hath set over us, who are to frame us, and we so to suffer them. Builders, in regard of ourselves first: then, such as are committed to us, by bond either of duty or charity, every one being, as St. Chrysostom saith well, *de subditâ sibi plebe quasi domum Deo struere,* 'of those under his charge, to make God an house.' As "stones;" it is said to us by St. Peter, *Super-ædificamini,* "Be ye built up," or framed. As "builders;" 1 Pet. 2. 5. it is said to us first by St. Jude, "Build yourselves in your Jude 20. most holy faith." Then by St. Paul, "Edify ye," or build 1 Thes. 5. ye "one another." "Be built," by obedience and con-formity: "Build yourselves" by increase in virtue and good works. "Build one another" by good example, and whole-some exhortation. The short is, this is to be our study, all: if we be but ourselves, every one in himself and of himself to build God an oratory. If we have an household, of them to build Him a chapel. If a larger circuit, then a Church. If a country or kingdom, then a *Basilica,* or Metropolitan Church, which is properly the prince's building.

This in the text, the builders here were in hand with, as a

Basilica; for it was the frame of the Jews' government, but is applied to all states in general. For Jewry was the scene or stage whereon the errors or virtues of all governments were represented to all posterity.

Four words there be in the text: 1. *Ædificantes,* "builders." 2. *Lapis,* "Stone." 3. *Angulus,* "a Corner," and 4. *Caput,* "the Head." From the first word, *Ædificantes,* this we have; that states would not be as tents, set up, and taken down, and removable. They would be buildings, to stand steady and fixed. Nothing so opposed unto a state, as not to stand.

2. From the second, *Lapis;* that this building would be, not of clay and wood, or, as we call them, paper walls; but stone-work, as strong, as defensible, as little subject to concussion, or combustion, as might be.

3. From the two parts specified, first, *Anguli;* this stone-work is not a wall forthright, to part in sunder, or to keep out, but it consists of divers sides: those sides meet in one angle where, if they meet and knit well, all the better will the building be.

4. *Caput.* And they will knit the better, if they have a good "head." For where they meet, no place so much in danger of weather going in, and making the sides fly off, if it want a covering. A head it would have to cover it; it is a special defence, and besides, it is a sovereign beauty to the whole building.

And that head would not be of plaister to crumble away, or of wood, to warp or rot with the weather; or of lead, to bow or bend, and to crack; but of stone, and the principalest stone that could be. The chief part it is, the head; the chief care and consultation would be, what stone meet for that place, for indeed it is all in all.

The first sense, Christ. That is the consultation here. Here is Christ, what say you to Him? He is "a Stone." 2. "A building Stone." 3. "A corner Stone." 4. "A head Stone." "A Stone:" so Acts 4. 11. the Prophets term Him. And so the Apostles, Peter [and] Dan. 2. 34. Paul. 1. In His Birth: Daniel's "Stone, cut forth without Zech. 3. 9. hands." 2. In His Passion: Zachary's Stone, graven and cut full of eyes, all over. 3. In His Resurrection: Esay's Isa. 28. 16. Stone, laid in Sion, *Qui crediderit non confundetur,* "he that

believeth in Him then, shall not be confounded," saith St.
Peter, *Hic est Lapis.* He is the Stone of our faith, saith 1 Pet. 2. 6.
St. Peter, *Lapis erat Christus.* And *Petra erat Christus,* 1 Cor. 10. 4.
saith St. Paul. He is "the Stone" of our Sacraments; the
Water of our baptism, and of our spiritual drink, both issue
from Him. "A Stone:" first, for His nature, of the earth
as stones are, out of Abraham's quarry, saith Esay, to shew Isa. 51. 1.
His humanity. And out of κατώτερα τῆς γῆς, "the very
lowest part of the earth," saith the Apostle, to shew His Eph. 4. 9.
humility. Indeed, nothing so subject to contempt, to be
trodden on, to be spurned aside, as it. And such was His
condition, *Vermis, non homo,* and *Lapis, non homo.* "A Ps. 22. 6.
Worm or a Stone, and no man."

A stone will endure much sorrow, nothing more. And 2.
who did ever suffer like Him? or, in His suffering, who
more patient, or still, or stone-like, than He?

But the chief virtue of a stone is, that it is firm and sure; 3.
and so is He. Ye may trust Him, ye may build on Him, He
will not fail you. What ye lay on Him is sure. David may
have sure footing and rest "his feet," Moses "his hands," Ps. 40. 2.
Jacob "his head," on this "Stone." This is it He hath His Ex. 17. 12.
Gen. 28. 11.
denomination from. He that trusts in Him, nothing, "not Mat. 16 18.
the gates of hell, shall prevail against him." Trustiness,
with *non confundetur,* the chief virtue of a stone, of Christ
and of those that are head-stones by, and under, Him.

But there are stones that lie scattered, that will neither
head well nor bed well, as they say, not meet to build
withal; meet for nothing but to hurl, and to do hurt with.
But Christ is a Stone to do good with, to build with. *Lapis
ad ædificationem.* And He loveth not to scatter, or be by
Himself; "His delight is to be with the sons of men," and Prov. 8. 31.
to grow with them into one frame of building.

"A Corner Stone." Of all the places in the building, 3.
that one special place liketh Him, where the sides meet—
there He is. To join together, "to make two one," He Eph. 2. 14.
loveth it above all; stretching Himself to both walls, that
both may rest on Him.

And lastly, *Lapis primarius,* "a Headstone." For there 4.
He should be, there is His right place, and it will never be
well with the building, till He be in that place, till Christ be

S E R M. 'Ακρογωνιαῖος, *Caput in omni procuratione,* "the highest and
VI. chiefest end of all." This He is, and in the end this He will
be; if not by men, yet by God.

But now we have to do with men, and we are to put it to
voices, their voices with whom He lived, what they think of
Christ for *Caput anguli.* It is returned, *Quem reprobaverunt;*
Lu. 19. 14. He is "refused." Will ye hear it from themselves? *Nolumus
Hunc regnare,* "We will not have Him King." Not in that
place, no head in any wise.

1. But *a quibus,* who were these? "These were foolish
Jer. 5. 4. people," that knew not the virtue or value of a stone; no
heed to be taken what they cry. We will get us with
Jer. 5. 5. Jeremy to men of skill, that know what stone is for every
place, professed builders by their trade. But these also
were no better conceited of Him than the other; for "do
Joh. 7. 48. any of the rulers make any account of Him?" as who say,
None of them neither, the very builders refuse Him too.

2. Well, we will make the best of it. It may be, not for
the head, but there be more places than that; if not allow
Him there, yet He may be in some else. *Improbaverunt* it
may be, but not *reprobaverunt;* 'disallowed,' but not 'cast
aside quite.'

We ask then, how far? Will ye put Him up the second
time, and to see the *quousque* in kind, will ye put up Ba-
Joh. 18. 40. rabbas with Him? *Non Hunc, sed Barabbam.* So it went,
that was their verdict. Now by this time it is *reprobaverunt,*
as flat as may be, a refuse indeed, and that with a foul indignity.

But these were but the vulgar again. What say the builders to this? He of them that took himself for a very Vitru-
vius, such a workman as he said all the rest "understood
nothing at all," the master-builder, Caiaphas, he was flat,
Joh. 11. *expedit,* "it was expedient He should die," be cast aside into
49, 50, the heap of rubbish, be put out of the building clean. This
is His doom.

1. Now, lay these together. To be refused is not so much;
it may be, it is of such as are ignorant. But to be "refused" of "builders," and those the chief, is much, for they
are presumed to be skilful. Again, to be disliked for the
chief place, not so much; if not for that he may be for

another. But to be utterly reprobate, that is, not refused 2.
for the head, nor refused for the corner, but refused simply
for any room at all; not in the top, nay not in the bottom;
not in the corner, nay not in any rank of the building; that
is as much as may be. And this was Christ's lot.

Yet this was all but in words, nothing was done to Him.
But there is a reprobation in deed, and that is yet far worse.
And to that they proceed, even to actual matters, to real
reprobation. Before they cast Him aside, this poor Stone,
they hacked and hewed it, and mangled it piteously; they
shewed their malice even in that too. *Cœlaverunt sculpturam* Zech. 3. 9.
Ejus, saith the Prophet, their tools walked on Him, "they
graved Him," and cut Him with a witness, and made Him
full of eyes on every side. What skilled that? What disgrace, or what sorrow is done to a stone? The stone feels
it not. The cry of *non Hunc,* or the edge of the graving tool,
affect it nothing. True: but He was *Lapis vivus,* "a living 1 Pet. 2. 5.
Stone," as Peter calleth Him, a Stone that hath life, life
and sense, and felt all; felt His graving, the edge and point
both; felt His despising, the scorn and malice both; of the
twain, this the more, but both He felt. When "they made Ps. 129. 3.
furrows on His back" with the scourges; when "they platted Mat. 27. 29.
the crown of thorns, and made it sit close to His head;"
when "they digged His hands and feet," He felt all. He
endured it patiently, *tanquam lapis ;* but He felt it sensibly, Ps. 22. 16.
tanquam vivus. Had quick sense of His pain in graving, had
lively apprehension of His contempt in refusing.

And these very two words in the text, *lapidem* and *reprobaverunt,* set out unto us both parts of His Passion fully.
As if He had been stone, so laid they on Him; as if He
had been a reprobate, so poured they all disgrace upon Him.
And even as a stone He was in His Passion. For as the
stones give against the weather, so was there not to be seen
upon Him a bloody sweat? Did He not give, as it were, of Lu. 22. 44.
Himself, against the tempest came? And when it came,
was it not so strange, even that which this living Stone suffered, as the dead stones that had no life, as if they had
had life and compassion of His case, rent in sunder with it? Mat. 27. 51.
Lapidem then is true.

And for *reprobaverunt,* that is as true. For how could

S E R M. they have entreated a reprobate worse than they entreated
VI.
Joh. 19. 29. Him? in His thirst, in His prayer, in the very pangs of
Mat. 27. 47. death, what words of scorn and spiteful opprobry! What
deeds of malice and wretched indignity! Of Himself it is
Phil. 2. 8. said, and by way of exaggeration, "He humbled Himself to
death, the death of the cross." Of them it may be no less,
reprobaverunt ad mortem, mortem crucis, 'they rejected Him
to death, the death of reprobates; the death whereunto a
curse is annexed, the death of the cross.' And never gave
Mat. 27. 60. Him over, till they brought Him, *Lapis ad lapidem,* into a
grave of stone, and rolled a stone upon Him, and there left
Him. And thus much for *Lapis Quem reprobaverunt.*

II. It is the feast of the Passover, we now pass over to His
other estate, His exaltation *ad Caput anguli.* Were it not
strange the stone should be rolled away, and this stone
should be digged up again, and set up in the *antes,* the place
most conspicuous, that is, made a corner-stone; and that in
the very top, the highest part of all, that is, made a Head-
stone? Were not this a strange pass-over from death to life,
from lowest reprobation to highest approbation, from basest
reproach to greatest glory?

But seeing builders, we see, may be deceived, and that *in
capite,* as we find here, and that, though Caiaphas be one of
them, and a stone may have wrong; would it not be well,
we called to scrutiny again? Is there any builder yet left
before whom we may bring the matter? Yes, there is.
"Every house is built of some man," saith the Apostle,
Heb. 3. 4. "but He That is the Builder of all, is God." He That set
up this great vaulted work of Heaven over our heads, That
Job 38. 6. "laid the corner-stone" of the earth, He is a Builder. But
Ps. 104. 3. He that "laid His chamber-beams in the waters," *et appendit*
Job 26. 7. *terram super nihilum,* " hangs this great mass, no man knows
upon what;" He that beginneth at the top, and builds down-
wards, Heaven first, and then earth, as He did; He passeth
all ours, He is a skilful Builder indeed. Is He of the same
mind? Offer Christ to His probation. He will *reprobare
reprobantes,* 'condemn them, that so refused Him,' and all
1 Pet. 2. 4. will turn quite contrary. St. Peter saith it; He was ἀπο-
δεδοκιμασμένος, "reprobate" with men, but ἐκλεκτὸς, "chosen" of God, ἐξουδενωμένος, "nothing worth" with them, but

ἔντιμος, " precious" with Him. Meet to be in the building ; nay, no building meet to be without Him. And in the building, if any part more object to the sight than other, there. And in that, if any place higher than another, there. *In ædificio, angulo ædificii, capite anguli* ; ' in the building, the corner of the building, the head of the corner ; that is in the highest place, of the chiefest part of all. This He thought Him, and as He thought Him, so He made Him ; and made Him so this day, the day of His resurrection. Whom they cast down, God lift up from the grave ; Whom they vilified, He glorified ; glorified, and made Him *Caput anguli,* " the Head of the corner."

How " of the corner ?" The corner is the place where two *Anguli.* walls meet, and there be many twos in this building. The two walls of nations, Jews and Gentiles ; the two of conditions, bond and free ; the two of sex, male and female ; the great two, which this day we celebrate, of the quick and the dead ; above all, the greatest two of all, Heaven and earth.

The two first meet in Him : there was a partition, but He down with it, *et fecit utraque unum.* So that there is neither Eph. 2. 14. " Jew nor Greek, neither bond nor free, neither male nor Gal. 3. 28. female, but all one in Christ Jesus ;" yea, the quick and the dead both live to Him. And all these, so many combinations, as in the centre, meet in Him ; and He, in the midst of all, draws all and knits all in one holy faith, and blessed hope of His coming ; one mutual and unfeigned love towards each other. *Ex te angulus,* well said Zachary. Zech. 10. 4.

And as unity is in the angle, so order is under the *Caput.* Head. As all one in Him, so He is Head of all. Head of the Jews,—Jesus in their tongue ; Head of the Gentiles,— Christ in their tongue. " Head of the Church ;" " Head of Col. 1. 18. all principality and power." Therefore this day, " Christ Col. 2. 10. That died rose again, that He might be Lord both of quick Rom. 14. 9. and dead." And of the great angle of all, consisting of Heaven and earth ; for all power was given Him in Heaven Mat. 28. 18. and earth, and He made Head of both.

Now then, will ye lay these together ? There can come 1. to a stone no greater dignity, than there to be in the head. 2. To any stone ; but it is much increased by that circumstance, that it is not only *lapis* barely, but *Lapis Quem reprobaverunt,*

S E R M.
VL

that now is there in the head; not any stone, but a Stone so refused, as we heard, for such a Stone there to be; from that *terminus a quo*, to come to this *terminus ad quem;* from so base an estate, there to be, that is a great increase to it.

3. And thirdly, by such a Person, a Builder so matchless, there to be, that is yet a degree higher; and this triplicity exalteth much His exaltation. That by God, and not God's suffering but His doing, and that *factum mirabile*, " His wonderful doing," it came to pass; as indeed, wonderful it is to see, that which all the world now seeth, Christ, That for the present was so strangely dejected, since to be so exceedingly

Phil. 2. 9, 10, 11.

glorified. So many knees to bow to Him, so many tongues to confess Him, His name to be above all names, Heaven and earth to be full of the majesty of His glory.

Now, from these words, *Caput anguli*, that which we learn morally is, to make much of the two virtues commended to us in these two words; 1. *virtus anguli;* 2. and *anguli sub Capite.*

First, the virtue of two walls united in one angle, that is unity. For Christ will not be *Caput maceriæ*, ' of a party-wall,' but of an angle joined. He is not of their spirit that, so they may be head, care not though it be never so broken a wall.

Secondly, not every unity, but *unitas ordinata*, that hath, or is under a head. For it is not *cujusvis anguli*, but *anguli cui Caput;* ' not of every angle, but of an angle the unity whereof is neither in the tail, nor in the sides, but in the head;' that is, commended to us, as unity against division, so order against confusion. They that can be content to corner well, but would be *acephali*, ' head-less,' have no head, please Him not. No more do they that would join, but would be *poly-cephali*, have a consistory of heads, ' many heads,' as many as the beast of Babylon. For sure it is, an angle can have no more heads but one. To love an angle well, but an angle that hath an head, and but one head. To love a head well, but a head, not of a single wall, but of an angle. Both these, and both to be regarded. They be

Zech. 11. 7. 10. 14.

Zachary's two staves, " bands," and " beauty," which uphold all government; break one, and the other will not long be unbroken. The head without unity, unity without the head; either without other will not long hold.

Both then, but especially unity, for that cometh in here, not necessarily, as doth the head, but extraordinarily. And therefore extraordinary regard to be had of it. For I was thinking why he should here in this second part say, that "He was made Head of the corner?" Why should it not suffice to have said, *factus est Caput,* and no more? Or if more, *factus est Caput ædificii?* To have said, 'He was made the Head,' at least-wise 'made the Head of the whole building?' Why must *anguli* be added? What needed any mention of the corner? No occasion was given, no mention was made of it in His refusing; the word "Head" would have served fully, to have set His exaltation forth. Some matter there was, that this word must come in. And sure no other, but to shew Christ's special delight and love of that place. At His rising this day, *stetit in medio,* and here He Joh. 20. 19. is come to His place again; for *stetit in medio,* and *Caput anguli,* come both to one. Therefore, that like love, like special regard be had by us of that place, and of the virtue of that place, unity; that it be sought and preserved carefully, that the sides fly not off, the well knitting whereof is the very strength of the whole building.

By Bede it is rendered as a reason why the Jewish builders [Bed. in refused our Saviour Christ for the head-place, *quia in uno* ^{Act. Apost.} *pariete, stare amabant.* 'They could endure no corner, they must stand alone upon their own single wall,' be of themselves; not join with Gentile or Samaritan. And Christ they endured not, because they thought, if He had been Head, He would have inclined that way. *Alias oves oportet Me* Joh. 10. 16. *adducere: alias* they could not abide. But sure, a purpose there must be *alias oves adducendi,* 'of bringing in others,' of joining a corner, or else we do not *facere secundum exem-* Heb. 8. 5. *plar,* build not according to Christ's pattern; our fashion of fabric is not like His. They that think to make Christ Head of a single wall are deceived, it will not be. They that say, So the Head, all is well, it skills not for the corner, err too. He is Γωνιαῖος, "a Corner-stone" first, and then Ἀκρογωνιαῖος, "a Head-stone" after. And they that had rather be a front in a wall, than in a meaner place *sub lapide angulari;* and they that stand upon their own partition, and will not endure to hear of any joining, care not what become of *angulus,* if

S E R M.
VI.

Phil. 2. 5.

Lu. 7. 35.

Ps. 118. 25,
26.

Zech. 4. 7.

Ps. 138. 2.

Joh. 11. 48.

1.
The second
sense, Da-
vid.

it were strucken out, "the same mind is not in them," in neither of them, " which was in Christ Jesus." His mind we see. He looks to the angle, as to the head; and to the head, as to the angle. And they build best, that build likest Him: "wisdom is justified of all her children."

1. And last, the duty of the whole second part, and so, this day's duty, is this. When the head-stone is brought forth and reared, as to-day it was, we are to prosecute it with Hosannah, and *Benedictus qui venit*, as it straightway followeth in the Psalm, with acclamation of " Grace, grace unto it." For so, saith the Prophet, *Lapis primarius* would be laid with rejoicing. Rejoicing, as in His regard that hath obtained His due, so even in the building's, that hath got such a Head; such and so gracious a Head as could endure thus to be refused by them, and yet admit, yea even those that so refused Him, if the fault be not in themselves, to be stones in His building for all that, and to be members of the body whereof He is the Head.

2. Then secondly, as God hath, so we to make Him Head. Actually we cannot, He is made to our hands, but in account we may; giving Him the highest place in all our respects, "magnifying His name and His Word above all things." "His Word," making it our chief ground; "His Name," and the glory of it, making of it our chief end. That other considerations carry us not away, as these builders here it did, of *Venient Romani*, or I wot not what; but that ever, as the heathen lawyer said, it be *potior ratio quæ facit pro religione*, 'the best reason that maketh best for religion,' and for the good of the body of this Head, that is, the peace of His Church. And this for *Lapis erat Christus*.

But *lapis erat David*, is likewise true. Therefore, that we do King David no wrong, let us shew how it fits him too; but briefly, because this is not his day. David was a " stone." The Jews say it was his nic-name or name of disgrace, that in scorn they called him so. For that all his credit, forsooth, came by casting a stone, and hitting Goliah by chance right in the forehead; and so they twitted him with that name. They gave it him in scorn, but he bare it in earnest. For sure much sorrow he endured, had that property of a " stone." And nothing could remove him, or make him shrink from his trust in God, or from his allegiance to Saul his liege-lord ;—that quality also.

And "refused" he was, not as Christ, we must not look 2. for that, neither in him nor in any. God forbid that any ever should be so refused as He. As Christ, none but Christ; No; but yet in his degree refused he was though. A hard time he had, and many hard terms, and hard usages he endured, for many years together; pursued and followed, and should have been no head, nay should have had no head if he had been gotten.

"Refused," and by whom? Even by Saul all his life- 3. time; and when Saul was dead, Abner "refused" him, and 2 Sam. 2. 8. set up another against him. And when he was out of his country in Gath, "refused" there too by the princes of 1Sam.29.4. Achish. And even at home by his own brethren and 1 Sam. 17. father's house. Yea, Samuel himself had given it away, 28. 1Sam.16. 6. the head-place, from him to Eliab, and so "refused" him, but for God. And these went then for the chief builders in Israel at that time. So the builders "refused" him.

But after all this, all this notwithstanding, this "stone became the Head," that is, David got the crown, and was 1 Sam. 15. King at last. For "head" is the King's name. So doth 17. Samuel call the King; so doth Esay; so doth Osee. But Isa. 7. 8. especially so Daniel in express terms, *Tu es caput aureum,* Hos. 1. 11. Dan. 2. 38. speaking to the king, "Thou art the head of gold."

"Head," and "of the corner;" that is, as some interpret it, of Judah and Israel. But that is thought somewhat hard. For those two were not two kingdoms, nor ever so reckoned, till Rehoboam's time. And what, if David had not happened to have been first King of one tribe, and after of all, should he have lost this name then? Should he not have been ἀκρογωνιαῖος? Shall no king be *caput anguli,* if he have but one entire kingdom? Shall not Solomon as well as David? No question but he shall.

The better part therefore think good to give it that sense which never fails in any state, and which sundry times ye shall find pointed at by David himself, as in the one hun- Ps. 115. dred and fifteenth Psalm before, and in the one hundred 10. 12. Ps. 135.19. and thirty-fifth after. Yea, even here in this Psalm in the beginning, *Domus Israel,* and *Domus Aaron,* "the House of

S E R M.
VI.
Israel, and the House of Aaron;" that is, the two estates, civil and ecclesiastical, which maketh the main angle in every government. God Himself hath severed them, and made these two but to meet in one; not one to malign and consume the other. And the happy combining of these two is the strength of the head, and the strength of the whole building. If it bear but upon one of them, it will certainly decay. It did so in Saul's time: he little regarded the Ark, and less the Priests. David saw Saul's error, and Pa. 75. 3. in his Psalm, where he singeth *Ne perdas* to a commonwealth, promiseth to have equal care of both pillars, and to uphold them both.

The first Book of Chronicles is sufficient to prove and persuade any, he dealt in both as chief over both. Not by right of priesthood, for none he had; and that of his prophecy is as cold. Others also did the like, Asa, Jehoshaphat, Ezekias, Josiah, that were no Prophets, nor ever so accounted.

[Phil.
Judæ.
περὶ τοῦ
τίς ὁ τῶν
θείων
πραγμάτων
κληρονό-
μος. circ.
med.]
In the law—it is Philo's note, both tables met in the fifth commandment which is the crown-commandment, as it were in an angle; which commandment is placed, saith he, ὡς ἐν μεσορίῳ 'as it were in the middle, or confines of both tables,' that of religion, and this other of justice civil; that with the right arm the Prince may support that, and with the left this, and so uphold both. And in the Gospel, Mat. 21. 42.
Heb. 7. 13.
14. Christ applieth this very verse to Himself, as Heir of the Vineyard. Heir He was not, but as King, not as Priest; He could not, for of that tribe He was not born, but was called to it as was Aaron.

Since then here we find both, and that David was both, it is no error I trust to call a King *caput anguli*; no more is it to call him *lapidem primarium*, or *angularem*, choose ye whether. The Persian, by the light of nature, called the King Ahashuerosh, that is, 'Sovereign head.' The Grecian, by the same light, called the King Βασιλέα, that is, βάσιν τοῦ λαοῦ, 'the base or corner-stone of his people.'

Shall I add this? This word "stone," which is here affirmed of David in this verse, is in the New Testament, five several times, turned by the Syrian Translator, Cephas; Mat. 21. 42.
Mark 12.
10.
Lu. 20. 17. thrice in the three Gospels, once in the Acts, and once in St. Peter. So that he did not think it strange to call King

David Cephas. So Cephas as well said of David as of Peter. Acts 4. 11.
And *tu pasces* as well said to David, as *pasce* to Peter. And 1 Pet. 2. 7.
2 Sam. 5. 2.
Zerubbabel hath in his hand the line, as well as Joshua the 1 Chron. 11.
High Priest, towards the building of the temple. The thing, 2.
Zech. 4. 10.
the duty itself, and the bounds of it, let us lay forth and
agree of as we can; but sure the name is not to be stood on,
it cannot be denied him.

And now to ourselves, to whom as "this is the day which 3.
The third
sense.
His Ma-
jesty.
the Lord hath made," touching Christ and His resurrection,
so is it likewise the day that He hath made the second time,
by making on it his Majesty head of this kingdom, the very
name[1] whereof hath affinity, and carrieth an allusion to the [1 *Anglia.*]
term *anguli* in the sound of it.

And neither were your Majesty without your part of re- 1.
fusing in a kind, but did participate somewhat of it with
David, though in a less degree. Good, and firm, and sure,
though your right were as any stone, yet allegations were
studied to subject it to question, yea to refusing. For did
nobody ever see a project drawn, wherein some other stone
was marked out to have been *caput anguli?* Yes, it is well
known, titles were raised and set on foot, and books written
to that end.

And they took themselves for no mean workmen that 2.
were the devisers of them, that both at home and abroad
contrived it another way, and plotted to have put you by,
and to have had some other head-stone of their own hewing
out in your room.

Yea, to make your case yet more like to Christ's case, 3.
even the High Priest, he that claimeth Caiaphas' place, he
and his crew had their hands in it. We may no less truly
say to them than St. Peter said to Caiaphas; *Quem vos,*
"Whom ye" would have cast aside, if ye might have had
your wills. And to that end had your first breves ready
drawn and sent abroad, and others in a readiness to second
them.

Yet for all their breves and bulls, this stone is the head 4.
for all that. *Factus* 'made' he is, and made by God. For
a Domino, God's doing it was evidently, that after so much
plotting so many years together, at the very time God bowed
the hearts of so many thousands, as it had been the heart of

SERM.
VI.
Ps. 64. 9. one man, to agree in one ; as that all that foresaw it thought it had not been possible, and all that saw it confessed it admirable, and "all men said, This hath God done, for they saw evidently it was His work."

4. The head you were then made, and head not of one angle, as you were before, for *caput anguli* I hold a King to be though he have but one kingdom, but *caput trianguli*, head now of three, even of the whole 'triangle.' So their titles were dashed, their plots disappointed, and all their devices Isa. 29. 16. as the potter's clay. Yours it was of right, and God hath brought you to it. So it is, and our eyes do see it, and our hearts do joy in it, and our tongues bless God for it ; and here we are this day with all praise and thanks to acknowledge it, that so it is. It is a part of this day's duty, that so we should acknowledge it, and give Him thanks for it That brought it to pass.

1. And may I not farther put you in mind of another making yet ? And it is not impertinent neither, to this day especially. For after the first making or placing, look how many after-attempts are made to unmake or displace the head-stone again ; so many times as it is heaved at to that end, and those attempts defeated, so many new placings, so many new makings, are we to reckon of. David was made head, not only when Saul and Abner sought to put him down, and were put down themselves, which was before he came to the crown ; but even after he had it, and had 2 Sam. 20. 1. worn it long, when Absalom and Sheba refused him being their head, and cried, " No part in David," and so sought to set him besides the throne.

2 Sam. 15.
31.
2 Sam. 17.
25. And builders there wanted not in that design : Absalom had Ahithophel and Amasa, two as principal master-builders, as then were any. When God brought David back to his seat again, and delivered him from them that sought to remove him from it, He did as good as place him in it anew. David himself saith so before, at the thirteenth verse. " He was shrewdly lifted at, and ready to turn over ; but God stayed him, and set him right in his seat again." And in very deed the verse next before, the twenty-first, where he saith, " God hath heard him, and was become his Deliverer," makes the writers to think this

Psalm was indited rather for this second, than for his first placing.

Now a like second making we may well remember, and we cannot do it better than upon this day. This day, as we shall see, hath an interest in it. That since your sitting in the seat of this kingdom, some there were, builders one would have taken them to be if he had seen them with their tools in their hands, as if they had been to have laid some foundation; where their meaning was, to undermine, and to cast down foundations and all; yea, to have made a right stone of you, and blown you up among the stones, you, and yours without any more ado.

And master-builders they had amongst them, so they will needs be accounted, that encouraged their hearts, and strengthened their hands to the work. And that they might do, there was no seal to hinder it; but disclose it that they might not, for fear of breaking a seal, there was a seal for that. And thus did they *ædificare ad gehennam,* ' edify their followers to hellward,' to set them forward and send them to their own place. That day which God undid that wretched design, and brought their mischief upon their own heads, that day did God make you *caput trianguli* the second time. That day that He brought you back, if not from death itself, yet from death's door, from the very gates of destruction, that day was a very Easter-day to you, though it were in November. And, ὡς ἐν παραβολῇ, "after a sort," a very resurrection; as very a resurrection as Isaac's was, which the Apostle there speaketh of. That day, the destroying Angel, I am sure, passed over you, and so it was truly the Feast of the Passover. Fit therefore to be remembered this day,—*hic est dies,* 'this is the day' of the Passover, this is Easter-day, the day of the Resurrection.

But to return to the first making of all. By the true course of the year, this month, being the very month, this day being the very day of that, of the first laying of this head-stone, we are as before *in Christo Domino,* so again here *in christo Domini,* to prosecute it with David's cry of *Hosanna,* and *Benedictus;* and with Zachary's acclamation of " Grace, grace unto it," even to this head-stone. " Grace," in His eyes That so made you; and again, " Grace" in their

Marginal notes:

2.

Acts 1. 25.
3.

Heb. 11. 19.

eyes and hearts to whom He so made you. But above all, the grace of all graces, that you may make Him ever your Ἀκρογωνιαῖος, "your stone of chief trust," and your mark of highest regard, in all your counsels and purposes, That so made you; and seek to reduce the *disjecta latera*, ' the sides and walls flying off,' of this great building for which the world itself was built, His Church, and reduce them to one angle, the greatest service that can be done Him on earth.

And so, He that this day made you the head, so make you, and so keep you long, and many days! He that refused them that refused you, refused them with reprobation, still may He so do, *toties quoties*, to their continual confusion; that the head over the triangle, and the triangle under the head, may many years stand fast and flourish, in all peace, plenty, and prosperity, health, honour, and happiness! And after all, He that hath crowned you here with two crowns already, crown you also with the third of glory and immortality in His Heavenly kingdom!

I have now done. Only I would move one thing, and it shall well agree with that hath been said of the corner-stone, and it shall serve to further our duty of thanks, and be a good closing up of the whole. Many ways was Christ, our blessed Saviour, a " Corner-stone;" among others, especially in this, saith St. Hierome; *Quando agnum cum pane conjunxit, finiens unum, inchoans alterum, utrumque perficiens in Semetipso.* One chief corner-point of His was, ' when He joined the Lamb of the Passover and the Bread of the Eucharist, ending the one and beginning the other, recapitulating both Lamb and Bread into Himself;' making that Sacrament, by the very institution of it, to be as it were the very corner-stone of both the Testaments.

No act then more fit for this feast, the feast of the Passover, than that act which is itself the passage over from the Old Testament to the New. No way better to express our thanks for this Corner-stone, than by the holy Eucharist, which itself is the corner-stone of the Law and the Gospel.

1.	And there is in it a perfect representation of the substance of this verse and text set before our eyes. Wherein two poor elements of no great value in themselves, but that they might well be refused, are exalted by God to the estate of a divine mystery, even of the highest mystery in the Church of Christ.

And a kind of resurrection there is in them, and therefore 2. fit for the day of the Resurrection, as ever in Christ's Church Easter-day hath pleaded a special property in them. Sown as it were, in weakness and dishonour; and, after they be 1Cor.15.43. consecrated, rising again in honour and power.

And that, a great honour and power, not only to represent, but to exhibit that it representeth, nor to set before us, or remember us of, but even to serve us for a corner-stone. First, uniting us to Christ the "Head," whereby we grow into one frame of building, into one body mystical, with Him. And again, uniting us also as living stones, or lively members, *omnes in id ipsum*, one to another, and all together in one, by natural love and charity. *Qui comedit de hoc* Joh. 6. 56. *Pane, et bibit de hoc Calice, manet in Me, et Ego in illo,* "He that eateth of this Bread, and drinketh of this Cup, abideth in Me, and I in him." There is our corner with Him. And again, *Unum corpus omnes sumus, qui de uno* 1Cor.10.17. *pane participamus,* "All we that partake of one bread or cup, grow all into one body mystical." There is our corner, either with other. By the same means expressing our thanks for it, and by the same possessing ourselves of it; sealing up both ways our duty to God for making Christ the Lord our greatest and chiefest, and for making His anointed this day, under Him, either in their several degrees, our ἀκρο-γωνιαῖος, "our chief, or head corner-stone." For which, together with all other His benefits, but especially as the time calleth to us, for these two, Christ's rising, and our Sovereign's raising to His royal place, render we, as we are bound, to God the Father, &c.

A SERMON

PREACHED BEFORE

THE KING'S MAJESTY, AT WHITEHALL,

ON THE TWELFTH OF APRIL, A.D. MDCXII., BEING EASTER-DAY.

---

1 CORINTHIANS v. 7, 8.

Purge out therefore the old leaven, that ye may be a new lump, as ye are unleavened; for Christ our Passover is sacrificed for us:

Therefore let us keep the Feast, not with old leaven, neither with the leaven of maliciousness and wickedness; but with the unleavened bread of sincerity and truth.

[*Expurgate vetus fermentum, ut sitis nova conspersio, sicut estis azymi. Etenim Pascha nostrum immolatus est Christus:*
Itaque epulemur, non in fermento veteri, neque in fermento malitiæ, et nequitiæ: sed in azymis sinceritatis, et veritatis. Latin Vulg.]

[*Purge out therefore the old leaven, that ye may be a new lump, as ye are unleavened. For even Christ our Passover is sacrificed for us:*
Therefore let us keep the feast, not with old leaven, neither with the leaven of malice and wickedness, but with the unleavened bread of sincerity and truth. Engl. Trans.]

SERM. VII.

[Joh. 2. 13.]

[Joh. 11. 55.]

THERE be two things give themselves forth upon the very first view of this text. 1. First, here is news, that we Christians, we also have "our Passover:" 2, Then, that in memory of it, we are "to keep a feast." *Pascha Judæorum,* "the Jews' Passover" we find in John, chapters two and eleven. *Pascha nostrum,* "our Passover," never till now. And indeed, to find a Passover in St. Paul's Epistle, and his Epistle not to the Hebrews but to the Corinthians, their Passover as well as his; for him to call, not his countrymen the Jews at Jerusalem, but the Gentiles at Corinth, to keep such a feast, is news indeed. But *Pascha nostrum,* the words be plain, one we have. *Itaque,* and "therefore let us hold a feast" for it.

And truly, upon this word, *celebremus,* may this feast of our Easter seem to be founded. There is not only a warrant, but an order for the making it a feast. And sure, howsoever it will fall out with other feasts, this of Easter, if there were nothing else but the controversy that was about the time of keeping it, in the very prime of the Primitive Church, even immediately after the Apostles, it were enough to shew it was then generally agreed of all, such a feast was to be kept And the alleging on either side—one, St. John's manner of keeping, the other, St. Peter's—proves plainly it is Apostolical, this feast, and that the Apostles themselves kept it. *Itaque celebremus,* "therefore let us keep it."

The word *itaque,* in the latter verse, is ever a note of a conclusion; and where a conclusion is, there is an argument, and so is the text. It standeth of an 1. antecedent, and a 2. consequent. 1. The antecedent, in these words: "Christ our Passover," &c. 2. The consequent, in these: *itaque celebremus, &c.* Supply but this maxim of reason and law —If we have one, we are to hold one; the text will make up a complete argument: but one we have, therefore we are to hold it. *Habendum et tenendum,* as our tenures run. The division.

, In the antecedent there rise these five points: 1. the main word "Passover," what is meant by it;—*Pascha.* 2. That we have one, in the word *nostrum.* 3. Who it is expressly; —Christ. 4. Christ how, or when? not every way, nor at every time considered; but as and when He was "offered up," *immolatus,* "offered up as a sacrifice." 5. And lastly, the word of our interest, *propter nos,* "for us;" that so we might pass over our sins, and be passed over by the punishment due to them. I.

In the consequent there arise two points: 1. There is an *itaque,* to conclude us to "keep this feast." 2. And there is a *non,* and a *sed,* to direct us how to keep it. The former binds us to *celebremus,* to celebrate a feast; or to *epulemur,* to make a feast. Both are read; and both well, for both are due. The latter, by *non in fermento, sed in azymis,* not so but thus, teacheth us how to hold it. How to keep a Pass- II.

over? but as a Passover should be kept. How was that? not with leaven, but with sweet bread. And then he takes off the veil from Moses' face, that under the legal types of leaven, and sweet bread, these evangelical duties are expressed unto us. By "leaven," is meant " malice and lewdness;" and so, we may not. By "sweet bread," is meant " sincerity and truth;" and so we are with them to "celebrate our feast."

So, in the antecedent, there is the 1. benefit, and the 2. means;—that is Christ's part. In the consequent, 1. the feast, and the 2. duty;—that is ours. Indeed, to the word "Passover," ye may reduce them all. 1. The benefit: for it is a "Passover," even the passing over of the destroyer. 2. The means: that is Christ, by the sacramental figure called the "Passover," as the means of it. 3. "The Feast:" whether that we solemnize, or that we are invited to, either is a "Passover." 4. And last our duty: for that is also a kind of "Passover," from *vetus fermentum,* to *nova conspersio.* So, 1. the benefit, 2. the means, 3. the feast itself, and 4. the duty of it, all are recapitulate in this one word "Passover."

The sum of all is, that we perform the duty that we so may partake of the benefit: all is but to conclude us *ad hoc festum, ad hoc epulum,* "to the feast and the feast of the feast," that we pass not them over. This is all that St. Paul here pleads for, and all that we. Enough, to let you see the text in the feast, and the feast in the text: in the text, the parts and the order of them.

I.
The an-
tecedent.
1. What is
meant by
Pascha.
Ex. 12. 26.
[¹ *èà, i. e.*
ảγαθá.]

Pascha, " a Passover." *Quænam est hæc religio,* (saith God) shall be our question? "What is the meaning of this observance," and what good is there in it? For, every feast is in remembrance of some benefit, ἑορτὴ, ὅτι ἐὰ¹ ὄρυυται. Passing over is, of itself, a thing indifferent; good or bad, thereafter as that is which passeth over us, or we over it. For if any good overpass us, we lose by it; but if any danger, we are the better. Again, if we pass from better to worse, it is a detriment, but if from a worse case or place to a better, it is a benefit. And this is a benefit, for here is a feast holden for it. Then did some evil pass over us, or we ourselves pass over into some better state.

The Law must be our line, to lead us all along this text:

the character of it is legal. How was it there? Evil passed
them; a destroying Angel, that "slew the first-born in every Ex. 12. 29.
house through Egypt," but passed them over, and touched
them not. And yet there was another: they passed out of
Egypt, to the land of promise, over the Red Sea. They
passed it well; as for Pharaoh and his host, they perished
in it. Ye shall find both these thus set down together;
Heb. xi. in the twenty-eighth verse, the destroyer did pass
over them; in the twenty-ninth verse, they did pass over
into Canaan. The Egyptians perished in both, had no Passover; God's people had.

But what is this to us? Here is *Pascha*, but where is 2. "Our
nostrum? We are not in Egypt, no fear of our first-born, What it is.
here is no destroying Angel; and we are far enough from
the Red Sea. What then, if our case fall out to be like, if
our danger as great, and so it will. Here we live, we call
it a "vale of misery;" in a world whereof Egypt is but a Ps. 84. 6.
corner, and was but a type; nor their Pharaoh but a limb
of the great Pharaoh that tyrannizeth here in this world.
2. We have every one a soul; it is not our first-born, it is
more, even *unicam meam*, as the Psalmist calleth it, the first, Ps. 22. 20.
and all that we have. 3. It skills not for the Angel; God's [See the Vulgate.]
wrath is still ready to be revealed on our sins: from that
cometh all destruction. The angels do but carry the "vials" Rev. 16.
of it. 4. And death will match the Red Sea; all must 1-17.
through it, and some pass well, but the most part perish.

Now then for *nostrum*. Our abode here is as dangerous
as theirs in Egypt; as many destroyers, yea as many croco-
diles too, and therefore we need a *Pascha*, to escape God's
wrath, to have it pass over us here.

And yet there rests another besides. For how well we
shall do with that former I know not, but to the latter we
must all come, to death, to the Red Sea brink; and there
either perish, or pass well over, one of the twain. Sure,
Pascha nostrum is not more than needs; *Pascha nobis opus
est*, ' we need one, a Passover,' no less than they.

Nay, I go farther, ours is such as theirs. Theirs is *nihil
ad nostrum*, 'nothing to ours.' For what talk we of a delivery of one poor nation, and that but from a bodily danger,
and but one neither? Call ye that a Passover? How much

SERM. VII.   more then ours, the great and general Passover that freeth

us? that freeth all mankind from the total destruction both of body and soul, and that by an eternal delivery both here

Mat. 3. 7.   and for ever? How to escape that, God's wrath, *ira ventura*, that is the true Passover. And what mention we Canaan? Is there any comparison between the two kingdoms of Canaan and Heaven, whither Christ shall make us pass? Indeed, *Pascha nostrum* is it, ours, and none but ours. Theirs but a shadow, ours the substantial, very Passover indeed. When all is done, *Pascha nostrum* is it.

Will ye give me leave to present you with a meditation upon this point? it will fit the feast well, and serve us for a preparation to our Passover, and I will not fetch it far, but even from the word Passover. For all the labour is, but to make us feel the want of it.

Ecc. 1. 4.   *Est sapientis querela, transire generationem, aliam succedere, aliam quoque transire.* It is that the Apostle tells us, and we

1 Cor. 7. 31.   feel it, *mundus transit*, that " the world passes." Παράγει,

1 Joh. 2. 17.   saith St. Paul, παράγεται, saith St. John, in the active and passive both ; " the world passeth away." *Et en Pascha, en transitus*, a kind of Passover of the world itself, of this tran-

Heb. 13. 14.   sitory world, as we term it, *ubi non habemus manentem, &c.* " where we cannot long have any abode."

2   But then, if we look home to ourselves, we shall find an-

Ps. 90. 10.   other Passover there, even that of the Psalm ; *Cito transit et avolamus*, " we pass as a shadow, as a dream, when one awaketh," we bring our years to an end, as it were a tale that is told. *Cito transit*, " so soon passeth it and we are

Jas. 3. 6.   gone." St. James very excellently expresseth it, τροχὸς, a very " wheel" of our nature whirling about; that the world passeth, but we faster than it.

3   But the third is the complaint indeed ; that transitory though this world be, and we yet more transitory, yet we cannot pass it quietly for all that. But some wipe we have of the Angel's sword; at least-wise in fear we live still of those

Ps. 91. 5, 6.   in the Psalm, *sagitta volans*, or *terror nocturnus*, or *incursus*, or *dæmon meridianus*. One of Egypt's ten plagues, one of

Rev. 6. 4-8.   the Angel's vials, or of the horses, red, black, or pale, are still abroad; much ado we have, without some mishap, to pass this life that passeth so fast.

But lastly, say that we have the good hap to scape well 4.
here, yet hence we must ere long to the Red Sea bank, we
must come to death all: and death is not *interitus*, 'a final
end,' but *transitus*, 'a passage over' to a new estate.   There
is the main peril, that we miscarry not—great odds there is,
for many do—but pass well over into the land of promise.

These four Passovers it will not be amiss to think of.   And
in all these, need we not one to help us well through, that
these perils may well pass us over?   Need we not one that
may make the Red Sea passable for us, that we may well
come to the land of the living?

And now then tell me, what is the sum of all our desires?
Is it not *bonum Pascha?*   While we are here, the destroyers
may pass, and when we go hence, we may well get over?   Is
it not *Sic transire transitoria, ut transeundo perveniamus ad
æterna?*   'So to pass these transitory things, that we may
well come to those that shall never pass?'   A good Passover
is our wish, and against we shall need it, a good one God
send us!   Upon the point, if we weigh well, *salus ipsa nihil
est nisi Pascha*, 'the benefit of all benefits, salvation itself,
is comprised in this word, is nothing but a Passover;' as
much in one word as the other, *transire a malo*, ' to be saved
from evil,' *transire ad bonum*, ' to be set safe in good.'   To
these two may all be reduced; this is all we need, and all we
seek.   And this *parasceue*, or "preparation," will set us in
hand to seek it, and make us say with our Saviour, *desiderio* Lu. 22. 15.
desideravi ut &c. "earnestly to desire, to have our part in
this Passover."

The next point: if we need one, and if we desire one, 3. Who it
where shall we have one?   *Quis revolvet nobis hunc lapidem?* is.
" Who will roll us away this stone," said the women this day. Mark 16. 3.
To our line again, the Law.   How did they there in the
type? for so it must be in the truth.   They had a means
that helped them through both, which, *per metonymian causæ*,
they called their Passover.   And it was a lamb.

Have we so?   Yes.   *Ecce Agnus Dei*, said the Baptist at Christ
the first sight.   But every lamb will not serve, it must be a "the Lamb of God."
Paschal lamb.   Is Christ that Lamb?   St. John puts it out
of question.   That which was said of the Paschal lamb, "ye Joh. 1. 29.
shall not break a bone of him," he applies to Christ, and Joh. 19. 36.

SERM. VII. saith, in Him the "Scripture was fulfilled." *Eodem tempore, illorum, et nostrûm, adductus in Festo ipso.*

4. "Christ offered in a sacrifice." Then a Paschal Lamb He is, and so in case to be made a Passover of. But a Passover He is not, till He be offered. For if ye mark it, offering is a passing over of that is offered, to Him we offer it to; offered He must be. *Et oblatus est,* saith Esay, "offered He was."

Isa. 53. 7. [See the Vulgate.]

Oblatus: so He may be, and yet alive; but the word is ἐτύθη, *immolatus,* "offered," and "offered in sacrifice." A live lamb is not it, it is a lamb slain must be our Passover. And Christ is a "Lamb slain," saith St. John, "from the beginning," and the sprinkling of His blood in Baptism maketh the destroyer pass over us.

Rev. 5. 12.
Rev. 13. 8.

As a peace-offering. There be many kinds of offerings; this determineth, which of them Christ was. Such an one, as we must *epulari;* that is, the peace-offering. For of the peace-offering, the flesh was to be eaten. Part God had, and part the offerer eat, in sign of perfect peace and reconciliation between them. Christ's blood not only in the basin for Baptism, but in the cup for the other Sacrament. A sacrifice—so, to be slain; a propitiatory sacrifice—so, to be eaten.

Lev. 7. 16, 17.

5. Our interest. *Propter nos.* Thus "Christ is a Passover." But where is *nostrum,* without which all this is nothing? *Propter nos,* "for us," that maketh it ours. That which is "for us offered" is ours, and we so reckon it. The lamb was not slain for itself— *Quid agnus committere?*—but for the first-born. So Christ, not for Himself, ("nothing worthy death in Him"—witness Pilate) but for us.

Ex. 13. 15.

Lu. 23. 4. 14, 15.

To save us from our sins. For us, that is for our salvation, to save us. Save us from what? From our sins. And here now, we are come to the point of the Passover indeed; the quitting us, and the manner of quitting us from our sins. All the business whereof was carried in the very manner of a Passover.

1. Ἀνομία. First, sin itself, what is it but a transgression or passing over the lines and limits of our duty, set us in the law of God? And why hovers the destroying Angel over us? Why goeth he not on his way, but seeks to bring destruction upon our heads? What is the mark he striketh at? What, but our sins? But for them, no destroyer should ever have power over us. But for them that hang

so heavy on us, and so press us down, we shall go through well enough.

Why then, *hic est omnis fructus ut auferatur peccatum;* 2. 'all is but this, to have our sins taken away.' And who shall take them away? *Ecce Qui tollit peccata mundi,* That Joh. 1. 29. "taketh away" ours, nay "the sins of the world."

How "taketh away?" "God hath taken away thy sin," 3. saith Nathan to David; the word is not *abstulit,* but *trans-* 2 Sam. 12. *tulit,* that is, *transferendo abstulit;* or as the Hebrew word is, 13. חעביר transire fecit. To take it from David, make it pass from him upon some other, that is, even the Son of David, Him God hath given us, to pass our sins over from us to Him.

And when that? when He was offered, made a sacrifice 4. for us. It is the nature of every sacrifice, *transferendo auferre.* He that offers it "lays his hands on the head of it," con- Lev. 1. 4. fesses his sins over it, and his just desert to be smitten by Lev. 3. 2. the destroyer; but prays he may put this offering in his own Lev. 8. 14. place, and what is due to him, that is death, may be trans- ferred from him, and light on the offering; that may serve, and he scape.

In all offerings thus it was, but in the Paschal lamb spe- 5. cially, that it hath carried away the name from all the rest, to be called the Passover only. In it evidently, the death of the first-born was translated over upon the poor lamb. The Ex. 13. 15. lamb died, the first-born was saved, his death passed over unto the lamb; that it was justly called the Passover, for so it was.

But much more justly Christ, Who sure was even a Pass- 6. over throughout from the first to the last. At the first: His birth, what was it but a Passover from the bosom of His Father to the womb of His mother, to take our nature? And His Circumcision what, but a Passover from the state of one free, to the condition of one bond, to undertake our debt? And at the last, His Resurrection, this day, what was it but a passage from death to life? and His Ascension another, *de mundo ad Patrem,* "from the world to His Father?" First and last, a Passover He was.

But above all, His death, His offering, was it. Then He 7. was *Pascha pro nobis* indeed. For then He passed over into the estate of us wretched sinners, laid off His own, as it

S E R M.
VII.

Isa. 53. 6.

2 Cor. 5. 21.

Gal. 3. 13.

Matt. 26. 39.

Lu. 22. 44.

II.
The conse-
quent.

Rom. 4. 25.

were, and took upon Him our person ; became *tanquam unus e nobis*, nay *tanquam omnes nos.* For God took from us, and laid them on Him, *posuit super Eum iniquitates omnium nostrúm,* "laid upon Him," our Passover, "the transgressions of us all." *Fecit peccatum,* "made Him sin for us"—there, our sins passed from us. *Fecit maledictum,* "made Him a curse for us ;"—there the punishment of our sins passed from us to Him. Then, and there, passed the destroyer over us.

Over us, to Him. But when he came at Him, he passed Him not, *Transeat a me calix* would not be heard, and it was *Pascha, non Pascha,* " a Passover" to us, no " Passover" to Him. We had one, He had none. Him it passed not, but light upon Him so heavy, that it made a sweat of bloody drops pass from Him, yea life and soul and all, ere it left Him. At which His Passion He was a right Passover, *Christus πάσχων, Christus Pascha.* Then He was *pro nobis,* then He was *nostrum;* " Christ," " Christ offered," " offered for us." Of which passing our sins to Him, and God's wrath over us, this day, and the action of this day, is a memorial.

And so let us pass over from the antecedent to the consequent, which is *itaque celebremus,* "therefore let us keep a feast." " A feast," and Christ slain, and so handled as He was ? A fast rather one would think. True, but that we heard again of ours; so did not they of theirs. For this He came again safe, and opened unto us a new passage by His second Passover. All we spake of right now was done the third day since, but we hold not our feast till this day. For till this day we knew not what was become of Him. Passed He was hence, but whether in His passage He had miscarried or no, we knew not. But now, this day, by His resurrection we know He is well passed over, and so *omni modo* a true Passover. So now we hold our feast, as a feast should be holden, with joy. And a double feast it is : 1. one, that by His suffering He passed from life to death for our sins; 2. a second, that by His rising again this day, He passed from life to death " for our justification." And so two Passovers in one. He died, and by His death made the destroyer pass over us; He rose again, and by it made death, as the Red Sea, passable for us. *Itaque celebremus, itaque epulemur.*

Ἑορτάζωμεν, the word is one, but two ways it is turned. 'Εορτάζω-
1. Some read, *celebremus.* 2. Some other, *epulemur.* But $\frac{\mu\epsilon\nu.}{Celebremus,}$
well : for first, it is kindly when we keep a feast, we make a *epulemur.*
feast. But this, this feast, is not celebrated *sine hoc epulo.*
If Christ be a propitiatory sacrifice, a peace-offering, I see
not how we can avoid but the flesh of our peace-offering
must be eaten in this feast by us, or else we evacuate the
offering utterly, and lose the fruit of it. And was there a
Passover heard of, and the Lamb not eaten? Time was
when he was thought no good Christian, that thought he
might do one without the other. No *celebremus* without
epulemur in it.

But first, will ye lay the former and this together, *immo-* 1. *Immo-*
latus and *celebremus,* and see how well it falleth out with us? $\frac{latus \ and}{celebremus.}$
Immolatus is His part, to be slain. *Celebremus* is ours, to
hold a feast. Good-Friday His, Easter-Day ours. His premises bitter, our conclusion joyful; a loving partition on His
part, an happy on ours.

Again, will ye lay *immolatus* to *epulemur?* That the Pass- 2. *Immo-*
over doth not conclude in the sacrifice, the taking away of $\frac{latus \ and}{epulemur.}$
sin only, that is, in a pardon, and there an end, but in a
feast, which is a sign, not of forgiveness alone, but of perfect
amity, full propitiation. Ye may *propius ire,* "draw near Heb. 10.22.
unto Him;" ye are restored to full grace and favour, to eat
and drink at His table.

Besides, there was an offering in *immolatus,* and here is
another, a new one, in *epulemur.* Offered *for* us there,
offered *to* us here. There *per modum victimæ,* here *per*
modum epuli. To make an offering of, to make a refreshing
of. For us in the Sacrifice, to us in the Sacrament. This
makes a perfect Passover. We read both in the Gospel,
πάσχα θύειν, "to sacrifice the Passover," and πάσχα φαγεῖν, Lu. 22. 7.
"to eat" it. It was eaten, the Paschal lamb, and it was $\frac{Mat. 26.17.}{Joh. 18. 28.}$
"a sacrifice;" it cannot be denied, there is a flat text for it. Ex. 12. 27.
Both propounded here in the terms of the text: 1. the Sacrifice in *immolatus,* 2. the Supper in *epulemur.*

Celebremus, and *epulemur.* There be that refer *celebremus*
to the day, *epulemur* to the action, and so it may well; both
day and action have interest in this text. And then the text is
against them that have never an Easter-day in their calendar.

SERM. But the fathers usually refer both to the action.   Their rea-
VII.
son, because in truth the Eucharist now in the Gospel is
that the Passover was under the Law, the antitype answering
to their type of the Paschal lamb.   It is plain by the immediate passage of it from the one to the other, that no sooner
done, but this began.   Look how soon the Paschal lamb
eaten, presently the holy Eucharist instituted, to succeed in
the place of it for ever.   And yet more plain, that this very
Scripture of my text was thought so pertinent, and so proper
to this action, as it was always said, or sung at it.   And I
know no cause but it might be so still.   Two things Christ

1 Cor. 11. there gave us in charge : 1. *ἀνάμνησις*, " remembering,"
24-26.
1Cor.10.16. and 2. *λῆψις*, " receiving."   The same two, St. Paul, but in
other terms, 1. *καταγγελλία*, " shewing forth ;" 2. *κοινωνία*,
" communicating."   Of which, " remembering" and " shewing forth" refer to *celebremus*, " receiving" and " communicating" to *epulemur* here.

1.*Celebre-*   The first, in remembrance of Him, Christ.   What of Him ?
mus :
In the   *Mortem Domini*, His death, saith St. Paul, "to shew forth
Sacrifice.
1Cor.11.26. the Lord's death."   Remember Him ?   That we will and
stay at home, think of Him there.   Nay, shew Him forth ye
must.   That we will by a sermon of Him.   Nay, it must be
hoc facite.   It is not mental thinking, or verbal speaking, there
must be actually somewhat done to celebrate this memory.
That done to the holy symbols that was done to Him, to His
body and His blood in the Passover ; break the one, pour
out the other, to represent *κλώμενον*, how His sacred body
was " broken," and *ἐκχυνόμενον*, how His precious blood was
" shed."   And in *Corpus fractum*, and *Sanguis fusus* there is
immolatus.   This is it in the Eucharist that answereth to the
sacrifice in the Passover, the memorial to the figure.   To
them it was, *Hoc facite in Mei præfigurationem*, ' do this
Lu. 22. 19. in prefiguration of Me :' to us it is, " Do this in comme-
1Cor.11.26. moration of Me."   To them *prenuntiare*, to us *annuntiare ;*
there is the difference.   By the same rules that theirs was,
by the same may ours be termed a sacrifice.   In rigour of
speech, neither of them ; for to speak after the exact manner
Heb. 10. 4. of Divinity, there is but one only sacrifice, *veri nominis*,
' properly so called,' that is Christ's death.   And that sa-
Heb. 9. 28. crifice but once actually performed at His death, but ever

before represented in figure, from the beginning; and ever
since repeated in memory, to the world's end. That only
absolute, all else relative to it, representative of it, operative
by it. The Lamb, but once actually slain in the fulness of
time, but virtually was from the beginning, is and shall be
to the end of the world. That the centre, in which their
lines and ours, their types and our antitypes do meet. While
yet this offering was not, the hope of it was kept alive by the
prefiguration of it in theirs. And after it is past, the memory
of it is still kept fresh in mind by the commemoration of it
in ours. So it was the will of God, that so there might be
with them a continual foreshewing, and with us a continual
shewing forth, the "Lord's death till He come again."
Hence it is that what names theirs carried, ours do the
like, and the Fathers make no scruple at it—no more need
we. The Apostle in the tenth chapter compareth this of 1 Cor. 10.
ours to the *immolata* of the heathen; and to the Hebrews, 21, &c.
habemus aram, matcheth it with the sacrifice of the Jews. Heb. 13.10.
And we know the rule of comparisons, they must be *ejusdem
generis.*

Neither do we stay here, but proceed to the other, *epulemur.* 2. *Epule-*
For there is another thing yet to be done, which doth pre- *mur:*
sent to us that which *celebremus* doth represent. From the In the
Sacrament is the applying the Sacrifice. The Sacrifice in Sacrament.
general, *pro omnibus.* The Sacrament in particular, to each
several receiver, *pro singulis.* Wherein that is offered to us
that was offered for us; that which is common to all, made
proper to each one, while each taketh his part of it; and
made proper by a communion and union, like that of meat
and drink, which is most nearly and inwardly made ours,
and is inseparable for ever. There, *celebremus* passeth with
the representation; but here, *epulemur,* as a nourishment,
abideth with us still. In that we "see," and in this "we Ps. 34. 8.
taste, how gracious the Lord is," and hath been to us. And
so much for these two as two means to partake the benefit,
and we to use them; and as duties required of us, and we
to perform them.

Will ye mark one thing more, that *epulemur* doth here
refer to *immolatus?* To Christ, not every way considered,
but as when He was offered. Christ's body that now is.

True; but not Christ's body as now it is, but as then it was, when it was offered, rent, and slain, and sacrificed for us. Not, as now He is, glorified, for so He is not, so He cannot be *immolatus,* for He is immortal and impassible. But as then He was when He suffered death, that is, passible and mortal. Then, in His passible estate did He institute this of ours, to be a memorial of His *passibile* and *Passio* both. And we are in this action not only carried up to Christ, (*Sursum corda,*) but we are also carried back to Christ as He was at the very instant, and in the very act of His offering. So, and no otherwise, doth this text teach. So, and no otherwise, do we represent Him. By the incomprehensible power of His eternal Spirit, not He alone, but He, as at the very act of His offering, is made present to us, and we incorporate into His death, and invested in the benefits of it. If an host could be turned into Him now glorified as He is, it Joh. 3. 14. would not serve; Christ offered is it,—thither we must look. Lu. 17. 37. To the serpent lift up, thither we must repair, even *ad* 1Cor.11.24. *cadaver;* we must *hoc facere,* do that is then done. So, and no otherwise, is this *epulare* to be conceived. And so, I think, none will say they do or can turn Him.

1.
Itaque:
We bound
to keep it.
Now all we have to do, is to shew what we think of this *itaque,* whether it shall conclude us or no; and that we shew it by our practice, for other answer the Apostle will take none. If we play fast or loose with it on this fashion, as divers do, upon the matter as good to say, The Holy Ghost cannot tell how to make an argument; Christ is offered, but no *itaque epulemur* for all that. Thus we will not say, for very shame. What then? will we *dispensare contra Apostolum,* which we blame as a foul abuse in the Pope? and yet I cannot see, but every mean person takes upon him papal authority in this case; and as oft as we list, dispense with the Apostle and his *itaque,* exempt ourselves from his conclusion:—that we will not seem to do. No, it is not at *itaque;* the truth is, it is at *non in fermento* we stick; we love our leaven so well, be it malice or be it some other leaven as bad, so well we love it, we will not part with it; we loath the lamb, rather than the leaven shall out. But in the mean time, there is no trifling with this conclusion, there is no dispensing with the Apostle; there is no wanton wilful

disabling ourselves will serve. *Itaque* will not be so answered; not, but with *epulemur.* It layeth a necessity upon every one, to be a guest at this feast. The Jews we know were held hard to theirs upon a great pain, to have, not their names, but their souls cut off from God's people. And is it a less trespass for Christians to pass by this Passover? or hath the Church less band to exact like care at our hands? No indeed; we must know the Holy Ghost can tell how to infer, and that this *itaque* of the Apostle's is a binding conclusion. To the next point. Ex. 12. 19.

Absolutely, we are to keep this feast, but not to keep it *quovis modo,* no matter how, prepared, unprepared, in any garment, in any sort. No; this *non* and this *sed,* not on that manner but this, shew plainly every manner will not serve. What then is the manner? "Not in old leaven." With the Passover he began, and he holds him to it still; that if it be a Passover, reason would it should be kept like a Passover, even in the same manner. Now the Passover was not a loose lawless thing, to hold it in any fashion, it skilled not how. No; it had his laws. Even that, *Hæc est lex Paschalis,* ye shall read it, Exod. xii. 43, "this is the law of keeping it." 2. Direction how to keep it.

Indeed, divers laws it had in type that concern us in truth; among the rest this, for one, in the text. The lamb would not be eaten with every kind of bread, every paste was not for this feast, not leavened in any wise. Such an antipathy there was between leaven and it, as it might not, I will not say come to the board, but not be endured in the house all the feast long, though it were neither tasted nor touched. If it were not thrown out, if any never so little of it remained in any corner, the law was broken, the feast illegitimate. To make it up then a perfect Passover, here is another yet, which I called our Passover duty; the not staying still in our old leaven, but passing over, as it were, to a new paste, a necessary condition for the right holding this feast. For sweet bread was so proper to the Passover, as ye shall find they be but two diverse names of one and the same thing. 1. *Non in fermento:* "not with the old leaven." Ex. 12. 19. Lu. 22. 7.

Omnia in figuram illis[1], saith the Apostle, "with them all was in type." What is the spirit of this letter? What meant by leaven? The Apostle tells us, the old leaven of Egypt is our former vicious course of life, soured with the 1Cor.10.11. [1 in figurâ. Vulg.]

leaven of the old Adam; and *nova conspersio*, is newness of
life. The time of offering the lamb, is the time of casting
out this. Meet, if we would have our sins pass from us, we
should pass from them also, and throw their leaven out.

And well is sin likened to leaven. Leaven will grow noi-
some, if it be kept long; and sin, if it have lain long in us, or
we in it, turns to a certain sourness, that we ourselves feel
an unpleasant savour or upbraiding of it in our souls. Our
Saviour felt it so, I am sure; the vinegar He took shewed
the relish of it. By which upbraiding, we find, we need an
expurgate for it, as it were a corrupt humour in our souls,
that needed to be purged out.

Generally, all old leaven whatsoever; namely, two sorts of
it, 1. κακία, and 2. πονηρία, turned " naughtiness and malice."
The words in their own nature—as they properly signify,
1. one noteth a loose licentious lewdness, lightly ending in
lust; 2. the other, an unquiet working wickedness, that will
take pains to do a shrewd turn, commonly the effect of malice.
The sins of lust are well set out in old corrupt leaven, for
so they end, mostwhat in corruption and rottenness. The
sin of malice likewise. For, as leaven, it makes men swell one
against another as if they would burst; and sour are the fruits
of it and unpleasant, as any leaven in the world.

These two to be cast out, as those that have a special antipathy with this feast and offering. For no agreement between a foul life, and the feast of an undefiled Lamb. Nor
no fellowship between sour malice, and the feast of sweet
bread. And these two are specially named, because they
were the faults wherewith the Corinthians specially were
leavened, to whom he writes. Incest, at the first verse, as
we know Corinth heard evil for looseness;—there is *nequitia.*
And again, swelling one against another at the second;—
there is malice.

As to rid ourselves of this leaven, so to furnish ourselves, as
Sed, &c. with new paste, with the two leaven-less virtues, " sincerity and
truth." " Sincerity," that is, cleanness of life, a word thought
to be taken from honey, which is then *mel sincerum* when it
is *sine cerá*, unmingled, ' without wax,' or any baggage in it.
Εἰλικρίνεια, the Greek word, is properly of uncounterfeit
wares, such as we may κρίνειν ἐν εἴλῃ, bring forth and shew

them in the sun; as need not the false light of a close shop to utter them. But truth that runs through all, flat against all kind of leaven, if it have any manner leaven, true it is not, and so out it must.

Of leaven in the Gospel, I find three sorts interpreted to our hands, that we cannot mistake. Christ willed His Disciples to "beware of the leaven of the Pharisees and Sadducees." It is after said, He meant it of their "doctrine," that was full of corrupt leaven. 1. The Pharisees', of the leaven of superstition consisting in phylacteries, phrases, and observances, and little else. 2. The Sadducees', of a leaven that smelt strong of profaneness, in their liberty of prophesying, calling in question Angels, and Spirits, and the Resurrection itself; 3. and a third leaven Christ names, "the leaven of Herod;"—beware that too: *Mark 8.15.* many times it is the bane of true religion, when God's truth and worship must be moulded up with Jeroboam's, and with Herod's ends; squared to them just as is fittest to do their turns, that Jeroboam may be safe. No superfluous *caveat*; many times, this marreth all. Let all be abandoned; Pharisees', Sadducees', Herod's, and the truth take place.

1. The leaven of doctrine. Mat. 16. 6. 12.

Now as in that place the Pharisees' leaven is "doctrine," so in another I find that Christ expounds it "hypocrisy;" and that is merely opposite to truth in meaning, speaking, and dealing. The Pharisee was a great dealer with this leaven. He had it on his face, to make him look sour; men might take notice when they fasted. He had it on his tongue;—Rabbi, O you teach the truth, you respect no *Mat. 6. 16.* man's person; when they sought to cut His throat. He had it in his whole course, all for show, to seem that they were *Mat. 23. 7.* not; Gabbatha without, and Golgotha within. *27.*

2. The leaven of life. Lu. 12. 1.

But yet even they, though they used it, they taught it not for a doctrine, nor avowed not the lawful use of it; that one might speak the one half without, and the other half within, as our Pharisees now do. Men, ye shall never have any sincere truth from them. Search them, they have still a piece of leaven in their bosom; speak so, and deal so, as if they would take the sentence by the end, and turn it clean against the Apostle; to purge out all his sweet bread, all sincerity and truth, and hold their Passover in leaven, or not at all. Antichrist's goat may be so eaten; the Lamb Christ cannot. To the Lamb's nature that is sincere, nothing so contrary as this, to mean, speak, or deal insincerely.

3.
The leaven
of company
corrupt in
life.
You see a leaven of doctrine and life; that is, the leaven of the Gospel. A third there is, the leaven of the Epistle, and that is of corrupt company; and that is, in very deed, the leaven of this text. For when the Apostle would have this leaven here purged, what means he? To have the incestuous Corinthian removed, and cast out of the fellowship of the faithful, by the censures of the Church. True; but those not in every man's power. But this is, to avoid and shun them and their company: so we may, and so we are bound to cast them out.

There is very great danger in persons so leavened, great scandal, even to the well-disposed; but far greater danger to the most, that will soon take this leaven; our nature is apt to take it, it is easily fermented that way. As much good leaven as will serve three pecks, so much evil will do more than serve three bushels, and never leave till it have soured them all. That, except this be looked to, all the rest will be to small purpose.

In religion.
Now, when St. Paul speaks of persons thus leavened, he means not only such as are lewd of life, tainted that way, but even such also as are unsound in matter of religion, and have a sour savour that way. Here to the Corinthians, he would have the incestuous person cast out, with his leavened life; but to the Galatians after, he presseth the same point against another kind, such as leavened the Gospel with Moses' ceremonies, and so corrupted the truth in religion; and them he would have cut off—both Corinthian and Galatian leaven, both must out. And mark; upon the same reason both, and in the very same words. That a little leaven doth not a little hurt, but otherwhile marreth the whole batch of bread. Evil doctrine is against truth, evil life against walking in the truth, evil company will bring us to both. Therefore away with them, but away with this especially. If they will not purge out their leaven, purge them out. And that especially, against this feast in the nature whereof there is a contrariety to all leaven.

Gal. 5. 3,
4, &c.
Gal. 5. 9,
12.

Gal. 5. 9.

Now then, this is our conclusion ; come we must, and *itaque celebremus.* This is our caution: thus we must come, *non in fermento, sed azymis.* If we say, it skills not whether we come, *itaque* meets with us; if we say, it skills not how we come, *non in fermento* meets with us too. It is with us here, as with the Prophet ; when he would heal one, the Hos. 7. 1. other breaketh forth. If we press *non in fermento,* we lose *itaque epulemur,* they come not at all; no feast. If we urge *itaque epulemur,* they come, how? leavened, and unleavened, all clap them down together. We need a *quomodo intrásti huc?* to keep some back; and yet we need a *compelle intrare,* Matt.22.12. to bring others in. But the manner, but the caution, re- Lu. 14. 23. member that. The main conclusion is that we come. The other we must not leave undone, but this peremptorily we are bound to do.

The Apostle binds us to do it; the time to do it, now. For if this follow—Christ is offered, therefore we are to come to His feast ; this will follow as strongly, Christ is now offered, therefore let us now come. Go by degrees: the Christian Passover, our Passover, a time it must have, some-time it is to be kept. We would do it at that time, when it were best for us to do it. When best for us to do it, but at the time He did it Himself? And that did He, even at this feast, now. Now then at this feast it is most kindly to do it; most like to please Him, and to prosper with us.

And indeed, if at any time we will do it, *Quando Pascha nisi in Pascha,* 'what time is the Passover so proper as at the feast of the Passover?' *Quando tempus epulandi, nisi quando tempus immolandi,* 'when the time of His receiving as at the time of His offering?' Therefore they both, the feast and the lamb, have one name, to shew the near con-junction that should be between them. When the day cometh, to remember what was done on the day, and so what we to do on that day. *Pascha quod celebramus,* to put us in mind of *Pascha quod epulamur.* For tell me, Will the sacrifice commemorative, or the Sacrament com-municative ever fall more fit, than when that was offered which we are to commemorate, and to communicate withal ? Is not the fittest time of doing it the time when it was done? of *hoc facite* then, when *hoc factum est ?* So that without any more ado, the season itself pleadeth for this effectually.

And now is the time of *expurgate* for our bodies, the corrupt humours that leaven it, now we cast them out. And why not now likewise, those that lie sour in our souls? And even nature's Passover, the general Passover is even at this time, both in Heaven and earth. Above in Heaven, where the sun having past over all the signs is come about, and renews his course at the first sign in the Zodiac. And beneath in earth, from the sharp time of winter, and fermenting time of the earth, to the renewing sweet time, the time of the spring, wherein there is *nova conspersio* in nature itself. And why should not the Passover of grace be now likewise in season, and have due concurrence with nature?

Sure all agree well, if we but agree ourselves. And if we agree for our parts to do the day's duty, Christ will not be behind with His, the day's benefit; but during our time and in the hour of death, be our true Passover; shielding us from all deadly mishaps while we here live, and giving us a sure and safe passage at our end, even a passage to the last and great Passover of all; the truth of that whereof theirs was the shadow, and ours the image now. For we have not yet done with our Lamb, nor the work of this Passover is not yet fully accomplished.

There is a farther matter yet behind; for as this feast looketh back as a memorial of that is already past and done for us, so doth it forward, and is to us a pledge of another
Rev.19.7,9. and a better yet to come, the feast of the marriage of the Lamb here That is our Passover, where whosoever shall be a guest, the Angels pronounce him happy and blessed for ever.

That is the last and great feast indeed, when all destroyers and all destructions shall cease and come to an end for ever-
Mat. 25.21. more, and we hear that joyful voice, *Transi in gaudium Domini,* "Pass over into the joy of the Lord," the joys of Heaven, joys not mingled with any sour leaven as this world's joy is, but pure and entire; nor transient as that of this world, and ever flitting and forsaking us then soonest when we think we have best hold of them, but permanent and abiding still. A Passover that will be never passed over, but last and con-

tinue a feast to all eternity. Of that, this here is a pledge, if we neglect it not as if it were not worth the taking. And He That at this time gave us this pledge, in His good time also bring us to the Passover whereof this is the pledge, even to the never-passing but everlasting joys and happiness, of His Heavenly kingdom, through the offering of His blessed Son the very Paschal Lamb! To Whom with, &c.

A SERMON

PREACHED BEFORE

THE KING'S MAJESTY, AT WHITEHALL,

ON THE EIGHTEENTH OF APRIL, A.D. MDCXIII., BEING EASTER-DAY.

COLOSSIANS iii. 1, 2.

*If ye then be risen with Christ, seek those things which are
above, where Christ sitteth at the right hand of God.*
*Set your affections, or minds, on things which are above; and
not on things which are on the earth.*

*Igitur, si con-surrexistis cum Christo, quæ sursum sunt quærite, ubi
Christus est in dextera Dei sedens.*
Quæ sursum sunt sapite, non quæ super terram.

[*If ye then be risen with Christ, seek those things which are above,
where Christ sitteth on the right hand of God.*
Set your affection on things above, not on things on the earth. Engl.
Trans.]

SERM.
VIII.

THE wisdom of the Church hath so disposed of her read-
ings in these great feasts, as lightly the Gospel lets us know
what was done on the day, done for us, and the Epistle what
is to be done by us. To instance in this present: *Surrexit
Dominus vere,* "The Lord is risen indeed," saith the Gospel.
In Quo con-surrexistis et vos, "and you are risen with Him,"
saith the Epistle.

2. That which is in the Gospel is Christ's act, what He
did; that which in the Epistle our *agendum,* what we to do.

3. Or rather both ours; 1. what He did, matter of faith;
2. what we to do, matter of duty, our *agendum* upon His act.

The common sort look to Easter-day no farther than
Easter-day fare, and Easter-day apparel; and other use they

have none of it. The true Christian enquireth farther, what is the *agendum* of the feast, what is the proper act of Easter-day? The Church hath hers, and we have ours. Nothing more proper to a Christian than to keep time with Christ, to rise with Him this day, Who this day did rise. That so it may be Easter-day with us as it was with Him; the same that was the day of His, be also the day of our rising.

Thus then it lieth. Christ is risen, and if Christ, then we. The sum. If we so be, then we "seek;" and that we cannot, unless we "set our minds." To "set our minds" then. On what? "On things above." Which above? Not "on earth," so is the text, but "where Christ is." And why there? Because, where He is, there are the things we seek for, and here cannot find. There " He is sitting;"—so at rest. And "at the right hand;"—so in glory. "God's right hand;"—and so for ever. These we seek, rest in eternal glory. These Christ hath found, and so shall we, if we make this our *agendum;* begin this day to "set our minds" to search after them.

Because it is to the Colossians, the *colossus* or capital point of all is, to rise with Christ; that is the main point. And if you would do a right Easter-day's work, do that. It is the way to entitle us to the true holding of the feast. That so we may, these two *opera Paschalia* are commended to us. "Things above," 1. to make them our search, 2. to fix our minds on them. These two we read, *quærite, sapite,* in the imperative; we may in the indicative as well; ζητεῖτε is *quæritis,* as well as *quærite,* and φρονεῖτε *sapitis,* as well as *sapite.* If ye read them *imperative,* thus: This ye are to do, "to seek," "to set your minds;" then be they *in præcepto* and *per modum officii,* 'by way of precept,' and 'in nature of a duty.' If you read them *indicative,* thus: "If you be risen, then you do seek, and set your minds;" then they be *in elencho,* and *per modum signi,* 'by way of trial,' and 'in nature of a sign.' Both well, and a good use of both.

The parts lie thus. Two things are supposed, two other The di- inferred, and a third two we are referred to, or given hope of. vision. The two supposed these; 1. Christ is risen, and 2. we with I. 1. 2. Christ: "If ye be risen with Christ." The two inferred these; "if risen," then 1. "to seek;" 2. then "to set our II. 3. 4. minds above, on things there, where Christ is." The two

SERM.
VIII.
—————
III. 5.
6.
7.
Heb. 1. 7,
&c.
[Epist. for
Christmas
day.]
Actsl.1,&c.
[For the
Epist. As-
cension-
day.]
he referreth to, or giveth hope of, rest with Him in glory. 1. Rest, to sit; 2. Glory, at the right hand. And God maketh up all the perfect number of seven, for eternal is the rest, and eternal the glory, that is at His right hand.

These we heard of at His birth, in the Epistle then. This we hear of again at His rising, or second birth, from the grave, in the Epistle now. This we shall hear of again at His Ascension too. This is remembered in all as the fruit of all, at every feast set before us as our hope and all we seek, to sit with Christ, at the right hand of God.

"If ye be risen." This seemeth *primá facie* to be but a single supposition, but being well looked into, resolves into two risings, 1. Christ's, and 2. ours; 1. He, and 2. we with Him. Of which the first, Christ's, doth *immutabiliter suppo-nere*, His needs no *if*. It is not if Christ be, but if we with Christ. For Christ is certainly. Three hundred years the world opposed it; thirteen hundred, ever since, the world hath supposed it. And so let us, and so pass to our own, and begin every year to lay our grounds anew; every Easter, to be teaching our rudiments over again.

There is an "if" that supposeth but *mobiliter*, may be or not be thereafter as we seek, and our minds be set. But yet, if ye mark it, is not His supposed by itself, and ours inferred upon His, but ours supposed likewise; His and ours both supposed under one, under one and the same *if*. And as they are close linked, that one supposition serveth for them, so are they woven together, that one preposition (σὺν) holdeth them, under one *si*, and one σὺν both. The Apostle hath framed a new word here, for the purpose, *con-surrexistis*. The resurrection we have heard of, the con-surrection we are now to hear and take notice of.

To set our suppose right, I ask two questions; 1. the one of these "if you;" 2. the other of these, "if you be risen." *Si vos,* "if you." Why, doth the Resurrection pertain but to some certain *vos?* Is it not *si omnes?* concerns it not all? As Christ died, so is He risen for all; and shall not all rise with Him? What do we then do with *si vos?* Yes, all rise with Him out of their graves, but not all rise to the right hand after-mentioned. A great part rise to stand on the left, not to sit on the right hand of God. With that the

Apostle here dealeth. The resurrection reacheth to all; this resurrection to such only as seek, and set their minds.

The other, "be risen," the tense, is that right? For ever, when we hear of the Resurrection, we are carried straight to that of the dead from their graves at the latter day. We conceive: Well, if He be risen we shall rise, *shall* in the future tense. But, here is news of another in the *preter* tense, for so it is, "be risen," not shall rise; be already, not shall hereafter. It cannot be taken of that which is to come; it should then be, *si consurgetis.* But needs of one present or past, it is *si consurrexistis.* 2. *Si con-surrexis-tis,* "if you be risen.'

How then? Fall we in with them *qui dicunt resurrec-tionem jam esse factam,* "that say the resurrection is already past?" Nor that neither. We are no Sadducees, nor we are not of Hymenæus' sect neither. But this we believe: as there is one to come of the body at the last and great resurrection, which he treats of to the Corinthians, so is there also one which we are to pass here, of the mind's, which here he commendeth to the Colossians. 2 Tim. 2. 18. 1 Cor. 15. *passim.*

And these two lead us directly to the two resurrections, which St. John after doth more expressly deliver, under the terms of "first" and "second." And this withal, that all the good or evil of that of the Corinthians, doth depend much upon the well or evil passing of this of the Colossians. Rev. 20. 6.

This we are to look after, to rise before, a resurrection now in being. This of ours imports us, we see, no less than Christ's own, which I wish well laid up in mind, since both are under one "if," supposed alike, one no less than the other. "Christ is risen" is not enough, nay is nothing at all, if that be all, if He be risen without us, He risen, and we lie still; if with this day's resurrection on His part there be not also a con-surrection on ours. [1 Cor. 15. 20.]

Now then we are to look to our *if,* that it supposeth aright. And if He be risen, to cry to Him *Trahe nos post Te,* "to draw us with Him," and not leave us still in our graves of sin. He said of Himself, that "if once He were exalted, He would" make His magnetical virtue to appear, and "draw all to Him." "All," but not all at once, but, as the Apostle saith, "each in his order." And that order is to begin with the soul first, and draw it. For the soul being, as Cant. 1. 3. Joh. 12. 32. 1 Cor. 15. 23.

SERM.
VIII.
[Conf.
Arist. Eth.
10. 7.]
the very philosophers have acknowledged—it is Aristotle's own word, ἄνωθεν 'from above,' will the more easily be drawn to τὰ ἄνω "things above." It is kindly, it is con-natural for it, to draw thitherward. And then after, in the second place, together with itself, to elevate and lift up the flesh thither with it. For, as well observeth Chrysostom, these two were not thus joined, the spirit and the flesh I mean, that the flesh should pull down the spirit to earth, but that the spirit should exalt the flesh to Heaven. And this subliming or lifting up the spirit, is the rising with Christ here in the text. The other in his time and turn to follow. But if this go not before, the other will not come after, take that for certain. This then to endeavour, and this day to set in hand with it. For this is the main point, that we find ourselves risen with Christ; find it, or procure it; find it already, or procure it as soon as may be.

II.
The
double
inference.
3. If we
" seek."
4. If we
" set our
minds,"
&c. " on
things
above."
Now thus we shall know if we be risen, and thus procure it if we be not; "if we seek, if we set our minds on things above," which is the double inference upon the former double suppose, which I divide into the 1. act, and the 2. object. The 1. act, *quærere* and *sapere*; the 2. object, *quæ sursum*.

Of the two acts, one referreth to action; seeking, is a matter of endeavour. The other to the affection; set your affection or mind, it is both. There be two works arguing the spirit; 1. motion, and 2. sense. Motion, in the one, Phil. 2. 5. seeking: Sense, in the other, so is it turned, Phil. 2. 5. *Idem sentite,* "let the same mind be in you." There is *motus læsus* in them that seek not; and *sensus læsus,* in them that savour not. To these two reduce all: 1. *Quærenda sapere,* and 2. *Sapienda quærere;* 'to mind what we are to seek,' and to 'seek what we mind.' Of these two 1. jointly first; 2. then severally; and 3. last of their order.

1.
The
two acts
jointly ;
" Seek,"
and " set
your
minds."
Jointly; for disjoined they may not be. One is little worth without the other. There be that seek, and be very busy in it, and yet savour not the things that are of God. So sought a great Apostle once, and our Saviour did not let to tell him of it; οὐ φρονεῖς, the very word here, " thou Mat. 16. 23. savourest not." Men that are possessed with false principles, and yet fall a seeking; zealous in their way, but want true Prov. 19. 2. knowledge to fix their minds aright. Now, " without know-

ledge," saith Solomon truly, "the mind is not good;" and we know, *mala mens malus animus*, 'the mind misled will set the affections awry straight.'

Will ye see them in kind? Look but to the end of the last chapter before. There they seek so, as they will neither taste, handle, nor touch. So seek as down they go to worship, not only God, but the Angels too. So seek, as "spare not their own bodies," and yet wrong all the while; and yet with all their seeking, not "risen with Christ" for all that. Why? For *quærunt, non sapiunt.* Col. 2. 21. 18. 23.

On the other side, there be that *sapiunt, non quærunt*, that *sapiunt quæ Christi, quærunt quæ sua,* 'savour Christ, but seek themselves.' Of whom the Apostle, they have knowledge competent, but without so much as a spark of true endeavour. *Pariter intelligunt nobiscum*, saith Augustine, *pariter non diligunt;* 'understand well enough, but coldly affected;' so, sit still and seek not. Phil. 2. 21.

So that both would be kept together, *quærite*, and *sapite* both. For as in the body natural it fareth between the stomach and the head—a rheumatic head spoils the stomach with distillations, and a distempered stomach fills the head with raw vapours, and soon mars the other, so it is here. Our mind mistaking misleads the affection, and a wrong set affection puts the mind out of frame. That in sunder they would not be, but joined ever. *Sapere* without *quærere* will not rise, but lie still; and *quærere* without *sapere* will rise, but lead you astray.

Now severally. If we be risen to move and to seek, that is, to resolve that, with sitting still without seeking, what we are here willed to seek will not be had. We shall not stumble on it, or hit upon it unawares; there needs a seeking. If our Saviour knew the way well, it is hard to hit, "and few there be that find it." The short; there goeth search and enquiry to it, pains and diligence are requisite; we shall not come thither with the turning of a gin. It were great folly, when we see daily things here beneath without travail will not be come by, once to think things above will drop into our laps without any seeking. 2. The acts severally. 1. "Seek." Mat. 7. 14.

To seek then, but to do it to purpose, for that which we call seeking is nothing less. Those, to whom the Prophet

SERM.
VIII.
Isa. 21. 12. Esay said, *si quæritis, quærite,* "if ye will seek, why then seek," do it in earnest; it seems they sought so slightly, so slenderly, as it deserved not the name of seeking. Pilate
Joh. 18. 38. asked, *Quid est veritas?* and then some other matter took him in the head, and so up he rose and went his way, before he had his answer; he deserved never to find what truth was. And such is our seeking mostwhat, seldom or never seriously, but some question that comes cross our brain for the present, some *quid est veritas?* so sought as if that we sought were as good lost as found. Yet this we would fain have go for
Isa. 21. 12. seeking, but it will not be. *O si quæritis quærite,* saith Esay, —look the place, "The morning comes, so doth the night," that is, our days spend apace, and we say we will seek. If we will, let us once do it indeed; seek it as they did this day,
Joh. 20. 4. follow it hard, make it our race with the one, our morning-work with the other.

2.
"Set your
minds." But we shall never seek as we should unless we put to the other word, set our minds on them. For will a man ever kindly seek that he hath no mind to? Never. The mind is all. Be it what it will, or whence it will, above or beneath, if we affect it not, we shall seek but faintly. That we may seek things above as it is meet, we must prize them, prize
Prov. 3. 14. them as "a silver mine," saith Solomon, as "a treasure hid
Mat. 13. 44. in a field," saith our Saviour, and go "sell all" to compass them. Then shall we seek to some purpose.

But in the word φρονεῖν there is more. There is, I told you, *idem sentite,* the sense—he that seeks, should have as well eyes to discern, as feet to go about it; it is no business for a blind man, no more than for a lame, to seek—and that is knowledge, which would be had too. To seek we know not what, is but to err, and never find that we seek for. To *quærere* then, but *sapere,* 'to be wise' in our seeking, to get us true directions; else for all our seeking we may be to seek still.

Which φρονεῖν is a word the Apostle much useth, as being very significant, full and forcible. Four things are in it; 1. To set the mind, the mind not the fancy; not to take up a fancy and fall to seeking as we see many now-a-days, no ground in the world but their own conceits. Yet seek they will needs, and have all the world follow them, and have nothing to follow themselves but their own folly. So as, being very idiots, they take themselves for the only men; and till they come into it, never was wise man in the world that knew what to seek, or how.

2. It is then an act of the understanding, φρονεῖν, but not of it alone, for then νοεῖν were enough. Yet the greatest part make no matter of it, but even *noëma*. It is, as to set our mind, not our fancy, so our mind, not only to know it, but to mind it. It is *sentire*, and *sapere;* and it is best seen in *sapite*, which is not only to distinguish tastes, but in and with the taste to feel some delight, to have a sense of the sweetness withal, which will make us seek it again *plus magis;* and without it our seeking will be but unsavoury.

3. So to savour it, as we hold *quærere* to be *sapere;* that to seek is our wisdom, that we do not *recte sapere*, unless we do *hoc sapere.* *Hæc erit sapientia vestra*, saith Moses, "this shall Deu. 4. 6. be your wisdom," before God and man, and you so to reckon of it: even this, to seek things above, and to think when ye are about that business, ye are about a point of high wisdom, and that to perform it well is the wisest action of our life.

4. To hold it our wisdom; and last, I ask what wisdom? Not that which doth contemplate, that is σοφία, but the active wisdom, for that is φρόνησις, *rerum agendarum.* To shew that not only our grounds for judgment, but our rules for action, are to be set thence. Thither to get us, thence to derive our reasons, why we do things, or leave them undone. Thus to cast with ourselves. This that now I am about, He That sitteth on high at God's right hand, what will He say or think of it? May I offer it to Him? Will He allow of it? Will He help me forward with it? Will He in the end reward me for it? Yea, even our πολίτευμα, as to the Phil. 3. 20. Philippians, is to be from thence, even the wisdom that swayeth there to be from above, *de sursum.* If it be not, St. James is somewhat homely with it. Jas. 3. 15.

By this time we know what it is to "seek," and what to "set 3. The our minds." But in the marshalling these there is somewhat, order. that *quærite* is called on first. 1. To teach us that it is the *Quærite,* First. first thing we are to have care of; Christ's *primum quærite* Mat. 6. 33. makes *quærite* to be *primum*, to stand first. That we then do it the honour to make it our first act, our rising with Him

Y

at this feast, the rising of the year; and on this feast, in the morning, the rising of the day. For then He rose.

2. 2. It is first called on, because, to say truth, there is more need of diligence in this business, than aught else. Always we have more ado to quicken the affection, than to inform the judgment. And that did they this day know, who sought before they had light, "while it was yet dark." So much did they know diligence to import in this business. The greatest defect is in that point, therefore it needs first to be urged. For though we see, yet we sit still and seek not.

III.
The thing referred to, or the object.
Quæ sursum.
Ps. 24. 6.
And now to the object. Of seeking we shall soon agree; *Generatio quærentium* we are all, saith the Psalm, even " a generation of searchers." Somewhat we are searching after still. Our wants or our wanton desires find us seeking work enough all our lives long. What then shall we seek, or where?

He, saith the Apostle, that will thus bestow his pains, let it be where? "Above." On what? "The things there," *quæ sursum*, he repeats in both, tells it us twice over; 1. *Quæ sursum quærite, quæ sursum sapite.* "Above" it must be.

And of this also we shall not vary with Him, but be easily enough entreated to it. We yield presently, in our sense, to seek to be above others in favour, honour, place and power, and what not? We keep the text fully in this sense, we both seek, and set our whole minds upon this. *Altum sapimus* Judg. 9.15. *omnes*; all would be above, "bramble" and all, and nothing is too high for us.

It is true here, for on earth there is a *sursum*, "above;" there be high places, we would not have them taken away, we would offer in them, and offer for them too, for a need. And there is a right hand here too, and some sit at it, and almost none but thinks so well of himself as why not he? Our Saviour Christ, when it was fancied that He should have been a great king upon earth, there was suing straight Mat. 20. 21. for his right-hand place. Not so much as good-wise " Zebedee's two sons" that smelt of the fisherboat, but means was made for them to sit there.

But all this while we are wide. For where is all this? Here upon earth. All our *above* is above one another here, and is ambitious above, and farther it mounteth not. But this is not the Apostle's, not the "above," nor "the right hand" he meaneth. No: not Christ's right hand upon earth, but that right hand He sits at Himself in Heaven. The Apostle saw clearly we would err this error: therefore, to take away as he goes all mistaking, he explains his "above" two ways. 2. *Privative: non quæ supra terram,* hear you, "not upon earth;" His "above" is not here upon earth. This is where not. 2. Then *positive:* to clear it from all doubt where, he points us to the place itself, "above," there "above" where Christ is, that is, "not on earth." Earth is the place whence He is risen. The Angels tell us, *non est* Lu. 24. 6. *hîc:* seek Him not here now, but in the place whither He is gone, there seek Him in Heaven. Heaven is a great circle; where, in Heaven? In the chiefest place, there where God sits, and Christ at His right hand.

So that upon the matter, the fault he finds, the fault of our "above" is, it is not above enough, it is too low, it is not so high as it should be. It should be higher, above the hills; higher yet, above the clouds; higher yet, higher than our eye can carry, above the Heavens. There now, we are right.

And indeed the very frame of our bodies, as the heathen 1. poet well observed, giveth thither upward: *cœlumque tueri* The reasons. *jussit,* and bids us look thither. And that way should our [Ovid. soul make; it came from thence, and thither should it draw Metam. 1. again, and we do but bow and crook our souls, and make 85-6.] them *curvæ in terris animæ,* against their nature, when we [Pers. Sat. hang yokes on them, and set them to seek nothing but here 2. 61.] below.

And if nature would have us no moles, grace would have 2. us eagles, to mount "where the body is." And the Apostle Lu. 17. 37. goeth about to breed in us a holy ambition, telling us we are *ad altiora geniti,* 'born for higher matters' than any here; therefore not to be so base minded as to admire them, but to seek after things above. For contrary to the philosopher's sentence, *Quæ supra nos nihil ad nos,* 'Things above they concern us not,' he reverses that; yes, and we so to hold, *ea maxime ad nos,* 'they chiefly concern us.'

Come to the last now. And why this place above? I 3. shall tell you: for there is Christ, and Him we seek to-day if it be Easter-day with us; and if we seek where He is, He

S E R M. is above certainly. But he implieth a farther reason yet,
VIII. because in very deed there with Him are the things which
we of all other seek for, and when all is done, all our seeking
is to them referred as to the end. We would not ever travail, but after our laborious toiling course here find a place
of rest, and this we seek. But not this alone, but a seat of
glory withal. Sit we would, but in some eminent place;
not at the left foot but at the right hand, in light and honour
as much as might be.

What "the   We seek rest; specially, they that are tossed in a tempest,
things
above" are. how do they desire a good haven, a harbour of rest! and sure
Rest.   here we "dwell in Mesech," meet with much disquietness.
Ps. 120. 5.
None but sometime hath sense of the verse in the Psalm:
Ps. 55. 6. " Oh that I had wings like a dove! then would I fly and be
at rest." And the more our *incolatus* is prolonged, the more
we seek it, find it how we may.

Mat. 11. 29.   And it is not the body's trouble so much, but *invenietis
requiem animabus,* to find rest to our souls;—that is it. And
the soul is from above, and but in her own place never finds
Ps. 116. 7. it. "Turn thee to thy rest O my soul;"—that is worth all.
Ps. 95. 11. But both are best, and not after all our turmoils here in this
world to hear, *non introibunt in requiem meam* in another
world, but to be cast into that place where there is no rest
Heb. 3. 11. day nor night; but enter into His rest, which in the Epistle
18, 19.   to the Hebrews he so much beats upon.

And verily if we seek rest, glory we seek much more. For
1. Glory. for it we are content to deprive ourselves of all rest, which
otherwise we love well enough. And a restless course we
enter into, and hold out in it all our life long, and all to win
it, though it be but a little before our death. For no rest
will satisfy or give us full content, unless it be on the right
hand.

These two then we seek for: where are they to be found?
Not in *quæ supra terram;* not here therefore, but folly to
seek them here. We are by all means to avoid their error,
Lu. 24. 5. that sought this day to "seek the living among the dead,"
a thing where it is not to be had.

Never seek to set up our rest here, in this tumultuous
Hos. 2. 15. troublesome place, "this vale of Achor" right, as Osee; this
Jas. 3. 6. τροχὸς, as St. James, a "wheel" ever whirling about, *quærens*
Mat. 12. 43.

requiem et non invenit eam. Where we shall soon be diseased
with a *surgite postquam sederitis*, 'after we sit a little, quickly
disquieted again.' The Prophet Micah tells us plain, *non* Mic. 2. 10.
habetis hic requiem, "here we cannot have it, this is not
our rest."

Nor never seek for true glory here: why? *Locus est puli-
cum et culicum*, 'It is the place of fleas and of gnats this.' In
the garden, the place of our delight, we meet with worms;
and there be spiders even in the King's palace. This place
of worms and spiders, call ye this the place of glory in dust
and cobwebs?

Say it be, yet such is the nature of these two such as they
be, the rest and the glory here, as they divide it still; have
ye one, ye must quit the other. They that are in glory have
not the quietest life; and they that are most at rest, farthest
off from being glorious. Rest is here a thing inglorious,
and glory a thing restless. Thus it stands with us: Issachar's Gen. 49. 14.
condition like some; rest is good though it be between a
pair of panniers. If that like us, we must live in this estate,
the most obscure of all the tribes. But if we will have a
name among the great ones of the earth, if be glorious, then
farewell rest; we must take our lot among them that live
not most at ease certainly. For here they meet not, but
are in sunder still.

But say yet we could make them meet, be at all ease and 7. "At the
in all glory together; seated, and seated "at the right hand" right hand of God."
both. Now come we to weigh the word *Dei*. The right
hand here, *super terram*, is not the right hand of God, but
of a man, which shall wither, and within a certain of years,
as the Prophet's term is, "fall from the shoulder." And so Job 31. 22.
this rest, and this right hand, we can have no hold of either.
It is said in the Acts, after two years Felix went his way, and Acts 24. 27.
another came governor in his place. And then the places
were changed—some were diseased; and so is the case of all
felicity here.

Upon the point then. Rest and glory we seek not barely,
but we seek them so as they may endure; and our wish is,
if it might be, even for ever. And this may be had, but it
will be had at no right hand but *ad dexteram Dei*, God's
only. Then seek them there. Not here, where either we

shall seek and not find them, or find one from the other; or
if both together, yet have no hold of them, but soon lose
them again.   Seek where we may, nay, where we shall be
sure to find them, where both will be had; and both together, and good assurance of both, even to eternity, as at
God's right hand, a right hand that withereth not.   If ye
seek rest, let it be in His "holy hill;" if glory, *gloria in ex-*
celsis, where Christ is already; set, so at rest; at the right
hand, so in glory; at God's right hand, and so, in both for
ever.   There they be, there "seek," there "set your minds."

Ps. 15. 1.
Lu. 2. 14.

   To withdraw ourselves, to sequester our minds from things
here below, to think of Him, and of the place where now He
is, and the things that will bring us thither.

The appli-
cation to
the time.
   It is a prerogative that a Christian hath, to make it Easter
any day in the year, by doing these duties on it.   They
come no day amiss.   But no day so fit as this day, the very
day of His rising.   Then of very congruity, we to rise also.
For no reason in the world, if He rise, that we should lie
still.   Nor is it good for us that He should rise without us,
and leave us behind in the grave of our sins still.   But when
He, then we too.

   Rising is not so proper to the day, but the two signs
or two duties, call them which ye will, are as proper.   For
this day was, indeed, a day of seeking.   "I know Whom you
seek, ye seek Jesus That was crucified," saith one Angel;
"Why seek ye the living among the dead?" saith another.
To rise when He rose, to seek Him when He was sought.
This day He was sought by men, sought by women.   Women,
the three Maries; men, the two Apostles.   The women at
charges, the Apostles at pains.   Early by the one, earnestly
by the other.   So there was seeking of all hands.

Mark 16. 6.

Lu. 24. 5.

   And they which sought not went to Emmaus, yet they set
their minds on Him, had Him in mind, were talking of Him
by the way.   So that these do very fitly come into the
agendum of this day; thus to seek and set our minds.   At
least not to lose Him quite, that day we should seek Him,
nor have our minds farthest from Him that day they should
be most upon Him.

Lu. 24. 13.

   The Church by her office, or *agendum,* doth her part to
help us herein, all she may.   The things we are willed to

To the Sa-
crament.

seek she sets before us, the blessed mysteries. For these
are from above; the "Bread that came down from Heaven," Joh. 6. 50.
the Blood that hath been carried "into the holy place." Heb. 9. 12.
And I add, *ubi Christus;* for *ubi Corpus, ubi sanguis Christi,
ibi Christus,* I am sure. And truly here, if there be an *ubi
Christus,* there it is. On earth we are never so near Him,
nor He us, as then and there. There *in efficaciá,* and when
all is done, efficacy, that is it must do us good, must raise us
here, and raise us at the last day to the right hand; and the
local *ubi* without it of no value.

He was found in the "breaking of bread:" that bread she Lu. 24. 30.
breaketh, that there we may find Him. He was found by 85.
them that had their minds on Him: to that end she will call
to us, *Sursum corda,* 'Lift up your hearts;' which, when we
hear, it is but this text iterated, "Set your minds," have
your hearts where Christ is. We answer, 'We lift them
up;' and so I trust we do, but I fear we let them fall too
soon again.

Therefore, as before so after, when we hear, 'Thou That
sittest at the right hand of the Father;' and when again,
"Glory to God on high," all is but to have this. But
especially, where we may *sentire* and *sapere quæ sursum,* and Heb. 6. 4.
gustare donum cæleste, 'taste of the heavenly gift,' as in
another place he speaketh; see in the breaking, and taste in
the receiving, how gracious He was and is; was in suffering
for us, is in rising again for us too, and regenerating us
thereby "to a lively hope." And gracious in offering to us [1 Pet.1.3.]
the means, by His mysteries and grace with them, as will
raise us also and set our minds, where true rest and glory
are to be seen.

That so at this last and great Easter of all, the Resurrec-
tion-day, what we now seek we may then find; where we
now set our minds, our bodies may then be set; what we
now but taste, we may then have the full fruition of, even of
His glorious Godhead, in rest and glory, joy and bliss, never
to have an end.

A SERMON

PREACHED BEFORE

THE KING'S MAJESTY AT WHITEHALL,

ON THE TWENTY-FOURTH OF APRIL, A.D. MDCXIV., BEING EASTER-DAY.

PHILIPPIANS ii. 8—11.

He humbled Himself, made obedient unto death, even the death of the Cross.

For this cause hath God also highly exalted Him; and given Him a Name above every name.

That at the name of Jesus every knee should bow, of those in Heaven, and in earth, and under the earth.

And that every tongue should confess, that Jesus Christ is the Lord, to the glory of God the Father.

[*Humiliavit Semetipsum, factus obediens usque ad mortem, mortem autem crucis.*

Propter quod et Deus exaltavit Illum, et donavit Illi nomen, quod est super omne nomen:

Ut in nomine Jesu omne genu flectatur cælestium, terrestrium, et infernorum,

Et omnis lingua confiteatur quia Dominus Jesus Christus in gloria est Dei Patris. Latin Vulg.]

[*And being found in fashion as a man, He humbled Himself, and became obedient unto death, even the death of the cross.*

Wherefore God also hath highly exalted Him, and given Him a Name which is above every name:

That at the Name of Jesus every knee should bow, of things in Heaven, and things in earth, and things under the earth;

And that every tongue should confess that Jesus Christ is Lord, to the glory of God the Father. Engl. Trans.]

SERM.
IX.
The sum.

"For this cause God hath exalted Him," saith the text; "Him," that is, Christ. And "for this cause" are we now here, to celebrate this exalting. Of which His exalting this is the first day, and the act of this day the first step of it; even His rising again from the dead. *Hæc est clarificatio Domini nostri Jesu Christi, quæ ab Ejus resurrectione sumpsit exordium,* saith St. Augustine upon this place; 'this now is the glorifying of our Lord Jesus Christ, which took His beginning at His glorious resurrection.' [S. August. Tract. in Joann. 104. 3.]

This is the sum and substance of this text set down by that learned Father.

By him also is it likewise divided to our hands; into *humilitas claritatis meritum,* and *claritas humilitatis præmium.* 'Humility, the merit of glory,' in the first verse of the four; and glory, the reward of humility, in the other three. Which two, here and ever, are so fast linked together as there is no parting them. I cannot but touch, and I will but touch, the merit in the first verse—it properly pertains to another day; and so come to *opus diei.* The division. I.

The matter of this day's exaltation is called here, His exaltation. II.

And is of two sorts. By God, in the ninth verse; and by us, in the two last.

By God; and that is double: of His Person; of His Name. Two *supers,* either, one. *Super-exaltavit Ipsum,* His Person; there is one in the forepart of the ninth verse. And *Nomen super omne nomen,* His Name; there is the other in the latter part of it. And this is God's. 1.

Then cometh ours. For God exalting it Himself, He will have us to do the like. And not to do it inwardly alone, but even outwardly to acknowledge it for such; and sets down precisely this acknowledgment, how He will have it made by us. Namely, two ways; by the knee, by the tongue. The "knee," to "bow" to it; the "tongue" to "confess" it. And both these to be general; "every knee," "every tongue." And not in gross, but deduced into three several ranks: all in "Heaven," all in "earth," all "under the earth;" which comprehends all indeed, and leaves none out. This acknowledgment, thus, but only, insinuated by the knee, is by the tongue more plainly expressed; and this is it, that Jesus Christ is the Lord, Lord of all those three. This to be done, and so done, as it redound all "to the glory of God the Father." 2. 1. 2. Phil. 2. 10, 11. 3. 4.

SE R M.
IX.

Phil. 2. 5.

But then last, take the use with us ; that since in Him His *humiliavit Seipsum* ends in *super-exaltavit Deus,* His humbling Himself in God's exalting, that "the same mind" be in us, and the same end shall come to us. As His end was, so ours shall be, "the glory of God the Father."

L

Phil. 2. 8.

Propter quod, " for this cause." We touch first upon this word. It is the *axis* and *cardo,* the very point whereupon the whole text turneth.

1.
Propter.

Isa. 22. 15.
Esther 3. 1.
Neh. 4. 1.

First, *propter ;* a cause there is. So God exalts ever, for a cause. Here on earth, otherwhile, there is an *exaltavit* without a *propter quod.* Some, as Shebna, Haman, Sanballat, sometimes exalted, no man knows wherefore. With God there goeth ever, with men there should go, a *propter quod* before *exaltavit.*

2.
Propter quod.

For a cause. For what ? " for this cause." And this now casts us back to the former verse where it is set down, *humiliavit ;* there it is for His humility.

Humiliavit.

Lu. i. 48.

2 Cor. 4. 6.

Now of all causes, not for that, if we go by this world, which, as the proverb is, was made for the presumptuous. Not for that virtue of all others. A virtue, before Christ thus graced it, so out of request as the philosophers—look into their Ethics, you shall not so much as find the name of humility in the list of all their virtues. Well, this cast virtue of no reckoning is here made the *propter quod* of Christ's exalting, as *respexit humilitatem* the ground of His Mother's *magnificat.* And He That by Him, "brought light out of darkness" at the first, will by Him bring glory out of humility at last, or this book deceiveth us. With God, it shall have the place of a *propter quod,* how poor account soever we make of it here.

1. *Ipse.*

Phil. ii. 6.

But this *quod* is a collective ; there be in it more points than one. I will but point at them.

Humiliavit Ipse, " He humbled." " He," which many times is idle, but here a circumstance of great weight. " He," so great a person, " being in the form of God, and without any disparagement at all, equal to God," as he tells us a verse before, " He humbled." *Ubi Majestatem præmisit, ut humilitatem illustraret ;* ' That discourse of His High Majesty was but to set out, to give a lustre to His humility.' For, for one of mean estate to be humble, is no great praise, it were a fault if he were not. But *in alto nihil altum sapere :* for a king, as David, to say, " I will yet be more humble ;" 2 Sam.6.22. for the King of kings, for Him, to shew this great humility, that is a *propter quod* indeed. *Humiliavit Ipse.*

Then secondly, that *humiliavit Ipse Se. Ipse Se,* and not 2. *Se. alius Ipsum,* that He was not brought to it by any other, but of His own accord, " He humbled Himself." There is a difference between *humilis* and *humiliatus.* One may be humbled, and yet not humble. Pharaoh was humbled, brought down, by his ten plagues. Simon of Cyrene, *anga-* Ex. 10. 16. *riatus,* to humble his neck under the cross. This was *alius* Mat. 27. 32. *ipsos.* But *Ipse Se,* is the true humility. For then it is *laudabili voluntate,* not *miserabili necessitate ;* ' of a willing mind, and that is commendable, not of force and constraint, for that is miserable.' " For this cause," that " He humbled Himself."

And thirdly, *humiliavit Ipse Se obediens.* It was not Ab- 3. *Obediens.* salom's humility, in show and compliment, and his heart 2 Sam.15.5. full of pride, disobedience, yea rebellion. And yet it is a glory for humility, that even proud men take a pride to shroud themselves in her mantle, that pride wears humility's livery. But it is not humble courtesy, but humble obedience, that is the *propter quod.* Till it come to that, many bear themselves in terms and show low *ad humum,* even touch the ground. But come once thither, to obedience; then give laws they must, but obey none; make others obedient, and ye will, but not *factus obediens,* not made themselves so. Christ was so " made." And " for this cause."

And something strange it is, why *humiliavit Ipse Se obe-* 4. *Factus. diens,* would not serve, and no more, but *factus* must be added. Somewhat there was in that. An obedience there is that cometh from the *dictamen* of natural reason ; in some things we so obey, we will do it because our reason so moveth us. That is, *obediens natus.* But some other there be, wherein there is no other reason to lead us to do it but only this, that it is enjoined us by a lawful superior, and therefore we do it, and for no other cause. This is *obediens factus,* and that in true proper terms is the right obedience indeed. All look to the former, and very few obey thus.

S E R M. But even so obeyed Christ, *et erat subditus illis.* And for

IX. this cause then, that He was *factus obediens.*

Lu. 2. 51.

5. *Usque.* And *obediens factus usque,* is a fifth. For the very size,
the extent of our obedience, is a matter considerable. For
Acts 26. 28. if we come to any, it is Agrippa's *in modico,* "in some petty
1 Sam.15.9. small matter." Or Saul's, in the refuse of the spoils little
worth. And that obedience is little worth, that is so shrunk
up. The drawing out, the *usque* of it is all in all. How far
obedient? until what? *usque quo?* Which very extent or
usque is many times as much worth as the obedience itself.
This also will come into the *propter quod.*

Phil. 2. 7. Now many *usques* there be in this of His! 1. *Usque
naturam hominis,*—thither. His very humanity had been
humility enough. 2. *Usque formam servi,* is more. How?
1 Sam. 25. Even "to wash the feet of thy servants," said Abigail, and
41.
Joh. 13. 5. took herself to be very humble in so saying. Thither He
came too.

6 *Mortem.* What say ye to *usque mortem,* the sixth point? *Mortem?*
that will stagger the best of us. We love obedience in a
Job 2. 4. whole skin; *usque* any thing, rather than that. And to say
truth, no reason in the world obedience should come to
Rom. 6. 23. that. "Death is the wages of sin," of disobedience. *Factus
obediens?* What, and *factus reus* too? Obedient, and yet
put to death? Heaven and earth should ring of it, if the
case were ours. Well, even thither came His obedience;
et, ne perderet obedientiam, perdidit vitam, 'and rather than
to lose His obedience, lost His life.' This is indeed, a great
propter quod.

7. *Mortem* Enough now, for death is *ultima linea* [1] we say. Nay,
autem cru- there is yet an *autem* more behind, to make it up full seven.
cis.
[[1] Hor. Ep. For one death is worse than another. And His was *mortem
1. 16. 79.] autem,* the worst death of all, the death of malefactors, and
of the worst sort of malefactors, *mortem crucis.*

Nay, if He must die, let Him die an honest, a fair death.
Not so; nay *morte turpissimá,* said they of it that put Him
Phil. 2. 8. to it, the foulest death of all other; *usque mortem, mortem
autem crucis.*

Died, and so died. Ever the *so,* the manner is more than
the thing itself, in all of Christ. To be born, so to be born,
Lu. 2. 7. *usque presepe,* 'to the cratch;' to die, nay so to die, *usque*

crucem, 'to the cross.' *Usque naturam hominis, usque for-mam servi, usque mortem malefici.* 1. So great a person; 2. Thus to humble; 3. Humble His Ownself; 4. To be obedient; 5. To be made obedient; 6. Obedient with an *usque,* so far; 7. So far as to death; 8. And to a death so opprobrious;—these extensives, and intensives put togteher, will I trust make up a perfect *propter quod.* And this for *humilitas claritatis meritum* in the first verse.

Now, for *claritas humilitatis præmium,* in the rest. And II. will ye observe how they answer one another? For *humilia-vit* there, here is *exaltavit;* for *Ipse* there, *Deus,* "God" Phil. 2. 9. here; for *Ipse Se, Deus Ipsum;* "He humbled Himself," "God exalted Him." For *humiliavit usque* there, here is *exaltavit super.* For *factus obediens* there, here *factus Do-minus.* For *mortem crucis,* "the death of the cross" there, here is "the glory of God the Father."

This exalting we reduced to two; 1. of His Person; 2. of *Super-exaltavit* His Name. Of His Person, in *super-exaltavit Ipsum;* of His *Ipsum.* Name in the rest of the verse.

To begin with His personal exaltation. *Super-exaltavit,* is a de-compound. There is *ex* and *super* both in it. His exalting hath an *ex,* whence or out of what; His exalting hath a *super,* whither or whereunto.

Ex, from whence? from the two very last words, *mortem* Ex. *crucis.* His raising to life opposed to *mortem,* the sorrows of death. The giving of His Name, to *crucis,* the shame of the cross. This day's *ex* was from death. His *humiliavit* had been *ad humum,* 'to the ground;' nay farther, into the ground; nay farther yet, εἰς κατώτερα, "into the very lowest Eph. 4. 9. parts of it." His *exaltavit* then was from thence, from death; and not "the gates of death"—then He was not in; Ps. 9. 13. nor "the jaws of death"—then He was not quite down; but Ps. 49. 15. from *inferiora,* and *interiora,* "the lowermost" and "inner- Prov. 7. 27. most" rooms of death. From under the stone—thence; Mat. 28. 2. from the dungeon, with Joseph; from the bottom of the Gen. 40. 15. den, with Daniel; from the belly of the whale, with Jonas; Dan. 6. 23. —all three types of Him; there is His *ex.* Jonah 2. 10.

Now then, whither? From death to life, from shame to Super. glory, from a death of shame to a life of glory. From the

SERM.
IX.
form of a servant in *factus obediens,* to the dignity of a Sovereign in *factus Dominus.*

Rom. 5. 15. But will ye mark again? For *non sicut delictum, sic donum,* saith he elsewhere; so here, not as His humbling, so was His exalting, but more. That of His humbling was dispatched in one verse; This of His exalting hath no less than three. So the amends is large, three to one.

But that is not it I mean, but this. *Super* is not thither only, but above and beyond it. From death to life; nay, Joh. 11. 44. *super,* more than so. Not to Lazarus' life, to die again, but Joh. 10. 10. to life immortal, *ut vitam habeat et abundantius habeat ;*—that *abundantius* is immortality. From shame to glory? only that? Nay, *super,* "to the glory of the Father," that is, 1 Pet. 1. 4. glory that shall "never fade," as all here shall. So downward, it was but *usque,* had his stint, so far, and no farther; upward now it is, *super,* no stint, but higher and higher still.

Lev. 23. 10. This day is the feast of the first fruits. On it, He had no more, but the first-fruits of His exalting. He was exalted, Jon. 2. 10. but with Jonah's exaltation only, from the lower parts to the upper parts of the earth. But we shall follow Him higher, to 2 Kings 2. the exaltation of Elias, *super,* 'above' the clouds; nay, *super,* 11. 'above' the stars, above the Heavens, and the Heavens of the Heavens, till we have brought Him from *de profundis* to *in excelsis,* 'from the lowest part of the earth' to 'the highest place in Heaven,' even to the right hand of God. And higher we cannot go.

Will ye observe yet once more a kind of omen or presage of both these exaltings, and that at the very time of His humiliation? For even that His humiliation was acted after the manner of an exalting, though in a mere mockery. For, to all their disgraces, they added this of scorn. They lift Judges 16. Him up upon His cross, for all the world as the Philistines 25. Mark 15. did Samson; set Him aloft "between the two pillars," to 16. 19. Mark 15.18. make sport at Him. This was His exaltation. And they gave Him a name too, Pilate's title over His head, and bowed their knees, and cried, *Ave Rex*—a kind of confession.

This, as they performed it, was *grande ludibrium ;* but as God turneth it, it was *grande mysterium.* For, to earnest

God turneth both. A kind of strife there seemed to be: the
lower they, the higher God; the more odious they sought to
make Him, the more glorious God; He exalted His Person,
instead of the cross, to His own high throne of majesty.
And instead of Pilate's title, gave Him a title of true honour,
above all the titles in the world.

And this for *super-exaltavit Ipsum.* And so I pass from the
exalting of His Person, the amends for *mortem,* and come to
the exalting of His Name, the amends for *crucis,* in the latter
part of the same verse.

"He gave Him a name." For without a name, what is *Dedit Ei*
exalting? What is His Nativity without an Epiphany? For *nomen.*
to those two may these two here well be compared. His resurrection is a very Nativity. To it doth St. Paul apply the
verse of the Psalm, *Hodie genui Te;* and this name-giving *Acts 13.33.*
is as the Epiphany, to make it apparent and known to the
world. And indeed, why are things exalted or lift up, but
that they may be in view, and notice taken of them? So
that they which be exalted, seem not so to be, till their so
being be made public, and there go a name of it abroad in
the world.

And sure, when men are so high as higher they cannot be,
as Kings, there is no other way to exalt them left us but this;
to spread abroad, to dilate their names. Which every noble
generous spirit had rather have than any dignity, though
never so high. For being in their dignities, how far will they
venture, even to jeopard dignity, life and all, and all but to
leave a glorious name behind them! That to give a name, is
even to exalt his very exaltation itself, and to make him,
that is at the highest, higher yet.

"A name He gave Him:" what name? not *inter* 'among' *Super om-*
the famous names on earth, but *super omne nomen,* 'above *ne nomen.*
them all.' Here is *super* upon *super,* another *super* to His
Name, no less than His Person. That above all persons, and
this above all names whatsoever. And now by this time His
exaltation is complete, and not one *super* to be added more.

This name is named in the verse, and it is "the Name of
Jesus." Of the giving first, and then of the *super,* of it. *Dedit Ei.*

Of the giving, three doubts arise: 1. How given Him, and
others had it also? 2. How given now, and He had it before,

SERM.
IX.

even in the womb of His mother? 3. How given Him of grace, and yet He deserved it? Propter quod.

1.
Others
had it.
Heb. 4. 8.
Hag. 1. 1.
Mat. 1. 21.

How is this name said to be given Him as some special dignity, and others had it beside and before Him? Jesus the worthy, the son of Nun; Jesus the high Priest, the son of Josedech, to say nothing of Jesus the son of Sirach. They had it, it is true, but not given them by God, as He by the mouth of the Angel, God's deputy. But they by men, had men to their god-fathers, as now we have a sect or society of Jesus; but they gave themselves the name, God never gave it them. He gave it here for *humiliavit*, a virtue they little regard; for he that doth but smell of it, is *eo ipso* not meet to be of that company. Other manner spirits they.

Sermon at
Christmas,
1610.
Zech. 8. 23.

I have before this told you of four main differences, between this Jesus and all others. This one now shall serve for all. All those Jesuses, and every one of them, had need of, and were glad " to lay hold of the skirts" of this Jesus, to be saved by Him : otherwise they had been falsely so called, lost men all. And so will be willing to resign this name to Him that He may bear it, at least with a main difference from them all.

Dedit Ei.
2.
He had it
before.
Mat. 27. 42.
Joh. 10. 18.
Heb. 5. 9.

But what tell ye us of it now after the Resurrection? Do not we know it was given Him, being yet in the womb? It was so, but by a kind of anticipation. For it never had the perfect verifying, the full Christendom, as they say, till this day. Not yet full three days since, they upbraided Him with it. Jesus a Saviour! A wise Saviour, and " cannot save Himself!" For He seemed to perish then, to lose His life in their sight; but now, this day "taking it again," He shewed He did but lay it down, He lost it not; He was now Jesus indeed, able to save Himself; and able to save all those that trust in Him for their salvation. So it was never in kind till now, but now it was.

Dedit Ei.
3.
He did
merit it.
1 Cor. 7. 3.

But if He gave it Him, and ἐχαρίσατο, "gave it Him of grace," where is the merit then? the *propter quod* we spake of, what is become of that? Safe enough for all this. That which is otherwise due, it may be so cheerfully parted with, as if it were a frank and free gift indeed. The Apostle elsewhere hath taught us to join *debita* and *benevolentia* in one; they will stand together well enough.

In many things we suffer slander by the Church of Rome;

in this among many, as if we pinched at Christ's merit, and
were loath He should be allowed Himself to merit aught,
because of this ἐχαρίσατο, that soundeth all upon grace.
Wherein it is well known, take the most can be made of it,
and we say no other thing than do their own schoolmen. It
is not *gratia adoptionis*, this, ' the grace of adoption,' as in us,
that is here spoken of; it is *gratia unionis*, 'the grace of
union.' And that grace Christ had. For seeing in the
humanity of Christ, there was not, there could not be, any
possibility of merit, to deserve the uniting itself, or the being
assumed into the Godhead; to be so assumed and so united,
was that grace we termed the grace of union. Other grace
we know none in Christ. But being once so united, there
was in Him to deserve, and deserve again, and that amply.
Propter quod, might then be truly said of Him every way.

This for the giving. But now, how is this Name said to be *Super*
" above all names?" what, above the Name of God? We *omne.*
may say with the Apostle when he saith, "God did give it "Above all
Him," "it is manifest He is excepted" That did give it Him. 1Cor.15.27.
But we need not so say, for this is one of God's own names.
" I am, saith He, and beside Me there is no Saviour." Isa. 43. 11.

How is it then given Him? *Accipit ut homo quod habebat
ut Deus;* ' What as God He had, as man He received;' with
His nature His name, and the chief of all His names, the
Name of a Saviour. For above all it is, above all to Him,
above all to us.

To Him: for though many titles of the Deity sound and Above all
seem to be more glorious, yet He esteems them all not like to Him.
this. Why? For no other reason but that they had not
nos homines, and *nostram Salutem*, in them. No name He
sets by like that, wherein with His glory is joined our safety.
And this of all He made choice of, as to Him above all, that
we might accordingly esteem of Him That esteems it above
all, only for our sakes.

But howsoever to Him, to us sure above all. For no name Above all
do we hold by, "no name under Heaven given us whereby to us.
we may be saved, but it." To us more worth it is than all; Acts 4. 12.
yea, I may say, than the very name of God. For "God in
Him reconcileth the world;" without Him is enemy to it, 2 Cor.5. 19.
and to us. So with this name there is comfort in the name

z

of God; without it none at all. The name sure which we
have use of above all. For it is the name which in the
depth of all our distress, by sin or by misery, we even adjure
Him by, *ut rem nominis impleat,* 'that He make good His
own name,' shew He bears it not for nought, and so save us;
that He would never so remember our wretched sins, as that.
thereby to forget His own blessed name, that name specially,
which He of all other most esteemeth, and so of all other will
least forget. To Him then and to us both, it is *nomen super
omne nomen.* And so let it be, even *suprema lex salus,* and
supremum nomen Jesus, 'to save the highest law, and the
name of a Saviour the highest name.' Let it so be, let it
ever stand highest, and let no name whatsoever get above it.
And so I come to the tenth verse.

Phil. 2. 10.
"At the
name of
Jesus."
"That at the name of Jesus," &c. To give Him such a
name, is one gift; to give Him, that for such an one it
should be reputed and taken, is another. For given it may
be on His part, and not acknowledged on ours. So that this
is a new degree.

That God, though He have so exalted it, yet reckons it
not exalted, unless we do our parts also, unless our exaltation
come too. At which words comes in our duty, the part that
concerns us. Thus to esteem it *super omne nomen,* "above
all," and in sign we so do, to declare as much. And therein
He leaves us not to ourselves, but prescribes the very manner of our declaration, how He will have it, namely, these two
ways; "The knee to bow to it," "the tongue to confess it."

"Knee"
and
"tongue."
Now these are outward acts, both. So then, first we are
to set down this for a ground, that the exalting of the soul
within is not enough. More is required by Him, more to
be performed by us. He will not have the inward parts
only, and it skills not for the outward members, though
we favour our knees, and lock up our lips. No, mental
devotion will not serve, He will have both corporal and vocal
to express it by.

Our body is to afford her part, to His glory; and the parts
of our body, and namely, these two, the knee, and the tongue.
Not only the upper parts, the tongue in our head, but even
the nether also, the knee in our leg. The words be plain, I
see not how we can avoid them.

For the "knee," two things : 1. He would have it "bow ;" "Knee
2. He would have it "bow" to His Name. "Bow," first; for 1.
what better way, or more proper, than by our humility to 2.
exalt Him Who for His humility was exalted? Or what
way more fit, to express our humility by, than by this sign
of humbleness? For a special way it is of exalting, or
making a thing high, by falling down and making ourselves
low before it. Then secondly, that God careth for our
knees, will be served with them. Negatively; He will not
have them "bow to Baal." Positively ; He will have them 1 Kings 19.
"bow" to Himself. Will ye believe Him if He bind it with 18.
an oath? "I have sworn," saith He, "by Myself, that Isa. 45. 23.
every knee shall bow to Me." And will ye make God for-
sworn? And it cannot be said, this is Old Testament, for
even in the New these very words are applied to Christ, as Rom.14.11.
meant to be fulfilled in and to Him.

But this here in the text is more strong, that it is assigned
Him, this honour, as a part of His reward for *mortem crucis.*
And shall we rob Him, or take from Him the reward of His
Passion ?

We begin our Liturgy every day with the Psalm—and we
had it from the Primitive Church, they did begin theirs with
the same—wherein we invite ourselves to it; "Come, let Ps. 95. 6.
us worship and fall down, and kneel before the Lord our
Maker." Shall we ever say it, and never do it? Is not this
to mock God ?

They in the Scripture[a], they in the Primitive Church [b],
did so, did "bow." And verily, He will not have us worship Him like elephants, as if we had no joints in our knees ;
He will have more honour of men, than of the pillars in the
Church. He will have us "bow the knees ;" and let us
"bow" them in God's Name.

To "bow the knee," and to His name to bow it; for this Bow to His
Name.

[a] Flexis Genibus Orantes Reges.
David, Ps. 95. 6. Solomon, 1 Kings
8. 54. Ezekias, 2 Chron. 29. 30.— Pro-
phetæ; Daniel, Dan. 6. 10. Ezra,
Ezra 9. 5. Micah, Mic. 6. 6.—Chris-
tus Ipse ; Luke 22. 41.—Apostoli ;
Petrus, Act. 9. 40. Paulus, Eph. 3.
14. Jacobus, Hegesip. 5 lib. apud
Hieron. [Tom. 4. p. 2. 101. *Ben.
Edit.*] Stephanus, Acts 7. 60. Ec-

clesia idque ipsa Pentecoste, Acts 20.
36. 21. 5.
[b] Euseb. Hist. l. 5. c. 5. Tertul.
contra Marc. lib. 3. cap. 18., et De
corona Mil. cap. 3. Athanas. in vitâ
Anton. fere in fine. Basil apud Œcum.
Nazian. Orat. 2. de Filio, Sive 36. Hieron. in Eph. 3. et in loc. Aug. de curâ
pro mort. gerend. c. 5. Theoph. Alex.
Ep. Pasc. 2. Cæsar. Arel. Hom. 34.

SERM.
IX.

Acts 1. 9.

Ps. 16. 2.

Ps. 111. 9.

Mat. 2. 11.

is another prerogative. He is exalted to whose person knees do bow; but He to whose name only, much more. But the cause is here otherwise. For His person is taken up out of our sight, all we can do will not reach unto it. But His name He hath left behind to us, that we may shew by our reverence and respect to it, how much we esteem Him, how true the Psalm shall be, " Holy and reverend is His name."

But if we have much ado to get it, "bow" at all, much more shall we have to get it done to His name. 1. There be that do it not.

2. What speak I of not doing it ? There be that not only forbear to do it themselves, but put themselves to an evil occupation, to find faults where none is, and cast scruples into men's minds, by no means to do it.

3. Not to do it at His name? Nay, at the holy mysteries themselves not to do it. Where His name is, I am sure, and more than His name, even the body and blood of our Lord Jesus Christ; and those, not without His soul; nor that without His deity; nor all these, without inestimable high benefits of grace attending on them. And yet they that would be glad and fain, a pardon for this life, or some other patent, with all humility to receive upon their knees; this so great, so high, so heavenly a gift, they strain and make dangerous, to bow their knees to receive it; as if it were scarce worth so much. But it hath ever been the manner in Christ's Church, whether we offer to Him, or[c] receive aught offered from Him, in this wise to do it.

But to keep us to the Name, this is sure, the words themselves are so plain as they are able to convince any man's conscience; and there is no writer, not of the ancient, on this place, that I can find, save he that turned all into allegories, but literally understands it, and likes well enough we should actually perform it.

Yet will ye see, what subtilties are taken up to shift this duty ?

All knees are called for, and all have not knees. Here are three ranks reckoned, and two of them have none. What is

---

[c] Chrysost. Hom. ad Pop. Antioc. 61.
Ambros. in Ps. 118. bis. Et lib. 3.
cap. 12. de Spir. S. Aug. Epist. 120.
cap. 27. Amb. Hex. lib. 6. cap. 9.
Hieron. in Isa. 45. 23. Cyril. in Isa.
tom. 4. Orat. 3. 1.

that to us? we have. To us it is properly spoken, and we to look to it. And if this were aught, that the spirits in Heaven and hell have no bodies, and so no knees, why, they have no tongues neither properly, and then by the same rule, take away confessing too, and so do neither.

But the Apostle, that in another place gives the Angels 1 Cor. 13. 1. tongues, "with the tongues of men and angels," might as well in this place, give them knees; they have one as much as the other. And in both places *humanum dicit*, he speaks to us, "after the manner of men," that we by our own Rom. 6. 19. language might conceive what they do. For sure it is, the spirits of both kinds, as they do yield reverence, so they have their ways and means to express it, by somewhat ἀναλογὸν to the knee. They do it their way, we to do it ours. And this is ours: let us look to our own then, and not busy our brains about theirs. But for us, and for our sakes, they are divers times expressed in the Revelation, even doing thus, Rev. 4. 10. "falling down before Him." Rev. 5. 8. 14.

Secondly, why to this name, more than to the name of Rev. 7. 11. Christ? There want not reasons why. 2. "The

Christ is not, cannot be, the name of God: God cannot name of be anointed. But Jesus is the name of God, and the chief Jesus." name of God, as we have heard.

The name Christ is communicated by Him to others, namely to princes; so is not Jesus, that is proper. *Ego* Isa. 43. 11. *sum, et præter Me non est alius.* And ever that which is proper is above that which is holden in common.

Christ is anointed to what end? to be our Saviour. That is the end then. And ever, the end is above the means; ever the name of health, above the name of any medicine.

But when we find expressly in the verse, this name is exalted above all names, and this act limited to it in direct words, and so this name above them in this very peculiar, why seek we any farther?

Thirdly, What? to the two syllables, or to the sound of 3. them? What needs this? Who speaks of sound or syllables? The text saith, do it to the Name. The name is not the sound but the sense. The caution is easy then, do it to the sense: have mind on Him that is named, and do His Name the honour, and spare not.

S E R M.
IX.
4.

Fourthly, but it cannot be denied but there hath superstition been used in it. Suppose there hath. And almost, in what not? In hearing of sermons now, is there not superstition in a great many? What shall we do then? Lay them down? abandon hearing, as we do kneeling? I trow not, but remove the superstition, and retain them still; do but even so here, and all is at an end.

Indeed, if it were a taken-up worship, or some human injunction, it might perhaps be drawn within the case of the 2 Kings
18. 4. brazen serpent. But being thus directly set down by God Himself, in us there may be superstition, in it there can be none. And if it be in us, we are to mend ourselves, but not to stir the act, which is of God's own prescribing. It was never heard in divinity, that ever superstition could abolish a duty of the text.

That we set ourselves to drive away superstition, it is well; but it will be well too that we so drive it away, as we drive not all reverent regard and decency away with it also. And are we not well toward it? we have driven it from our head, for we keep on of all hands; and from our knees, for kneel we may not—we use not, I am sure. Sure heed would be taken, that by taking heed we prove not superstitious we slip not into the other extreme before we be aware, which of the two extremes religion worse endureth, as more opposite unto it. For believe this, as it may be superstitiously used, so it may irreligiously be neglected also.

Look to the text then, and let no man persuade you but that God requireth a reverent carriage, even of the body itself; and namely, this service of the knee, and that to His Son's Name. Ye shall not displease Him by it, fear not; fear this rather for the knee, if it will not bow, that it shall be stricken with somewhat, that it shall not be able to bow. And for the Name, that they that will do no honour to it, when time of need comes, shall receive no comfort by it. And so I leave this point.

The
tongue.
Ps. 30. 12.
Ps. 57. 8. For the knee is not all, He farther requires somewhat from the tongue. And reason: that member of all other the Psalmist calls our "glory," a peculiar we have more than the beasts; they will be taught to bow and bend their joints, we have tongues besides to do something more than they. And

indeed, the knee is but a dumb acknowledgment, doth but signify *implicite;* but a vocal confession, that doth utter our mind plainly. And so is looked for at our hands.

This he calls ἐξομολόγησις. Three things are in it; first To con-
fess. λόγος—speak we must, say somewhat. And secondly, ὁμοῦ, do it together; not some speak, and some sit mute. And thirdly, ἐξ, speak out, not whispering or between the teeth, but clearly and audibly. And this is ἐξομολόγησις. And it was the praise of the primitive Church, this, that jointly they did it and aloud; that their Amen, as St. Hierome saith, was [S. Hieron. like a clap of thunder, and their Allelujah as the roaring of 2. Prooem. the sea; and no praise it is to us, who as our joints are stiff Galat.] to bow, so our voices are hoarse to confess. We can neither see the former, nor scarce hear the latter; as if, there being but two duties in the text, we meant to suppress them both.

The "knee" and the "tongue." Why the knee first? why "Knee" begins He there? They be marshalled right. For having first, and then by our "knee" bowed, put ourselves in mind of due regard "tongue." of Him in fear and reverence, we are then the fitter to speak of Him and to Him with that respect is meet; and not be so homely with Him as in their gesture and speech both some are, as if they were Hail fellow, even familiar with God. And all forsooth, as they call it, to cast out the spirit of bondage. From a heart possessed with the humble fear of God, from such an heart, confession is ever most kindly; faith being as the heart, and fear being as the lungs—so the Fathers compare them; it will get an heat and an over-heat, our faith, if by fear, as cool air, it be not tempered; but faith and fear together make the blessed mixture.

The tongue and "every tongue," as the knee and "every "Every knee;" they to bow all, and these all to confess. But for "Every all that, not all alike. They in Heaven "cast down their tongue." crowns, and fall down" themselves of their own accord; and Rev. 4. 10. confess Him singing, as at His birth, and in the Revelation, Lu. 2. 14. Rev. 15. 3. divers times. They under the earth do it too, but not *ultro,* Rev. 4. 8. Rev. 5. 9. are thrown down, and even made His "foot-stool." So down Ps. 110. 1. they go, though sore against their wills; and confess Him Mark 9. 26. too though roaring, and as it were upon the rack. They on 2. earth, as in the midst, partake of both. The better sort, with the Angels, get them to their knees gladly, and cheerfully

SERM. confess Him. The rest, as Infidels and some Christians little
IX.   better, are forced to "fall backward," and made in the end
3.
Joh. 18. 6. to cry *Vicisti Galilæe,* though "they gnaw their tongues"
Rev. 16. 10. when they have done.

So we see our lot; one way or other we shall come to it
all: if not now, *in die illo,* which is the reason that the
Rom. 14. Apostle applieth this place in Esay to Christ's sitting in
11.
judgment at the latter day. Exalted He shall be with our
[Isa. 45. good wills, or whether we will or no. Either fall on our
21.]
knees now, or be cast flat on our faces then; either confess Him *cantando,* with Saints and Angels, or *ululando,* with
devils and damned spirits. For the Father will be glorified
in the Son, by the glorious confession of them that yield, or
the glorious confusion of them that stand out.

"Every   The tongue and "every tongue;" that is, every speech,
tongue."
dialect, idiom, language in the world, stand charged with
Ps. 150. this confession. *Omnis spiritus,* "every spirit" to give breath,
ult.
and *omnis lingua,* "every tongue" to be as a trumpet to sound
it forth. And where are they then that deny any tongue the
faculty here granted, or bar any of them the duty here enjoined? That lock up the public confession, the chief of all
other, in some one tongue or two, and send forth their *super-
sedeas* to all the rest? No, His title here hath more tongues
than Pilate's on the cross; that had but three, this hath
"every tongue," what, where, whose-soever, none except. A
præludium whereof was in the "tongues" sent from Heaven,
Acts 2. 4. whereby every nation under Heaven "heard, each in their
11.
own tongue spoken," *magnalia Dei,* the glad tidings of the
Gospel.

"Confess   But though thus many tongues, yet one confession. Even
that Jesus
Christ is   this, that "Jesus Christ is the Lord." And a blessed con-
the Lord."
fession is it, this, that Jesus, that is, a Saviour, that He, that
such a one, "is the Lord;" that not a fleecer or a flayer, but
a Saviour hath the place. 2. That Christ, that is, one which
saveth and cureth *unctione non punctione,* with anointing not
with searing or pricking—that we acknowledge Him to be
"the Lord." "Lord" before by that He is Son, and now
Lord again by virtue of His *propter quod.*

"Lord" whereof? Nay not qualified of such a place,
barony, county, signory, but Lord *in abstracto.* But if we

will qualify Him we may. Lord of these three ranks of con-
fessors here in the verse, and of those three places and re-
gions that contain them: 1. "Lord of Heaven"—He gave Mat. 16. 19.
"the keys" of it. 2. Lord of earth—He hath "the key of Rev. 3. 7.
David," and if of his, of every kingdom else. 3. Lord of Rev. 1. 18.
hell, for lo, "the keys of hell and of death." "Of death," to
unlock the graves; "of hell," to lock up "the old dragon" Rev. 20. 2,
and his crew, into the bottomless pit. A great Lord; for 3.
whither shall one go to get out of His dominion.

Well, if it be but to confess this, that is no great matter,
we will not stick with Him: who cannot say, "Jesus Christ
is the Lord?" That "can no man," saith the Apostle—say 1 Cor. 12. 3.
it as it should be said, "but by the Holy Ghost." For confessing Him Lord, we confess more things by Him than one.
For two things go to it. 1. St. Peter gives us one, 2. St. Paul,
the other. 1. *Domine salva, pereo,* saith St. Peter; "Save Mat. 14. 30.
Lord, I sink:"—a Lord to save. 2. *Domine quid me vis* Acts 9. 6.
facere? saith St. Paul. "Lord what service wouldst Thou I
should do?"—a Lord to serve.

St. Peter's we like well, to succour and save us, when we
are in any danger; He shall hear of us then. But St. Paul's
Quid me vis facere? when it comes to that, then our confession fumbles and sticks in our teeth. Nay then, *Quis est* Ps. 12. 4.
Dominus noster? we have no Lord, we then. So we play
fast and loose with our confession; fast at succour, loose at
service; in at one, out at the other.

But what speak I of doing His will? when, if He do not
ours in each respect; if we have not this or that when we
would, we fall from confessing, and fall to murmuring. And
it fareth with us, not as if He were Lord and we to do His
will, but as if we indeed were the lords and He to do ours:
as if there were nothing between us and Him, but He to do
our turns, and then, *Tu autem Domine,* His Lordship were
expired and at an end.

Upon the point thus it is; we confess it the wrong way,
the Lord to be Jesus, but not Jesus to be the Lord. O Lord,
be Jesus; but not, O Jesus, be Lord. O Lord, be Jesus to
save us; but not, O Jesus, be Lord to command us. So that
all our *humiliavit* still is without *factus obediens.*

Ye see then, it is worth the while to confess this, as it

SERM.
IX.

should be confessed. In this wise none can do it but "by the Holy Ghost." Otherwise, for an *ore tenus* only, our own ghost will serve well enough. But that is not it. *Quid me vis facere?* is it that makes "the Lord." He tells us so Himself, and with a kind of admiration that any should

Lu. 6. 46.

think otherwise; "How call ye Me Lord," saith He, "and do not as I will you?" As much to say as, It is to no pur-

Mat. 7. 21.

pose, though you say *Domine, Domine;* double it, and treble

Tit. 1. 16.

it too, it will go for no confession, if a *factis negant* come in the neck of it, if St. Paul's *Quid me vis facere?* be left out.

"Confess to the glory of God the Father."

And this is yet more plain by the last words of all, namely, that this confession is so to be made, as it redound "to the glory of God the Father." Whose great glory it is, that His Son is Lord of such servants, that men shall say, See what servants He hath! How full of reverence to His Name! How free, how forward to do His will! Herein is His Name much magnified. As on the other side it must

Rom. 2. 24.

needs be "evil spoken of, and that among the very heathen," when not a knee got to bow; when this syllable, Lord, comes out of our mouth, but no *Quid me vis facere?* to follow it. When they see how unservice-like our service is, how rude our behaviour toward Him and His Name, Whom we term Lord indeed, but use Him nothing so. But come hither into His presence, and carry ourselves here for all the world as the fellow did before Augustus, of whom Mæcenas well said: *Hic homo erubescit timere Cæsarem.* And so we, as if we were ashamed to seem to bear any reverence at all to Him, or His name. It would not be thus. I am privy there is no one thing doth more alien those that of a simple mind refuse the Church, than this, that they see so unseemly behaviour, so small reverence shewed this way. But sure, the Apostle tells us our carriage there should be such, so decent, as if a stranger or unbeliever should come into our assem-blies, the very reverence he there seeth, should make him

1Cor. 14.25.

fall down and say, "Verily God is among us," to see us so respectfully bear ourselves in the manner of our worship.

"Jesus is the Lord to the glory of God the Father."

This confession that "Jesus is the Lord," is to be "to the glory of God the Father:" so we take it one way. Or this confession is to be, "that Jesus is the Lord to the glory of God the Father:" so another way. And both well. To

" confess" that He is " the Lord," that all His Lordship is not to His own glory, but to His Father's. Think not then that *gloria Filio* shall abate aught of *gloria Patri.* The Son is " Lord to the glory of His Father," and not otherwise. Let that fear then be far from us, that in exalting the Son we shall in the least minute eclipse the glory of His Father. Here is no fear of emulation, that it will prove the case of Jupiter and Saturn. No, so blessed is the accord of this Father and this Son, as the Father thinketh it some blemish to His glory, if so profound humility, so complete obedience, He had not seen highly rewarded with *super* upon *super.* And the Son will admit of no glory that shall impair His Father's in the least degree; for lo, " He is Lord to the glory of God His Father." This is the end of His, of Christ's, and the same may be the end of all exaltations; that a Saviour ever may be " Lord,"—hold that place, and hold it and be " Lord," not to His own, but " to the glory of God," even " God the Father."

The end of all, and we must needs know and take that with us, for which all this here is brought. And it is a lesson, even His *Discite a Me;* and it is a pattern, even His *exemplum dedi vobis,* to commend unto us the virtue of the text, the *propter quod* of the feast, even humility; *hoc erit signum,* it is His sign at Christmas. As His sign then, so His *propter quod* now at Easter; so the virtue of both feasts. I will offer you but three short points touching it. *The conclusion.* Mat. 11. 29. Joh. 13. 15. Lu. 2. 12.

It is no humble man is set before us here, it is the Son of God, and Himself God; *et quomodo non humiliatur homo, coram humili Deo?* How is not the son of man humble, and the Son of God is? Even for Him to love it, for His very Person. 1. *Humiliavit.* Christ's Person.

And in this verse He is not barely set out to us, but in it and by it bringing to pass the works of our redemption, which cannot but extraordinarily commend this virtue to us; in that it hath pleased God to do more for us in this His humility, than ever He did in all His Majesty, even to save and redeem us by it. To love it then, if not for Him, yet " for the work's sake." 2. Work. Joh. 10. 38. Joh. 14. 11.

But specially, which is the third, for the *propter quod* in the text; if not for the work, yet for the reward's sake. That 3. Reward.

SERM.
IX.
as Christ was no loser by it no more shall we, for all this glory here, the way to it, is by the first verse. *Humiliavit* is the beginning, and the end of it is exalting. That the mother, this the daughter; all riseth from *humiliavit Ipse Se.*

Jas. 4. 10.
1 Pet. 5. 6.
Humiliamini ergo, saith St. James; *humiliamini ergo,* saith St. Peter; and after it there followeth still, *et exaltabit vos Deus,* a promise of a like glorious end. And what saith the

Phil. 2. 5.
Apostle here? "This mind," saith he, "was in Christ," and it was φρονεῖν, a wise mind; that we count it a wise mind, and worth the carrying, and carry it; and it shall carry us to the same journey's end it brought Him, even "to the glory of God the Father." This for humility.

Obediens Domino.
And what? Shall we not give some light trial of our obedience also, to aver our confession, that He is our Lord? It would be by *Domine, quid nos vis facere?* that is the true trial. Say then *Domine, quid nos vis facere?* and He will answer us, *Hoc facite in Mei memoriam.* Will ye know what

[Luke 22. 19.]
I would have you do? "Do this, in remembrance of Me." In sign that I am Lord, do but this; here is a case of instance, and that now, even at this very present, a proof to be made. By this we shall see, whether He be Lord or no.

2 Kings 5. 13.
For if not this, but slip the collar here, and shrink away; *si rem grandem dixisset,* in a far greater matter, how would we stand with Him then? We were wrong before; here is the sound and syllables we spake of, here it is. For all is but sound and syllables, if not this.

Heb. 6. 9.
But of us, "I hope for better things," that by our humble carriage and obedience, at least in this, we will set ourselves some way to exalt Him, in this His day of exaltation; which, as it will tend to His glory, so will He turn it to matter of our glory, and that in His kingdom of glory; or to keep the word of the text, "in the glory of God the Father." That so we may end, as the text ends. A better or more blessed end there cannot be. And to this blessed end He bring us, That by His humility and obedience, hath not only purchased it

[1 Joh. 2. 1.]
for us, but set the way open, and gone it before us, "Jesus Christ the Righteous," &c.!

A SERMON

THE KING'S MAJESTY AT WHITEHALL,

ON THE NINTH OF APRIL, A.D. MDCXV. BEING EASTER-DAY.

JOHN ii. 19.

Jesus answered and said, Dissolve (or destroy) this Temple,
  and within three days I will raise it up again.

Respondit Jesus et dixit eis Solvite Templum hoc, et in tribus diebus
  excitabo illud.

[*Jesus answered and said unto them, Destroy this Temple, and in*
  three days I will raise it up. Engl. Trans.]

HE "answered and said" this to the Pharisees, who sought ^{The occa-} "a sign" of Him the verse next before. A sign they would ^{sion:} have, and He tells them, a sign they should have. Them- ^{Joh. 2. 18.} selves should minister Him occasion to shew a sign, the like was never shewn. For destroy Him they should, His body so, and He within three days would raise it again from death to life.

But this answer of His is a figurative speech, and runs ^{The} under the terms of the Temple. The reason whereof was, ^{speech, figurative.} they were then in the Temple; there, fell out this question. And as it appeareth in the verses before, much ado there had been between them, and that a long time, about the Temple.

Now His manner still was—the place, the time, the matter in hand, ever to frame the tenor and terms of His speech, according to them. And so, now being in the Temple, He takes His terms from thence, even from the Temple.

But He doth, as I may say, *solvere Templum hoc,* loose ^{The figure} and undo this term for us; for within a verse we are told, ^{inter-preted.} this Temple is no other than "the Temple of His body." ^{Joh. 2. 21.}

SERM.
X.

Now the rest follows of itself. The *solvite* is a taking Him in sunder, His soul from His body; the *excitabo* is the setting them together, and raising them up again. And both these "within three days," the only word in the text wherein there is no figure.

How a sign in the true sense.

And this now was His sign, and a great sign it was. Great, even in their sense if it had been but of the pile of building, as they took the word Temple. But greater far, far another manner sign in His sense, in the true.

For, as for that Temple, Zerubbabel and Herod had raised it, and other great persons as great buildings as that. But the Temple of the body, if that were once down, all the Temple-builders that ever were, with all their care and cost could never get it up more. Therefore in His, in Christ's sense, it is far the greater sign, than as they fancied it.

Lu. 16. 30.

Indeed, so great a sign as he that was in hell fire could not devise, nor did not desire a greater. If but Lazarus, "if but one come from the dead," then, then regard him; that sign out of question. Why here is one come from the dead, and this day come, and a greater than Lazarus. I trust then we will regard Him, we will regard this sign, and not be worse than he in hell was. Let us then regard it.

The division.

The ground of the sign, and of all here, is *Templum hoc.* About it two main acts, they shew forth themselves; the razing of it down in *solvite*, the raising of it up in *excitabo*. These in figure. Answerable to these, this temple is Christ's body. The razing it down, is Christ crucified and slain. The raising it up, is Christ restored to life.

Of which two, to divide it by the persons, *solvite* is their part, *excitabo* His. That, His Passion by their act—*solvite;* This, His Resurrection by His own,—*excitabo.*

Now this He saith shall be done, and saith farther shall not be long in doing, no longer than three days. And within the compass of the time limited He did it; for this is now the third day, and to day by sun-rising it was done.

I.
II.
III.
IV.

So upon the matter, there come to be handled these four points: I. That Christ's body is *Templum hoc.* II. The dissolution of it by death, in *solvite.* III. The rearing it up again by His resurrection, in *excitabo.* IV. The time to do it in, three days.

By which circumstance of three days, and this day the
third of them, cometh this time to claim a kind of property
in this passage of Scripture. And that, two ways.

For first, at this feast were these words here spoken; you
may see they were so, at the thirteenth verse before, at the
feast of Easter.

And secondly, at this feast again were they fulfilled after;
the *solvite* three days since, the *excitabo* this very day. So at
this feast the promise, and at the very same the accomplishment of it. The accomplishment once, the memorial ever.

Being then at this very time thus spoken and done; spoken
here now, done three years after; being, I say, spoken and
done, and at this time spoken and done, never so fit as now.

Solvite Templum hoc. Templum hoc, we begin with. It
is a borrowed term, but we cannot miss the sense of it; for
both are set down here to our hand, the wrong sense and the
right. The wrong, the next verse of all, for the material
Temple. So the Pharisees took it, and mistook it. The
right, the next verse after, for the "Temple of His body."
So they should have taken it, for so He meant it. *Ipse autem
dicebat, &c.* "But He spake of the Temple of His body."
And He knew His own meaning best, and reason would
should be His own interpreter.

And this meaning of His it had been no hard matter
for them to have hit on, but they came but a birding, but
to catch from Him some advantage, and so were willing to
mistake Him. At this they caught as an advantage we see,
and laid it up for a rainy day, and three years after out they
came with it, and framed an indictment upon it, as if He
had meant to have destroyed their Temple.

But was it likely, or could it once be imagined, He meant
to destroy it? It was God's house. And "the zeal of God's
house," but even a verse before "consumed Him." And
doth His zeal now, like the zeal of our times, consume God's
house? What, and that so quickly? but a verse between?
But even very now He purged it, and did He purge it
to have it pulled down? That were preposterous. Now,
it was purged, pull it down? Nay, pull it down, when it
was polluted: now it is cleansed, let it stand. To reform
Churches, and then seek to dissolve them, will be counted

I.
The two
senses of
*Templum
hoc.*
Joh. 2. 20.

Joh. 2. 21.

Mat. 26. 61.
Mark14.58.

The Phari-
sees' sense
could not
be true.
Joh. 2. 17.

S E R M. among the errors of our age. Christ was far from it. He
    X.
———— that would not see it abused, would never endure to have it
destroyed; specially not when He had reformed the abuses;
and yet more specially, not even presently upon it, they
might be sure.

But that which must needs lead them to the right meaning was, that these words, *Templum hoc,* He could not say
them, but by the manner of His uttering them, by His very
gesture, at the delivery of this particle *hoc,* they must needs
know what Temple it was He intended. It was easy to
mark whether He carried His hand, or cast His eye up to
the fabric of it, or whether He bare them to His body;
which one thing only was enough to have resolved them of
this point, and to quit our Saviour of equivocation.

The true   We will then wave theirs as the wrong meaning, and take
sense.   it, as he wisheth, who "leant on His breast" and best knew
Joh. 13. 23.
His mind, of "the Temple of His body."

1.   But what resemblance is there between a body and a
A body,   Temple? or how can a body be so termed? Well enough;
a temple.
for I ask, why is it a Temple? What makes it so? Is it not
Joh. 2. 16. because it is *Domus Patris Mei,* as He said a little before,
because God dwelleth there? For as that wherein man
dwells is a house, so that wherein God, is a Temple properly. That I say wherein, be it place or be it body. So
come we to have two sorts of Temples; Temples of flesh
and bone, as well as Temples of lime and stone. For if our
bodies be termed houses, because our souls, tenant-wise,
abide and dwell in them; if because our souls dwell they
be houses, if God do so they be Temples: why not? Why
1 Cor. 6. 19. not? why "know ye not this," saith the Apostle, "that your
very bodies, if the Spirit of God abide in them," *eo ipso,*
"Temples they be"—such as they be? But then they be
so specially, when actually we employ them in the service
of God. For being in His Temple, and there serving Him,
then if ever they be *Templa in Templo,* 'living Temples in a
Temple without life. A body then may be a Temple, even
this of ours.

2.   And if ours, these of ours I say, in which the Spirit of God
Christ's   dwelleth only by some gift or grace, with how much better
body a
"temple." right, better infinitely, His body, Christ's, "in Whom the
Col. 2. 9.

whole Godhead, in all the fulness of it, dwelt corporally!" "Corporally" I say, and not spiritually alone as in us; by nature, by personal union, not as in us by grace, and by participation of it only. Again, if ours which we suffer oft to be polluted with sin, that many times they stand shut up, and no service in them for a long season together, how much more His that never was defiled with any the least sin, never shut but continually taken up, and wholly employed in His Father's service? His above all exception, His without all comparison certainly. Alas ours but tabernacles under goatskins; His the true, the marble, the cedar Temple indeed. Christ's body then a Temple.

But a Temple at large will not serve. It must be *Templum hoc*, that very Temple they took it for. And so we to proceed yet farther, and to seek a congruity of His body with the material Temple it was taken for, to which there is no doubt His intent was to resemble it.

8. Christ's body, "this Temple," or *Templum hoc*.

The Rabbins, in their speculative divinity, do much busy themselves to shew, that in the Temple there was a model of the whole world, and that all the spheres in Heaven, and all the elements in earth were recapitulate in it. They were wide. The Fathers took the right, and bestowed their time and travail more to the point, to shew how that Temple and all that was in it was nothing else but a compendious representation of Christ, for Whom and in Whose honour was that and all other true Temples. And this they did by warrant from the Apostle, who in Heb. ix. aimeth at some such thing.

Heb. 9. 5.

Now the points of congruity they found were many, they may be reduced to these four: 1. Whether you look to the composition or parts of it; 2. Or, to the furniture, and vessels of it; 3. Or, to what was done in it; 4. Or, to what was done to it, that is, what first and last befel it. In all which they hold, that *Templum hoc* might more truly be affirmed of Him That was in the Temple, than of the Temple He was in.

Christ's body, *et Templum hoc* wherein the like.

The last of the four, what was done to that Temple, what befel it, and so what befel the Temple of Christ's body, that I take to be most proper to this text, and to that we have in hand. For to go through all four, would take up a whole sermon. So I take myself to the congruity only.

A a

SERM.
X.

Mark then what befel either: by that shall you best find that *fata utriusque Templi,* 'the destinies of both Temples' were alike.

Ps. 132. 6.
Mat. 2. 1.
[Ps. 87. 5.]

They began alike. The first news of the Temple was heard " at Ephratah," which is " Bethlehem." So was it of Him, for "there was He born."

Like in *solvite, et excitabo.*

Like in their beginnings, and in their ends no less. I appeal to this text, and content me with those two He insists on Himself. Both were destroyed, both were reared again, that in all things His Body and His Temple might be suitable.

2 Chron. 36. 19.
Ps. 137. 7.

That Temple was destroyed by the Chaldees: "down with it even unto the ground." Imitated by them here: down with it, even into the ground. For they never left it, till they had Him there, past *excitabo* as they thought, past rising any more. But as the Temple after it was so razed

Hag. 1. 14.

had an *excitabo*, was raised again up by Zerubbabel, so was this too. *Solvite* took place, but there came an *excitabo*

Hag. 2. 9.

after, that made amends for it. And as " the glory of the second house was greater than the first," so the estate He rose to, far more glorious than that He was in before.

And mark, I pray you, if these two were not to be seen as brim in the little glasses about it, as in the great mirror itself. For the Temple was as a great mirror, and the furniture as so many little glasses round about it. Take but the ark, the epitome as it were of the Temple. The two tables in it, the

Col. 2. 3.
Ex. 32. 19.
Ex. 34. 4.

type of the true " treasures of wisdom and knowledge" hid in Him, they were broken first—there is *solvite;* but they were new hewn and written over again,—there is *excitabo.* " The pot of manna," a perfect resemblance of Him (the *urna* or the vessel being made of earth, so earthly; the manna, the con-

Ex. 16. 20, 24.

tents of it, being from Heaven, so Heavenly;) the manna, we know, would not keep past two days at the most—there is *solvite;* but being put into the *urna,* the third day it came

Ex. 16. 33.

again to itself, and kept in the pot without putrifying ever after—there is *excitabo.* Aaron's rod, the type of His Priesthood and of the rule of souls annexed to it, that rod was

Nu. 17. 8.

quite dead and dry, but revived again and " blossomed," yea " brought forth ripe almonds." In every and in each of them His destiny Whom they represented, *solvite* and *excitabo* in all.

But the end is all in all; and in respect of that, of the end, well saith Ambrose of His body, *Vere Templum in quo nostrorum est purificati peccatorum;* 'Truly a Temple He, no Temple ever so truly, as wherein was offered up the true propitiation for, and the true purification of our sins,' and of us from them; which is the end of all temples that ever were or shall be, and was but shadowed in all besides, but in this truly performed. [S. Ambros. in Ps. 47. Enar. circ. med.]

There, the only true holocaust of His entire obedience which burnt in Him bright and clear, from the first to the last, all His life long. [See Lev. 6. 9.]

There, the only true "trespass-offering" of His Death and Passion, the *solvite* of this Temple, satisfactory to the full, for all the trespasses and transgressions of the whole world. [See Lev. 5. 6.]

There, the "meat and drink-offering" of His blessed Body and most precious Blood. [See Lev. 2. 1.]

And the *exta* of this sacrifice, the fat of the entrails of it, that is the love wherewith He did it, "the desire," the longing desire He had to it; that, that, was the perfect offering, that "set at one all things both in Heaven and earth." That whatever was *sub figurâ in Templo illo*, was really and in truth exhibited *in Templo hoc.* Lu. 12. 50. Lu. 22. 15. Col. 1. 20.

And judge now whether the sign were not well laid by our Saviour in the Temple, which was itself a sign of Him. And whether as He said in a place, *Ecce major Templo hîc*, so He might not have said *Ecce majus Templum hîc*, when He was in the Temple; 'behold, a greater, a truer Temple now in the Temple,' than the Temple itself. Mat. 12. 6.

Now to the second main point, *solvite.* 2. The saying it first, the executing it after. The *solvite*, and the *solutum est.* II. A solvite, the saying.

1. First, by *solvite*, that is, dissolving, is meant death. *Cupio dissolvi*—ye know what that is; and *Tempus dissolutionis meæ instat*, "the time of my dissolution," that is, my death, "is at hand." For death is a very dissolution, a loosing the cement the soul and body are held together with. Which two, as a frame or fabric, are compaginate at first; and after, as the timber from the lime, or the lime from the stone, so are they taken in sunder again. But death is not this way only a loosing, but a farther than this. For upon the loosing the soul from the body, and life from both, there 1. *Solvite.* Death a loosing. Phil. 1. 23. 2 Tim. 4. 6.

SERM.
X.
follows an universal loosing of all the bonds and knots here;
of the father from the son, and otherwhile of the son from
the father first; of man from wife, of friend from friend, of
prince from people :—so great a *solvite* is death, makes all
that is fast loose, makes all knots fly in sunder.

2. *Solvite.*
Violent.
2. And all this in natural death. But a farther matter
there is in *solvite.* For that is against nature, *aliis solventi-
bus,* by the hands of other that are the *solventes,* them to
whom this is spoken. This temple drops not down for age
or weakness, dissolves not of itself; others, they to whom
solvite is here said, they pull it down. It is then no natural
but a violent death, this. Well therefore turned *solvite,* " destroy it;" there is no destruction but with force or violence.

3. *Solvite.*
Voluntary.
3. So violent though on theirs, as voluntary yet on His
part. Not against His will quite, not by constraint; for He
Himself That is to be dissolved, He it is doth here say *solvite.*
He could have avoided it, if He would; He would not; in
sign He would not, we see, Himself saith *solvite.* And *solvite*
He must have said, He must have said it, or they could not
have done it. It had passed all their cunning and strength
to have undone this knot ever, but that He gave way to it.

4. Gave way to it, I say, that we take not this *solvite*
otherwise than He meant it. It is not of the nature of a
charge, this, nor we so to conceive it. Very expedient it is
that we know the nature of *solvite Templum.*

2. *Solvite
Templum,*
no com-
mandment.
Rom. 2. 22.
Solvite Templum is no commandment, be sure, in no sense;
He commands not any Temple, not that they themselves
meant, to be destroyed; it were sacrilege that, and no better.
And sacrilege the Apostle ranks with idolatry, as being full
out as evil, if not worse than it.

But indeed worse; for what idolatry but pollutes, sacrilege
pulls quite down. And easier it is to new-hallow a Temple
polluted, than to build one anew out of an heap of stones.

And if but to spoil a Church be sacrilege, as it is granted,
yet that leaves somewhat, at least the walls and the roof, so
Ps. 137. 7.
it be not lead; to leave nothing, but " down with it," is the
cry of Edom, the worst cry, the worst sacrilege of all, and
never given in charge by God to any, we may be sure.

1 Kings
8. 18.
2 Chron.
6. 8.
For God Himself said to David with His own mouth,
" Whereas it was in thine heart to build Me an house, thou

didst well that thou wert so minded." "Didst well?" well done, to think of building? then *a sensu contrario,* evil done to think of dissolving. And that which is evil Christ will never enjoin.

But what is to be thought of *solvite Templum,* I would have you to judge by these two, they be both in the text. 1. To whom this is spoken. 2. And what is meant by it. *1. To whom* *Solvite* *Templum* *is said.*

1. To whom this is spoken. *Distingue tempora* is a good rule; so is *distingue personas.* Distinguish the persons then, give every one his own, it will make you love *solvite Templum* the worse, as long as you know it. *Solvite?* To whom is this spoken? Who be they? The Pharisees. To them is this speech directed. That is made their work, work for a Pharisee, to dissolve Churches. And so it was. For as hot and holy as they seemed, with their "broad phylacteries" and "long prayers," our Saviour saith "they loved the gold of the Temple better than the Temple." So do their posterity, to this day. To the Pharisees then with them, to their marrows[1], that would fain hear *solvite* given in charge. The other person is Christ; Christ's word and work both is *excitabo; excitator Templorum* He, a raiser of them, a raiser of them when they be down, we see here. They will not let them stand when they be up. Christ, He sets them up for His part; when you will have them down, you must bespeak some Pharisee, and they will do it, *leviter rogati.* For as His speech to them is *solvite et excitabo,* so theirs to Him may seem to be *excita et solvemus.* Set up as many as He will, they will down with them; first with *Templum hoc,* then with *Templum illud,* and so one after another, if they may have their will; they lack but one to give the *solvite* to them, and to set them on work. *Distingue personas* then, and they to whom *solvite* is said, are but bad persons certainly, and fit for a bad business. *Mat. 23. 5, 14.* *Mat. 23. 17.* [1 The word "marrow" is used to signify an equal match.]

2. Will ye mark again, what is meant here by it, by destroying the Temple? What, but even the killing of Christ? Now the suiting and sorting of these two thus hath but an evil aspect neither, but this worse than the former though. And I wish but this one point well printed in all men's minds. *Solvite Templum, quid vult dicere? Solvite Templum, id est, occidite Christum;* that he that goes about to 'dissolve the *What is* *meant by* *solvite* *Templum.*

SERM.
X.

Church, it is all one as if he went about to make away Christ.' One of these is implied under the other. Enough, I think, to take off the edge of any that are glad to hear, and ready to catch *solvite Templum* out of Christ's mouth, but quite besides His meaning. For His meaning was, and it was one special end of Christ's comparing His body to the Temple, to shew, He would have us so to make account of the Temple, and so to use it, as we would His own very body; and to be as far from destroying one, as wewould be from the other. This may suffice, to let you know the nature of *solvite Templum* once for all, that you be not mistaken in it.

3. *Solvite Templum hoc.* Not by way of command,

3. Of *solvite Templum* I say. But now, to come to *solvite Templum hoc*, to "the Temple of His Body." Concerning it, that it should enter into any man's heart to think, Christ would open His mouth to command or to counsel His own making away, that is, the committing the most horrible foul murder that ever was—God forbid! It was a sin out of measure sinful, that, if ever any were. And give me any religion rather than that, that draweth God into the society of sin; makes Him, or makes Christ, either Author or Adviser, Commander or Counsellor, of aught that is evil. Any, I say, rather than that.

But by way of prediction.

Isa. 47. 1.

1. How then? if no command, what is it? All that can be made of it, say the ancient Fathers, is but either a prediction in the style of the Prophets, "Come down Babel,"—that is, Babel shall be brought down; so *solvite*, "ye shall destroy," to warn them what He saw they were now casting about, and whither their malice would carry them in the end, even to be "the destroyers and murderers" of

Acts 7. 52.

the Son of God.

By way of permission.

2. Either this, or at most but a permission, which in all tongues is ever made in this mood, in the imperative. So we use to say, Go to, do an ye will, or do what ye will with my body, when we mean but sufferance for all that, and no command at all. For all the world this *solvite* to them, as

Joh. 13. 27.

fac cito to Judas after. *Quod facis*, "that which you are resolved to do," and have taken earnest upon it, *fac*, "do it," and *fac cito*, "do it out of the way," which yet, it is well known, was nothing but a permission, and not a jot more.

2. But should such, so foul an evil as that, be permitted

though? No, nor that neither, simply; it is not a bare per- Permitted
mission, but one qualified, and that with two limitations,— for a
greater
Will ye mark them? 1. For first, He would not suffer any good.
evil at all, least of all that, but that out of the evil He was
able, able and willing both, to draw far a greater good.
Greater for good I say, than that was for evil. And that
was *solutionem peccati ex solutione Templi.*

For we are not to think, that He would thus down with
it, and up with it again, only to shew them feats and tricks
as it were to be wondered at, and for no other end. No,
the end was the destroying of sin by the destroying this
Temple. It went hard, *et væ tibi atrocitas peccati nostri,*
' and woe to the heinousness of our sins,' for the dissolving
whereof neither the Priest might be suffered to live, nor the
temple to stand; but the Priest be slain, and the Temple be
pulled down, Priest and Temple and all be destroyed. But
sin was so riveted into our nature; and again, our nature so
incorporate into His, as no dissolving the one without the
dissolution of the other. No way to overwhelm sin quite,
but by the fall of this Temple. The ruin of it like that of
Samson's. That the destruction of the Philistines, this Judges 16.
30.
" the dissolving of all the works of the devil." It is St. 1 Joh. 3. 8.
John's own term, *ut solveret opera diaboli.*

2. But neither was this enough yet, neither would He for Permitted,
all this have at any hand let it go down, but that withal He for another
as good.
meant to have it up again presently. Never have said *solvite,*
but with an *excitabo* straight upon it; which is a full amends,
so that the Temple loses nothing by the loosing.

The world with us hath seen a *solvite,* without any *excitabo;*
down with this, but nothing raised in the stead. But that is
none of His; *solvite* without *excitabo,* none of Christ's. We
see with one breath He undertakes it shall up again, and
that in a short time; there is amends for *solvite.*

And so now with these two limitations, under these two
conditions—1. one, of a greater good by it: the other of
another as good or better in lieu of it—may *solvite* be said
permissive; and otherwise not, by any warrant from Christ
or from His example.

And thus you have heard what He saith. Will ye now 2. *Solvite,*
see what they did, what became of this *solvite* of His? the doing.

Solvite, saith He, and when time came they did it. But He said *solvite,* that is "loose," and they cried *crucifige* at the time, that is, fasten, "fasten Him to the cross;" but that fastening was His loosing, for it lost Him and cost Him His life, which was the *solutum est* of this *solvite.*

For indeed, *solutum est Templum hoc,* this Temple of His body, the Spirit from the flesh, the flesh from the blood was loosed quite. The roof of it, His head, loosed with thorns, the foundation, His feet, with nails. The side aisles as it were, His hands both, likewise. And His body as the body of the Temple, and His heart in the midst of His body as the *Sanctum Sanctorum,* with the spear loosed all. What He said they did, and did it home.

More than *solvite.* Nay, they went beyond their commission, and did more than *solvere.* A thing may be loosed gently, without any rigour; they loosed Him not, but rudely they rent and rived Him, one part from another, with all extremity; left not one piece of the *continuum* whole together. With their whips they loosed not, but tore His skin and flesh all over; with their hammers and nails they did not *solvere,* but *fodere* His hands and feet; with the wreath of thorns they loosed not, but gored His head round about; and with the spear point rived the very heart of Him, as if He had said to them, *Dilaniate,* and not *solvite.* For as if it had come *è lani-endá,* it was not *corpus solutum,* but *lacerum;* 'His body not loosed, but mangled and broken,' *corpus quod frangitur;* and His blood not easily let out, but spilt and poured out, *sanguis qui funditur,* even like water upon the ground. Well is it turned "destroy;" it is more like a destruction than a solution, more than *solvite* it was sure.

1Cor.11.24.
Mat. 26. 28.

The *solvite* of this Temple sensible. Now will ye remember? This was a Temple of flesh and bone, not one of lime and stone. Yet the ragged ruins of one of them demolished will pity a man's heart to see them, and make him say, Alas poor stones, what have these done! yet the stones neither feel their beating down, nor see the deformed plight they lie in. But He *sic solutus est ut Se solvi sentiret,* 'the solution of His skin, flesh, hands, feet and head, He was sensible of all;' He saw the deformity, He felt the pains of them all.

So saw and so felt as with the very sight and sense, before

it came, there befel Him another *solvite*, a strange one; The *sol-vite* of this sweat.

solutus est in sudorem, the orifices of the veins all over the texture of His body were loosed, and all His blood let loose, Lu. 22. 44. that He was all over in a strange sweat, stood full of great drops of blood—a *solvite* never heard of nor read of, but in Him only.

And yet another *solvite*. For, that *solvite Templum hoc* The *solvite* of the veil. might every way be true, in all senses verified, what time the veil of His flesh rent, that His soul was loosed and departed, at the very same instant "the veil of the material Temple, Mat. 27. 51. that split also in two from the top to the bottom," as it were for company, or in a sympathy with Him; that it was literally true, this *solvite*, and of the Temple that they meant. And so, two *solvites* of both Temples together at once.

One more yet, and I have done with *solvite*, and that is The great *solvite* at His Passion. a *solvite* in a manner of all, of the great Temple of Heaven and earth. For the very face of Heaven, then all black and Mat. 27.51, dark at noon-day yet no eclipse, the moon was at the full, 52. the earth quaking, the stones renting, the graves opening as they then did, shewed plainly there was then toward some universal *solvite*, some great dissolution, as the philosopher Dion. then said, either of the frame of nature, or of the God of Areop. [See Lard-ner's Cred. Works, 7. 387, 8.] nature.

Cast your eye thither, look upon that, and there you shall see *solvite Templum hoc* plainly, and what it means. And it had been enough, if they had had any grace, even to have pointed them to the time when this *solvite Templum hoc* was fulfilled by them. And this for both *solvite* and *solutum est*, their part, which was His Passion, by their act.

Now, to answer them two, to *excitabo* and *excitavit*, His III. part, His resurrection, by His own. 1. *Ex-citabo* the saying.

And first to *excitabo*. Hitherto we are not come, but now we come to the sign, for the sign is in *excitabo*.

Ex excitabo, "And I will raise it up." Which is spoken, as it were, by way of triumph over all they could or should do to Him. Go to, "dissolve it, destroy it," down with it; when you have done your worst, it shall be in vain, *excitabo illud*, my power shall triumph over your malice; "I will raise it, I will up with it again."

But to loose and to raise, these two are not opposite;

SERM.
X.
Excitabo
how op-
posed to
solvite.
rather, to loose and to set together again. Raising is opposed
to falling, and resurrection to ruin, properly. But it comes
all to one. Upon the dissolving of any frame, straight down
it drops. This goodly Temple of our body, on the decking
and trimming whereof so much is daily wasted, loose the
soul from it but a moment, and down it falls, and there it
lies like a log we all know. In opposition to this fall, it is
said He will raise. But He will do both; as it was loosed
ere it fell, so will He set it together ere He raise it again.

    Excitabo illud. Three points there are in it: 1. the act,
2. and the Person, in *excitabo*, and 3. the thing itself in
illud.

Excitabo,
the act, as
from sleep.
    1. The act. The word He useth for it, ἐγερῶ, in propriety
is a raising from sleep; and sleep, we know, is far from
destruction. It is to shew us first what a strange metamor-
Ps. 16. 9.
phosis He would make in death, turn it but into a *requiescet,*
and a *requiescet in spe,* and there is all. So made He His
1Cor.15.20.
own, so will He make ours. This day "Christ is risen again,
Dan. 12. 2.
the first fruits of them that sleep;" and the rest "that sleep
in the dust," when their time comes, shall do the like.

    2. To shew, secondly, they should miss of their purpose
quite. They reckoned indeed to destroy Him; they were
deceived, they made Him but ready for a night's rest or two.
They made full account, death had devoured and digested
Him too; they were deceived, it was not so, death had but
Jon. 2. 10.
swallowed Him down, as the whale did Jonas, upon the
third day to cast Him up again.

    3. To shew, thirdly, not only that this He would do, but
with what ease He would do it. With no more difficulty
than one is waked up after a night's rest; with no more ado
than a knot that is but loose and untied, is tied again.

Excitabo,
the Person.
He Him-
self.
    But besides the act, we are to look to the Person in *exci-
tabo.* It is not, Destroy you, and some other shall raise it;
but I, even I Myself, and none but Myself, will do it; *nec
alienâ virtute sed propriâ,* 'and by none others beside, but by
Mine own proper virtue and power.' An argument of His
divine nature. For none ever did, none ever could do that.
Raised some were, but not any by himself or by his own
power, but by a power imparted to some Prophet by God
for that time and turn; Christ, by none imparted from any

other, but by His own from Himself. And let it not stumble
any that elsewhere the Father is said to raise and exalt Him;
that is all one. Both will stand well. The same power the
Father doth it by, by the same doth it He. There is but one
power of both; of both, or of either of them, it is alike truly
verified. This for the Person.

Now for the thing, *illud*. *Templum hoc* before, and *illud* *Illud.*
here: *hoc* and *illud* are not two, but one and the same. Not The same
Temple, in
solvite hoc, et suscitabo aliud; 'down with this, and I will up substance.
with another in the stead.' No; but *idem illud,* 'the very
same' again. The very same you destroy, that and no other
will I rear up again. With us, with the world, it is not so:
when we fall to dissolve a frame of government, suppose of
the Church, it is not *solvite hoc, et excitabo illud;*—no, but
excitabo aliud. We raise not the same but another, quite
another, nothing like it, a new one never heard of before.
But let them keep their *aliud,* and give us *illud* again. *Illud*
we love, it is Christ's *excitabo,* that; and if we follow Christ
in His raising, the same again, or not at all.

But though *illud* be the same again in substance, yet not Not the
in quality the same for all that; but so far different, as in same,
in quality.
that respect it may seem *aliud,* 'another' quite. At least
well may it now be called *illud,* as it were with an emphasis,
as qualified far beyond that it was before, when it was but
Templum hoc. And to say truth, if it be but the same just,
and no whit better, as good save His labour and let the first
stand. For it is but His labour for His travel, if nothing
won by it.

But if, though the same yet not in the same, but in a far
better estate than before; "cedar for mulberry, marble for Isa. 9. 10.
brick," as the Prophet speaks; then ye say somewhat, and
then we will be content to have it taken down.

And such was the estate of this Temple after the raising;
and such was it to be, for "the glory of the second house Hag. 2. 9.
was much greater than of the first." Which increase or
bettering is implied in the word *excitabo.* It is, I told you,
a rising up after sleep. Now in the morning after sleep, the
body riseth more fresh and full of vigour, than it was over
night when it lay down. The Apostle speaks it more plainly:
Templum hoc, saith he, at the loosing it was "in weakness, 1 Cor. 15.
42, 43.

SERM. dishonour, mortality;" *Templum illud,* at the raising it is
X. "in power and honour, and to immortality."

And sure, one special reason of the dissolving this Temple
was, that, as then it was, *solvite* might be said of it, it was
dissoluble. But being now raised again, it is faster wrought,
indissoluble now ; no *solvite* to be said, not to be loosed ever
any more. This for *excitabo illud.* Now the last point, of
the time. The sign is in that too.

IV. And when this? Within what time? "Within three
The time. days." Which words seemed to affect them most; all their
"Three exception lay to them. He looked not like one that would
days." build Churches. But let that pass, were He never so likely,
He takes too small a time for so great a work as they thought.
But if we agree once of His power to raise from death, the
time will slide, we shall never stick at it much, but agree of
that quickly. He that can raise from the dead—ten thousand Churches will be built one after another, before one be
raised thence—to Him that is able to do that, forty-six hours
are as good as forty-six years, all one. Nay, even forty-six
minutes, but that it was held fit He should lie longer in His
grave than so, that there might be the surer certainty of
His death. Otherwise, years, days or minutes, to Him are
all alike. The sign is in both, but to say truth in *excitabo,*
rather than in the three days. For to the power of *excitabo,*
nullum tempus occurrit.

Why three. But why three days just? Neither more nor less? Because, elsewhere He saith, no other time but Jonas' that
should serve Him. No other than Moses' time, forty days,
in His fasting. No other than Jonas' time, three, in His
rising. Content to keep time with His Prophets before
Him. Far from the humour of some, that must vary—no
remedy. If Jonas three, they must four, or three and a half
at least. If Moses forty, they must be a day under or over,
have a number, have a trick by themselves beyond others
still, else all is nothing worth. Far from them I say, and
to make us far from them; by His example to keep us to
that which others before us have well and orderly kept.

2. *Ex-* Now to the *excitavit* of this *excitabo.* Thus He said it
citavit, should be, *et fuit sic,* "and so it was." He would raise it
the doing. —*dixit;* and He did raise it—*factum est.* His dissolution

lasted no longer than His limitation beforehand set. That was not *post tres,* but *in tribus;* not 'after, but within the compass of three days.' And He came within His time, for this is but the third day, and this day by break of day was this Temple up again.

This then being the day, not only of *excitabo* but of *exci-* 1. Our tavit illud,* of the setting it up, accordingly we this day to these. duty upon celebrate the *encænia,* or new dedicating of this Temple. A To rejoice. dedication was ever a feast of joy, and that great joy. Every town had their wake in memory of the dedicating of their Church. That we then hold it as a feast of joy, that we be glad on it; as glad, nay more glad to see it up again this day, than the third day since we were sorry to see it down in the dust. To *solvite,* "down with it," Edom's cry, be- longs Jeremy's Lamentation; to *excitabo,* this day's work, [Lam. 2. 2.] Zachary's joyful shout or acclamation, *gratiam gratiæ,* "grace Zech. 4. 7. upon grace," and joy upon joy, and thanks upon thanks. Grace, joy, and thanks with an emphasis, for it is now *illud* with an emphasis indeed.

But our joy will quickly quail, if we no good by it. I ask For our then, what is all this to us? And I answer with the Apostle, good. Rom. 3. 2. *Multum per omnem modum.* 1. For first, this *solvite* of His By *solvite.* is a *solvite* to us; a loosing us, not only from our sins, "the cords of our sins" here, as Solomon calls them, but "the Prov. 5. 22. chains, the everlasting chains of darkness" and of hell, there Jude 6 due to them, and to us for them.

2. Then this *excitabo* is not to end in Him. What we By *excitabo.* believe He did for that Temple of His body natural, the same we faithfully trust He will do farther for another Temple, the Temple of His body mystical. For His mysti- cal as much as for His natural, for whose sake He gave His natural body thus to be dissolved. Of which mystical body we are parts, and the whole cannot be without his parts; every of us members of this body for his part, every one living stones of this spiritual Temple. *Dissipentur illa, re- staurabit denuo,* saith Origen, 'scattered we may be, He will [Conf. Orig. gather us again;' loosed, He will knit us; fall down and die, in loc.] He will set us together and set us up again. "After two days Hos. 6. 2. He will revive us, and in the third day raise us, and we shall live in His sight," saith the Prophet Osee, of us all.

SERM.   And this is to us all matter of great joy. For to this
X.
—————— *solvite* in the end we must all come; *statutum est hominibus,*
Heb. 9. 27. "there is an act passed" for the dissolution of these our
earthly tabernacles. Loosed they shall be, spirit from flesh,
flesh from bone, each bone from other—no avoiding it.

2. Our mo-   All our care to be this, how to come to a good *excitabo.*
ral duty.   Good I say, for *excitabo* we shall never need to take thought
for; we shall come to that, whether we care for it or no.
But to a good *excitabo,* such an one as He, as Christ, as this
Temple is come to, that is, to a joyful resurrection as we call
it. That is worth our care, for in the end that will be
worth all.

To make   That shall we come to, if we can take order that while we
our bodies
temples.   be here, before we go hence, our bodies, we get them tem-
plified as I may say, procure they be framed after the similitude of a Temple, this Temple in the text; for if it be *solvite
Templum,* at the dissolution a Temple, a Temple it will rise
again, there is no doubt of that.

Our bodies, as we use the matter—many of us, are far from
Temples; rather *prostibula* than *Templa,* ' brothel-houses,
brokers'-shops, wine-casks, or I wot not what, rather than
Temples.' Or if Temples, Temples the wrong way, of Ceres,
Bacchus, Venus; or, to keep the Scripture phrase, of Chemosh, Ashtoreth, Baal-peor, and not *Domus Patris Mei,* as
this here He speaks of.

But if this be the fruit of our life, and we have no other
but this, to fill and farce our bodies, to make them shrines of
pride, and to maintain them in this excess, to make a money-
change of all besides, commonwealth, Church and all; I
know not well what to say to it, I doubt at their rising they
Rev. 3. 12. will rather make blocks for hell fire, than be made "pillars
Heb. 9. 11. in the Temple of God," "in the holy places made without
hands."

Otherwise, if they prove to be Temples here, let no man
doubt then, let them be loosed when or how they will, He
that raised this Temple, so they be Temples, will raise them
likewise; and that, to the same glorious estate Himself was
raised to.

The moral   A course then must be taken, that while we are here, we
solvite of
them.   do *solvere Templa hæc,* ' dissolve these Temples' of Chemosh

and Ashtoreth, and upon the dissolution of them we raise
them up very Temples to the true and living God; that we
down with Beth-aven, "this house or shop of vanity," as by
nature they are, and up with Bethel, "God's house," as by
grace they may be.

For a *solvite* and an *excitabo* we are to pass here in this The moral.
life, and this, this *excitabo*, in the first resurrection here to be *Excitabo.*
passed. "He that hath his part in this first, he shall not fail Rev. 20. 6.
but have it in the second."

If then Temples they would be, that we so make them, for
to make them so is the *excitabo* of this life.

And so shall we make them, even Temples; and no way That they
sooner, than if we love this place, the Temple, well, and love may be
temples.
to resort to it, and to be much in it. By being much in it,
we shall even turn into it. And sure, if ever we have *aliquid
Templi*, 'any thing of a Temple' in us, then it is when we are
duly and devoutly occupied and employed, they and we, in
His worship and service. Then are we Temples.

But to be Temples is not all, we are farther to be *Templum* Temples.
hoc, "this Temple;" and this was "the Temple of His Body." *Corporis
sui.*
And that are we, if at any time, then certainly when as if we
were Temples in very deed, we prepare to receive, not the
Ark of His presence, but Himself, that He may come into us
and be in us; which is at what time we present ourselves to
receive His blessed Body and Blood; that Body and that
Blood which for our sakes was dissolved, dissolved three days
since when it suffered for our sins. And this day raised again,
when it "rose for our justification." Rom. 4. 25.

Which when we do, that is, receive this Body or this
Temple, for *Templum hoc* and *Hoc est Corpus Meum* are now
come to be one, for both *Templum hoc* and *corpus hoc* are
in *Templum corporis Sui* ; and when the temples of our body
are in this Temple, and the Temple of His Body in the
temples of ours, then are there three Temples in one, a
Trinity, the perfectest number of all. Then if ever are we,
not Temples only, but *Templa corporis Sui*, 'Temples of His
Body,' and this Scripture fulfilled in us.

This are we when we receive. Now at no time is this act This feast
of receiving so proper, so in season, as this very day—so hath a fit time
for it.
Christ's Church thought it, and so practised it ever—the very

day of this His *excitabo*, the day of His rising, and by means of it, of our raising ; our raising first, to the life of righteousness, to the estate of Temples here in this world, and after, of our raising again to the second, the life of glory and bliss, of glorious temples in the world to come, which is the *excitabo* when all is done. What time they and we shall be loosed as now from sin, so then from corruption; and raised and restored, as now to the estate of grace, so then to the state of glory, and glorious liberty of the sons of God. To which happy and blessed estate, may He raise us all in the end, That this day was raised for us, &c.!

A SERMON

PREACHED BEFORE

THE KING'S MAJESTY, AT WHITEHALL,

ON THE THIRTY-FIRST OF MARCH, A.D. MDCXVI. BEING EASTER-DAY.

---

1 PETER i. 3, 4.

Blessed be God and the Father of our Lord Jesus Christ,
*   Which according to His abundant mercy hath begotten us*
*   again unto a lively hope, by the resurrection of Jesus Christ*
*   from the dead,*
To an inheritance incorruptible and undefiled, and that fadeth
*   not away, reserved in Heaven for you.*

[*Benedictus Deus et Pater Domini nostri Jesu Christi, Qui secundum*
*   misericordiam Suam magnam regeneravit nos in spem vivam, per*
*   resurrectionem Jesu Christi ex mortuis,*
In hæreditatem incorruptibilem, et incontaminatam, et immarcescibilem,
*   conservatam in cælis in vobis.*   Latin Vulg.]

[*Blessed be the God and Father of our Lord Jesus Christ, Which*
*   according to His abundant mercy hath begotten us again unto a*
*   lively hope by the resurrection of Jesus Christ from the dead,*
To an inheritance incorruptible and undefiled, and that fadeth not
*   away, reserved in Heaven for you.*   Engl. Trans.]

THE sum of this text, and if ye will the name of it too, is The sum. set down in the very first word of it. It is a *Benedictus;* the first word is so. The first word *Benedictus,* and if you look, the last word is "for you." Give me leave to read it "for us," to put in ourselves, seeing to us and for us it was written. So a *Benedictus* it is, from us to God, for something coming from God to, or "for us."

Something? Nay many. *Benedictus* is but one word, but the first word; the rest of the words of both the verses, are "for us" all.

B b

And many they are. We reduce them to three: 1. Our regeneration which is past; 2. Our hope, which is present; 3. and our inheritance, which is to come. 1. Regenerating or begetting, is of itself a benefit; we get life by it, if nothing else. 2. But to beget to an inheritance, is more than simply to beget. 3. And yet more than that, to beget to such an inheritance as this, of which so many excellent things are here spoken.

Three then, in this: 1. To be begotten; 2. To be begotten to inherit; 3. To be begotten to inherit such an inheritance.

But then, an inheritance is no present matter. All heirs be "heirs under hope," *usque dum,* "till the appointed time." So comes hope in. Therefore, first "to hope." After, to the thing hoped for, the "inheritance" itself. There is a resemblance of both these in the two seasons of the year. At this time, the time of Christ's resurrection, and of our celebrating it, "to hope," as to the blossom or blade, rising now in the spring; to the "inheritance"—that, as the crop or fruit to come after at harvest, and the "harvest" of this crop, saith our Saviour, "is the end of the world."

We are not yet come to the point. "Regenerate" whereto? "to a lively hope." "Hope," whereof? of an "inheritance." "Inheritance," what manner one? Such as is here set down.

But all these whereby? *Per resurrectionem,* "by the resurrection of Christ." All by Him, all by that. This "by" is the main here. This διὰ the διὰ πασῶν that runs through all this text. For all arise from Christ arising from the dead.

Now if from Christ rising, then from Christ at this feast. For this is the feast of Christ's rising, and so this the proper *Benedictus* for this feast. We had a *Benedictus* made by Zachary, St. John Baptist's father, for His Birth, for Christmas-day, known by the name of *Benedictus.* We have here now another for His rising, for Easter-day, of St. Peter's setting. And this it is.

For the order, we will put the words in no other, for we can put them in no better than they stand; every one is in his due place, from the first to the last.

Tit. 3. 7.
[Gal. 4. 2.]

Mat. 13. 39.

Lu. 1. 68.

The division.

1. " God" first, and the true God, " the Father of our Lord Jesus Christ." 2. Then " His mercy," the cause moving. 3. Then " Christ's resurrection," the means working. 4. Then " our regenerating," the act producing.

Producing 1. " hope," first, of the inheritance; 2. then after, the " inheritance" we hope for. Of which, two points there are: 1. How it is qualified; " uncorrupt, undefiled, not fading,"—every one hath his weight. 2. Then, how seated; even, " in Heaven:" there it is, there " kept" it is. And which is the capital chief point of all, " kept for us" there.

Now then for these. 1. For His " mercy," first. 2. For our " regenerating by His mercy." 3. For the " hope" of this " inheritance," 4. but more for the " inheritance" itself, specially such an one, so conditioned as here is set down. 5. For " keeping it for us in Heaven," in this verse. 6. For 1 Pet. 1. 4. " keeping us" for it on earth, the next verse. For these all; but above all, for the means of all, the rising of Christ, this day's work, the dew of this new birth, the gate of this hope, the pledge of this inheritance. For these, owe we this *Benedictus* to God. And this day are we to pay it, every one of us. It is a sin of omission not to do it; he that doth not, is a debtor.

To God the Father, the *Qui* ; and to Christ our Lord, the *per Quem*, by Whom and by Whose rising, lose this life when we will, we have hope of a better; betide our inheritance on earth what shall, we have another " kept for us in Heaven." Thus, every one naturally ariseth out of other.

" Blessed be God." Yea, blessed, and thanked, and 1. praised; *Benedictus, magnificat, jubilate*, and all. All; but *Benedictus:* here " blessed" suits best,—that the best and most proper God. return for a blessing. That we " inherit," is the " blessing ;" 1 Pet. 3. 9. the hope is a " blessed hope ;" but the " inheritance" is the state of blessedness itself. Therefore, *Benedictus bene dicitur*, 2. *Benedictus* is said well. Said well of God, " Who is above God. all blessed for ever :" well also of a father, *Benedictus* a fit Rom. 9. 5. term for him. And God, in the tenor of this whole text, is brought in as a " Father," " a Father begetting ;" begetting us first by nature, begetting us again in it by grace.

But thereby hangs a scruple, for what are we that we Bless God
B b 2 we may.

should take upon us to bless God? St. Peter says it here; St. Paul seems to gainsay it. "Without all question," saith he, "the less is blessed by the greater." And is He less, or we greater, that we should offer to bless Him? And if not as "God," not as a "Father," the next word. For, shall the child presume to bless his father? It becomes him not. He us then, and not we Him.

Yes, He us, and we Him too. We have so many texts for it, I make no doubt but there is blessing both ways. Of the many, I remember that one of St. Paul's *Benedictus Deus Qui benedixit nos,* "Blessed be God for blessing us." As if they were reciprocal, these; one the echo, the reflection of the other. Equal they are not. It were fond to imagine the father gives the child no other blessing, but the child can give him as good again. No: *aliter nos Deum, aliter Deus nos;* otherwise God blesseth us, and the parent who represents God in begetting our bodies, and the Priest who represents Him in begetting again our souls. Otherwise, we them. God's is real, ours but verbal. His *cum effectu,* ever; ours, if it be but *cum effectu,* that is all. His operative, ours but optative. What then? he that wisheth heartily, would do more than wish if his power were according. Even that then, in want of power to shew a good will, I know not how, but we take it well ever. God doth I am sure, as appeareth by the goat's hair of the Old Testament, and by the widow's mites in the New. And this is St. Peter's, but expressing a good mind only. And without all question thus, the greater may be blessed even of the less; not *tanquam potestatem habens,* but *tanquam vota faciens.* So we may say *Benedictus Deus,* and let us then say it.

What say we then, when we say *Benedictus?* It is a word compound. Take it in sunder, and *dicere* is to say somewhat, to speak, and that we can; and *bene* is, speaking to speak well, and that we ought. To speak is confession, to speak well is praise; and praise becometh Him, and us to give it Him.

Put together in one word, and then *benedicere* 'to bless,' in the phrase of ours and of all tongues else, is not so much *omnia bona dicere,* 'to speak all good of Him,' as *omnia bona vovere,* 'to wish all good to Him.' And that becomes Him too; not only *laus* but *votum*, specially, where *votum* is *totum*, where we have little else left us but it.

And what good can we wish Him that He hath not? *Bonorum nostrorum non eget*, saith the Psalmist, nor *Bene-* Ps. 16. 2. *dictionum* neither. We can add nothing to Him by our *Benedictus*; say we it, say we it not, He is blessed alike.

True; to Him we cannot wish—not to His person, but to In His His Name we can, and He is blessed when His Name is Name. blessed; we can wish His Name more blessedly used, and not in cursing and cursed oaths, as daily we hear it.

And to His Word we can, we can wish it more devoutly In His Word. heard, and not as a few strains of wit, as our manner is.

Yea, even to His Person we can. There is a way to do In His Person that, inasmuch as He and His Church are now grown into as united one, make but one person; what is said or done to it, is said to His Church. or done to Himself. Bless it, and He is blessed.

In a word then, to bless God is to wish His Name may be glorious; to wish His Word may be prosperous; to wish His Church may be happy. By wearing of which Name, and by hearing of which word, and by being in, and of which Church, we receive the blessing here upon earth that shall make us for ever blessed in Heaven. This we say, if we mark what we say, when we say, " Blessed be God."

" God, and the Father of our Lord Jesus Christ." This "God, and the Father is *stylo novo*, the style of the New Testament; ye read it of our Lord not in the Old, no, nor in Zachary's neither. Between that Jesus Christ:" of Zachary's, and this of St. Peter's, it fell out, this. The The style of the sun was yet under the horizon when Zachary made his, but New Testament. now up and of a good height. And thereupon, this taken 1 Cor. 1. 3. up by St. Peter here; by St. Paul, 1 Cor. 1. Ephes. 1. and Eph. 1. 3. upon great reason.

1. " Blessed be God." Say that, and no more, and never 1. To sever a Jew, Turk, or Pagan, but will say as much. " Blessed be all false God," we; " blessed be God," they. It is never the worse gods. for that. But yet, seeing the world then was, still is, full of " many gods," and " many lords," it would be known which 1 Cor. 8. 5. God. For we would not bestow our *Benedictus* upon any but the true God; neither they, nor we, I dare say. Which is then the true God? *Pater Domini nostri Jesu Christi;* and he that is not so, is a false feigned God, is an idol.

SERM.
XL.

Put them to it then, put this addition to, and neither Turk, Jew, nor Pagan will say after you; none but the Christian. For this is the Christian man's *Benedictus.*

Now ever since idolatry first took head, it hath been held fit, they that are God's chosen people of all the people upon earth, they should have some mark of severance to distinguish, as theirs the true God, so themselves the true worshippers from the false. So to settle our *Benedictus* right upon the right God, this is added.

2. As His best title.

2. For this cause, but not for this alone. When we bless Him, I dare say we would bless Him with His best title. So hath it been ever. You shall observe in titles ever, upon the

Jer. 23.7,8.

coming of a greater the less is laid down. "No more, The Lord liveth That brought thee out of Egypt, but, The Lord liveth That brought thy captivity from the North." And now no more that neither, for here is one that after it came puts them down all, as being indeed the greatest of them all, the greatest that ever was, or that ever shall be. One, which when we add, we set our *Benedictus* at the highest.

For, if this be to be God, to be bounteous, beneficial, as we seem to think, when we say *homo homini Deus,* in nothing was God ever so beneficial, so bounteous, and so in nothing

Joh. 3. 16.

ever so God, as in "sending His only-begotten Son into the world." In that God specially, and for that specially to be "blessed." And because a greater than His Son He hath not, and so a greater than this shall never come, therefore this shall never be laid down. This shall be His title for ever, for ever to have a place, and a chief place, in our *Benedictus.*

3 .To bring Christ in too.

And yet there is another, on Christ's behalf—"our Lord;" even to bring Him in too. For, seeing all that which follows comes not but by the rising of Christ, and so by Christ, I see not how well we can leave Him out. All the good that comes to us, as it comes to us from God, so it comes to us by Christ. God the *Qui,* Christ the *per Quem.* God the cause—from Him cometh all, God and all. Christ the means—by Him cometh all, God and all. All things from God, and nothing from God immediately, but *mediante Christo.* He the cause mediate, the Mediator, the Medium. No *Benefactus,* and so no *Benedictus,* without Him.

This is most plain in this here. *Benedictus Deus Qui generavit Christum,* first, " That did generate Christ," before *Benedictus Deus Qui regeneravit nos,* " that did regenerate us." If He not generate, we not regenerate; then no children, then no inheritance, then all this text void. For in Him this text, and all other texts are " yea and Amen." [2 Cor. 1. 20.]

By this time we see why this addition. 1. It is His title of severance; 2. It is the highest title of His honour; 3. It takes in Christ Who would not be left out in our *Benedictus. Dixit Dominus Domino meo,* " the Lord said to my Lord," to take both Lords in, and leave neither out. And so shall we knit it well to that which follows. [Ps. 110. 1.]

From the party whom, we pass to the cause why. For we say not this *Benedictus,* as we say many an one here, without any cause, *Benedictus* for nothing; nay, otherwhile a *Benedictus* for a *malefactus,* for a shrewd turn; yea, and glad and fain too. No, here is a *Qui,* and in this *Qui* there is a *quia.* That doth it, that is, for doing it; " that regenerates us," that is, for regenerating us, for God is ever aforehand with us. *Regeneravit* is the *preter;* that is past before any *Benedictus* can come from us. [3. The cause why.]

Pater qui Regeneravit follows well, is kindly. For generation, it is *actus paternus,* ' the proper act of a father.' But before we come to it, let us not stride over that which in the text stands before it—*secundum misericordiam.* God did this, did all that follows, but upon what motive?' " According to" what did He it? " According to His mercy." And mercy accords well with a father; no compassion, no bowels like his. And as well with *regeneravit,* for " of His own good-will begat He us." How else? when as yet we were not, what should move Him but His mere mercy? Well therefore said, *regeneravit secundum;* for regeneration is but *secundum,* but " a second," not a first. Would ye have a *primum,* ' a first' for it? that first is His mercy ever. [1. "Mercy.]

But the benefits ensuing are too great to run in the common current of mercy. As they then are, so is the mercy that goes to them. " Great:" therefore " according to His great mercy." " Mercy" the thing, " great" the measure. And " great" would not be passed by, lest we pass not [" His abundant, or great mercy."]

SERM.
XI.
greatly by it; lest we conceive and count of it, as but of some ordinary matter.

His mani-
fold mercy.
But indeed πολὺ is rather *multa,* than *magna;* a word of number, rather than magnitude. The meaning is; no single mercy would do it—no, though great, there must be many. For many the defects to be removed, many the sins to be forgiven, many the perfections to be attained; therefore, " according to His manifold mercy."

"According" is well said. For that indeed is the chord, to which this and all our *Benedictusses* are to be tuned. That the centre, from which all the lines are drawn. The line of Lu. 1. 78. Christ's birth in Zachary's *Benedictus,* "through the tender mercies of our God, whereby the Day-spring from on high did" lately "visit us." The line of Christ's resurrection, in St. Peter's *Benedictus,* "according to His manifold mercies," whereby this Day-spring from on high doth now visit us. The line of all the rest, if we had time to go through all the rest.

At all times mercy cometh in, at no time out of time I trust, we shall die with it in our mouths. Let us make much of it while we live, never pass by it but say it, say it as oft as we can; " blessed be God," blessed be His mercy. "God" that doth it; " His mercy, according to" which He doth it. Doth it, and doth all else, at this and all other feasts; at Easter, at Christmas, the Fifth of November, and all. " Blessed be He for His mercy; yea, many times blessed for His manifold mercies."

4.
*Regenera-
vit nos.*
2. Hath
begotten
us again.
"Mercy" then first; *regeneravit secundum,* the act of this mercy the second, that is *regeneravit. Regeneravit* may be said with reference to Christ. *Generavit Christum, regeneravit nos,* and not amiss. But better and more properly, both to us. *Generavit nos,* 'begot us' first in Adam to this; *regeneravit nos,* 'begot us again' in Christ, the second Adam, to the hope of a better life.

But why is it not so then, *Qui generavit* without *re?* Why begin we not with that? Verily, even for that, even for our natural generation, we owe Him a *Benedictus.* But what should I say? Unless, beside our first *generavit,* we be so happy as to have our part in this second *regeneravit,* the former I doubt will hardly prove worth a *Benedictus.* But if

this come to it, then for both a *benedictus* indeed. Otherwise as our Saviour said to Nicodemus, " no man, unless he Joh. 3. 3.
be thus born again," by his first birth, be it never so high or
noble, is a whit the nearer this inheritance following. For
all our goodly *generavit* we so much boast of, it would go
wrong with us but for this. Well therefore may we all say,
Benedictus Qui regeneravit.

Now *re* hath in it two powers, *re* is 'again, the second "Again,"
time;' so it suits well with *secundum*, it is the second. For second
two there be: 1. that old creation, 2. and the "new crea- time.
ture" in Christ. And two births;—we see it daily. A child Gal. 6. 15.
is brought into the world, but it is carried out again to the
Church, there to be born and brought forth anew, by the
Sacrament of Regeneration.

But *re* is not only again, but again, as it were, upon a loss. "Again,"
Not a second only, but a second upon the failing of the first. upon a
So doth *re* imply ever. Re-demption, a buying again upon loss.
a former aliening. Re-conciliation, upon a former falling
out. Re-stitution, upon a former attainder. Re-surrection,
upon a fall taken formerly. Re-generation, upon a former
degenerating from our first estate.

Our first would not serve, it was corrupt, it was defiled, it
did degenerate. Degenerating made us *filios iræ*; and *ira* Eph. 2. 3.
principis, much more *ira Dei, mors est.* So children of death, Prov.16.14.
death and damnation; and there left us, and all by means of
the corruption and soil of our former degenerate generation.

Never ask then *Quid opus est re? Re* cannot be spared.
There was more than need of a new, a second, a re-generation, to make us children of grace again, and so of life;
which He hath given us power to be made "by the washing Tit. 3. 5.
of the new birth," "the fountain which He hath opened to Zech. 13. 1.
the House of Israel for sin and uncleanness"—even for the
sin and uncleanness of the first. Will ye have it plainly?
Benedictus Deus Qui generatos ad mortem, regeneravit ad
vitam; or, *Qui generatos ad timorem mortis regeneravit ad*
spem vitæ. That we, we that were begotten to the fear of
death, or to a deadly fear; us He hath begotten anew to
the hope of life, or " to a lively hope."

This act of regenerating is determined doubly; εἰς is
twice repeated. 1. "To hope" first; 2. then, "to the in-

SERM.
XI.
heritance :" ye may put them together, "to the hope of an inheritance." But thus parted they stand, because of our two estates, to serve them both: 1. "hope" in this life, 2. "inheritance" in that to come; "hope" while here in state of grace, "inheritance" when there in state of glory.

In Spem.
"To hope."
But because, as we said, an "inheritance" is no present matter—it is to come and to be come to ; from begetting we step not straight to entering upon our inheritance, but the state of heirs is a state of expectancy, and so a fit object for hope, *donec,* "till" the time come. Therefore we begin with that, *regeneravit in spem.*

There needs no great *Benedictus* for *in spem ;* hope is no great matter. For what is hope ? What but *vigilantis somnium,* 'a waking man's dream ?' And such a hope indeed it may be, for such hopes there be many in the world. But this is none such.

To shew it is none such, it is severed by two terms ; 1. *Regeneravit,* and 2. *Vivam.* They are worth the marking, both.

1. *Spem generatam.*
1. *Regeneravit* first ; that it is *spes generata,* which implies there is another but *inflata,* but 'blown into' us, or we sprinkled or perfumed with it. Such there is, but not this; but this is *per viam generationis,* and *generatio,* we know, *terminatur ad substantiam,* 'brings forth a substance.' So this a substantial hope, called therefore by St. Paul, "the helmet" of hope, "the anchor" of hope, things of substance that will hold, that have metal in them.

1 Thes. 5 8.
Heb. 6. 19.

2. *Spem vivam.*
2. Then mark *vivam.* And *vivam* follows well of *regeneravit.* For they that are begotten are so to live, to have life. *Vivam* also imports there is a dead, or a dying hope; but this is not such, but a living.

Nay, *viva* is more than *vivens;* "lively," than 'living.' Where *viva* is said of aught, as of stone or water, the meaning is they spring, they grow, they have life in themselves. And such is the water of our regeneration ; not from the brooks of Tema, in Job the sixth, that in summer will be dry, but the water of Jordan, a running river. There, Christ was Himself baptized: there He began and laid the Sacrament of our new birth, to shew what the nature of the hope is it yields, even *viva,* with life in it.

Job 6.
15—20.
Mat. 3. 13

And indeed, *regeneravit* is a good verb to join with hope.
There is in hope a kind of regendering power; it begets
men, as it were, anew. And *viva* is a good epithet for it.
When one droops, give him hope, his spirits will come to
him afresh; it will make him alive again, that was half dead.
As Jacob, when he was put in hope to see Joseph alive, it is
said, *Revixit spiritus Jacob*, " his spirit revived in him;" he Gen. 45. 24.
shewed, *spes* was *viva*, hope was a reviver.

Never so well seen, this, as this day, in them that went to
Emmaus. With cold hearts—cold and dead, God wot, till
they heard the Scriptures opened to this point; and then,
" did we not," said they, "feel our hearts warm, nay hot, Lu. 24. 32.
within us?" Such a vital heat, they found and felt, came
from this hope. For, to say truth, what is it to give life to
them that have it already, *dum spiro*, that are alive, that can
fetch their breath? it is not worthy, that, to be called *spes
viva*. *Spes viva* indeed is that which, when breath and life
and all fail, fails not; that that then puts life into us, *dum
expiro*, when life is going away; that, when this life we must
forego, bids let it go; when that is gone, shews us hope of
another.

This is *viva* indeed. Nay this is *vita*, for the hope of that
life immortal is the very life of this life mortal. And for
such a hope, *Benedictus Deus*, " Blessed be God."

And whence hath it this life? The next word shews it, *Vivam, per*
vivam, per resurrectionem. The viveness, as I may say, the *resurrec-*
tionem
vivacity, the vigour it hath from Christ rising, and by His *Jesu*
Christi.
rising opening to us the gate of life at large. What life?
Any life? this life? No; *vivam, per resurrectionem.* Not
this here, *falsi seculi vita*, as even the heathen man called
it, but the other, the life by the resurrection, the true life
indeed. Not to live here still as we do, but to rise again
and live as Christ this day did. That so we mistake not
the life, and take the wrong for the right. For so shall we
mistake in our hope also, as commonly we do.

For shall we do hope no wrong? The truth is, hope hears
evil without a cause. The fault is not hope's, the fault is
our own; we put it where we should not, and then lay the
blame upon hope, where we should blame ourselves for
wrong putting it. For if ye put it not right, this is a general

SERM.
XI.

Isa. 36. 6.
Job 8. 14.
Ecclu.34.2.

rule: As is that we hope in, so is our hope. "Ye lean on a reed," saith Esay. "Ye take hold by a cobweb"—Job. "Ye catch at a shadow," saith the Wise Man. And can it be then but this hope must deceive you?

Wis. 13. 10.

We for the most part put it wrong, for we put it in them that live this transitory perishing life; we put it in them that must die, and then must our hope die with them, and so prove a dying hope. "Miserable is that man, that among the dead is his hope," saith the Wise Man. The Psalm

Ps. 146.
3, 4.

best expresseth it: "our hope is in the sons of men," and they live by breath, and when that is gone, "they turn to dust;" and then there "lies our hope in the dust." For how can ever a dying object yield a living hope?

[Rom.5.5.]

But put it in one that dies not, that shall never die, and then it will be *spes viva* indeed. No reed, no cobweb-hope then, but helmet, anchor-hope; "hope that will never confound you."

1 Tim. 1. 1.

And who is that, or where is he, that we might hope in him? That is *Jesus Christus spes nostra*, "Jesus Christ, our hope"—so calls Him St. Paul. Such shall their hope be that have Christ for their hope.

Yet not Christ in every way considered: not as yesterday, in the grave; not as the day before, giving up the ghost upon the cross; dead and buried yields but dead hope. But in *Jesus Christus hodie*, 'Jesus Christ to-day,' that is, *Christus resurgens*, 'Christ rising again;' Christ not now a living soul, but a quickening Spirit.

Lu. 24. 21.

In Christ's life then, but not in His mortal life. They that so hoped in Him, to Emmaus they went this day with *nos autem sperabamus*, "we did hope;" "did" while He was alive, but now, now He is dead, no more hope now. And for two days, as He was, so was their hope, dead and buried; and if He had risen no more, had been quite dead for ever. But this day He revived and rose again;—so did their hope too.

To this life we are regenerate by the resurrection of Christ;—right. As to death generate by the fall of the first Adam, so to life regenerate by the rising again of Christ, the second.

And these two, resurrection and regeneration, match well.

The regeneration of the soul is the first resurrection; and the resurrection of the body, is the last regeneration. So doth our Saviour Christ term it: "in the regeneration, Mat.19.28. when the Son of Man shall sit"—that is, at the general resurrection. So was His own; His resurrection, His regeneration. "This day have I begotten Thee," the verse of Ps. 2. 7. the Psalm, the Apostle applies to Christ's eternal generation. Heb. 1. 5. But so doth he to His resurrection also, for then was Christ Acts 13. 33. Himself regenerate as it were, begotten in a sort anew, and brought forth out of the grave, as out of the womb, the very womb wherein He was born to the immortal, that is, to the true life.

"By His resurrection." And if ye ask how, Esay tells us; there goeth from His resurrection an influence, which shall have an operation like that of the dew of the spring; which when He will let fall, "the earth shall yield her dead," as at Isa. 26. 19. the falling of the dew the herbs now rise, and shoot forth again. Which term therefore, of regenerating, was well chosen, as fitting well with His rising and the time of it. The time, I say, of the year, of the week, and if ye will, of the day too. For He rose in the dawning—then is the day Lu. 24. 1. regenerate; and in *primâ Sabbati* — that, the first begetting of the week; and in the spring, when all that were winter-starved, withered and dead, are regenerate again, and rise up anew.

We pass now to the "inheritance." But as we pass, will 2. *In hæ-* ye observe the situation first? It is well worth your observ- *reditatem.* ing, that the resurrection is placed in the midst, between our *inherit-* hope and our inheritance. "To hope" before it—before the *ance.'* resurrection, hope; but after "to the inheritance" itself, to the full possession and fruition of it. So from the estate of hope, by the resurrection as by a bridge, pass we over to the enjoying our inheritance. And that falls well with the feast, which is the feast of the Passover. The resurrection is so too; pass we do from *spes* to *res*. So passed Christ; so we to pass. Every word stands exactly in his place and order.

An inheritance accords well with "according to His mercy." We have it not of ourselves, or by our merits— by the πολύ of them; but of Him, and by His mercies, and the πολύ of them; else were it a purchase, and no inheritance.　It comes to us freely, as the inheritance to children.

Well with " mercy ;" and well with *regeneravit.* For the inheritance is of children, pertains to the children, either of generation by nature, or of regeneration by grace. By the former He is *Pater Domini nostri,* by the latter He is *Pater noster.*

But yet for all that, *ad hæreditatem* is a new point. Begetting is, properly, but to life, and nothing else ; the greater part by far are begotten so. To inherit besides, not one of a thousand. Ask poor men's children, ask younger brethren. But this here not in *vivam* only, but in *hæreditatem* also, and these are two. 1. To be begotten, *vivam* ; 2. to be heirs, *hæreditatem.* It is not Lazarus' resurrection, to rise again to the condition he had before. It is Christ's rising, to receive " an inheritance" withal.

Nor shall we need to doubt any prejudice to God, from Whom it comes, by our coming to this inheritance. *Vivam* and *hæreditatem,* there, will stand well together ; here they will not. Here the inheritance comes not but by the death of the party in possession, but there, no prejudice to the ancestor ; he dies not for the heir to succeed. There is *successio minorum sine recessione majorum.* A succession, as of lights ; the second burns clear, yet the first goes not out, but burns as clear as it.

Nor no prejudice to the heir neither ; to us by Him, nor to Him by us. It is not as here, one carries it from all, and all the rest go without ; or, if they come in, his part is the less. No ; it is of the nature of light, and other such spiritual things, as sounds and smells, which be *omnibus una, et singulis tota.* If there be a thousand together, every one sees, hears, smells as much, as he should do, if there were no more but himself alone. Such is this, not *erga aliquos vestrûm,* but *erga vos.*

And as we said, One thing it is to be born, another to be so to inherit, so say we again now : One thing to be born to an inheritance, another to such an inheritance as this here. For in inheritances there is great odds, one much better than another, even here with us ; but this better, incomparably better, another manner inheritance far than any

with us here. We would know what manner one, and St.
Peter gives us a little overture, how it is conditioned, that we
may know it is worth a *Benedictus. E theologiâ negativâ* he
doth it; there is no other way to describe things to come,
but by removing from them such defects as, we complain,
are incident and encumber all we can inherit here.

Three they are, 1. *Corrumpi,* 2. *Contaminari,* 3. *Marcescere ;* 'corruption, soil, and fading,' to which *nos nostraque,*
'we and all ours' are subject. Of which three, 1. Corruption refers to the very being itself; 2. Defiling, to the sincere and true being, without all foreign mixture; 3. Fading,
to the beauty, the prime and flourishing estate, that each
thing hath.

The substance, that corrupts and comes to nothing, sup- 1. "Incor-
pose by death, for corruption is contrary to generation. The ruptible."
undefiled pure estate, that is soiled and imbased by some
bad thing coming to it from without, as it might be by infection or sickness. And though both these hold, the best
estate long will not, but lose the lustre by-and-by, and fade
away of itself. St. Peter enlarges this after in this chapter,
taking his theme from the voice in Esay 40. "All flesh 1 Pet. 1. 24.
is grass, and all the glory of it as the flower of the grass." Isa. 40. 6.
The grass itself lasts not long, but the flower of the grass
nothing so long as the grass itself. Let there be no blasting
to corrupt it, no canker to defile it, yet of itself it falls off,
and leaves the stalk standing.

It is now the time of flowers, and from flowers doth the
Apostle take his term of *Marcescere.* It is properly the
fading of the rose. Straight of itself doth the rose *marcere,*
and the violet *livere,* 'wax pale and wan.' Their best, their
flourishing estate they hold not long; neither the flowers
that are worn, nor they that wear them neither—they, nor
we; but decay we do, God wot, in a short time.

And as we, so they; as the heirs, so the inheritances
themselves. Their corruptible hath not put on incorruption 1 Cor. 15. 53.
neither. They corrupt daily, we see, from one to another.
One man's inheritance corrupts, by another man's purchase.
To them that had them, and have them not, they are corrupt.
And not that way alone; divers other escheat for want of
heirs, confiscate for some offences, rioted and made away by

SERM. unthriftiness; the heir stripped and turned clean out, the in-
XI.
———— heritance wasted and quite brought to nothing. At least, if
not they to us, we to them corrupt, which comes all to one.

"Unde-   But say, they stand and corrupt not, another complaint
filed."
there is; their soil, their μιασμòς, is but too evident. They
soil us, their soil we brush off, wipe, rub, wash off daily; in
summer dust, in winter dirt; these, and sundry like *inquina-
menta mundi*, nothing in this region but subject to soil.
Why, the "inheritance" itself, we call it soil; and how can
it then but soil us? or how can there be here any undefiled
inheritance?

3. "That   But make them and keep them as clean as you can, take
fadeth
not."   them even at the best, yet fade they do sensibly; Jonah's
Jon. 4. 7. worm, once a year, bites them by the root and they wither.
Every year at least they fall into a *marasmus*, lose flowers
and leaves and all, till they be regenerate by a resurrection,
or rise again by a regeneration, as it were; till this time,
the time of the spring come about, and bring them forth
new again.

So whatsoever we here can inherit, is subject to one, nay
to all of these. It corrupts, takes soil, fades. Is it not so?
find we not St. Peter saith true? find we it not by proof
daily? One or other, are we not still complaining of, specially
of the fading? For though they fade not of themselves, yet
to us they fade. The fading to us, even before themselves
fade. We are hungry, and we eat. Eat we not till that fades,
and we as weary of our fulness, as we were of our fasting?
We are weary and we rest; rest we not till that fades, and
we as weary of our rest, as ever we were of our weariness?

Yes indeed so it is, and that so it is, is the very faithful-
ness of the creature to us. Thus by these defects to tire us,
and not suffer us to set our rest upon them, upon any inheritance here, but to chase us from themselves, and force us
up to God the Creator, with Whom there is "an inheritance
laid up," in danger of none of these. But 1. "uncorrupt,"
that shall hold the being, and none ever disherit or disseize
us of it; 2. "undefiled," that shall hold the assay, and never
be imbased by any bad mixture; 3. and "that shall never
fade or fall into any *marasmus*, but hold out in the prime
perfection it ever had. And if there be upon earth a state

like this, it is now, at this time. Now, all things generate anew; the soil of winter is gone, and of summer is not yet come. Now nothing fades, but all springs fresh and green. At this time here, but at all times there, a perpetual spring, no other seasons there but that. For such "an inheritance," "Blessed be God!"

But where may this be? For all this while we know not "In Heaven." that. Only this we know, wherever it is, it is not here—upon earth no such seat. All here savour of the nature of soil, *corrumpi, contaminari, marcescere,* are the proper passions of earth and all earthly things; but "in Heaven" it may well be. There is no contrary to corrupt, *nihil inquinatum,* nothing to defile there. And there all things keep and continue to this day in their first estate, the original beauty they ever had. There then it is, and we thither to lift up our hearts, whither the very frame of our bodies gives, as if there were somewhat remaining for us there.

It is thought, there is some farther thing meant by St. Peter—he writes to the dispersed Jews—and that by *in cœlo* he gives them an item, this inheritance is no new Canaan here on earth, nor Christ any earthly Messias to settle them in a new land of promise;—no, that was for the Synagogue, ἥτις θνητὴ θνητοῖς ἐπηγγέλλετο θνητά, was itself mortal, is dead and buried since, and so had but mortal things to promise to her children whom she did generate to mortality. The Church of Christ, "the heavenly Jerusalem," hath other Gal. 4. 26. manner of promises to her children, regenerate by the im- [Heb. 12. 22.] mortal seed of the Word and Spirit of God. To them she holdeth forth things immortal and heavenly, yea Heaven and immortality itself.

"In Heaven," then. There it is first, and there it is "Reserved in Heaven." "kept;" the being there one, the keeping another. For that there it is "kept," is happy for us. Earth would not keep it; here it would be in hazard, there is great odds. For my part, I give it for lost, if in this state we were possessed of it; it would go the same way Paradise went. Since it would be lost in earth, it is "kept" in Heaven. And a *Benedictus* for that too, as for the regenerating us to it here on earth, so for the keeping, the preserving of it there, in Heaven.

c c

"Kept," and "for us kept," else all were nothing: that makes up all, that it is not only preserved, but "reserved for us" there. As *Benedictus* the Alpha, so this the Omega of all.

But "reserved," as the nature of the word is, and as the nature is of things hoped for, yet under the veil; for *spes* Rom. 8. 24. *quæ videtur non est spes.* But time shall come, when the veil shall be taken off, and of that which is now within it there 1 Pet. 1. 5. shall be a revealing, as followeth in the next verse. And so all begins and ends, as the Bible doth. As the Bible with Genesis, so this text with regeneration; as the Bible ends in the Apocalypse, so this here with a revelation.

Only it stayeth till the work of regeneration be accomplished. Generation and it take end both together, and when generation doth, then shall corruption likewise, and with it the state of dishonour which is in foulness, and the state of weakness which is in fading; and instead of them, incorruption comes in place with honour and power. And these three, 1. incorruption, 2. honour, and 3. power, make the perfect estate of bliss to which Christ this day arose, and which shall be our estate at the Resurrection. That as all began with a resurrection, so it shall end with one. Came to us by Christ's rising now, this first Easter; and we shall come to it by our own rising at the last and great Easter, the true Passover indeed, when from death and misery we shall pass to life and felicity.

Now for this "inheritance" which is bliss itself, and in the Heb. 6. interim for the "blessed hope set before us, which we have 18–20. as an anchor of our soul, steadfast and sure, which entereth even within the veil, where Christ the forerunner is already seized of it" in our names and for our behoofs, for these come we now to our *Benedictus.*

For if God "according to His manifold mercy," have done all this for us, we also according to our duty, as manifold as His mercy, are to do or say at least somewhat again. It accords well that for so many *beneficia,* one *Benedictus* at least. It accords well, that His rising should raise in us, and our regenerating beget in us some praise, thanks, blessing at least; but blessing fits best with *Benedictus.*

First then, *dictus;* somewhat would be said by way of

recognition, this hath God done for us and more also, but this, this very day. Then *bene* let it be, to speak well of Him for doing thus well by us; a verbal *Benedictus* for a real blessing is as little as may be. For the inheritance which is blessing, for the hope which is blessed, for the blessed cause of both, God's mercy, and the blessed means of both, Christ's resurrection this blessed day, "Blessed be God!"

But to say *Benedictus* any way is not to content us, but to say it solemnly. How is that? *Benedictus* in our mouth, and the holy Eucharist in our hands. So to say it; to seal up, as he in the old, his *quid retribuam* with *calicem salutaris,* "the cup of salvation," so we in the new, our *Benedictus* with *calix benedictionis,* "the cup of blessing which we bless in His Name." So shall we say it in kind, say it as it would be said. The rather so to do, because by that "cup of bless-ing" we shall partake the "blood of the New Testament," by which this inheritance, as it was purchased for us, so it is passed to us. Always making full account, that from "the cup of blessing," we cannot part but with a blessing. _{Ps. 116. 12, 13. 1Cor.10.16.}

And yet this is not all, we are not to stay here but to aspire farther, even to strive to be like to God; and be like God we shall not, unless our *dicere* be *facere* as His is, unless somewhat be done withal. In very deed there is no blessing, but with *levatâ* and *extensâ manu,* "the hand stretched out:" —so our Saviour Himself "blessed." The vocal blessing _{Lu. 24. 50.} alone is not full, nor the Sacramental alone without *Benedic-tio manus,* that is, the actual blessing. To leave a blessing behind us, to bestow somewhat for which the Church, the poor in it, so, shall bless us, and bless God for us. In which respect the Apostle so calleth it expressly, εὐλογίαν *benedic-* _{2 Cor. 9. 5.} *tionem,* and by that name commends it to the Corinthians. And that is the blessing of blessings, when all is done; that is it for which *venite benedicti* shall be said to us, even for _{Mat. 25. 34.} parting with that here which shall feed, cover, and set free the hungry, naked, and them in prison. That shall prove the blessing real, and stick by us, when all our verbal bene-dictions shall be vanished into air.

So for a treble blessing from God, 1. our regenerating, 2. our hope, 3. our inheritance, we shall return Him the same number, even three for three. 1. *Benedictus* of the voice and instrument; 2. *Benedictus* of the sign and Sacrament; 3. and *Benedictus*, of some blessed deed done, for which many blessings upon earth, and the blessing of God from Heaven shall come upon us. So, as we say here, *Benedictus Deus*, "Blessed He," He shall say, *Benedicti vos*, "Blessed ye." The hearing of which words in the end shall make us blessed without end, in Heaven's bliss. To which, &c.

A SERMON

PREACHED BEFORE

THE KING'S MAJESTY, IN THE CATHEDRAL CHURCH AT DURHAM,

ON THE TWENTIETH OF APRIL, A.D. MDCXVII., BEING EASTER-DAY.

MATTHEW xii. 39, 40.

*But He answered and said unto them, An evil and adulterous
generation seeketh a sign, but no sign shall be given unto it,
save the sign of the Prophet Jonas :*

*For as Jonas was three days and three nights in the whale's
belly, so shall the Son of man be three days and three nights
in the heart of the earth.*

[*Qui respondens ait illis, Generatio mala, et adultera signum quærit ;
et signum non dabitur ei, nisi signum Jonæ Prophetæ.*

*Sicut enim fuit Jonas in ventre ceti tribus diebus et tribus noctibus,
sic erit Filius hominis in corde terræ tribus diebus et tribus noctibus.* Latin Vulg.]

[*But He answered and said unto them, An evil and adulterous generation seeketh after a sign ; and there shall no sign be given to it, but
the sign of the Prophet Jonas :*

*For as Jonas was three days and three nights in the whale's belly, so
shall the Son of man be three days and three nights in the heart of
the earth.* Engl. Trans.]

"THE sign of the Prophet Jonas" is the sign of the Resurrection, and this is the feast of the Resurrection. Being
then the sign of this feast, at this feast to be set up; *signum
temporis in tempore signi,* 'the sign of the time at the time of
the sign,' most properly ever.

The words are an answer of Christ's in this verse, to a motion of the Pharisees in the last. They "would see a sign." The answer is negative, but qualified. There is in it a *non,* and a *nisi; non dabitur,* "none shall be given them." Indeed "none should," they were worthy of none. Yet saith He not *non* simply, His *non* is with a *nisi—non dabitur nisi;* it is with a limitation, with a but, "none but" that. So *that,* so one shall be. In the *non* is their desert, in the *nisi* His goodness That, though they were worthy none, yet gives them one though.

Gives them one, and one that is worth the giving. Put *non* and *nisi* together, it is a *non-nisi.* If you speak of a sign, none to it; a sign, *instar omnium.*

This sign is "the sign of the Prophet Jonas." Of him divers other ways, and namely this; that as he "was in the whale's belly," so was Christ "in the heart of the earth." There they were either.

And that which makes up the sign, "three days" apiece; three days, and no longer.

And then, as Jonas cast up by the whale, so Christ rose again from the dead, and both the third day. So that upon the matter, the substance of this sign is Christ's resurrection, and the circumstance of it is this very day.

We will divide it no otherwise than already we have: 1. into the *non, non dabitur;* 2. the *nisi, non dabitur nisi;* 3. and the *non-nisi, non nisi signum Jonæ.*

I.   The *non,* the denial first; *non dabitur eis.* And the reason is in *eis,* in the parties. For they 1. an "evil, and 2. adulterous," and a 3. "generation" of such—three brands set upon them; *eis,* "to them," to such as them, "no sign" to be "given;" none at all.

II.   Then the *nisi; non dabitur nisi.* For though they were such as little deserved any, yet Christ of His goodness will not cast them quite off. "None" He will give "but." So one He will give, a sign they shall have.

III. And that no trivial or petty sign, to give it His due, but in very deed a *signum non nisi; non nisi signum Jonæ,* that is, *insigne signum,* 'a sign signal:'—mark them all, none like it.

And that is "the sign of the Prophet Jonas," coming forth

of the whale's jaws, half out and half in. In which sign there are upon the point three *sicuts*.

1. The parties first; as Jonas, so "the Son of Man," that is, Himself.

2. Wherein, the place. That as the one was "in the whale's belly," so was the other "in the bowels of the earth."

3. Last, in time. Either, "three days and three nights" just, and but three days, and then forth again. There they were, and there both the same time; the places diverse, the time the same.

So Jonas, the sign of Christ; and the whale's belly, the sign of Christ's grave. Jonas' three days, the sign of Christ's three days, 1. Good Friday, 2. yesterday, 3. and to-day.

Which three days, when we shall come to calculate them, they will give us three stands, and make as it were three signs in one, each day his several sign.

The letter of the text saith, there they were; 1. we are carried then to ask, How came they thither? The text saith, there they were but "three days;" 2. we are carried then to ask, How came they thence?

1. Jonas' state before he came into the whale; 2. his state while there; 3. his state getting thence.

Conform in Christ. 1. Good-Friday, when as Jonas went down the whale's throat, so Christ laid in His grave. 2. Easter-eve, while there He lay. 3. And this which is now the third day, when as Jonas cast up on dry land, so Christ risen from death to the life immortal.

So have you, as in a sign, set forth: 1. Christ's death by Jonas' drowning; 2. Christ's burial, by Jonas' abode there; 3. Christ's resurrection by Jonas' emersion again.

As *Christus sepultus* by *Jonas absorptus*, so *Christus resurgens* by *Jonas emergens*. 1. Jonas' going down the whale's throat, of Christ put into His sepulchre; 2. Jonas' appearing again out of the whale's mouth, of Christ's arising out of His sepulchre. All in Jonas shadowed, and in Christ fulfilled.

In these three days these three signs, and in them three keys of our faith, three articles of our creed; 1. *mortuus*, 2. *sepultus*, 3. and *resurrexit*, 1. Christ's death, 2. burial, and 3. rising again.

SERM.
XII.
——
Ps. 86. 17.
And last what this sign portends or signifies. That whatsoever it was to them, to us it is *signum in bonum,* 'a sign
boding good to us-ward,' a sign of favour and good hope
which we have by the resurrection of our Saviour. Specially,
if we have the true signature of it, which is true repentance.

[I.]
The denial
of a sign.
*Non da-
bitur.*
Judges 6.
36, &c.
2 Kings
20. 8-11.
To "ask a sign," is of itself not evil; good men, holy
Saints have done it. Gideon asked one of God and had it;
he is painted with the fleece, that is, the sign given him, in
his hand. Ezekias asked one and had it too: "in the sun-
dial of Ahaz, the shadow went ten degrees back." Yet this
suit here is denied by Christ, and Christ denieth nothing
that is good; specially, not with hard terms as here we see
He doth.

The rea-
son, in *eis,*
the men.
Somewhat is amiss sure, and it is not in the sign or in the
suit, but in *eis,* the men; the suit was not evil, the suitors
were. In three words, three brands set upon them: 1. "evil,"
2. "adulterous," 3. "a generation of evil and adulterous."

They were
"evil."
Mat. 12. 22.
1. "Evil." There be marks of evil-minded men even in
their very suit. They "would see a sign." If they had
never seen any before, it had not been evil, but they came
now from a sign; they had scarce wiped their eyes since
Mat. 12. 10. they saw one, the sign of "the blind and dumb" man, made
to see and speak immediately before, it was *spirans adhuc,*
'yet warm,' as they say. That they saw, and saw they not
a sign? A little before even in this very chapter, a withered
hand was restored to another. What, could they not see a
sign in that neither? Go back to the chapters before, ye
shall have no less than a dozen signs, one after another;
Mat. 12. 38. and come they now with a *volumus videre?* They would have
that shewed them that, when it is shewed, they will not see;
a bad mind this, certainly.

Nay mali-
ciously
evil.
2. Nay worse yet; for ye shall note malice in them, which
is the worse kind of evil. For if ye mark, this *volumus* of
theirs is with a kind of spite, with a kind of disgrace, to
those he had shewed before. They would see one, as who
should say, those were none they had seen, that was none
they saw, even now. Maliciously: if He shewed none, then
He was no body, could not indeed shew any, and so vilify
Him with the people. If He shewed one, then carp and
cavil at it, as they did at that even now; say, it was done by

the black art. So cavil out one, and call for another, to deprave that too.

3. Nay, which is worst of all, "evil and absurd" men, saith the Apostle. When is that? *Vidi iniquitatem et contradictionem,* saith the Psalmist; ye shall see how absurdly they contradict themselves. But even now they charged Him to work by the devil; and here now they come, and would have Him shew a miracle. The devil cannot shew a miracle; a trick of sorcery he can—such may be done by the claw of the devil; miracles not, but "by the finger of God," by power divine. Him then, Him Whom they even now had pronounced to deal with the devil, Him come they to now for a miracle. So absurdly malicious, as they cared not in their malice to contradict themselves. To men so "evil," so maliciously evil, so absurdly evil, *signum non dabitur eis.*

And absurdly evil.
2 Tim. 3. 13.
Ps. 55. 9.

[Lu. 11. 20.]

Well, howsoever they might err that way, the men otherwise to be respected; they were so virtuous men, so straight livers. See ye not their phylacteries, how broad they wear them? Nor that neither, saith Christ, but "evil, and adulterous" too. As of evil minds, so of evil lives too. Ye shall come now to the uncasing of a Pharisee; for Christ lifts up their phylacteries, and shews what lurks under them.

For by "adulterous," I understand not as if He charged them they were born of adultery, came into the world the wrong way, the seed of Canaan and not of Judah; as having nothing in them of the Patriarchs, so nothing less than their children of whom they bear themselves so much. This is *adulterina* rather than *adultera;* 'children of the adulterers, rather than adulterous themselves.' And that was no fault of theirs, and Christ upbraideth no man but with his own faults.

Nor I understand it not of spiritual adultery, though that way they might be charged, as leaving Him the true Spouse, the true Messias; taking no notice of Him, passing by Him, went after such as had adulterate the truth of God by devices of their own taking up; not with idolatry perhaps, but which is an evil, and differs but a letter, with idiolatry; for to worship images, and to worship men's own imaginations, comes all to one. That they were faulty of, and I pray God we be free. But this is mystical adultery, and I would

S E R M.
XII.
make, as no more miracles, so no more mysteries than needs I must.

For my part I see no harm to take the word in the native sense without figure, for men given to commit that sin, the sin of adultery. For, for all their deep fringes, all was not well that way, as is plain by John the eighth; where, not one of them durst take up a stone, to cast at the woman taken in adultery, but slunk away one after another, till there was not one left. Christ toucheth upon that string, to shew what heavenly men these were, that would have a sign from Heaven, and none else serve them. Were not these meet men to sue for a sign? Were not a sign even cast away upon them?

Joh. 8. 1-9.

"A gene-
ration" of
such.
But this is not all. For this they were, saith our Saviour, not here and there a man of them, but the whole bunch was no better; not the persons only, but the generation so, not a good of them all. And such you shall observe there be; not only such men, but such generations of men and faults— suppose of lying, swearing and such like, rooted in a stock; kept even *in traduce*, as it were, and derived down *ab avis atavisque*, 'from the father to the son,' by many descents, in a kind of hereditary propagation.

Prov. 30.
11-14.
Solomon in his time noted four of them: 1. One, a "generation" unkind to their "parents," and their children so to them for it: 2. Another, "pure in their own eyes:" 3. A third of "high eyebrows:" 4. A fourth, cruel-hearted, whose " teeth were as knives" to shred the poor of the earth, shred them small.

Such were these, and adultery made way for such. For *ubi corrupta sunt semina*, 'where a general corruption that way,' no good to be hoped for, the country will not last long. By this Christ had said enough, and shewed that *non dabitur eis*, is a fit answer for these.

Now, this ye shall mark; the worse the men, the more importune ever, and the harder to satisfy. They must have signs, and signs upon signs, and nothing will serve them; as no less than four several times were they at Christ. 1. Here; 2. in the sixteenth chapter; 3. Mark the eighth; 4. Luke the eleventh. And still to see a sign. As oft as they came, this had been their right answer; to dispatch them with

Mat. 16.
Mark 8. 11.
Lu. 11. 29.

a *non dabitur*, and no more ado. Other answer let them have none, even absolutely none at all, for none they should have had.

Yet saith He not, none they shall have. He will be better to them than they deserve; Christ will be Christ, *redit ad ingenium;* forgets now all He had said erewhile. And "an evil and adulterous generation" though they be, yet "a sign" they shall have for all that. Not simply "none" then, but *non nisi,* "none save;" the negative is qualified, so qualified as upon the matter it proves an affirmative. The *nisi* destroys the *non; non dabitur nisi,* that is, *dabitur.* So one they shall have, though not now presently at their *volumus,* at their whistling as it were, but after when He saw the time. And though perhaps not such an one as they would have fancied, yet such an one as they rather need, and would do them more good; that is, one for their want, not for their wanton desires.

II.
The denial qualified: *non nisi.*

And that is the reason why none but it, for no sign needed but it. For without others, well they might be; without this, they or we could not well be. For *oportuit Christum vati,* "It behoved Christ, Christ ought to die," and rise again.

Lu. 24. 26.

None but that? Why afterward, between this and His Passion, He shewed divers others, and how then saith He, none but it? Signs indeed He shewed, yet not any of them so pregnant for the purpose they sought, as was this. They sought a sign of the season, as by the sixteenth chapter is plain, that this was the time the Messias was to come. To put them out of doubt of that; to that point none so forcible as His death and rising again, figured in that of Jonas. That, and none but that. All He did else, the Prophets had done the like; given signs from Heaven, which they here sought, yea even raised the dead. But raise Himself being dead, get forth of the heart of the earth when once He was in, that passed their skill, never a Patriarch or Prophet of them all could do that; *non nisi,* none but He. So as therein He shewed Himself indeed to be the true and undoubted Messias, and never so else in any sign of them all.

Mat. 16. 4.

For signs being compounded of power and goodness, not power alone but power and goodness, that is, the benefit or good of them they be done for; never so general, so univer-

SERM.
XII.
sal, so great a good, as by Christ's death, as it might be
Jonas' casting in; nor ever so great, so incomparably great a
power, as by raising Himself from death to life, set forth in
Jonas' casting up again; those twain, by these twain, more
manifest than by any another. The sign of the greatest love
and power—love to die, power to rise, that ever was wrought.

This sign
*signum non
nisi*, a sign
para-
mount.
This *nisi* then is a *non nisi* in a new sense, a none-such,
a sign paramount. All else nothing in comparison of it.
I keep you too long from it.

The sign is laid in the Prophet Jonas, *sicut Jonas*, and we
are much bound to God for laying it in him; they, and we
both. And Jonas is a *non nisi*; such a sign for us, and
besides so many peculiars of Christ in him, as in effect no
sign but he.

For them,
*Propheta
peccator.*
First, for them, for "an evil and adulterous generation,"
no sign so meet to be given as he. For Jonas, and *non nisi
Jonas*, was *Propheta peccator*, 'the trespasser or sinning Prophet,' among them all. Sinners I know they were all, they
confess as much themselves; but for transgressing the express commandment of God, in not obeying God's immediate
call, therein none of the rest to be tainted, he only was *Propheta fugitivus*, fled touch, was in the transgression; sent to
Nineveh and went to Joppa; sent East, and went flat West;
and was even taken with the manner as we say, and arrested
in the very flight. For "an evil and an adulterous generation" this was a good sign say I; and so might they, if they
knew their own good. For them and for us, and in a word
for all sinners; for he is *Propheta peccator*, and so *Propheta
veccatorum*. And Christ is pleased to pick out His fugitive
Prophet, His runaway, and make him, a sinner and such a
Rom. 8. 3. sinner, His sign. As to come Himself "in the similitude of
sinful flesh," so to make sinful flesh His similitude, to come
into a *sicut* with. All, that sinful flesh might have hope in
the *signatum*, in Him of Whom this was the sign. This,
theirs, and ours.

For us,
*Propheta
gentium.*
The next is ours, and we highly to bless God for it; that
being to set His sign in a Prophet, He would do it in him,
choose him out to make him His pattern, who was *Propheta
Gentium*, 'the Prophet of the Gentiles,' sent to prophesy to
Nineveh that were heathen, as we and our fathers were.

And in that a *non nisi* too, for none but he was so, never a Prophet of them all sent to the heathen; the rest to the Jews, all. This sending of his to the Gentiles, was to us of the Gentiles, "a gate of hope," that in former ages, and long before Christ came in the flesh, we Gentiles were not forgotten. Even then, sent God a Prophet to Nineveh. And what was Nineveh? the head city of the Assyrians, the greatest monarchy then in being, and so the principal place of all paganism. That thus *in signo*, we were not forgotten, a sign it was, no more should we be *in signato*, but Christ be to us, as Jonas to them, "a light to lighten the Gentiles," and "His salvation to the uttermost parts of the earth." Isa. 49. 6.

Hos. 2. 15.

Lu. 2. 32.

Let me add this yet more, to our comfort. This Jonas whom He thus sent on this errand to the Gentiles, what was he? Of all the Prophets, all whose prophecies we have remaining on record in the Bible, the four great, the twelve less, of them all, all the sixteen, he was the first in time, senior to them all. Plain by 2 Kings 14, that he prophesied long before any of them. For it is there said, that his prophecy came to pass in the days of Jeroboam the Second, who lived the same time with Uzziah in Judah. And in Uzziah's time, the eldest of all the rest did but begin to prophesy. So his was done, before theirs was begun. Him that was thus first in the rank of them all, did God send to us Gentiles; to us first, before any to the Jews. A sign we were not last—nay first in His care, in that visited by Him first, as to whom He sent the first of all the sixteen. And I may say to you, this was to them an item, as if God were now to turn Gentile, as looking that way, having a mind to them then even in Jonas' time; they to come in shortly, and the Jews to be shut out; and that, as they had then priority *in signo*, so should they no less, *in signato*, and "the fulness of the Gentiles come in" before the conversion of the Jews. This to us sinners, to us Gentiles, to us "sinners of the Gentiles," was *salutare signum*, 'a healthful sign,' every way.

Primus Propheta- rum.

2 Kings 14. 25.

Rom. 11. 25.

[Gal. 2. 15.]

These three are put, on the by. In the main point of the text and of the time, two more.

He, and *non nisi*, none but he, had the honour to be a *piacularis hostia*, as it were, for the casting him into the sea served in a sort as a kind of 'expiatory sacrifice,' as far as to

1.
Jonas sig- num non nisi, as piacularis hostia.

SERM.
XII.
[1Joh.2.2.]

the temporal saving of the ship he sailed in. And therein as a meet sign he expressed Him Whose death was after the full and perfect "expiation of the sins of the whole world."

2.
As *Propheta redivivus.*

Then again Jonas, and *non nisi*, only he, was *propheta redivivus;* that is peculiar, above them all. He the only Prophet that went down into the deep into the whale's belly, and came forth again alive. Dead he was not, but *lege viventium,* 'after the law of the living,' one thrown overboard into the sea in a tempest to all intents may be given for dead, and so I dare say all the mariners in the ship gave Jonas. That he came out again alive, it was by special grace, not by course of nature. For from the whale's belly he came for all the world as if one should have come out of his grave, risen again.

1 Kings
17. 23.

Among the Jews it goes for current—the Rabbins take it up one after another, that this Jonas was the widow of Sarepta's son, the child whom Elias raised from death to life. If so, then well might he be a sign; a sign—dead in his cradle once, as good as dead in the whale's belly, now again. In both resembling Him Whose sign he was, if both be true; but one is most certain, and to that we hold us. And this is indeed the main *sicut*, the *sicut* of the text and of the day.

3.
As "three days and three nights in the whale's belly."
Gen.39.20.
Dan. 6. 16.

One more, and I have done, and that is of the time—precise "three days and three nights;" for in this a *non nisi.* For none but he so; just three, neither more nor less. For I ask, why not the sign of Joseph or of Daniel? Joseph was in the dungeon, among condemned persons to die; Daniel, in the lions' den, as deadly a place as the whale's belly; yet neither of them made the sign of Christ. Why? Joseph was in his dungeon too long; Daniel, too short—but a night; not long enough to represent Christ being in His grave. Only Jonas' time, just. And the time is it here. Else might the others have been His sign well enough, for the matter, if that had been all.

Lu. 24. 21.

But the time is still stood on, and the days numbered, that His Disciples, that all might know how long He would be from them, and not a day longer. And this, not without good cause. This day was but the third day, and this day they were at *sperabamus,* "did hope;" did, but now do not, their hope was fallen into a tertian, that it was time He

were up again. This sign set that they might know for
a surety, by this day at the farthest they should hear of
Him again.

Of which three. To verify His being there three days,
it is enough if He were there but a part of every one
of them, for it is not three whole days. As in common
phrase of speech, we say the sun shone or it rained these
three days past, though it did not so all day long but some
part only of each. And if it rained at all in every of them,
we say true, it is enough. And so here, the first day of the
three, Jonas was in the ship, and Christ on the cross till
Friday, somewhat before the sun-set. All the second day
Jonas was in the whale, Christ in His sepulchre. The third
day Jonas came out of the whale, and Christ out of His
grave, as it might be about the sun-rising, for this day both
suns rose together.

To verify the three nights. That do we reckoning, as did
the Jews, and that by warrant out of Genesis the first, the
evening and the morning but for one; so drawing still the Gen. 1. 5. 8,
precedent night, and counting it with the succeeding day. &c.
So do they still the night past with the day following, as
in Genesis they are taught; and we doing so, it will fall
out right.

To the *sicut* then of these three days. There is in each of The *sicut*
them set down a several state of Jonas, and so of Christ. of these
1. Their going thither; 2. their being there; 3. and their
coming thence.

Thus fell it the first day. Jonas was at sea in a ship; 1. In their
"a great tempest came," so great as the ship was upon thither.
casting away. Good-
Friday.
Of tempests, some are of course, have their causes in Jon. 1. 4, 5.
nature; and in them art and strength will do good. With
Jonas here it did not prevail a whit. Thereby they knew it
to be one out of course, of God's immediate sending.

God sends not such tempests but He is angry; He is not
angry but with sin. Some great sinner then there is in the
ship, and if the ship were well rid of him, all would be calm
again.

To lots they went; Jonas was found to be the party.

Being found, rather than all should be cast away, he bid

SERM.   frankly, *tollite me et projicite,* "take me, cast me into the
XII.   sea."
Jon. 1. 12.
        Cast in he was, and the storm ceased straight, the ship
[Gen. 1. 5.] came safe home.   "And the evening and the morning were
the first day."

Will ye see now what was acted in Jonas, actually fulfilled
in Christ? But first will ye note that what is in the Old
Testament written of Jonas, is not only *historia vera,* but
Eph. 5. 32. *sacramentum magnum,* not a bare story only, but beside the
story, pregnant also with "a great mystery." Not only
a deed done, but farther a sign of a deed to be done, of
a far higher nature; *dico autem in Christo,* "I speak it as
of Christ" and His resurrection. Of that history this the
mystery, this the *sacramentum magnum.*

Will ye note again? it is on Christ's side with advantage.
Mat. 12. 41. *Sicut Jonas,* saith this verse. But *ecce plus quam Jonas,* saith
the next, and both may stand; there may be a *sicut* where
yet there may be a *plus quam,* a likeness in quality where
an exceeding in degree though. Indeed, *sicut* makes not a
non nisi, plus quam doth; and we then so to remember the
sicut in this, as we forget not the *plus quam* in that. No
more will we.

And now weigh them over well, and whithersoever ye look,
ye shall find a *plus quam.* *Plus* in the ship, in the tempest,
in the cause, in the danger, in the casting in, in the coming
out again; in every one, a *plus quam.* All that was in Jonas,
in Christ more conspicuous, and after a more excellent
manner; *in signato,* than *in signo.* That so in this, as in all
Col. 1. 18. else, "Christ may have the pre-eminence."

To begin then. It is no new thing to resemble the Church,
the commonwealth, yea the world to a ship. A ship there
was, not a small bark of Joppa, but *plus quam,* a great ark
or argosy, wherein were embarked all mankind, having their
course through the main ocean of the world, bound for the
port of eternal bliss. And in this great carrick, among
the sons of men, the Son of Man, as He terms Himself, becomes also a passenger, even as did Jonas in his small
bottom of Joppa.

Then rose there a tempest. A tempest itself, and the cause
of all tempests, the heavy wrath of God, ready to seize upon

sinners, which made such a foul sea as this great ship and all
in it were upon the point of being cast away. The *plus* here
is plain, take it but as it was indeed literally. For what a Mat. 27.
tempest was there at Christ's death! It shook the Temple, ^{51, 52.}
rent the veil, cleft the stones, opened the graves, put out the
sun's light, was seen and felt all the world over, as if Heaven
and earth would have gone together. But the miserable
storm, then, who shall declare?

And no marvel; there was a great *plus* in the cause. For
if the sin of one poor passenger, of Jonas, made such a foul
sea, the sins of the great hulk that bore in it all mankind
together in one bottom, what manner tempest think you were
they like to raise? In what hazard the vessel that loaden
with them all! But one fugitive there; here all runaways
from God—masters, mariners, passengers, and all.

Now the greater the vessel, the more ever the danger. With
Jonas, but a handful like to miscarry; in this, the whole mass
of mankind like to perish. So in the peril *plus* too.

The storm will not be stayed neither, till some be cast
into the sea; and some great sinner it would be. And
here the *sicut* seems as if it would not hold; here the only
non sicut Jonas. For Jonas there was the only sinner, all
besides in the ship innocent poor men. Here Christ only
in the ship, innocent, no sinner, all the ship besides full
fraught with sinners; mariners and passengers, grievous sinners all. Here it seems to halt.

And yet I cannot tell you neither, for all that. For in
some sense Christ was not unlike Jonas; no, not in this
point, but like Jonas, as in all other respects, so in this too.
Not as considered in Himself, for so He knew no sin; " but 2 Cor. 5. 21.
Him that knew no sin, for us made He sin." How? by lay-
ing " on Him the iniquities of us all," even of all the sons Isa. 53. 6.
of men upon this Son of Man. And so considered, He is
not only *sicut,* but *plus quam Jonas* here. More sin on Him
than on Jonas; for on Him the sins of the whole ship, yea
Jonas' sin and all.

For all that here is another *plus,* though. For what Jonas
suffered, it was for his own sin, and *merito hæc patimur* might Lu. 23. 41.
he say, and we both with the thief on the cross. But Christ,
what had He done? It was not for His own, it was for other

S E R M.
XII.
————
Ps. 69. 4.
1 Pet. 3. 18.

men's sins He suffered, " He paid the things He never took."
So much the more likely was He to satisfy, "the just for the
unjust," the Lord for the servant; much more than if one
sinner or servant should do it for another.

Jon. 1. 12.
Joh. 18. 8.

Yet was Christ, as was Jonas, content to be thrown in.
Tollite Me, said Jonas; *sinite hos abire,* said Christ, "Let
these go." Take me, my life shall answer for theirs, as it
did. As content, said I? Nay, *plus,* 'more.' For with
Jonas there was no other way to stay the storm, but overboard with him. But Christ had other ways, could have
stayed it with His word, with His *obmutesce,* as He did the

Mat. 8. 26.
Mat. 3. 15.

eighth chapter before, needed not to have been cast in, yet
"to fulfil all righteousness," condescended to it though, and
in He was thrown, not of necessity as Jonas, but *quia voluit;*

Isa. 53. 7.
[Vulg.]

and *voluit, quia nos salvos voluit,* 'would have us safe,' and
His Father's justice safe, both.

Now to the effect. Therewith the storm stayed, God's
wrath was appeased, mankind saved: here the *plus* is evident. That of Jonas was but *salus phaseli*—no more; this
was *salus mundi*—no less. A poor boat with the whole world,
what comparison? And the evening and the morning were
Good-Friday, Christ's first day.

2. Their be-
ing there.
Easter-eve.

To Jonas now *secundo;* he was drowned by the means.
Nay, not so. God before angry, was then pacified; pacified, not only with the ship, but pacified with Jonas too;
provided a whale in show to devour him; indeed not to devour, but to preserve him; down he went into her belly.

There he was, but took no hurt there. 1. As safe, nay
more safe there than in the best ship of Tarshish; no flaw
of weather, no foul sea could trouble him there. 2. As
safe, and as safely carried to land; the ship could have
done no more. So that upon the matter he did but change
his *vehiculum,* shifted but from one vessel to another, went
on his way still. 3. On he went as well, nay better than
the ship would have carried him. Went into the ship—the
ship carried him wrong, out of his way clean, to Tarshish-
ward. Went into the whale, and the whale carried him
right, landed him on the next shore to Nineveh, whither
in truth he was bound, and where his errand lay. 4. And
all the while at good ease as in a cell or study, for there he

indited a Psalm, expressing in it his certain hope of getting ^{Jon. 2. 2. 6.} forth again. So as in effect, where he seemed to be in most danger, he was in greatest safety. Thus can God work. And the evening and the morning were Jonas' second day.

The like now in Christ, but still with a *plus quam.* Do. but compare the whale's belly with "the heart of the earth," and you shall find, the whale that swallowed Christ, that is, the grave, was another manner whale, far wider-throated than that of Jonas. That whale caught but one Prophet, but Jonas; this hath swooped up Patriarchs and Prophets and all, yea, and Jonas himself too. None hath scaped the jaws of it.

And more hard getting out, I am sure—witness Jonas. Into the whale's belly he went, and thence he gat out again. After he gat thence, into "the heart of the earth" he went, and thence he gat not; there he is still.

The sign lies in this, by the letter of the text. And in Christ the sign greater. For though to see a whale tumble with a Prophet in the belly were a strange sight, yet more strange to see the Son of God lie dead in the earth; and as strange again, to see the Son of man to rise from the grave again alone. A double sign in it.

"The heart of the earth," with Justin Martyr, Chrysostom, Augustine, I take for the grave; though I know Origen, Nyssen, Theodoret take it for hell, for the place where the spirits are, as in the body that is the place of them. And thither He went in Spirit, and "triumphed over the powers and principalities" there, in His own person. But for His body it was the day of rest, the last Sabbath that ever was; and then His body did rest, rest in hope—hope of what? that neither His soul should be left in hell, nor His flesh suffered to see corruption. For Christ had His Psalm too, as well as Jonas. David composed it for Him long before —the sixteenth Psalm, the Psalm of the Resurrection. And so the evening and the morning were Christ's second day, Easter-eve.

Now to Jonas' *ultimo.* Jonas' hope failed him not; the whale's belly that seemed his tomb, proved his womb or second birth-place. There he was, not as meat in the stomach, but as an embryo in the matrix of his mother.

[Justin. Mart. Quæstion. et Respons. ad Orthodox. 64. Chrysost. et Origen. in loc. Greg. Nyss. in Christ. Resurrect. Orat. 1. circ. init. S. August. Epist. 102. 34. Theodoret. Com. in Jon. 2. 3.] Col. 2. 15. Ps. 16. 10. 3. In their coming thence. Easter-day.

Strange! the whale to be as his mother, to be delivered of him, and bring him forth into the world again. So forth he

Jon. 2. 10. came, and to Nineveh about his business. Thither he went, to bring them out of the whale's belly too. And the evening and the morning were Jonas' third day.

Now the whale could not hold Jonas, nor more could the grave Christ longer than this morning, after break of day, but forth came He too. And with a *plus quam,* in respect of Jonas. It was in strict speech with Jonas no resurrection, for the truth is, he was never dead; never he, but *putative.* But Christ was dead, stark dead indeed, slain out-right upon

Joh. 19. 34. the cross, His heart pierced, His heart-blood ran out. And

Mat. 27. 66. for dead taken down, laid in, sealed up in His grave, a stone rolled on Him, a watch set over Him. Made sure, I trow, and yet rose for all that.

Another. Jonas rising, the whale gaped wide, and strained hard, and up came Jonas. It was long of the whale, not of him or any power of his. But Christ, by His own power,

Acts 2. 24. brake the bars of death, and "loosed the sorrows of hell, of which it is impossible He should be holden."

A third. Jonas rose but to the same state he was in before, but mortal Jonas still. When he scaped, he drew his chain after him, and by the end of it was plucked back again afterward. But Christ left them, and linen clothes and all, in the grave behind Him; rose to a better, to *ultra*

Rom. 6. 9. *non morietur,* never to die more, He.

And in a word, the great *plus quam.* Jonas was but *ejectus in aridam,* but Christ was *receptus in gloriam.* And in sign of it, the place whereon Jonas was cast, was dry land or cliffs, where nothing grows. The place wherein Christ rose, was a well-watered garden, wherein the ground was in all her glory, fresh and green and full of flowers at the instant of His rising, this time of the year. So, as He went lower, so He rose higher than ever did Jonas, with a great *ecce plus quam.*

And yet behold, a greater than all these. For Jonas, when he came forth, came forth and there was all; left the

Mat. 12. 42. whale as he found it. But *ecce plus quam Jonas hîc, plus quam* indeed. Christ slew the whale that devoured Him, in the coming forth, was *mors mortis;* He left not the grave as He found it, but altered the property, nay changed the very nature of it by His rising.

Three changes He made in it very plainly: 1. Of a pit of perdition which it was before, He hath made it now an harbour of rest, rest in hope. Hope of a new, not the same it was before, but a better far, with a great *plus quam.*

2. Made it again, as the whale to Jonas was, a convoy or passing boat to a better port than any is in our Tarshish here; even to the haven of happiness, and Heaven's bliss Acts 2. 26. without end. This for the soul.

3. And for the body, made the grave as a womb for a second birth, to travail with us anew, and bring us forth to life everlasting; made *cor terræ ventrem ceti,* 'the heart of the earth to us, as the belly of the whale was' to Jonas, which did not still retain him. That did not him, nor this shall not us; shall not hold us still, no more than the whale did him, or the grave did Christ. There shall be a coming forth out of both. And when God shall speak to the earth, as to the whale He did, the sea and grave both shall yield Rev. 20. 13. up their dead, and deliver them up alive again.

The very term of " the heart of the earth" was well chosen. There is heart in it. For if the earth have an heart, there is life in it, for the heart is the fountain of life, and the seat of the vital spirits that hold us in it. So there is, we see; for the earth dead for a time, all the winter—now when the waters of Heaven fall on it, shews it hath life, bringing forth herbs and flowers again. And even so, when the waters above the Heavens, and namely the dew of this day distilling from Christ's rising, shall in like sort drop upon it, it shall be, saith Esay in the twenty-sixth chapter, " as the dew of Isa. 26. 19. the herbs," "and the earth shall give forth her dead." " Dead" men, as it doth dead plants, now fresh and green again in the spring of the year. And so the evening and the morning were Christ's third day, this day, Easter-day morning.

Thus many ways doth this *sicut* hold, and hold with a *plus quam.* Were it not great pity now that Christ Who is so many ways *plus quam Jonas,* for all this should come to be *minus quam Jonas,* in this last, the chief of all? For this is the chief. Jonas, after he came out of the whale, brought to

SERM. pass that famous repentance, the repentance of Nineveh.
XII. At Jonas' preaching they repented at Nineveh, at Christ's
Jonah 3. 5. they did not in Jerusalem.

We shall mend this, if we be as the Ninevites, repent as
they. As they? *Absit ut sic,* saith St. Augustine, but adds
then, *sed utinam vel sic.* As they? God forbid we should be
but as they; as Christ was more than Jonas, so Christians
should be more than Ninevites. Well, in the mean time, I
would we were but as they; but so far onward, never plead
for a *plus,* but be content with *sicut,* and never seek more;
but that we must, for less sure we cannot be. Christ to be
plus quam Jonas, we to be *minus quam Ninivitæ*—it will not
fit, it holds no proportion.

What this The *sicut* ye see, and the *plus quam,* both. Now what is
sign por- the profit of this sign of the Prophet? This sign being of
tends. Christ's giving, Christ gives no sign, but it is *signum in*
Ps. 86. 17. *bonum,* "a sign for good," a good sign; and a good sign is
a sign of some good. Of what good is this a sign? Of hope
of coming forth sure. Coming forth whence? From a whale.
What is meant by the whale? the deliverance most-what is
as the whale is. And three whales we find here: 1. Jonas'
whale; 2. Christ's whale; 3. and a third; and hope we
have, to come forth of all three.

First Jonas' whale. Death it was not, it was but danger,
but danger as near death as could be, never man in more
danger to escape it than he; if not in death, in Zalmaveth,
Ps. 23. 4. "in the vale of the shadow of death" it was.

Of any that hath been in extreme peril we use to say,
He hath been where Jonas was. By Jonas' going down the
whale's throat, by him again coming forth of the whale's
mouth, we express, we even point out the greatest extremity,
and the greatest deliverance that can be. From any such
danger, a deliverance is a kind of resurrection, as the Apostle
plainly speaks of Isaac; when the knife was at his throat, he
Heb.11.19. was "received from the dead," ὡσεὶ ἐν παραβολῇ, though
yet he died not. This for the feast of the Resurrection.

And thus was Jonas a sign to them of Nineveh. As he
escaped, so they—he his whale, they theirs, destruction,
which even gaped for them as wide as Jonas' whale. And
as to them a sign this, so to us. And this use we have of it;

when at any time we are "hard bestead," this sign then to be [Isa. 8, 21.] set up for a token. And there is no danger so deadly, but we may hold fast our hope, if we set this sign before us, and say —What? we are not yet in the whale's belly; why, if we were there, from thence can God bring us though, as Jonas He did.

Jonas' whale was but the shadow of death; Christ's was death. And even there in death to be set up. And we not in death itself to despair, but with Job to say, yea, "Though Job 13. 15. He kill me, yet will I trust in Him." My breath I may, my hope I will not forego; *expirare possum, desperare non possum.* Here now is our second hope; to come forth, to be delivered from Christ's whale, from death itself.

But if the whale be, or betoken, the death of the body, it doth much more the death of the soul. So shall we find another whale yet, a third. And that whale is the "red dra- Rev. 12. 3. gon," that great spiritual Leviathan, Satan. And sin, the very jaws of this whale, that swoopeth down the soul first, and then the body, and in the end both. Jonas had been deep down this whale's throat, before ever he came in the other's; the land-whale had devoured him, before ever the sea-whale meddled with him. In his flight he fell into this land-whale's jaws before ever the sea-whale swallowed him up. And when he had got out of the gorge of this ghostly Leviathan, the other bodily whale could not long hold him. And from this third whale was Jonas sent, to deliver the Ninevites; which when he had, the other, of their temporal destruction, could do them no hurt. Their repentance rid them of both whales, bodily and ghostly, at once.

Here then is a third cape of good hope, that though one had been down as deep in the entrails of the spiritual great Leviathan as ever was Jonas in the sea-whale's, yet even there also not to despair. He That brought Jonas from the deep of the sea, and David "from the deep of the earth," his Ps. 71. 20. body so; He also delivered his "soul from the nethermost Ps. 86. 13. hell," where Jonas and he both were, while they were in the transgression.

And now by this are we come to the very signature of this sign, even to repentance, which followeth in the very next words, "for they repented at the preaching of Jonas." Jonas Mat. 12. 41.

preached it, and indeed none so fit to preach on that theme, on repentance, as he, as one that hath been in the whale's belly; in both the whales, the spiritual whale's too, for Jonas had been in both. One that hath studied his sermon there, been in Satan's sieve, well winnowed, *cribratus Theologus*, he will handle the point best, as being not only a preacher but a sign of repentance, as Jonas was both to the Ninevites.

And as Jonas, so Christ; how soon He was risen, He gave order straight "that repentance," as the very virtue, the Lu. 24. 47. stamp of His resurrection, and by it "remission of sins should be preached in His name to all nations."

But, indeed, if you mark well, there is a near alliance between the Resurrection and Repentance; reciprocal, as between the sign and the signature. Repentance is nothing Eph. 2. 1. but the soul's resurrection; men are "dead in sin," saith the Apostle, their souls are. From that death there is a rising; else were it wrong with us. That rising is repenting; and when one hath lain dead in sin long, and doth *eluctari*, 'wrestle out of' a sin that hath long swallowed him up, he hath done as great a mastery, as if with Jonas he had got out of the whale's belly; nay, as if with Lazarus he had come out of "the heart of the earth." Ever holding this, that Mary Magdalene raised from sin, was no less a miracle than her brother raised from the dead.

And sure, repentance is the very virtue of Christ's resurrection. There it is first seen, it first sheweth itself, hath his first operation in the soul, to raise it.

This first being once wrought on the soul from the ghostly Leviathan, the like will not fail but be accomplished on the Eph. 5. 32. body from the other of death, of which Jonas is here *mysterium magnum; dico autem in Christo.* For in Christ this sign is a sign, not betokening only, but exhibiting also what it betokeneth, as the Sacraments do. For of signs, some Mat. 12. 41. shew only and work nothing; such was that of Jonas in itself, *sed ecce plus quam Jonas híc.* For some other there be that shew and work both—work what they shew, present us with what they represent, what they set before us, set or graft in us. Such is that of Christ. For besides that it sets before us of His, it is farther a seal or pledge to us of our own, that what we see in Him this day, shall be accomplished in our own selves, at His good time.

And even so pass we to another mystery, for one mystery leads us to another; this in the text, to the holy mysteries we are providing to partake, which do work like, and do work to this, even to the raising of the soul with "the first resurrection." And as they are a means for the raising Rev. 20. 5. of our soul out of the soil of sin—for they are given us, and we take them expressly for the remission of sins—so are they no less a means also, for the raising our bodies out of the dust of death. The sign of that body which was thus "in the heart of the earth," to bring us from thence at the last. Our Saviour saith it *totidem verbis,* "Whoso eateth My flesh Joh. 6. 54. and drinketh My Blood, I will raise him up at the last day" —raise him, whither He hath raised Himself. Not to life only, but to life and glory, and both without end. To which, &c.

A SERMON

PREACHED BEFORE

THE KING'S MAJESTY AT WHITEHALL,

ON THE FIFTH OF APRIL, A.D. MDCXVIII., BEING EASTER-DAY.

---

1 Corinthians xi. 16.

But if any man seem to be contentious, we have no such custom, neither the Churches of God.

Si quis autem videtur contentiosus esse, nos talem consuetudinem non habemus, neque Ecclesiæ Dei.

[*But if any man seem to be contentious, we have no such custom, neither the Churches of God.* Engl. Trans.]

SERM. XIII.

THIS is no Easter text as we are wont to have, nothing of the Resurrection in it. It is not for the day.

1. How the text may serve for Easter.

It is not directly, but if it should happen there were any contention about Easter, that would bring it within the word "contentious" here. Specially, if that contention about Easter were, whether it hath been ever a custom in the Church of God, for that would bring it within in the word "custom" here mentioned; and so would it both ways fall within the compass of the text. The custom of Easter made a contention, would make it an Easter-day text.

The text two ways qualified. 1. *Videtur.* "Seems."

I say not any such contention there is, I desire to proceed, as the Apostle doth, without the least offence. 1. He saith not, there be any "contentious," but "if any seem to be." That any be "contentious," it may not be said. They will deeply protest that from their hearts they abhor all contentions, and desire to walk peaceably. Be not then, but "seem to be."

2. Nay, not "seem to be" neither, St. Paul says not so 2. *Si quis,*
"If any."
much; says only, *si quis,* "if any;" puts but a case, and
there is no harm in that. No more will we, go no farther
than the text: "If any such seem to be," this text tells what
to do; if none be, none "seem to be," it is but a case put.
And so by way of supposition be all said that shall be. All upon

Upon the view, three points give forth themselves: 1. supposi-
tion.
Here are contentions: and 2. here are customs; and 3. cus- The di-
vision.
toms opposed to the contentions. These the three heads.

To break them yet farther into certain theses or propo- I.
Conten-
sitions, to proceed by. 1. First, it should seem there were tions.
contentions in the Apostle's times. 2. Contentions about
what? About matter of circumstance. So was this here,
whether men were to pray uncovered, and women veiled or
no? 3. And that there were which did not only contend,
but which is more, were even "contentious" about these.
4. For those that were so, here is a *si quis* set up, "if any
seem to be" such, what to do to them.

Not to pass them in silence and say nothing to them, but II.
this to say; "we have no such custom, nor the Churches of The
Church-
God." And so oppose the Churches' custom to contention. customs.

In which saying, there are these heads: 1. First, that the
Church hath her customs. 2. As she hath them, so she may,
and doth allege them. 3. And allege them finally, as the
Apostle here, we see, resolveth the whole matter into them,
as into a final resolution. 4. And all this by Scripture confirmed, even by this Scripture, on which the customs of the
Church are grounded, and the power that shall be ever in
them, to overrule the "contentious."

And let not this move you that it seems to be negative, *Non habe-*
mus talem.
Non habemus talem. As this time twelve-month *Non dabitur* Mat. 12. 39.
nisi, a negative in show, proved an affirmative, *Dabitur, sed* The text
the last
non nisi; so will this *Non habemus talem* prove to *habemus,* year.
sed non talem. "Custom" we have, but "none such." To Negative
in shew;
apply it to the Apostle's purpose: "none," to sit covered at Affirma-
tive in
prayer, *non talem,* "none such," but the contrary rather; to effect.
be uncovered then, *talem,* such is our custom, such an one
the Church hath.

Where, because the negative refers not to *habemus,* but to The two
marks of a
talem, and a custom is not therefore good, because we have right cus-
tom.

SERM.
XIII.

III.
The
Church-
custom for
keeping
Easter.

There
wants not
Scripture
for Easter.
Epist. 119.
cap. 14.
[55. 15. B.]

Ps. 118. 24.

1 Cor. 5. 7, 8.

But the
Church's
custom is
more
kindly.

The use of
the third
point
about
Easter.

it, but because it is *talem,* so qualified. The *talem* to be,
1. First, if "we," that is, the Apostles have had it, if it were
Apostolic; the *non talem* to be, if our new masters have
taken it up the other day, and the Apostles never knew it.
2. The *talem* to be, if "the Churches of God" in general
have had it, if it be Catholic. The *non talem* to be, if the
Church of Corinth, or some one Church perhaps had it, but
the rest never had any such.

Then, will we descend to shew the keeping of Easter, to
be such, ever in use with "the Churches of God" from the
time of the Apostles themselves. Which, if we can make
plain, here is a plain text for it; that if one should ask,
What Scripture have you why Easter may not be laid down?
it may well be answered, *Non habemus talem consuetudinem,
nec Ecclesiæ Dei.* Custom to keep it we have—the Apostles,
the Church had it; but to abolish it, "such custom have we
none," we depart from them both if we do.

Protesting yet, that we have no purpose to wave Scripture
quite for the keeping of Easter. St. Augustine is plain : *Hoc
ex authoritate divinarum Scripturarum, per anniversarium
Pascha celebratur;* 'Even by authority of divine Scripture
it is, that every year Easter is kept solemnly.' We have
touched two Scriptures heretofore; "The day, which the
Lord hath made," applied ever to this feast. That text for
the Old. And for the New Testament that verse in this
Epistle, "Christ our Passover is offered, let us therefore keep
a feast."

But every thing standeth safest and surest upon his own
base, and the right base of this I take to be custom. We do
but make ourselves to be pitied otherwhile, when we stand
wringing the Scriptures, to strain that out of them that is
not in them, and so can never come *liquide* from them, when
yet we have for the same point the Churches' custom clear
enough. And that is enough, by virtue of this text. There
is and shall be enough ever in this text, to avow any custom,
—the Apostles, the Churches of God had it; to disavow any
—the Apostles, the Churches of God had it not.

The fruit of our labour will be this I hope at least, to con-
firm us in the keeping of it. We keep Easter, many of us,
we know not upon what ground. By this we shall see we

have a ground for that we do; we do no more than the Churches of God, than the Apostles have done before us. So, our ears shall hear the voice in Esay behind us, *Hæc est* Isa. 30. 21. *via,* "This is the way," *ambulate in eâ,* "walk in it" as you do, you are in the right, and there hold you.

"If any." This "if" I take it, is no idle *if,* no vain sup- L. position; to say, "if there be any," where there were none. No; contentions there were. When? when "we"—who be they? St. Paul and his fellow Apostles, when they lived. 1. And "the Churches"—what Churches? the Churches under $\frac{\text{Conten-}}{\text{tions in}}$ them, of their times. In the very prime of the Primitive $\frac{\text{the Apo-}}{\text{stles' time.}}$ Church then were there contentions.

And those not with an enemy without, Jew or Gentile— that were πόλεμος, 'war' abroad; this is νεῖκος, but 'a jar' at home, among themselves. That former abroad they re- present by Ishmael and Isaac, and they were of two venters. Gal. 4. 29. This latter at home, by the two twins in Rebecca's womb. Gen. 25. 23. I fear the time; else could I let you see this strife, in every Church of them.

This I note first, that we may not ξενίζεσθαι, to use St. Peter's term, "think it strange," if there be contentions 1 Pet. 4. 12. in our times. They shall be no strangers with us, in ours; they were not with them, in theirs. Neither contentions, in this verse; nor "schisms" in the next, the eighteenth; nor "heresies," in the nineteenth, next to that. It is of "the fiery trial" St. Peter speaks it, of persecution; it is as true of the watery trial of contention. As true it is of the last as of the first Church, "I proved thee also at the waters of Ps. 81. 7. strife." Those waters, the waters of Meribah, will hardly be drained ever.

There were contentions then; about what? For though $\frac{2.}{\text{Conten-}}$ peace be precious, yet of such moment may the matters be, tions about as they are to be contended for, yea even to the death. For $\frac{\text{matter of}}{\text{circum-}}$ what then were these? For nothing but a matter of rite— stance. men praying, whether they should be uncovered: women, 4, 5. whether veiled or no. For a hat and a veil was all this ado. It was not about any the high mysteries, any of the vital parts of Religion, Preaching, Prayer, the Sacraments; only about the manner how, the gesture and behaviour where- with; in what sort to carry themselves at Preaching, Prayer, the Sacraments; about matter of circumstance merely, and nothing else.

And even these, even the meanest things would be done "for the better," not "for the worse," saith the Apostle in the next verse. And the more order, the better. So the Apostle had set order for them, and *inter alia*, for this too. Other his ordinances, he saith, they remembered well, but not this; this was opposed. For with some all is not worth a rush, if they see not farther than their fellows, nay their betters, then; if they find not somewhat to find fault with, if it be but a ceremony. And to pick a quarrel with a ceremony is easy. A plausible theme, not to burden the Church with ceremonies; the Church to be free, which hath almost freed the Church of all decency.

3.
Yea, contentiousness, which is more than contention.
About such points as these were there that did not only contend, but that grew contentious. Νεῖκος is one thing, to contend; φιλονεικία another, to be "contentious." The Apostle saith not, if any contend; but *si quis contentiosus*. And *osus* is full; φίλε is one that loves it, is given to it. Strange any such should be, but the Apostle's "if" proves to be no if. We see it daily in persons but meanly qualified, God wot, yet so peremptory, as "if the word of God had come, if not from them, yet to them only, and none besides." Good Lord! Why should any love to be "contentious?" Why? It is the way to be somebody. In time of peace, what reckoning is there of Wat Tyler, or Jack Straw? Make a sedition, and they will bear a brain with the best. Primianus and Maximianus were the heads of the two factions of Donatists in St. Augustine's time. He saith, it was well for them that faction fell out; else Primianus might have been *Postreminianus*, and Maximianus be *Minimianus*, well enough. But now in schism either of them was a jolly fellow, head of a party. This makes we shall never want contentious persons, and they will take order we shall never want contentions.

4.
Such contention not to be neglected.
Well, if any such should happen to be, what is to be done in such a case? What saith the Apostle? Saith he thus? Seeing it is no greater matter, it skills not greatly whether they do it or no, covered or bare, sit or kneel, all's one; sets it light, and lets it go. No; but calls them back to the

"custom" of the Church, will not have them swerve from
that, makes a matter of it. For we see he presses the point
hard, spends many words, many verses, even half the chapter
about it.

Why doth he so? For two reasons. 1. First, he likes not Not any
contention at all. Why? If it be not taken at the first, tion.
within a while, within one verse after, ye shall hear of a
"schism,"—look the eighteenth verse; and within a little
after that—look but to the nineteenth, ye shall have a flat
"heresy" of it. The one draws on the other; if the contentious humour be not let out, it will fester straight, and prove
to an apostume.

2. Nor, he likes not the matter wherefore, though it seem No, not in
but small. St. Paul knew Satan's method well; he seems these
small mat-
somewhat shamefaced at first, asks but some small trifle. ters.
Give him but that, he will be ready for greater points. If he For, from
win ground in the Ceremonies, then have at the Sacrament; nies to Sa-
if he can disgrace the one, it will not be long but ye shall craments.
hear of him at the other.

Speak I beside the book? was it not so here? At the very
next verse, there he falls in hand with an abuse of the Sacrament, and that takes up the rest of the chapter.

For when they had sat covered at prayer awhile, they grew
even as unreverent, as homely with the Sacrament; eat and
drunk there as if they had been at home, *in triclinio,* that the
Apostle is fain to tell them at the twenty-second verse, they
had homes to be homely at: the Church, the house of God—
they were to be used with greater reverence. "He did not
commend them" for this their rude carriage, at the Sacrament. "Did not commend them?" you know what that
meaneth—*minus dicitur, plus intelligitur,* he blamed them
much for it.

Then are we to make stay at these less matters at first, as
the Apostle doth. To think the Wise Man's counsel worth
the following, *ne sit tibi minimum, non negligere minima,* [Comp.
"count it no small matter, not to neglect small matters." Ecclus.
19. 1.]
What so small as an hair? when these small hairs were gone Judges 16.
from Samson, his strength left him. In itself, in his own 19.
nature, a rite is not so much. This is much, that by it they

learn to break the Church's orders, and that thereby they are fleshed to go on to greater matters.

II.
To these conten- tions, the Church- custom opposeth.

Opposing then to these, what course takes he? Lays for his ground this, *non habemus talem.* The force of his reason is, If "we," if "the Churches of God" had any such custom, it were somewhat, that were warrant enough for a Rite. But now, we and they both have none such, nay we and they have the quite contrary; therefore, let us hear no more of it.

1.
The Church hath her customs.

Where, it is plain, the Apostle is for the Church-customs. 1. And first, that she hath them. Every society, beside their laws in books, have their customs also in practice; and those, not to be taken up or laid down at every man's plea-

Pand. 1.
Tit. 3. de legib. 35.
[36.]

sure. The civil law saith this of custom, *Imo magnæ autho- ritatis hoc jus habetur, quod in tantum probatum est, ut non fuerit scripto comprehendere necesse.* Men, it seems, had a great good liking to their customs, that they remembered them without book, that they never needed to be put in writing, as their laws and statutes did. Now as every society, so the Church, besides her *habemus legem,* hath her *habemus consuetudinem* too. There is such a thing as *mos populi Dei.*

And fear not traditions a whit. Those respect *credenda,* 'points of doctrine;' these but *agenda,* 'matters of practice,' and that, not in points of substance, reach only to matter of circumstance, go no farther. Nor do we even them with, much less oppose them to, that which is written. Never any custom against that; no custom that comes from the will or wit of man, against Scripture which comes from

Mat. 23.23.

the wisdom and will of God. But *hæc oportet facere, et illa non omittere.* Only so.

The Apo- stles and their Churches had their customs.

The Church then hath her customs. I add, these "we" here, that is, the Apostle had them, and the Churches under them had theirs. It was but early day then, yet had they their customs, even then. At the writing of this Epistle, it was not at the most thirty years from Christ's Ascension. If that were time enough to make a "custom," now after these twenty times thirty years, and thirty times thirty years, and a hundred years to spare, shall it not be a "custom" now by much better right? A custom is susceptible of more and less; the farther it goeth, the longer it runneth, the more strength it gathereth; the more grey hairs it getteth, the more venerable it is, for indeed the more a custom it is.

Now then as the Church hath them, so she stands upon them; fears not, we see, to allege them, to say *habemus*, or *non habemus*. *Habemus*, to uphold an ancient good one; *non habemus*, to lay down an evil one new taken up. *2.
The Church allegeth her customs.*

Here, *negative, non habemus talem*. As our Saviour likewise—*a principio non fuit sic*. And yet by implication this here is, One we have, but not such an one. And our Saviour's there, A way there was "from the beginning," but this was not it. *In the negative. Mat. 19. 8.*

But otherwhere, it is *positive* also, to affirm and to maintain a good; and men positively referred to know, what hath been the use in former times. *In the affirmative.*

Higher than Moses we cannot go. Moses as a law-giver, one would think, would be all for law. He is *positive* full for custom too. "Enquire," saith he, "of the days that be past, how it hath gone since the day God created the earth." And that, in the second edition, or setting forth of the Law. *Hath ever so alleged. Moses. Deu. 4. 32.*

Job is for it too. "Enquire, I pray you, of the former age, and set yourselves to ask after the Fathers, for we are but of yesterday—shall not they tell you," thus, and thus it was in their times? *Job 8. 8.*

And say not the Prophets the same? "Stand upon the ways"—it is Jeremy, "and there look for the good old way, and that way take, it is the only way to find rest for your souls." *The Prophets. Jer. 6. 16.*

To all which agreeable is that wherewith I will shut up this point, which all the Fathers in the first Nicene Council took up, and which ever since hath been the Church's cry, τὰ ἀρχαῖα ἤθη κρατείτω, *mos antiquus obtineat*, 'let old customs prevail,' let them carry it. By this you see, *habemus consuetudinem* hath been counted a sound allegation, not only from the Apostles', but even from Moses' time. *The Fathers. [Can. 6.]*

And now for the *talem*, for it is not the *habemus* that binds, but the *talem*. Not because we have it, but because it is so qualified. It is not every custom, hand over head, we may stand on. Why binds not this? 1. Because, though it may be it was at Corinth, *Ecclesia Dei*, "a Church of God," *3.
The badges of a right custom, two.*

E e

one Church, yet *Ecclesiæ Dei*, the other "Churches" of God had it not; the word is plural. 2. Because, though it hath liked some not long since to like well of it, yet the Apostles never knew it; or the other way, if it have liked them to dislike it and lay it down, yet the Apostles liked it well enough.

Non talem, saith the Apostle, "none such." *Qualem* then? How shall we do to know the right *talem?* Thus. *Non talem* is here opposed to two; to "the Churches of God," to *nos,* that is, the Apostles.

If it be
*Ecclesi-
arum Dei.*
If it be but of some one Church, but at Corinth alone, it is too narrow; not large, not general enough. If it be but taken up by some of our masters of late, it is too fresh, it is not ancient enough; *non talem,* "no such."

But by these two, we know our right *qualem.* If it be *Ecclesiarum,* that is, if it be general; if *nos* come to it, that is, the Apostles, if it be ancient; then is it rightly qualified, then it is as it should be, then it may be alleged and stood upon, then it will bind; and then, if any oppose, *videtur conten-tiosus esse.*

I begin with the Church, in the plural. Every Church hath power to begin a custom, and that custom power to bind her own children to it; provided her private custom affront not the general, received by all others, for then binds it not. By the rule in the mathematics, ever *totum est parte majus;* and by the rule in the morals, ever *turpis pars omnis toti non congrua.*

As neither is any particular Church bound to the private custom of another, like particular as itself is. But if the other Churches' custom have also been the general custom of the Church, then it binds and may not be set light, for then
Epist. 118.
cap. 5.
[54. 5. B.]
said it must be that St. Augustine doth say, If the whole Church usually have observed aught, to go from that or to question whether it be to be observed, *insolentissimæ insaniæ est.* It savours of a distemper coming of a heat or humour
Prov. 13.
10.
of pride, for "only by pride," saith Solomon, "cometh contention." This for the Churches' custom.

If *nos,*
that is,
the Apo-
stles had it.
But if to this we add, or rather if before this we set this, *nos,* the Apostles had it too, that it is Apostolic; we have then said as much as in this point can be said, as much as

may content any that is not " contentious," that is not more
wedded to shew his wit than to seek the truth, and more
set φυλάττειν τὴν θέσιν, 'to maintain his own position,' than
to regard the Churches' peace. For sure, if a custom be to
be esteemed by antiquity, such a custom is *ab heroicis usque
temporibus*, for they be our heroes. 2. If it be to be esteemed
by the author, what authors more worthy in themselves, more
worthy of our imitation, than they? Nothing can be devised
more reasonable than that in the one hundred and eighteenth
Quæst. ad Orthod. in Justin Martyr, That of, and from, whom [*Respons.
ad fin.*]
we received τὸ εὔχεσθαι to pray; of and from them, we
should also receive τὸ πῶς εὔχεσθαι, how and when, at what
time, at what feasts to do it. Their example, that is, the
Apostles', the Church commended to her children to prac-
tise—a better she could not; that practice in time grew to
a custom. That custom is *talem*, may safely be alleged.

Lastly, as this sheweth it may be alleged for a good argument in Divinity, so doth it 1. what the men are, against
whom; 2. what the matters, wherein; 3. what the penalty,
whereupon it may be alleged. {4. The use of this argument from custom.}

1. Whom against. This may be alleged against *si quis
videtur contentiosus esse*, such as are, or at least " seem contentious." *Habemus*, or *non habemus consuetudinem*, is their
proper answer. No reasoning with such, it will be to small
purpose, they will be *sine fine dicentes*. St. Augustine saith
well, they cannot distinguish between *respondere posse*, and
tacere nolle, they take them for all one. So they cry loudest
and have the last word, they take it they have answered sufficiently. Against these it lieth most properly. None so ready
a way to stop their mouths, for custom is matter of fact,
habemus or *non habemus* may be put to the twelve men, and
there is an end. St. Paul then using it here against these,
teacheth us to use it against the like. Against such parties,
against *si quis videtur contentiosus esse*, to put it upon this,
Is there a custom, or is there none? {Against what parties.}

Specially, if the matter be of the nature of this here in the
text, where the question seemed to concern but matter of
circumstance and outward order, there hath it his right use,
that the proper place of it. You will say, But had it not
been good though to have used some reason for it? It had, {In what matters.}

E e 2

and the Apostle used divers, if that would have served—from the signification at the third verse, from decency at the thirteenth, from nature at the fourteenth. But to say the truth, such he saw a wrangling wit would elude. The nature of the question afforded none other. It was well observed, and set down for a rule by the philosopher, That in moral matters, men may not look for mathematical proofs, the nature of the subject will not bear them. If not in moral, in ritual much less; they of all other least susceptible of a demonstrative reason.

The Apostle saw this, and therefore finally resolves all into the Churches' practice, by custom confirmed in matters of this kind, enough of itself to suffice any that will *sapere ad sobrietatem.* In so doing, as he took the right course we are sure, so he taught us by his example in points of this nature, of ceremony or circumstance, ever to pitch upon *habemus* or *non habemus talem consuetudinem.* This to be final.

Upon what penalty.

2. And then follows upon what penalty. Upon no other pain, but to be pronounced to be fallen into the Apostle's *si quis,* to be taken and declared *pro contentioso.* Then if any for every point of rite that takes him in the head, will hazard the Church's peace; will not *acquiescere,* but set himself against the Church's custom, he knoweth his doom here. For it turns back *reciproce.* As, if any be " contentious," the Churches' custom is against him, so if any turn upon the Churches' custom, be against it, it is no good sign; *videtur* saith St. Paul, to the Apostle " he seems" so, and he had his eyes in his head. And what such seemed to him, they may well seem to us; and we take them for no less that are like stirring in matters of no more weight. And so an

The argument final.

end of this matter. For the Apostle, when he had said this, thought he had said enough, needed to say no more. The Churches' custom shall ever be of force, to overrule such as are contentious. And when St. Paul had said this, he had said. And so have we.

III.
The keeping Easter is such a custom.

This then being set down, That customs so qualified are to be kept, shall we now go on to the hypothesis that the keeping of Easter is such? And now I would the hour were to begin again, so much is to be said for it.

One foot of our compass we fix in the Apostles' times.

Of the Resurrection. 421

The other, where? They appoint us Gelasius' time who was fast upon the five hundredth year. Be it so.

From the Apostles' age which ended with St. John, who survived Christ sixty-eight years, and died the year 102, under Trajan, to Gelasius' age. Of these five hundred, the first hundred years are for *nos*, the Apostles' time. From thence, the four hundred years following, are for the Churches'. Which four hundred we may divide again into two even moieties—two hundred under persecution, two hundred under peace.

To prove then our *habemus consuetudinem,* we cannot better begin than with this in the text, the contentions that from the beginning rose about it. Those very contentions prove it. It must *be* that must be contended for, and then it must be, when it is contended for. These three things in this one proof. 1. The contentions that were about it, even presently upon the Apostles' times; 2. The great care had, and continual pains taken to lay them down, that is, the Churches' contending for the feast; 3. The censuring of those that took them up, with St. Paul's *contentiosus* here, and with somewhat more; of Blastus, at Rome in Europe; or Crescentius in Egypt, for Africa; of Audæus, in Syria, for Asia;—these were the principals, these were all written up in the black book, by those that registered the heretics; by Tertullian, Epiphanius, Philastrius, Augustine, and Theodoret, all five.

But as God would have it, the question never was of the feast itself, but of the time of it only. All kept Easter, though not all at one time. For the keeping they had the Churches' custom; for the time of keeping, they had their own;—the feast of the Christians, the time of the Jews.

And I will tell you how this came, first. From St. James, who was the first, there were successively one after another fifteen Bishops of Jerusalem, all of them of the Circumcision. These, the sooner to win their brethren the Jews, condescended to keep their Easter, XIV.° *Lunæ,* as they did. That which was by them thus done by way of condescension, was after by some urged as a matter of necessity, as if it were not lawful but on that day to hold it.

The first that it took thus in the head, Tertullian in the end of *De Præscriptione* saith, was one Blastus about the days

The time to make this custom. How long the Apostles'. 100. How long the Churches'. 400.

Proofs for the custom of the Churches. 1. Proof. From contentions about it. 2. The Church took part with Easter. 3. Censured ever for heretics, that against it. Tert. *de Præscr.* c. 53. Epiphan. *Hæres.* 30. Syn. Antioch. Can. 1.

The contention not about the feast, but the time only.

How the contention first came.

Tertull. *de Præscr.* 53. Iren.

S. E R M.
XIII.
Frag.
Epiph.
Hær. 30.
sive 50.
[Vid. Dion.
Petav.
Animad.
ad Hæres.
50.]
of Commodus.   He began a schism.   And Irenæus presently wrote *De Schismate contra Blastum.*   But after, from schism Blastus fell to heresy, and began that of the *Quartodecimani ;* to whose manner of keeping it, for the most part, other heretics did cleave, leaving the Churches' custom of purpose since they were departed from her.

Great pity some in our days had not been then living to have advised the Church to have saved her pains, and never have striven so about it; the shortest way was to have made no more ado, but kept none at all.   But *non habemus talem consuetudinem,* would have been their answer.   But you will easily guess, if these for not keeping it at the right time were scored up for heretics, what would become of them that had been against the keeping of it at all.

None
against
Easter, but
Aërius.
Epiph.
Hæres. 75.
[3.]
1 Cor. 5.
7, 8.
Till now in our days, there was never any such but Aërius; he took it away clean, as Jewish.   His reason was, saith Epiphanius, scorning it because "Christ our Passover is offered." "Christ our Passover is offered, let us therefore keep a feast," saith St. Paul.   Let us therefore keep none, saith Aërius, holden for so saying for little better than crazed.   There was never any Council called about him; but as Aërius was his name, so was his opinion, and so it vanished into air, and was blown over straight.   Otherwise all heretics, an Easter they had; not so much as the Novatians that called themselves *Cathari,* that is, the Puritans of the Primitive Church, but one they had; but like good fellows, by their *Canon adiaphorus,* they left every one at liberty, so he kept one, to keep it whether way he listed; but keep one he must.   This contending about this custom from the beginning, sheweth from the beginning such a custom there was.

All else
keep Eas-
ter, the
old Puri-
tans, the
Novatians,
and all.
Socr. l. 5.
c. 20. [21.]

2. Proof
from the
*Cycli Pas-
chales.*
1.
[See Bing-
ham, vol. 7.
97. new
edit.]
Next we avouch the *Cycli Paschales,* for the keeping it right, which were indeed the Church's yearly Calendar, which to this day the Greek Church call their πασχάλιον, made of purpose for the just keeping it, at the very time.   A pregnant proof for this custom, if there were none but it.   By Hippolytus, first, a famous Bishop and holy Martyr—his was the sixteen-year Canon, set forth by him so timely, as it ended in the first year of Alexander Severus.

2.   And after him, that of eight years devised by Dionysius Bishop of Alexandria, who was a Martyr also, and of high

account ever in the Church. And both these under the persecution.

Then came Eusebius, whose device the Golden Number was, or cycle of nineteen years. His held till Theophilus of Alexandria's began. Now the time of the setting his is recorded to have been the year 380. ^{3.}

3.
4.

Prosper came after him, and he set another. And last came Victorinus of Aquitaine about the year 460, not much before Gelasius. Two more came after these before it was fully settled, but we will not pass our bounds. If no such custom were, what needed all these pains, all this ado, in these cycles setting, and calculation of times? It shews the great esteem the Church had the feast in, that it was so careful of the precise time of it every year.

5, 6.

1. Victor. Capuanus.
2. Dionys. Exiguus. See Bingham 7. 103. new edit.

And there was reason for it. Otherwhile they were at an after-deal, about the time. The year 454, within a year or two after the Council of Chalcedon, all were at a stand. Easter fell so high in April, they were in a doubt they had been wrong; yea Leo himself, that then lived, and all. Presently fell Leo to writing of letters about, to all reputed any thing seen that way. To the Bishop of Lilybæum[1] in Sicily. To the Bishop of the Isle Coos[2]. To the Emperor Marcian[3] himself, and to the Empress[4] to solicit him, that he would not fail but send to Proterius Bishop of Alexandria to help them out; as he did. And the like fell out in St. Ambrose's time. Damasus and all were to seek about it, and he then fain to clear it by his eighty-third Epistle to the Bishops of Æmilia.

The use of the *Cycli Paschales.*

[1] Pascha-sinus. Ep. 68. 4.
[3] Julianus. Ep. 65.
[2] Ep. 64. al. 94.
[4] Ep. 65. al. 95.

Now, upon the consulting of the Bishop of Alexandria there hangs a third proof—the *Paschales Epistolæ* yearly sent abroad by that See, to this end. Leo[1] confesseth to the Emperor, that because they of Egypt were held for the most skilful in the mathematics, best at calculations, it was by the first Council at Nice laid upon them, this trust, yearly to calculate the day exactly, and to give notice of it in time to other Churches, yea, to Rome and all.

3. Proof. From the *Paschales Epistolæ,* or λόγοι ἑορταστι-κοὶ of the Bishop of Alexandria. [1 Leon. Ep. 64. 1.]

And it was *antiqua consuetudo,* saith Cassian, who lived with Chrysostom, and was his Deacon, that every year, the morrow after the *Epiphania,* the Bishop of Alexandria sent abroad his *Paschales Epistolæ,* to warn Easter over the world,

Collat. 10. 1.

S E R M.
XIII.

Concil.
Carthag.
III.
Cap. 41.

L. 1. c. 6.

Eccl. Hist.
7. 20.
Niceph.
6. 18.
4. Proof.
Job 8. 8.
From the
Fathers
in the
Churches'
peace, the
latter two
hundred
years.
By the
Homilies
upon
Easter-day.

1. *In
Pascha.*
[Orat. Se-
cund. init.]

And when after, by reason of wars in the spring time, in many places they were intercepted that they came not time enough, order was taken anew by the great Council of Africa, that letters for warning Easter should come forth sooner, by the one-and-twentieth of August every year, that so they might have time to come whither they were sent soon enough.

These *Paschales Epistolæ* were ever famous and of high account, for other good matter contained in them. Three of them of Theophilus we have extant, so highly esteemed by St. Hierome, as he took the pains to turn them into Latin, and to him we owe them. But though by the Nicene Council this was laid upon the Bishop of Alexandria, I would not have you conceive it began then. Ruffin saith, the Council did but *antiquum Canonem tradere*, ' deliver the old Canon' that had been before in use. For long before, Eusebius mentioned those *Paschales Epistolæ* sent about by Dionyse, Bishop there, even under the persecution.

Now if we follow Job's advice, and set ourselves to "ask of the Fathers," we shall find *habemus talem consuetudinem*, clear with them for it. 1. Those first, that lived after the Churches' peace; 2. Then those, that during the persecution. Those in the Churches' peace, four ways: 1. By the Homilies or Sermons made purposely by them, to be preached on this day. We have a full jury, Greek and Latin, of them ; and that, of the most chief and eminent among them: St. Basil, Nazianzen, Chrysostom, Nyssen, Theophilus Alexandrinus, Cyril, Chrysologus, Leo, &c. And yet I deal not with any of those in Ambrose, Augustine, Maximus, now extant; I know they are questioned. I rely only on the report of St. Hierome and Gennadius, who saw the right copies, and what they saw have reported.

I will give you a taste of one. It shall be Nazianzen, surnamed the Divine, and so one that knew what belonged to Divinity. Thus begins he a Sermon of his upon it. ' Easter-day is come, God's own Easter-day ; and again I say, Easter-day is come, in honour of the Trinity ; the feast of feasts, the solemnity of all solemnities, so far passing all other feasts, holden not only by or for men, but even in honour of Christ Himself, as the sun doth the stars.'

And in his Funeral Sermon for his father, having occasion but to name it by the way, for that his father once, brought to the last cast in a sickness of his, suddenly, as it were by a miracle, recovered upon an Easter-day morning. 'It was,' saith he, 'Easter, the great and famous feast of Easter, the queen and the sovereign of all the days in the year.' That in his days they had sure such a custom. [S. Greg. Naz. Orat. 19. vol. i. p. 304. ed. Colon. 1690.]

And so it seems they had in Ignatius' days, for from him borrowed he that term of lady and queen of days, out of his Epistle *ad Magnesianos.*

2. By the hymns set for this day, to be sung on it. By Prudentius that lived in St. Ambrose's time. By St. Ambrose himself. Before him by St. Hilary. But Paulinus I insist on. He, in his panegyric for Felix, sets down in particular all the feasts in the year, as they were then in use among them; Easter for a chief feast. He lived with St. Augustine. A pregnant record for the Church's custom then. *By the hymns upon Easter-day.*

3. By their writings. 1. Some of them in their commentaries, as St. Hierome, and namely on the Galatians, and on that place, "ye observe days." 'If that be a fault,' saith he, 'we Christians do incur that fault, all. For we keep,' by name, 'Easter, but not the Jews' Easter of unleavened bread which the Apostle excepts to, but the Christian Easter of the Resurrection of Christ.' 2. Some, by way of Epistles and answers; as St. Ambrose's eighty-third Epistle, full to it; St. Augustine's hundred and eighteenth, and hundred and nineteenth, set Epistles concerning questions about it. 3. Some, by their πολεμικά. As Epiphanius, the treasure of antiquity in his fiftieth, seventieth, and seventy-fifth heresy, *ad oppositum.* Positively, in his Compendium of the true Church's orders, at the end of his Pannarium, whereof one is πανήγυρις μεγάλη ἐν τῇ ἡμέρᾳ τοῦ Πάσχα, 'the great solemnity upon Easter-day.' 2. As St. Augustine expressly *contra Adimantum,* the sixteenth chapter, and the thirty-second book against Faustus, that found fault the Church kept it, yet kept it not as the Jews, confesseth the one—the Church's keeping, traverses the other, that she ought, neither at that time, nor in that manner to keep it, as they did; and that at large. *By their writings touching Easter.* [16. 3.] [32. 11.]

4. Some, by short Treatises, as Ambrose *De mysterio Paschæ;*

SERM.
XIII.
and some by full books, as Eusebius, who wrote a book of the whole order of the Churches' Service then, dedicated it to Constantine, was by the Emperor highly commended for it.

By matters of fact.
Of Chrysostom.
Socrat., lib. 6. c. 18.
4. Lastly, as by writing, so by matter of fact. As Chrysostom, who when he was deposed, and so enjoined not to come in any Church; yet Easter-day coming, so loath he was not to keep it, as he got him *in Thermas Constantini*, a spacious great building for the public bath of the city, and there held his Easter, with a very great company, that would not forsake him. As Athanasius, who being accused to Constantius the Emperor for keeping the feast of Easter in the great Church at Alexandria, then but newly finished and as yet not dedicate, he lays the blame from himself upon the people, that would have kept it there, do what he could, the other Churches were so narrow, and the concourse to the feast so great, as he saith, it would have done the Emperor's heart good to have seen it.

Of Athanasius.
Apolog. ad Constantium.
[14.]

And in his Epistle *ad Africanos*, with open mouth he crieth out upon the Arians, that came in military manner to instal their new Bishop, and the many outrages by them done. Above all, that not only they did those outrages, but did them of all days upon Easter-day, *Et ne ipsum quidem Dominicum diem sanctissimi festi ullâ in reverentiâ habuere*, 'and had not in any reverence, not the very Sunday of that most holy feast.'

Custom for the three holy days at Easter.
Hom. 1. in Pasch.
[See Bp. Sparrow's Rationale. p. 139. New Edit.]
Not the Sunday; for we are to know, the custom that is continued with us still they then had, to keep two days beside the Sunday, three in all: for the Latin Church, plain by St. Augustine *de Civitate Dei*, 22. 8.—*in tertium Festi diem*; for the Greek, by Nyssen, who expressly termeth it τριήμερος προθεσμία.

Thus, all these ways, by singing, by saying, by writing, by doing, all bear witness to it; and I may safely say, there is not one of them but one of these ways or other, he hath his hand in it, and among them they make up a full proof, of this *habemus consuetudinem*.

5. Proof. From the Councils.
The Nicene.
[See Bingham 7. 90.]
From the Fathers I pass to the Councils, and plead it by all the four. The Nicene first.

1. Two causes there were, saith Athanasius *de Syn. Arim. et Sel.*, of the assembling that Council. *Nam et claudicabant*

circa festum, and he makes that the first cause, 'They halted about the feast, kept it not uniformly;' and that was set straight against Crescentius. And the Deity of the Son of God was questioned, and that was put into the Nicene Creed, against Arius. You have the Council's Epistle for the settling it; you have the Emperor's *Sacra* for the ratifying it, directed *Ad omnes Ecclesias,* in the third book of his life, by Eusebius. Theod. l. 1. c. 9. Socrat. l. 1. c. 9. [De Vit. Constant. 3. 14.]

2. For the two General at Constantinople. As Constantine in the first, so Theodosius at this was not behind. His law remains, whereby he provided that for fifteen days, from the Sunday before the day till the Sunday after, no process should go forth, none should be arrested; a general cessation of all, both processes and proceedings, in honour of the high feast. That you have Easter-day, and the custom of holding it solemnly, in the body of the law too, in Theodosius' Code. The second of Constant. [Cod. Justin. lib. 3. tit. 12. de Feriis leg. 8.]

3. At the third, of Ephesus, there have you, in the 2. Tom. c. 32, Rudius, Hesychius, and Ruffin, three *Quartodecimani* heretics, publicly in the face of the Council, recanting their error, subscribing, and promising ever after to conform and keep their Easter after the custom of the Churches of God. At Ephesus. [Con. vol. 1. 1029-30. Venet. 1585.]

4. And at the fourth, of Chalcedon, the sixth session, the Emperor being there then present in person, the whole Council with one voice made this acclamation, *Unum Pascha orbi terrarum;* thanks be to God, 'One Easter now, and but one, all the world over.' At Chalcedon. [Lab. 7. 178.]

But before all these, the Nicene and all, by a dozen years at least, was the Council of Arles, and in it this custom proclaimed. I mention it, not so much for the antiquity, as that by it appeareth how the custom of Easter went here with us in this realm; for at it was present and subscribed the Bishop of London, Restitutus. A plain argument we had such a custom then. Custom in England. [Con. Arelat. c. 1. Lab. 1. 1427.]

And for the other realm, Gelasius shall speak. In a Synod of seventy Bishops, where he and they decreed what books were to be read, what not, they say there was then a poem of venerable Sedulius, who had the addition of Scotus for his nation, which they do *insigni laude præferre,* that is, 'very highly commend.' Sedulius entitles it his *Opus Paschale,* and begins it with *Paschales quicunque dapes*—as it Custom in Scotland. Sedulius. [Lab. 8. 150.]

S E R M.
XIII.
were inviting his readers, his countrymen I dare say specially, if they will come to it, to a feast upon Easter-day.

Custom in both.
Constantine.
[Euseb. Vit. Constant.3.19.]
But for both, none so worthy a witness as the Emperor Constantine, who in his rescript about Easter, directed to all Churches, expressly nameth this isle, the isle of Britanny, among those places, where this custom was duly and orderly observed.

6. Proof.
From the Fathers in the first two hundred years of persecution.
Two, between peace and persecution.
Lactantius.
Pierius.
Hier. de Scr. 76.
All this while the Church had rest. During the persecution how went it? Two we will take in, in the passage between the times of peace and persecution.

1. Lactantius, the most part of his life lived under the persecution, but died in the Church's peace. 2. So did Pierius of Alexandria, for his excellent learning called Origen the younger. In Lactantius' seventh book, and nineteenth chapter, there is a plain testimony for the solemn keeping of Easter-eve. And Pierius, saith St. Hierome, hath a long sermon upon the Prophet Osee, made by him and preached at the solemn assembly on Easter-eve. And if the eve were so held, we make no doubt of the day.

Under the persecution.
The fact of Philip the Emperor.
L. 6. c. 34.
1. Now in the midst of the persecution there fell out a special case of Philip the Emperor, supposed to have given his own and his son's name to the Christian profession, as Eusebius reporteth. In sign thereof he on Easter-eve offered to join himself at the Church-service, as knowing that to be their chiefest solemnity; which they failed not to keep, no not then, when their case was at the hardest.

Euseb. l. 7. c. 22.
Dionys. Alex.
2. And even then at Alexandria, Dionysius, the Bishop there held this custom. Thus writes he to Hierax, a Bishop too, and to others, out of prison, That though the persecution then raged much, and the plague more, yet were the Christians even then so careful not to break this custom as they kept their Easter, some in woods, some on ship-board, some in barns and stables; yea they in the very gaol, keep it they did even then, persecution and plague both notwithstanding.

Cyprian.
Epist. 20. 24. 75.
[Ed. Baluz.]
3. Cyprian held this custom; not by his Homily—I wave it as doubtful, but in four of his Epistles I find it. I name but one, his fifty-third. Some had consulted him in a question of some difficulty. He writes back, It was now Easter, his brethren were from him, every one at his own

charge, solemnizing the feast with their people. So soon
as the feast was over, and they met again, they should hear
from him, he would take their opinions, and return them
a sound answer.

4. Origen had this custom. In his eighth against Celsus
frankly he confesseth, That other feasts, Easter by name,
the Christians held them; and that, as he saith, σεμνότερον,
'in more solemn manner' than Celsus, or any heathen men
of them all held theirs.

5. Tertullian had this custom. Many places in him. Tertulli-
Only one I cite, in the fourteenth chapter, *de jejunio.* *Quod* anus de Corona
si omnem in totum devotionem dierum erasit Apostolus, cur Mil. c. 3. Ad uxo-
Pascha celebramus annuo circulo? 'If it were the Apostle's rem l. 2. c. 4. Contr.
mind to raze out all devout observing of days quite, how Marc. 4. 3.
comes it to pass, we celebrate Easter yearly, at the circle 5. 4.
of the year turning about.'

6. Irenæus had this custom. His Epistle to Victor shew- Irenæus
eth it; to Victor, and to many more, saith Eusebius, about apud Euseb.
that question—understand still the question of the time, not l. 5. c. 24.
of the feast. A book also we find he wrote *de Paschate*, in
the 115th *Quæst.* in Justin Martyr. So he will be for it,
certainly?

7. And it is strange, even during the persecution, how Seven
many books we find written to deduce the custom by. books then writ-
1. Beside that of Irenæus, 2. One by Anatolius the great ten for it. Euseb.
learned Bishop of Laodicea; 3. By Theophilus Bishop of l. 7. c. 32. Hieron.
Cæsarea, and 4. by Bacchyllus Bishop of Corinth, either of Cat. Script. Eccl. 24.
them one. 5. Another by Hippolytus, that made up the 35. 38. 43,
first cycle. Yet, 6. another by Clemens Alexandrinus. And 44. 61. 63.
last, which indeed was first in time of all, two books, 7. by
the holy Martyr and Prophet Melito, Bishop of Sardis, in the next
age to the Apostles themselves, set forth by him as he saith,
at the time of the feast, and in the very holy days of it.

Nay, there wanted not Councils then neither, and that in 7. Proof.
seven several parts of the world at once; all in the midst From Councils
of the fervor of the fiery trial, when the Church, God wot, in the per-
could but evil intend it. It was no time to contend then, secution.
but it shews they made a matter of it, and no slight reckon- 1. Pales-tine.
ing of the retaining it. Else might they have slipt it with- 2. Pontus.
out any more ado. 3. Osroena.
4. Italy.
5. France.

SERM.
XIII.
6. Græcia.
7. Asia
Minor.
Euseb. l. 5.
c. 23.
Enough, I trow, to shew, such a custom there was in all
the Churches these parties lived in, which were all the
Churches God then had. They must needs seem " contentious," that will contend against all these. I see not
how they can scape the Apostle's *si quis*, that do. And this
I say, if some one example of some eminent man of worth
will serve to make an authority, if that; then this cloud of
witnesses, and those, 1. not persons, but whole Councils and
Churches; 2. not in some one region, but in divers, all the
world over; 3. and that not for one time, but so many
ages successively continued, from generation to generation;
what manner of authority ought that to be? the greatest
sure, and none greater, but of God Himself.

Proofs.
That this
custom
was Apo-
stolic.
1. Proof
by testi-
mony.
Augustine
[Ep. 54. 1.
B.]
Now to *nos*, that is, to the Apostles themselves. First,
that it was a custom Apostolic and so taken, St. Augustine
is direct in his one hundred and eighteenth Epistle to Janua-
rius, who had purposely sent to him to know his opinion
touching certain questions, all of them about Easter. Thus
saith he there. ' For such things as come to us not by writing,
but by practice, and yet such as are observed quite through
the world, we are given to understand they come commended
to us and were instituted either by the Apostles themselves, or by General Councils, whose authority hath ever
been accounted of as wholesome in the Church.' Now what
be those things so generally observed *toto orbe terrarum?*
These; that the 'Passion, the Resurrection, the Ascension
of Christ, and the coming of the Holy Ghost from Heaven,
anniversariâ solennitate celebrantur, are yearly in solemn
manner celebrated.' 'And,' saith he, 'if there be any beside these,' for these are most clear.

First, he is clear, it was the custom of the Church, far
and wide the world through. Then, that it must either by
the Apostles be institute, or by some Council. Not by any
Council. Many met about the time—about the feast never
any; that not questioned at all, taken *pro confesso* ever,
Lib. 4.
de Bapt.
con. Donat.
cap. 24.
and so Apostolic. They be his own words, 'If the whole
Church observe any thing, not having been ordained by
some General Council,' *rectissime creditur*, 'we are to believe' *rectissime*, 'by as good right as any can be, right in
the superlative, that it came to us,' *non nisi ab Apostolis,*

'from the Apostles, and from none else,' nor by any other way. So St. Augustine is for *nos habemus talem.* So he held it.

An hundred years before him, Constantine is as direct in his Epistle *Ad omnes Ecclesias.* Many remarkable things there are in that Epistle. 1. 'The most holy feast of Easter,' four times he calleth it, that is the good Emperor's style; 'In so great a matter, in so high a feast of our religion to disagree,' ἀθέμιτον 'utterly unlawful.' And 3. τί κάλλιον, τί σεμνότερον, 'what more honest, what more seemly, than that this feast should be inviolably kept, by which we hold our hopes of immortality?'—Mark that reason well.

But for Apostolic? " Be it lawful for us Christians," saith he, 'rejecting the Jewish manner, that day' ἣν ἐκ πρώτης τοῦ πάθους ἡμέρας ἄχρι τοῦ παρόντος ἐφυλάξαμεν, 'which day ever since the very first day of His Passion we have to this present kept, to transmit the due observing of it to all ages to come.' Mark the words, 1. 'They had kept Easter from the first day of Christ's Passion, till that present time.' 2. And after that, 'We have received it of our Saviour.' 3. And yet again, 'which our Saviour delivered to us.' And concludes, that 4. accordingly, 'when he came among them, he and they would keep their Easter together.' Nothing can be more full than in his time this custom was, and that it was reputed to have come from the Apostles, as begun from the very day of Christ's Passion. Which Leo shortly but fully expresseth, *Legalis quippe festivitas dum mutatur, impletur.* 'The legal feast of the Passover, at the fulfilling of it was changed, both at once.' Fulfilled and changed, at one time both. No distance between. And fulfilled, I am sure, it was in the Apostles' time, and so changed then also.

If you will see it deduced in story, that may you too. Thus of himself Irenæus writeth, that he was brought up in Asia under Polycarpus; and that he, young though he were, observed and remembered well all his course of life. And namely, how coming to Rome in Anicetus' time, he kept his Easter there. Not when Anicetus kept it, but keep it he did though. In the keeping they agreed, in the time they differed. Either held his own.

Constantine. Euseb. l. 3. 18. vita Constantini.

[Ibid.]

Leo, Hom. 7. [1.] de Passione.

2. Proof by story. Euseb. 4. 1. c. 24. Iren. l. 3. c. 3. Tertul. de Præscript. c. 32. Polycarpus kept Easter with St. John

SERM.
XIII.
and the
rest of the
Apostles.
Μετὰ
'Ιωάννου
τοῦ μαθη-
τοῦ τοῦ
Κυρίου
ἡμῶν, καὶ
τῶν λοί-
πων 'Απο-
στόλων
οἷς συνδιέ-
τριψεν
ἀεὶ τετη-
ρηκότα.
Euseb. l. 5.
24.
St. Philip
the Apo-
stle kept it.
3. Proof
from the
Lord's
Day.
Rev. 1. 10.
Ps. 118.
22. 24.
Aug. Ep.
119.[55.B.]
13.
Dies Do-
minicus
Christia-
nis resur-
rectione
Domini
declaratus
est et ex
illo habere
coepit festi-
vitatem
suam.

Polycarpus then kept Easter. Now Polycarpus had lived and conversed with the Apostles, was made a Bishop by them, Bishop of Smyrna—Irenæus and Tertullian say it directly, and he is supposed to be the Angel of the Church of Smyrna; and Polycarpus, as saith Irenæus, kept Easter with St. John, and with the rest of the Apostles, *totidem verbis.*

Polycrates in his Epistle there, in Eusebius, expressly saith that St. Philip the Apostle kept it. If St. Philip and St. John, by name, if the rest of the Apostles had it, then *nos habemus* is true; then it is Apostolic.

But yet we have a more sure ground than all these. The Lord's Day hath testimony in Scripture—I insist upon that; that Easter-day must needs be as ancient as it. For how came it to be "the Lord's Day," but that, as it is in the Psalm, "the Lord made it?" And why made He it? but because on it, "the Stone cast aside," that is Christ, "was made the Head-stone of the corner?" that is, because then the Lord rose, because His resurrection fell upon it?

Now what a thing were it, that all the Sundays in the year that are but abstracts, as it were, of this day, the very day of the Resurrection, that they should be kept; and this day, the day itself, the prototype and archetype of them all, should not be kept, but laid aside quite, and be clean forgotten? That the day in the week we should keep; and the day of the month itself, and return of the year, we should not keep? Even of very congruity it is to be as they, and somewhat more.

Take example by ourselves. For his Majesty's deliverance the fifth of August; for his Majesty's, and ours, the fifth of November, being Tuesday both ;—for these a kind of remembrance we keep, one Tuesday every week in the year. But when by course of the year in their several months, the very original days themselves come about; shall we not, do we not celebrate them in much more solemn manner? What question is there? weigh them well, you will find the case alike. One cannot be, but the other also must be Apostolic.

4. Proof
of the
Church's
custom of
Easter.
1. The

1. For the last proof I have yet reserved one; or rather, three in one. 1. The custom of Baptism, known to have been ministered as upon that day, all the primitive Church through. A thing so known, as their Homilies *de Baptismo*

were most upon that day. St. Basil I name. In his upon custom ot Baptism.
Easter-day, he shews the custom of baptizing them, and the 2. The custom of the cen-
reason of it.

2. The use of the keys, at that time specially. Then were sures then deter-
the censures inflicted; then were they released. 1. Inflicted. mining.
Against that time, did St. Paul cut off the incestuous person,
that a little leaven might not sour them all. Even against
the time that "Christ our Passover was offered, and they 1 Cor. 5.
therefore to hold this feast." 2. Released. So you shall find 7, 8.
the Council of Ancyra, elder than that of Nice, order, the Can. 5.
censures should determine all, endure no longer 'than the
great day'—so in their common speech they termed Easter,
and then all to be restored. 3. To which purpose the Coun- Can. 5.
cil of Nice took order, there should be in Lent a Synod
yearly to this end; that by it all quarrels being taken up,
and all things set straight, they might be in better case to
come with their oblation at Easter to the Sacrament.

And last, by the never broken custom of a solemn Eu- 3. The cus-
charist, ever upon this day. Origen in his seventh upon tom of a
Exodus, he saith, our Easter-day far passeth the Jewish Commu-nion.
Easter. They had no manna on theirs—the Passover was
eaten in Egypt, manna came not till they were in the wilderness—but we, saith he, we never keep our Passover, but we
are sure of manna upon it, the true Manna, "the Bread of John 6.
life that came down from Heaven." For they had no Easter 50. 58.
then without a Communion.

Leo joins both, he might well all three. *Paschalis quippe* Hom. 6.
solennitatis hoc est proprium, 'This is a peculiar that Easter- [1.] de Qua-
day hath,' *ut in eâ tota Ecclesia remissione gaudeat pecca-* drag.
torum, 'that on it, all the whole Church obtaineth the remission of their sins.' One part, *qui sacro Baptismate renas-*
cuntur, by virtue of the solemn Baptism then ministered;
the rest, by benefit of the Eucharist they then receive, *ad*
rubiginem mortalitatis,—it is his term, 'to the scouring off
the rust, which our mortality gathereth' by the sins and
errors of the whole year.

I will conclude all with the words which St. Ambrose
concludes his eighty-third, his Paschal Epistle with, to the
Bishops of Æmilia: *Ergo, cum tot veritatis indicia concur-*
rant, juxta majorum exemplum, Festum hoc publicæ salutis

læti exultantesque celebremus ; ' Since then there be so many
proofs for this truth that thus meet, according to the example of our forefathers, let us with joy and gladness keep this
feast of our common salvation.' How? *Sumamus spiritu
ferventi Sacramentum in azymis sinceritatis;* ' Let us receive the holy Sacrament, with the sweet bread of sincerity.'
*Postes nostros, ubi est ostium verbi, sanguine Christi, in fide
passionis coloremus.* ' The posts of the door of our mouth,
that is, our lips, let us dye them with the Blood of Christ,
in the faith of His blessed Passion.' Ensuing the steps of
the Apostles and the Churches of God, all, with whom joining in both, let us expect the blessing of God upon us, &c.

END OF VOL. II.

Made in the USA
Las Vegas, NV
05 August 2022

52689277R20267